ALSO BY KEITH O'BRIEN

Charlie Hustle: The Rise and Fall of Pete Rose, and the Last Glory Days of Baseball

Paradise Falls: A Deadly Secret, a Cover-Up, and the Women Who Forged the Modern Environmental Movement

Fly Girls: How Five Daring Women Defied All Odds and Made Aviation History

Outside Shot: Big Dreams, Hard Times, and One County's Quest for Basketball Greatness

HEARTLAND

HEARTLAND

A FORGOTTEN PLACE, AN IMPOSSIBLE DREAM, AND THE MIRACLE OF LARRY BIRD

KEITH O'BRIEN

ATRIA BOOKS
New York   Amsterdam/Antwerp   London
Toronto   Sydney/Melbourne   New Delhi

ATRIA
BOOKS

An Imprint of Simon & Schuster, LLC
1230 Avenue of the Americas
New York, NY 10020

For more than 100 years, Simon & Schuster has championed authors and the stories they create. By respecting the copyright of an author's intellectual property, you enable Simon & Schuster and the author to continue publishing exceptional books for years to come. We thank you for supporting the author's copyright by purchasing an authorized edition of this book.

No amount of this book may be reproduced or stored in any format, nor may it be uploaded to any website, database, language-learning model, or other repository, retrieval, or artificial intelligence system without express permission. All rights reserved. Inquiries may be directed to Simon & Schuster, 1230 Avenue of the Americas, New York, NY 10020 or permissions@simonandschuster.com.

Copyright © 2026 by Keith O'Brien

All rights reserved, including the right to reproduce this book or portions thereof in any form whatsoever. For information, address Atria Books Subsidiary Rights Department, 1230 Avenue of the Americas, New York, NY 10020.

First Atria Books hardcover edition March 2026

ATRIA BOOKS and colophon are registered trademarks of Simon & Schuster, LLC

Simon & Schuster strongly believes in freedom of expression and stands against censorship in all its forms. For more information, visit BooksBelong.com.

For information about special discounts for bulk purchases, please contact Simon & Schuster Special Sales at 1-866-506-1949 or business@simonandschuster.com.

The Simon & Schuster Speakers Bureau can bring authors to your live event. For more information or to book an event, contact the Simon & Schuster Speakers Bureau at 1-866-248-3049 or visit our website at www.simonspeakers.com.

Interior design by Jill Putorti

Manufactured in the United States of America

1 3 5 7 9 10 8 6 4 2

The Library of Congress Cataloging-in-Publication Data has been applied for.

ISBN 978-1-6682-1170-0
ISBN 978-1-6682-1172-4 (ebook)

Let's stay in touch! Scan here to get book recommendations, exclusive offers, and more delivered to your inbox.

For Mark Price,
in memoriam

For Andrew Bauer,
who reads it all

and for Golch, Wenner, Voegele, and Patel,
who will complain if they aren't mentioned here

"Larry Bird, distilled, is a very private person who was thrust into a very public place. And that was hard. It was hard for him and it was hard for the people who were trying to support him."
—CRAIG MCKEE, FORMER ASSISTANT SPORTS INFORMATION DIRECTOR, INDIANA STATE UNIVERSITY

"If Bill Hodges hadn't been as persistent as he had been, Larry Bird might never have existed in any of our minds. I believe that with all my heart."
—JACKIE MACMULLAN, FORMER *BOSTON GLOBE* REPORTER

"I like to tell people that we hit the lotto. We were in the right place, at the right time, with the right person: Larry Bird."
—RICH NEMCEK, BACKUP GUARD, INDIANA STATE

CONTENTS

Author's Note	xi
Introduction	1
Part I: The Boy on the Boulevard	7
Part II: The Most Nowhere Place	43
Part III: The Harry and Larry Show	67
Part IV: Cinderella in Middle America	139
Part V: Afterlife	249
Acknowledgments	285
Notes	289
Bibliography	349
Photograph Credits	351
Index	353

AUTHOR'S NOTE

THIS STORY IS A work of nonfiction, built with the help of diaries and journals, television footage and radio archives, thousands of newspaper and magazine articles, court records, military records, genealogical research, memoirs penned closer to the moment, and more than two hundred hours of interviews with the people who lived it—the players, the coaches, their families and friends, and the reporters covering the story at the time. Almost everyone participated, except Larry Bird, who elected not to be interviewed.

The narrative takes no license with facts, characters, scenes, or chronologies. If something appears in quotes here, it means it is verified—taken directly from a memoir, a recorded interview, television footage, or a press account, or, in rare instances, confirmed by reliable sources who were there.

Every effort has been made to portray the events as they occurred, to depict emotions as they were felt at the time, and to document them as accurately as possible for history.

INTRODUCTION

Piscataway, New Jersey
March 14, 1978

LATER, WITNESSES WOULDN'T BE able to decide if Larry Bird threw an elbow or a punch. All they knew for sure was this: A fan was down, blood was everywhere, the guy was headed to the hospital, the season was over, and security couldn't get Bird off the floor fast enough. They needed to save him from himself.

That it was ending like this—in chaos, in New Jersey—was hard for people back home to imagine. Bird had started the season on the cover of *Sports Illustrated*, a lightning-bolt moment for him and all of western Indiana. He had finished the year as a first-team All-American, and in between, he had pulled off the impossible: He'd made Indiana State relevant. The long-forgotten Sycamores—in the overlooked city of Terre Haute, at the crossroads of America, and on the way to nowhere—became part of the national sports conversation for the first time ever. They proceeded to win their first 13 games. By mid-January 1978, they had climbed all the way to No. 4 in the basketball polls. They were better than Bobby Knight's Hoosiers—the standard that mattered most in Indiana—and the only person who wasn't surprised was the Sycamores' head coach, Bob King.

King, who was prematurely old with achy knees, white hair, and a heart that was getting weaker by the day, had logged enough miles over the years on little propeller planes and crowded charter buses to know that what he had in this team was special. In addition to Bird, King had two seven-footers under the basket, a senior point guard with experience, a bench filled with young players willing to do anything, and an athlete from Anderson, Indiana, who complemented Bird in every way: Harry Morgan. Harry was Black while Larry was white, was fast while Larry was slow, could jump while Larry couldn't, and loved to talk while Larry didn't, and together they were a show. "The Harry and Larry Show," reporters called them, and Harry liked to point out that his name came first on that marquee, even if it was Larry who had appeared on the cover of *Sports Illustrated*, and not him.

But since mid-January and the No. 4 ranking, the feel-good story of Indiana State had crumbled into dust in a way that Bobby Knight never would have tolerated. King sabotaged himself again and again with strategic errors and poor decisions. His assistant coaches argued with each other. Players lost confidence in themselves, and Bird lost one of the few things that mattered to him: his privacy. He recoiled from the spotlight that season, like a spider seeking safety in the shadows. Bird didn't want to talk to reporters about himself, his life, his family, or his past. He wanted to dodge all of it. He said he just wanted to play basketball.

At this exact moment, the Sycamores stopped winning. They lost five in a row, then six of seven, then seven of ten, and the losing streak almost ensured their banishment to Piscataway, New Jersey, on this Tuesday night in mid-March 1978. Instead of playing on national television in the NCAA tournament against the best teams in the country, Indiana State was playing Rutgers in the NIT—the "Not Important Tournament," reporters joked. The game was airing on local TV and cable channels, if viewers could find them on their dials. And it was ending in typical fashion for Larry Bird and the Sycamores: They were blowing this game, too.

With 3:42 to go, the Sycamores had the ball and the lead, 56–53. They just needed to avoid mistakes against the Scarlet Knights in the final minutes and they would be staying on the East Coast, advancing to the NIT semifinals, and salvaging their season by playing that weekend in basketball's most hallowed hall: Madison Square Garden. But on the next two possessions, the Sycamores turned the ball over. The Knights scored both times to take a one-point lead. King froze on the bench—paralyzed, it seemed, with indecision. Larry Bird failed to get off a shot in the waning seconds. The Knights won the game, 57–56, and their fans stormed the floor to celebrate, jumping around Bird—and then jumping *on* him.

"Birdshit!" one fan shouted as he pounced on Bird's back. And that's when Bird threw the elbow or the punch—the incident that nobody wanted to talk about after the game, but that everyone saw with their eyes wide open. Rick Shaw, the team's beefy manager, who had been tasked over the season with protecting Bird from the media, tried to get there in time to stop it from happening. But he was too late.

"The guy's nose exploded like a ketchup bottle," Shaw recalled. "Blood went everywhere."

Paramedics moved in to carry the fan away, a blood-soaked bandage wrapped around his head, but no one was coming to help the Sycamores. After the game, in the belly of the arena, the players sat in silence, pondering everything they had just lost and were still about to lose.

Both seven-footers, and the starting point guard, would be gone before next season. Harry Morgan would be gone, too—headed, he hoped, for the NBA. Some underclassmen weren't sure if they were coming back. Bob King and his two assistants would never sit on the bench together again. By the fall, one of them would be rushed to a hospital. Another would quit in disgust. And no one knew what was going to happen with Larry Bird now that the season was over. Maybe he'd leave school one year early and jump to the NBA with Harry Morgan. Or maybe Bird would disappear. Again.

He had vanished before, after all. In some ways, he was vanishing even then, shrinking from the moment at the arena in New Jersey. Bird was there, but he wasn't. He was hiding from reporters who had questions about the incident on the floor at the end of the game.

"What happened?" the press shouted as Bird walked to the bus sometime later.

"Huh?" Bird replied.

"You were there—what happened in the end?"

"I don't know."

That night, the players managed to acquire some beer and sneak it into their hotel rooms in New Jersey. A few of them drank too much, washing off the Rutgers loss, and the flight home the next day out of Newark was a hard one. One player vomited several times in the plane's tiny bathroom while others stared out the windows on takeoff, looking down at New York City in the distance. They'd probably never be back.

But this wasn't the end; it was the beginning. The characters had assembled. The cast was all there. The people who would write one of the greatest American sports stories of all time—an underdog basketball tale for the ages—were on that plane. They were in that quiet locker room in New Jersey. They were on campus that spring in Terre Haute and they were about to achieve the rarest thing in sports: immortality. People in western Indiana would soon be writing songs about them, lining the streets for them, filling arenas for them, building statues for them, opening museums for them, and crying for them, because they loved them.

It's a narrative that's almost impossible to imagine today in an era when college basketball players jump from school to school, leave through the transfer portal in the middle of March, play for the highest bidder, chase lucrative deals funded with name, image, and likeness money, live on campus as millionaires, cash in, check out, and rarely stay in one place long enough to leave any legacy at all. In the spring of 2025 alone, more than a thousand college basketball players entered the portal after the NCAA tournament—enough players to create rosters that would fill an entire 68-team bracket and then some. The games were over, but the real madness had just begun. Young athletes were on the move. Coaches were scrambling to sign them, and booster clubs in charge of doling out the cash stood at the ready, their checkbooks open.

It's a flawed system that has created a new world. As one booster club president put it, "The day of the retired number is gone." But it would be wrong to believe that Larry Bird and his Indiana State teammates played in an innocent time. The professionalization of college sports had begun years before Bird and his teammates ever showed up on campus. By the early 1970s, college coaches had turned recruiting into a pseudoscience. College boosters were bending rules to land the best players. Network executives were leveraging America's growing interest in sports to give viewers more college basketball, in better time slots. NBC started airing NCAA tournament games in prime time. Ratings soared. Three separate times in the first half of the decade—in 1972, '73, and again in '75—NCAA tournament games set viewership records for the most-watched game. University presidents began to take notice, realizing there was money to be made. And one other cohort of people turned out in droves to chronicle—and contribute to—this craze: sportswriters. Flush with expense accounts financed by advertising dollars, reporters at the biggest newspapers and magazines started to travel the country, hoping to discover the next great basketball hero. Put simply: Larry Bird didn't create the wave; he rode it.

Like most waves, this one started small. It was just a ripple in the darkness, at first. Anyone could have missed it, and Bird himself nearly did. Basketball fans might have never known his name. But within five years, this wave rolled across the landscape, picking up everything in its wake: Bird, his teammates, his coaches, and sometimes even his opponents. Each of them would be forever defined by what happened in this little window of time. Each of them would not be able to forget, especially later on cool nights in March, and each of them would be stunned by the final result in 1979. At the end of that year, Indiana State would play in front of the largest audience in American basketball history and capture the hearts of a nation.

It's an epic story that no one saw coming, least of all the people on that plane, flying out of Newark one year earlier in 1978. The Sycamores had blown the game against Rutgers. They had squandered their one chance. They were tired and broken and they were returning home to the only place that wanted them at the time, the only place that cared.

They were going back home to Indiana.

Part I

THE BOY ON THE BOULEVARD

1

IN THE BEGINNING, THE boy didn't like basketball as much as he seemed to like just being with his brothers. Larry Bird would spill out of his home in West Baden Springs and tumble down the hill with his older brothers, Mike and Mark, to shoot hoops at the small, yellow-brick water plant on the edge of the Lost River.

It was a rudimentary setup. The Emmons family, who ran the water pumps and lived upstairs, had drilled a telephone pole into the ground near the settling basin and then attached a backboard to it at roughly regulation height. There was no pavement to make a court. The kids played on grass, beating it down with their sneakers. And if someone threw up a bad shot, the ball could carom off the hoop and roll down the hill to a low point, where the rains pooled after a storm.

But to the local kids, maybe the Birds most of all, the hoop was a miracle. It gave them a place to gather and a reason to get out of the house. Sometimes the boys even played there when it snowed. Butch Emmons, who was the oldest of the group by far, would grab a shovel, clear the court, and they'd play in the cold. The only problem was, they didn't always have a roster spot for Larry. In the schoolyard picks at the water plant, Larry would get left out because he was significantly younger than the other boys. He was small, and anyway, Mark Bird was better—the best shooter, inside of 15 feet, that some locals had ever seen.

Later, the Birds would move out of West Baden and into French Lick, a short trip about two miles down State Road 56—the boulevard, as locals called it. After that, the Birds didn't come by the water plant much anymore. But Butch Emmons would never forget how upset Larry would get when he didn't get picked in the games out there. Larry seemed to take it personally, like it disgusted him, and it wouldn't be the last time that Emmons saw Larry have his boyhood dreams get crushed on a basketball court.

In the years ahead, Emmons graduated from college, returned to French Lick to work as a teacher, got the job as the seventh-grade basketball coach in town, and was on the floor the night his friend, eighth-grade coach Roger Fisher, had to let young Larry go. Larry had made Fisher's team; he was good enough to play. He just wasn't coming to practice, Emmons said, and Fisher finally made the difficult choice to send Larry away, even though the school, the coaches, and everyone else in French Lick knew what Larry was facing at home.

2

LARRY'S FATHER, JOEY BIRD, had blue eyes, ruddy skin, and a pleasant demeanor. People liked him. But he had been making poor choices since at least the early 1940s.

Joey never finished eighth grade in West Baden. He didn't go to high school, and in the spring of 1944, Joey, still just 17 years old, walked away from the best job a kid from rural Indiana with a seventh-grade education could ever hope to get. He was employed that spring as an ammunition loader at a federal munitions plant—a sprawling, newly built center 25 miles away that would manufacture American bombs for decades to come. It was the sort of job that savvy locals kept forever, riding the plant's steady wages and federal benefits straight to the middle class. But not Joey. In late April 1944, five months before his 18th birthday, he had his father sign the paperwork to send him off to war.

It probably sounded romantic. At the moment that Joey enlisted, the local newspaper, the *Springs Valley Herald*, was filled with exciting dispatches of West Baden and French Lick boys fighting the enemy overseas, winning medals for bravery, surviving firefights with Germans, taking command of naval warships, dying with honor in Saipan, and running into their brothers and classmates at the front. But there was nothing romantic about enlisting as an apprentice seaman with the US Naval Reserve, as Joey Bird did that April. He wasn't going to be a hero;

he was going to be swabbing decks. And according to his military record, he got into trouble almost immediately.

That summer, while still at basic training in Illinois, Joey went AWOL from his base and faced punishment as a result. The following spring, while in port in South Carolina, he was caught drinking liquor on his ship, and again faced consequences. And once at sea in the summer of 1945, steaming into the Pacific, Joey seemingly did little to excel. He earned no weapons qualifications. He didn't learn to scuba dive and couldn't salvage anything if it sank to the ocean floor. He was a "crew messman"—a job that typically entailed serving food and clearing dishes in the mess hall belowdecks.

Joey was still young then; he had time to get things right. But his problems continued after he returned to the US in June 1946. His ship landed in California on a Saturday and docked at Treasure Island, in the heart of San Francisco Bay. With the city beckoning across the water, Joey secured a weekend pass and promptly lost all his personal belongings for reasons unknown. He returned to West Baden, still mourning his lost stuff, and worked in a shoe factory over in Paoli for a while. There he met a nice girl, Georgia Kerns.

Georgia was tall and fair, from the hills outside of French Lick, and sweet on Joey. But bad luck struck Joey Bird yet again. Georgia left the shoe factory for a job at the paper cup plant in French Lick. The young couple lost touch, and Joey quickly moved on, too. In 1949 he found himself reenlisting to go to Korea.

This time he wasn't going to be serving food on a ship. He was a foot soldier in the 25th Infantry Division, a grunt in the thick of the fight, shivering in a foxhole in the cold Korean winter, waiting for the Chinese to attack in the dark, dodging their bullets, and retreating at dawn as dead bodies piled up in the snow. The experience shook Joey so much that he wrote a story about his long and dreadful winter fighting the communists. In early 1951, his account landed in the hands of the editors at the *Springs Valley Herald*, and in March of that year, they printed Joey Bird's first-person tale of valor and bravery on the front page for everyone to read.

Joey Bird had finally gotten the hero treatment, and he returned home that summer to get the girl, too. On a Saturday night in late September 1951, Joey Bird married Georgia Kerns in a small, private ceremony at a minister's house over in Shoals. It was a moment to celebrate, and there would be a bridal shower a few weeks later. But the wedding wouldn't be anything like the grand celebrations that other soldiers were having that fall after returning home from the front.

Georgia's father, a concrete finisher, had advised against this marriage, and at least one of Georgia's sisters had her own concerns, because of how Joey had changed since returning home from Korea. He was no longer a teenager sneaking liquor onto his ship or a young man who enjoyed a beer or two. He was an adult, drinking at times to get drunk, lashing out at ghosts in the night, haunted by nightmares of whatever had happened in Korea, and on his way to becoming the father of six kids, including four born in four years in the 1950s—Mike, Mark, Linda, and Larry.

3

LARRY LOVED HIS FATHER. Sometimes, his older brother Mark wondered if Joey was Larry's best friend. But by the time the Birds moved into French Lick in the 1960s—and Larry got sent away from the eighth-grade team—Joey's problems were taking a toll on the family. They moved a lot. Money was tight. Georgia would soon have to take on two jobs to help pay the bills and Larry seemed to seek refuge outside the house, running with a small crew of French Lick boys: Mike Cox, John Mills, and Gary "Herbie" Wyman.

The four boys did just about everything together. They rode bicycles out to the golf course, with Larry often sitting on the handlebars of Herbie's bike because he didn't have one to ride himself. They searched for lost balls in the weeds and sold them back to golfers for nickels, dimes, and quarters. They used the proceeds from their sales to go to the movie theater or stuffed the money in their pockets and went mushroom hunting instead on a piece of land that Herbie Wyman's family had outside of town.

Back at Herbie's house later—always Herbie's—they'd fry up the mushrooms in the kitchen and then, with their fingers dripping with grease, they'd head to the little court next to the grade school to play basketball.

In those days, no one thought Larry was going to be great. Not even Larry. He was just like the rest of them: scrappy, competitive, and looking to have fun. If Larry had a dream, it was just that he might one day make the varsity team at Springs Valley High School, like his older brother Mark. No one in Larry's crew thought bigger than that. And no one in the crew asked questions about why Larry and his older brothers sometimes lived with Georgia's mother, Granny Kerns, in a little house on the hill behind the grade school, or why the crew of friends was hardly ever in Larry's house at all. But the adults in town knew.

Joey Bird couldn't shake the nightmares—some nights, he'd wake up swinging—and perhaps to numb the pain, he became a regular at the local bars. Folks would find him at the Colonial in downtown French Lick or at the Jubil Bar on the boulevard in West Baden, drinking away his paycheck and trying to steer clear of trouble. The latter wasn't always easy. In addition to the bars, French Lick had a brothel. Men often drove over from Paoli or Jasper to visit the women there, and things sometimes went sideways after midnight. From time to time in the 1970s, men fought and even killed each other in the parking lot outside the Jubil, fighting over women and nothing. And according to Georgia's sister, Virginia, Joey was soon fighting, too: He was fighting Georgia. "There were times when Joey was drinking that he became abusive to Georgia," Virginia wrote later in a family history. One day, Virginia recalled, Georgia even turned up with a black eye. "Joey had hit her, breaking her glasses and forcing her to flee."

In August 1972, about two weeks before Larry would start his junior year at Springs Valley High School in French Lick, Georgia had finally reached a breaking point. She filed for divorce, making public a private disaster that had been building from the moment that Joey stepped off that ship in San Francisco years before. He moved back into his parents' house in West Baden while Georgia and the kids stayed right where they were: in a little house on Washington Street in French Lick, not far from the high school and the railroad tracks.

They were moving on alone, and young Larry did his part to provide in these years. He got jobs delivering newspapers, stocking shelves in a local market, or putting up hay over at Wilstem Farm, a piece of land on the road to Paoli. Baling hay was hard work, hot and miserable, especially if Larry was assigned to toil in the barn instead of the field. Temperatures could soar to over 100 degrees in there, and no matter where Larry was assigned, the barn or the field, he'd leave his shift with scratches up and down his forearms, as if he'd done battle with a feral cat.

But Larry didn't complain. By the late summer of 1972, he had grown to about six foot three. He was only 155 pounds, a scarecrow in the field at Wilstem Farm, yet he could throw a hay bale as far as any boy in town. Barry Wilson, one of Larry's high school classmates, would later tell folks that Larry could take a bale and toss it nine feet into the air, up onto the wagon or into the barn, like it was nothing. Whether that was true or not, this was: Larry loved working outside. With his father gone, he needed the job. And there was a side benefit to the work, too: It seemed to make Larry stronger. The kids in town saw it with their own eyes that summer as Larry graduated to the most important basketball court in town. He was no longer playing on Butch Emmons's ramshackle hoop at the water plant or on the little court outside the grade school in French Lick. He was playing on the outdoor basketball court on the boulevard in West Baden, just down the road from the Jubil Bar.

People came from three counties to play ball on that court. The local coaches often came out to watch, curious to see how the boys stacked up against each other and the out-of-towners. And by the fall of 1972, both Larry Bird and Mike Cox—two members of the French Lick crew who liked to fry up mushrooms in Herbie Wyman's house—were good enough on the boulevard to attract the interest of Springs Valley varsity coach Jim Jones.

Jones was more than just a coach in French Lick; he was a father figure, a taskmaster, a mentor, and a local icon who knew everybody and had coached almost every kid in town since 1962, including Mike Bird, Mark Bird, and Larry himself. Jones was the first person to ever show Larry how to hold the ball, how to cradle it in his hand. He kept the Valley gym open whenever he could, encouraging kids to play, and had created a system for basketball success along the way. From biddy ball to summer camps, grade school to high school, everyone in town coached the game and played the game the way Jim Jones wanted.

For him, it was about fundamentals and versatility. He wanted kids to be able to go left or go right. Dribble with both hands. Score with both hands, too. Make every pass possible—left-handed, right-handed, over the head, or off the dribble. And for the kids who were good enough to make his high school team, the Springs Valley Blackhawks, there was an expectation that they would work. Jones wanted his players starting their days by shooting free throws in the gym before school and ending their days running. At Valley practices in the 1970s, kids were forced to run up and down the length of the court, again and again. Or worse, they had to run the steps in the gym, up and down every aisle, all the way around, until their quads burned.

Granny Kerns sometimes had to wake Larry for the early-morning free-throw shootaround during Larry's sophomore and junior years at Springs Valley. "Larry," she'd say, nudging him in the dark, "those other boys are down there." Other days, Jones roused Larry himself. He walked into Granny's house in the dark, cognizant of the troubles that Larry was facing at home and worried that Larry wouldn't come to school at all if Jones weren't there to demand it.

But no one could keep Larry off the court on the boulevard. Folks would drive by—headed to the Jubil, Shorty's pool hall, the JayC food mart, the laundromat, the barbershop, or the Shell station—and see Georgia Bird's quiet, long-legged son out there in his sneakers, shooting and shooting. Everyone saw him, except for maybe Georgia herself. Around the time of the divorce, she was busy working different jobs in town, including one as a cook at Flick's Restaurant.

Flick's was a short walk from just about everything in French Lick—the feed store, the bottling factory, the railroad tracks, and the four places that mattered most to Larry: his home, his grandmother's house, the high school, and the gym. And Larry and his teammates became fixtures at Flick's. The restaurant understood that folks in town were hurting, and it priced the menu accordingly. Mini-burgers were just 29 cents, or four for a dollar.

But mostly, the kids went to Flick's because Georgia was there—a warm presence, in a friendly place, happy to cough up her tip money to Larry so that he could get himself a heaping plate of those mini-burgers.

"You always have tons of money," Larry remembered telling his mother with awe one day as she placed coins and dollar bills in his hand.

It wasn't true, but Georgia had a way of putting people at ease—even strangers, like the handsome young college basketball recruiter who started showing up in French Lick near the end of Larry's junior year. His name was Dave Bliss. He was interested in Larry, and Bliss's good looks, blond hair, and blue eyes weren't the only things that opened doors for him.

Bliss worked for Bobby Knight—the most important man in Indiana.

4

DAVE BLISS HAD BEEN with Bobby Knight for years, going back to their days at Army in the late 1960s, and so he'd seen it all: the shouting, the cursing, the badgering of the refs, the technical fouls, the ejections, and Knight's stern and unwavering sense of right and wrong. Once, on a road trip to Madison Square Garden in New York in 1968, Knight refused to let the Army players arrive at the Garden early to watch Elvin Hayes and the No. 1–ranked Houston Cougars play in the afternoon game. Knight only wanted them thinking about their own opponent that evening, NYU. "I'll be damned," Knight scowled, "if I let them watch Houston."

The players didn't complain—at least not publicly. That would have been insanity. Knight let them know up front: "To play for me, you will do it my way or not at all." They had to fall in line, and Knight's young assistant, the newly commissioned Private First Class Dave Bliss, with his blond hair shaved into a tight crew cut, was happy to follow the rules, too. He was learning from Knight. "I feel that I am studying under *the* outstanding young coach in basketball today," he said in 1968. Most of all, Bliss was learning how to recruit, and he was doing it under the hardest possible circumstances: the bloodiest year of the Vietnam War.

As the 1968 basketball season began, more than 300 American servicemen were dying in Vietnam every week, and these deaths had tangible trickle-down ramifications for Knight's basketball program. Most teenage boys had no interest in playing basketball at Army, only to then potentially get shipped off to some jungle in Indochina to die, when they could play at a different college and possibly avoid military service altogether. As a result, Knight instructed Bliss that if they were ever going to succeed at West Point, he needed to outwork other recruiters. Bliss needed to do things that they'd never do, go places they'd never go, stay longer, listen better, be smarter. And because it was Bobby Knight speaking, Bliss did as he was told.

He would read a hundred newspaper clippings every day, tracking good players who also had decent grades and happened to live in cities or homes that leaned pro-war, sympathetic to the military hawks in Washington. Then, once Bliss had dozens of potential targets in mind—he needed dozens because most kids would still say no—he'd hop on a C-130 out of McGuire Air Force Base in New Jersey and be gone for weeks, living out of Ramada Inns, Howard Johnsons, and army-issue rental cars. To stay awake at the wheel, driving from Mobile to Jacksonville or Fresno to Stockton, Bliss would buy 10 packs of chewing gum, dump all the sticks into a single plastic bag, grab them by the handful, the flavors all mixed up, and then just drive. When the gum went hard in his mouth, he'd spit it out and start over, chewing more gum and logging more miles. And when he reached his final destination, Bliss would ease into a parking spot, walk into the high school gymnasium, find the kid he wanted, and turn on the charm that Bobby Knight couldn't teach and didn't have. With his handsome face and his Ivy League education from Cornell, Bliss could charm just about anyone.

That it worked at all at Army was a testament to Knight's intensity and genius, but also the perseverance of assistants like Bliss, who lived on the road. In Knight's six seasons at Army, the Cadets went 102–50—a minor miracle that got the attention of lots of people, including the board of trustees at Indiana University in March 1971.

The trustees, at the time, were in the midst of an existential crisis. The Hoosiers hadn't won a national title in 18 years, since Bobby "Slick" Leonard hit a free throw in the waning seconds of the title game in 1953 to beat Kansas. And the current squad didn't appear poised to achieve anything anytime soon. Indiana had finished last in the Big Ten Conference in three out of the last four seasons. Alumni had started to grumble about coach Lou Watson, who was one of their own but had lost control. Just before the last game of the 1970–71 campaign, the Hoosier players did the unthinkable: They went over Watson's head to complain to the university president about playing time and alleged favoritism shown to the star of the team.

Watson, a man of principle, resigned immediately. "I'm not bitter about the situation," he told reporters who called him at his house that day. Watson was just clear-eyed about the reality: He couldn't coach a team like this. And the basketball beat writers in Indiana agreed. The writers—who were old and white, and had been entrenched in their jobs covering Indiana basketball since the mid-1940s—wrote columns bemoaning the privileged, self-absorbed "trouble-makers" who had taken down Watson and poisoned the Hoosier locker room. "A bunch of guys in short pants," one columnist complained, "whose loyalty doesn't extend past their reflection in the mirror."

It was time for new leadership. It was time for discipline. It was time for someone who wasn't going to indulge player complaints over just about anything. It was time for Bobby Knight. The Army coach, then just 30 years old, got the job at the end of March 1971 and, upon his introduction, refused to apologize for anything. Not his "earthy American language." Not his ugly treatment of referees, and not his off-color remarks, either. At times, he would openly mock female coaches who attended his seminars, harassing them in front of auditoriums full of male coaches, who laughed and laughed. And none of this mattered because Knight had come to Bloomington to win, and winning came at a cost that university officials were willing to pay.

On the day he was introduced in Bloomington, wearing his customary short-sleeved button-down shirt and dark, conservative tie, Knight told Hoosier fans that they could expect a few things. His teams were going to play man-to-man defense. His players were going to be tough. He wasn't going to put up with the childish machinations that had taken down Lou Watson. He wasn't going to tolerate prima donnas, either. "You build winning teams on character," Knight said at his opening press conference, "not characters." And he promised Indiana fans that he and his staff were getting started right away. They were going to recruit high-quality homegrown Indiana basketball players who would do anything to win. In fact, Knight said he wasn't even going home—he wasn't even going to see his wife, Nancy—until he had landed the recruits he needed.

Then, Knight brought Dave Bliss to Bloomington and they started all over again. They were going to work just as hard as they always had. Bliss was going to read his newspaper clippings every day, make his player lists, and hit the road. Only this time, Bliss was going to have a team of managers working to clip the articles out of the papers for him. He wouldn't have to travel as far. He wasn't going to need as much chewing gum. And he wasn't going to face rejection like he had at Army. Knight and Bliss were going to be able to have their choice of recruits at Indiana. They were going to skim the cream right off the top.

Kids like Larry Bird—if they were good enough for an offer, if they were worthy of Bobby Knight, if they were deserving of being an Indiana Hoosier—wouldn't be able to say no.

5

BLISS FOUND LARRY BIRD the way that good recruiters often found kids in those days: by accident.

Bliss attended a Springs Valley game during the 1972–73 season to watch Bird's teammate Steve Land—a senior who was two inches taller than Bird, 50 pounds heavier, and a scorer who was making headlines across the state. In one game that January, Land set a Valley record when he put up 41 points in a win over North Knox. This sort of kid was worth the drive from Bloomington, 50 miles due south on country highways. But while Bliss was watching Steve Land, he found himself distracted. He couldn't take his eyes off Bird.

He was smaller than Land, it was true. And his lack of heft could hurt him at times. Physical opponents could make Bird uncomfortable, push him around. But in Bliss's estimation, Bird had attributes that most high school players—including Steve Land—did not have, and never would. Bird always played with his hands up, ready to catch a pass, throw a pass, take a shot, block a shot, or defend the lane. These hands, Bliss thought, allowed Bird to do almost anything on the floor. But it was his feet that made him notable. Bird was slotted at forward for the Springs Valley Blackhawks, yet he played like a guard. He could bring the ball up the floor better than just about anyone, anticipate plays before they happened, see the floor in three dimensions as if from above, and make a pass to a teammate with heat, and sizzle, and perfection, as the teammate cut to the basket for an easy lay-up. It was no wonder that Steve Land was scoring 40 points against the likes of North Knox, Bliss thought. Larry Bird was making it happen. And Bliss and other Indiana assistants moved in to do their job. They started laying the groundwork with Bird's high school coach, Jim Jones.

Jones didn't appreciate lots of things about Bobby Knight—namely his treatment of women and the way he berated his players at times. That wasn't the way Jim Jones operated. But Jones, a graduate of Indiana University, had grown close with Knight since he took the job in Bloomington in 1971. Knight invited Jones to work his summer basketball camps and even attend practices. Through opportunities like these, Jones got to know Knight and found him to be kind, a gentleman, even. At one point around 1972, Knight learned that Jones's son, Tom, then about 10, loved cheering for the Boston Celtics and their great swingman, John Havlicek, and not long after that, a gift arrived for Tom: a Havlicek-signed photo, courtesy of Bobby Knight.

Knight saw Jones as a friend, or at least an ally, and Bliss came to believe that he could rely on Jones. He could call him anytime. Find out Bird's schedule. Stop by a Springs Valley shootaround. Arrange to bump into Bird on a water break. Chat him up. Try to make it seem casual and also make it count. Bliss wanted his conversations with Bird to be the best thing Bliss did all day, even if Bird didn't engage with Bliss and hardly spoke. Even if he only uttered two words. Then Bliss would leave, headed back to Bloomington, hoping that Jim Jones would do the rest, convincing Bird that Bloomington was his future. "I just know," Bliss said later, "that he was in his ear all the time."

Larry Bird, by this point, was developing the qualities of the man he'd later become. He was uncomfortable with strangers and distrustful of out-of-towners who wanted something. He'd shut down if he thought he'd been wronged, and he could vanish right in front of people's eyes, disappearing into a dark, deep well of silence. But there was another side to him—a side that the kids saw. This version of Larry Bird had a knack for deadpan humor, searing sarcasm, and wild, harebrained ideas. Around the time that Bliss was taking an interest in him, Bird borrowed the compact Chevrolet pickup truck that belonged to his childhood friend Herbie Wyman, and used it, Wyman recalled, for an unusual purpose: mowing grass. Bird and some other boys strung some lawn mowers behind the Chevy, Wyman said, and made quick work of a grass-cutting job, so that they could all go fishing instead. Bird apparently loved the idea. Wyman said Bird drove the truck that day, towing the lawn mowers behind it, and the kids knew a few other things about Bird that most people didn't. He believed in his basketball ability at all times; he didn't mind pronouncing his greatness out loud, if only to friends; and he wasn't just stubborn—Bird could be loyal. If he said he was going to do something, he did it, which is maybe why he agreed to let Dave Bliss into his life, just a little. At one point, Bird even took Bliss mushroom hunting in French Lick, like he was part of the crew.

Bliss's plan was working. He was getting closer to Bird every day, and then, to Bliss's surprise, it all fell apart. In late June 1973, shortly after the end of Bird's junior year, Jones made an announcement that stunned everyone: He was stepping down as head basketball coach at Springs Valley.

The reasons for the decision, Jones said later, were complicated. He was burned out; the team was losing three starters before the next season; his son, Tom, was playing middle school basketball now; Jones wanted to be at Tom's games; and he thought it best to cede the job to his assistant, step back, and spend the year—Bird's senior year—serving only as the Springs Valley athletic director.

Bird and his friend Mike Cox were running around downtown when they got the news. Both of them felt like crying, and Dave Bliss didn't feel much better. The scaffolding he had carefully constructed around Bird, with Jones's help, crumpled to a heap on the gym floor. Bliss was going to have to start over now with Jones's replacement, Gary Holland, a young assistant from Paoli with no ties to Bloomington whatsoever. Holland had played his college ball at the University of Louisville. And Bliss was starting over with Holland at the worst possible time.

In the summer and fall of 1973, Bird grew about four inches, until he was roughly six foot seven and recruiters were coming to see him from across the Midwest. A kid this tall, and this good, would not go unnoticed—even here, in French Lick.

Dave Bliss's secret was out.

As Larry adapted to his new body and the attention that it was attracting, his mother just tried to keep up. That fall, classmates recalled, Georgia had to extend Larry's pants by sewing swatches of fabric to the leg bottoms. "It wasn't even matching," said Barry Wilson, one of Bird's teammates. But the Valley kids understood. Many of their parents were also making concessions and bargains to get through the week and make sure there was enough money for groceries at the JayC food mart on Friday. And anyway, no one was going to make fun of Larry Bird. With the extra height, he towered over just about everyone in town and had become the greatest basketball player the kids had ever seen.

In the third game of the Valley season in December 1973, Bird broke Steve Land's short-lived scoring record, putting up 43 points on Orleans.

He then broke his own record a month later, hanging 55 on Corydon. In a five-game stretch around that time, Bird personally scored 192 points, more than some *teams* compiled in that time period. He was averaging more than 30 points a game and was executing plays that people in the little gyms of southern Indiana had never seen before.

When opposing teams were inbounding the ball after a Valley basket, Bird would pretend he was running back on defense and then pluck the pass out of the air for an easy lay-up. When thicker players boxed him out with their bigger bodies, he'd use his long arms to reach up and over them and tip rebounds to himself. And finally, he had developed one last trick that kids in town liked to employ on the outdoor courts, and that one teacher liked to use, too. When opponents were guarding Bird close, he would sometimes hold the ball behind the defender's head. And when this defender turned around to find it, Bird would pull it back and shoot. College coaches had to see this prospect for themselves, and they descended on French Lick to meet Larry Bird.

Most of them didn't get much traction. Often, they didn't even get to talk to Bird at all. Gary Holland and Jim Jones had erected a wall around the boy in an effort to protect him. At one point that winter, a Kansas State assistant traveled 600 miles to French Lick and didn't even get the chance to introduce himself to Bird, much to his frustration. At least the visit helped him understand where Kansas State stood in the Larry Bird sweepstakes. In the gym that night in French Lick, he got the sense that Bird was going to play for Bobby Knight at Indiana. And if not Indiana, then maybe the University of Louisville, Holland's alma mater. At least three Louisville coaches visited French Lick in January 1974 alone, and one of them, Bill Olsen, an assistant to head coach Denny Crum, checked in with Holland all the time. Olsen wanted Holland to know that Louisville had graded Bird, that Bird had scored a 92, that this score was "the highest rating that any player had ever gotten," and that they would be back to see him again soon. "Best wishes for the rest of your season . . ."

By then, lots of people were weighing in on where Bird should go to college, including, it seemed, half the town. So, Holland tried to stay out of it. He tried to say nothing. But on the same day that Olsen wrote to him in early 1974, passing along Bird's high grade, a third school moved in that Holland could not ignore. The University of Kentucky wanted to invite Larry, his parents, and Holland down to Lexington for a visit—an invite that Larry had to accept, and did.

Dave Bliss was in trouble. He was in danger of losing Larry Bird, and there was maybe only one way to salvage the situation now.

Bobby Knight needed to get to French Lick.

6

ON A FRIGID EVENING near the end of January 1974, Bliss and Knight drove south from Bloomington, down into the valley, to watch Bird play in one of the most important high school basketball games of the year: a Tuesday-night battle against Jack Butcher's high-flying, big-talking, elbow-swinging Loogootee Lions.

Loogootee (pronounced luh-GOH-tee) was only about 20 miles from French Lick. But in the minds of the teenagers, it was a world apart. Many Loogootee parents worked at the federal munitions plant outside of town—the place where Joey Bird had briefly found employment in 1944. Thanks to these jobs, some Loogootee kids felt empowered to look down on French Lick. They called it "a dirty, little, poor, unkempt town." They bought slightly nicer cars than their counterparts at Springs Valley and used them to cruise the streets of Loogootee at night, driving the loop. They'd go from the high school to the carhop and back again, or they'd just park their cars in the pasture at Baker's Farm and drink beer and make out around a bonfire.

But regardless of how they felt, where they drove, or what they did, Loogootee always beat Valley. Every year, like a rite of winter. Loogootee won by 17 points in January 1972, during one of the worst stretches of Jim Jones's coaching career. Loogootee won by two points in January 1973, when Bird was called for charging with 15 seconds to go and turned the ball over. And Loogootee was poised to win again now, in January 1974, even though the Lions' tallest player was at least four inches shorter than Larry Bird. Coach Butcher, on his way to 806 career wins, the most in Indiana high school basketball history at the time, would find a way.

Butcher didn't believe his team could truly stop Bird. "He's too mobile," the iconic coach said that week, "and too good an outside shooter." But Butcher knew how to work the refs, how to craft a game plan, and how to put his players in a position to win. On the perimeter, he had his own son, Bill, playing point guard. Inside, he had Wayne Flick, the son of one of those munitions workers, ready to bang with Bird. And perhaps most important, he had a fan base that traveled.

Gary Holland knew he was in trouble on the night of the Loogootee game when he pulled up outside the Springs Valley gymnasium and couldn't find a parking spot anywhere. He had arrived early, long before tip-off, and still there was nowhere to park. People had been there for hours, waiting in line, and now they were packed inside.

Estimates would vary as to how many people were there that night. Some said it was 3,000. Others said it was at least 4,000. The number seemed to grow with time, until everyone in the county was there. What's clear is that the crowd easily exceeded the gym's official capacity of 2,700, and it was quite possibly double the size of French Lick itself. The gym was, in effect, a town within a town. People were sitting on the edge of the floor. They were stacked in the aisles. They were perched on the windowsills up in the rafters or they were standing shoulder to shoulder on the mezzanine, watching condensation drip off the support beams along the ceiling and fall to the basketball court like rain. Managers and support staff had to keep mopping up the floor so that the players wouldn't slip in the water. But nothing was stopping this game.

The Lions were there. The Blackhawks were ready. A radio station out of Jasper would broadcast the event live across southern Indiana, and Bird was animated beforehand, urging on his team to win, as Bobby Knight slipped in through the back door to assume his position near the floor with Dave Bliss.

It was time to play.

Bird got his points early, scoring 10 in the first quarter alone. But Loogootee was still up at the break, 18–14, and Coach Butcher was about to make it harder for Bird. At the first intermission, he assigned Wayne Flick to cover him from now on. Anytime Bird got near the paint, Flick was to front him while a second player squeezed Bird from behind.

It was a modified double-team, and it worked, but everything at this point was working for Loogootee. As Flick neutralized Bird, Bill Butcher kept scoring, slicing through the Valley defense. Holland realized he had a problem. His guards were too slow and too small to stop Butcher. Valley fell behind by 10 points in the second quarter and the game began to slip away.

Yet somehow Valley closed the gap in the waning moments of the half. Loogootee came out cold to start the third quarter. Bird, who couldn't score inside with Loogootee's double-team all over him, started taking what the Lions were giving him: 25-footers from the corner. The shots fell. Rebounds went his way, too, as Bird used his long arms to reach over Flick and tip the ball back to himself, and suddenly, Valley had a lead, 33–32.

The gym in French Lick hadn't been this loud since at least 1958, the year that Valley went undefeated and advanced all the way to the state championship game. But Loogootee's point guard, Bill Butcher, was unruffled by the crowd noise and the presence of Bobby Knight. Butcher claimed he didn't even see Knight. Didn't even care. He was just locked in on scoring, and Flick was locked in on something else. He didn't like that Bird was going over his back to tip the rebounds to himself, and the next time Bird tried to do it—with 10 seconds left in the third quarter—Loogootee sent him a message. An elbow landed in Bird's chest—"right in the sternum," Flick recalled—and Bird fell to his knees on the floor.

Bird would get up and play on, but he was unable to unspool any magic in the fourth quarter. Flick held him to eight points in the final minutes and 28 for the game, Bird's lowest scoring total in almost a month. Bill Butcher hit the game-winner: a 10-foot baseline jumper that made his father furious, until the ball rattled around and fell in. And then Bird's friend Beezer Carnes frittered away the last chance that Valley had. Beezer called a time-out in the final seconds—a time-out that Valley didn't have—and it was over.

Loogootee 66, Springs Valley 63.

The Valley boys had lost again. Bobby Knight slipped out the back door unnoticed, and no one was more upset about the outcome than Bird. After the game, according to Wayne Flick, Bird left the locker room, walked past a Loogootee fan bus outside, took grief from the kids on the bus, and gave it right back to them.

Bird raised a fist and a finger, Flick said, and greeted them all with an obscene gesture.

7

COACH HOLLAND HEARD THE story about the middle finger later and didn't flinch. It wasn't the worst thing Bird could have done in that moment, with a bus full of Loogootee kids yelling at him. At least he didn't fight them, Holland said. At least he didn't holler.

But with his team, Bird stayed positive. He didn't question Holland's coaching, like some people did that week in conversations at the Jubil Bar or at Flick's, and he didn't blame Beezer for calling a time-out they didn't have. He just said that he looked forward to beating Loogootee the next time, in the second round of the playoffs that March, in the regional tournament.

The locals were certainly excited about that possibility. In the days before the playoffs began late that winter, businesses paid to take out a two-page advertisement in the *Springs Valley Herald* celebrating each member of the team. And after Valley won the sectional and advanced to the regionals, as expected, people in French Lick pulled out all the stops. On the morning of the regional tournament, they held a pep rally in the gym, arranged for a police escort for the team bus, and drove as a town, as a community, to the host site in a place called Washington, 40 miles away. With one more win, the Valley Blackhawks would get the Loogootee Lions again, just like they wanted.

But it didn't work out that way. Loogootee lost its morning game while Springs Valley won. And instead of facing the Lions in a revenge rematch that night, Bird was now in an unexpected situation. He was facing Jim Pentzer of the Bedford Stonecutters, and Pentzer was waiting for Bird. He had had been thinking about him for weeks, actually. Pentzer believed that Bird's stats were inflated because he was playing against small towns. He thought that Bird would struggle against a bigger school like Bedford. Pentzer didn't understand why Bird was getting so much press, and he really didn't like the way that Bird taunted his opponents by dangling the ball behind their heads and tricking them into turning around. If Bird tried it on Pentzer, it wasn't going to work. "I'm not going to turn around," he told his teammates that week. "I'm staying right on him."

Pentzer—a high school senior, bound for a 39-year career as an educator in Indiana schools—had done his homework on Bird. And because he had prepared, Pentzer planned to bedevil Bird with one more tactic. He was going to get low on the block, bang him around, and maybe even pinch the back of Bird's legs to start the game, as the Bedford coaches had instructed him to do many times before. "You pinch their legs," Pentzer said, "to see if they've got hair."

Whatever Pentzer did that night, it worked. Bird played his worst game of the year, scoring just 15 points. Valley lost by three and Pentzer became a basketball folk hero in Bedford, as the Stonecutters moved on to the semi-states. In the days to come, Bedford High would present Pentzer with a bundle of feathers tied with a red ribbon, because he had clipped Bird's wings and ended Bird's high school career.

Bird rode home on the Valley bus to face his life away from the court: his parents' divorce, his father's problems, and his shrinking options for college. Around that time, Joe B. Hall, the head coach at the University of Kentucky, decided that Bird was too slow to play in Lexington. It didn't matter that Bird had made a visit to campus that winter at Hall's invitation, or that Hall's graduate assistant had been showering Bird with praise since January. Instead of signing Bird, Hall was taking three kids from Kentucky, one from Manchester, Ohio, and a different star who was voted the most valuable player in the state of Louisiana in 1974: Rick Robey.

It was a disappointment for Bird, but he didn't have time to linger on it. The day after Bedford beat Valley in the regional final, Bird was getting phone calls at the house from a school that *did* still want him: Indiana. Dave Bliss sat in a hotel room in Champaign, Illinois, calling Indiana's top eight recruits, including Bird, and by the end of the night, Bliss had made a decision. He would be happy, he told himself, if Bobby Knight signed any three of Bliss's top eight players. "As long as Bird is one!" Bliss wrote in his journal. He believed Bird to be the best of the bunch. "Guy is going to be really good."

But phone calls from Champaign weren't going to close this deal. It was time for Knight to return to French Lick.

The meeting happened in Jim Jones's house on Skyline Drive, above the neighborhood where Bird ran around with his friends, and Coach Jones's wife, Joyce, would remember later that the very best version of Bobby Knight was there.

He was humble that evening, interested in Bird, and excited to sell Indiana basketball in Coach Jones's living room. But Knight seemed perplexed as to why he was having to sell his product so hard, why Bird wouldn't just sign. He left French Lick without a deal—cause for concern—and Bliss's thoughts turned again to Louisville. At the same time that Knight was making his visit to Jones's house, Denny Crum's assistant, Bill Olsen, was trying to convince Bird to come south for a visit. Olsen believed that if Bird saw Louisville, met Crum, went out to Crum's farm outside the city, and laid his eyes on Crum's homestead, Bird would realize that Louisville wasn't all that different from French Lick and agree to go there.

The only problem was, Bird wasn't listening. He had dug himself in the way he often did, forcing Olsen into a realization. With the clock ticking and Indiana circling, Olsen couldn't wait for Bird to go to Crum. He needed Crum to go to Bird.

8

THE MORNING OF THE trip to French Lick, Olsen had a simple hope: He didn't want to die. Crum was driving like a maniac on the rural Indiana roads, Olsen said. Too fast for his taste.

In fairness to Crum, they were in a bit of a hurry. Gary Holland had arranged for Crum to meet Bird in the Valley gym before school started. It was Louisville's only shot; Crum and Olsen couldn't be late, and they weren't. They survived the drive and walked into the gym right on time, to have a morning chat with Larry Bird.

Crum was 37 years old that spring, with a car dealer's smile, a perfect coif of hair for television, and limited Division I coaching experience. He had only been the head coach at Louisville for three seasons. But already, he knew he was good. He had played at UCLA for the great John Wooden. He had impressed Wooden with his will to compete in just about anything: basketball, card games, and practice. Crum had led Louisville to the Final Four in his very first season as head coach in 1972, and figured he'd be back soon, in part because he had confidence in how he handled his players. He didn't come down hard on them, with lots of annoying rules. The players could drink beer if they wanted. Smoke cigarettes, too. "Hell," Crum said in 1974, "I go out at night and drink a beer and horse around." Why couldn't they? Crum didn't care what his players did, as long as they showed up on time and were ready to work.

He was positioning himself, in effect, as the anti–Bobby Knight, and he was succeeding. Crum had a salary like Knight's ($30,000). He had a record that was better than Knight's (70–19 in the past three years). And, most persuasive of all, he wasn't Knight. Not even close. On weekends, Denny Crum rode a motorcycle in the hills around his farm, and he drove it fast, too.

"Let's be realistic," the Louisville coach liked to say. "Times have changed."

Now Crum was talking to Larry Bird in the Valley gym—and he was failing to break through, just like Bill Olsen had before him. Bird was polite to Crum, but he was also steadfast. He wasn't interested in Louisville, Bird said, and no, he wasn't interested in visiting. After being snubbed by Joe B. Hall and Kentucky, Bird had decided that he wanted to stay close to home. Any trip across the river, Olsen recalled Bird saying, was going to be a waste.

"A waste of your money," Bird said, "and my time."

But Crum had just made an 80-minute drive to be in French Lick; he wasn't taking no for an answer. So he considered the situation for a moment and then challenged Bird. Crum suggested that the two of them play a game of H-O-R-S-E, right there in the gym, right then. If Bird won, Crum said, Bird could do whatever he wanted. If Crum won, however, it was settled: Bird was visiting Louisville.

Bird accepted Crum's terms and Olsen took a seat in the bleachers, ready for the show. From time to time, Crum would issue a similar challenge to his college players. It was a way of testing their mettle—and his. And Crum usually came out on top, because he had developed a trick shot that was hard to make. Crum would take the ball down into the corner, about 26 feet away from the basket, and would set his feet out of bounds, behind both lines. From this point on the floor, any shot had to be taken at an off-kilter angle. Perhaps more problematic, it would have to clear the backboard from behind. To make it from here, Crum would have to arc the ball into the rafters, send it over the board, and somehow find net—a feat he pulled off many times, but players rarely did. "I don't remember a player ever beating him," Olsen said years later.

Bird was in trouble; Olsen knew it. Then, to make matters worse, Bird made a strategic error. In Olsen's memory, Bird deferred to Crum and told him he could shoot first. "So Denny shoots a free throw," Olsen recalled. "Makes it. Bird matches. Then, Denny takes him to his trick shot—deep in the corner where the sideline and the baseline come together."

At this point, Olsen knew what was coming. In work shoes, not sneakers, and dress clothes, not sweats, Crum set up in the corner, toed the line, sized up the goal, and released the perfect shot. Even decades later, Olsen could see it in his mind, arcing up toward the rafters, sailing over the backboard, going halfway down the orange cylinder on the other side, and then rattling up and away.

Crum had missed. In and out.

Later, when Crum would tell this story—to reporters, boosters, and fans—he was honest about what happened next that morning: Larry Bird beat him in that game of H-O-R-S-E, he conceded. But Olsen said that Crum didn't tell the full truth. Crum didn't admit, he said, that Larry Bird didn't miss a single shot the rest of the morning, as Crum missed them all.

"Five straight," Olsen said. "H-O-R-S-E."

The pair raced back to Louisville empty-handed, and Bird soon walked into Jim Jones's office and announced his intentions. The boy, still just 17 years old, was choosing Indiana. Bobby Knight even drove over again, in mid-April, for a small signing ceremony in the Valley gym—a moment that one of Bird's classmates captured in a photograph and that the *Springs Valley Herald* published a few days later.

In the photo, Bird stands on the floor wearing an Indiana T-shirt under some sort of windbreaker. Holland is at his right. Knight is at his left. There is space between them, as though the three men didn't want to get too close, and there is one other notable detail about the image.

None of the men are smiling.

9

IT SHOULD HAVE BEEN Larry Bird's greatest summer; it wasn't. For starters, he was becoming aware that his father was overwhelmed. Joey Bird was still living with his parents in West Baden that summer and still struggling to hold down a job. And Larry seemed to be starting to see his father in a different light. He knew Joey had always liked to buy rounds of drinks for people—"in return for the drinks they bought for him," he said later. Now it was clear that he was really struggling. "Dad was strapped."

Some weeks, according to Larry, his father was almost broke after meeting his legal obligations to support his mother. He'd only have about $20 left for himself—barely enough to get through the week. And amid these quiet struggles at home, Larry Bird was embarrassed that summer on the basketball court. Indiana sportswriters snubbed him again and again. They didn't care that he had averaged 30 points and 20 rebounds a game as a high school senior. The writers tended to agree with Jim Pentzer: Bird had done it against inferior competition.

Or maybe he hadn't done it at all. Most people who voted for the postseason awards had never seen Bird play, had never set foot in French Lick, and the awards played out accordingly. Voters didn't consider Bird for the coveted title of Mr. Basketball. The Associated Press didn't name him first- or second-team all-state. As far as the Associated Press was concerned, there were at least 15 players in Indiana in 1974 who were better than he was.

Jerry Birge, a sportswriter for *The Dubois County Daily Herald*, 15 miles southwest of French Lick, knew what this was. "A first-class rook job," Birge wrote that spring. He believed Bird had been robbed, and the writer decided to go to work for him, using his column to politick for Bird. The efforts helped lead to one important accolade: Bird was named to the Indiana high school all-star team, one of the greatest honors an Indiana player can receive. But the roster was loaded with players who had been getting more attention all season. The team's coach, Kirby Overman, was under pressure to play the state's co–Mr. Basketballs as well as other big names. Bird thought he spent too much time on the bench during the all-star games and let his frustration boil over in the team's final game that summer, against Kentucky's best high school players at Hinkle Fieldhouse in Indianapolis. Bird refused to reenter the game after sitting out for most of the second half, and, according to reporters, he cried in the locker room afterward, complaining about Overman. "I don't like the coach," Bird said, putting it plainly as always.

Overman understood why Bird felt that way: The kid was disappointed, and probably a little humiliated. French Lick and West Baden had emptied out to spend the day at Hinkle Fieldhouse, cheering on the local boy. Perhaps more important, Bird's friends were there. They piled into the back of Herbie Wyman's Chevy pickup, riding in the truck bed, with the wind in their hair all the way to Indianapolis, just to see him play.

Still, it wasn't a great look for Bobby Knight or his young recruit from French Lick. One of the most prominent sportswriters in the state, Bob Hammel, accused Bird of "petulance born of embarrassment." This was a quality that would not be tolerated when Bird reported to campus in Bloomington later that summer. The Hoosiers were coming off a 23-5 season. They had a roster populated with future NBA players. They had no room on the bench for a freshman from some little town in the southwest corner of the state moaning about playing time.

But Bird understood the deal. He knew that what he had done to Overman was wrong. He wasn't going to act that way with Knight, and he claimed to be excited about going to college on the day he left French Lick in August 1974. Bird caught a ride to Bloomington from his uncle Amon, his mother's brother, because his mother had no car. He was bringing just one bag of clothes. He had $75 in his pocket and, at the end of the day, he had a new home in a dormitory: McNutt Quad.

McNutt had a reputation for two things that Bird liked—or would come to like: beer and basketball. Half of Bobby Knight's team lived at McNutt, including every freshman on the Hoosier roster and four players later selected at the top of NBA drafts. That August alone, there were five future NBA players moving into the dorm rooms, 42 years of future NBA service greeting their roommates, and 37,780 future NBA points unpacking their bags. In short, Knight had placed Bird with his people.

But they weren't just clumped together for companionship; they were at McNutt because it was a short walk to the gym, the arena, and a handful of outdoor basketball courts, where the guys sometimes gathered. On a sprawling campus, the players were close to what mattered most to them: basketball. And when they weren't playing, there were plenty of activities at McNutt to keep them occupied—namely, parties. The McNutt kids were known for throwing ragers, complete with kegs, eight varieties of alcohol, and women. At one of these parties, male students had to pay six dollars at the door, while the female students got in for free.

It should have been a good fit for Bird; he even knew people on campus, people from back home. His high school girlfriend—a cheerleader named Janet Condra, with long hair, fair skin, and a warm smile—lived in the dormitory next door, a five-minute walk away. This could have worked.

But Bird was troubled in Bloomington almost from the start. McNutt housed some 700 kids—about one-third of the population of French Lick—and Bird found the campus outside the dormitory walls to be bewildering. At any given moment that August, 30,000 students were eating in the dining halls, drinking beers on Fraternity Row, trying out for the tennis team, attending the president's welcome picnic, auditioning for the fall production of *Man of La Mancha*, or piling into cars to go to the drive-in movie theater off campus. This wasn't a college. "It was more like a whole country," Bird said later. He felt like a foreigner in this place. He didn't even fit in with his roommate, Jim Wisman, a fellow freshman on the basketball team.

Wisman would later earn notoriety for two moments that weren't about him. The biggest of these involved Bobby Knight in early February 1976. Indiana was playing Michigan at home in front of 17,000 fans. Late in the first half, Wisman committed back-to-back turnovers under his own basket, and Knight responded by grabbing him by the jersey with such anger that it drew the eye of *Indianapolis Star* photographer Jerry Clark. The *Star* stripped Clark's photos across the front page the next morning, above the banner, showing Knight in full snarl with a fistful of Wisman's jersey. In one of the images, Wisman looked worried. And as folks in Indiana woke up to the photos, they began to question their coach for the first time. Maybe he wasn't a disciplinarian, they thought. Maybe he was just unhinged—a charge that Knight denied as he tried to make two other seemingly unhinged decisions. He blamed Clark and the *Star* for his problem and said he wanted to ban all photographers from the next Hoosier home game.

This was Jim Wisman's most famous moment, but maybe only just barely. The second was about Bird—Jim Wisman and Larry Bird in McNutt Quad in the late summer of 1974. The two freshmen likely ended up there together for the simplest of reasons: They were the last two recruits in need of a roommate, and they didn't seem all that different, at least from afar. Wisman was the son of a postal carrier in Quincy, Illinois, a small city on the banks of the Mississippi River. He was white, like Bird; Midwestern, like Bird; small-town, like Bird. And if it didn't work out between Wisman and Bird, there were lots of other basketball players for them to befriend at McNutt. They could hang with the two other freshmen on the team, who were living down in room 386, roll with upperclassmen Quinn Buckner and Scott May, or find future NBA No. 1 draft pick Kent Benson somewhere in the same dorm. It would be fine.

But the room assignment, random as it was, revealed something important about the operation at Indiana: Bliss had recruited Bird, chasing him for a full year, and Knight had signed him in that joyless ceremony in the Valley gym the previous April. But Knight had failed to get to know Bird at all. And it didn't take long for people to realize that pairing Wisman with Bird was a mistake. Wisman was polite and articulate—a good kid, Bliss said, but also different. "He was," Bliss realized too late, "maybe the antithesis of Larry." Bird had that one bag of clothes that he had thrown in the trunk of his uncle Amon's car, while Wisman had arrived on campus that August with a full wardrobe. On the day they moved in, Bird watched Wisman unpack, thinking, *"Man, I don't have nothing."* Teammates who visited their room that August left with the same feeling. John Laskowski, a senior guard, remembers going there to welcome the two freshmen and seeing three things in their room that he would not be able to forget: Wisman's full closet, Bird's empty one, and the wide gulf that seemed to exist between two new roommates. "It was just kind of two different worlds," Laskowski said. Even Wisman's generosity didn't help. At some point, he told Bird he could borrow his clothes, and he loaned Bird money when Bird's $75 ran out. But Wisman was almost seven inches shorter than Bird; most things in that closet weren't going to fit him. And by early September, Bird began asking himself a question: *"How can I keep wearing Jim Wisman's clothes and accepting Jim Wisman's money?"*

In dark times like these, Bird had typically sought solace in one place—the basketball court. He'd go to Butch Emmons's old hoop at the water plant on the banks of the Lost River, to the Springs Valley gym at six o'clock in the morning with Coach Jones, or to the asphalt court on the boulevard down the road from the Jubil Bar in West Baden. And there he'd stay, shooting and shooting. But Bird couldn't find any peace at Indiana. In pickup games in the Hoosiers' arena, Assembly Hall, his new teammates treated him poorly, Bird thought. He complained later than Kent Benson took his ball. Sometimes, in the schoolyard picks before scrimmages, he wasn't selected at all, like those long-ago days at the water plant. Then, in early September, he injured his toe while playing on the outdoor courts. In addition to everything, Bird was now hobbled, limping off to class on an enormous campus that was 15 times bigger than French Lick.

It all began to pile up inside of him until he began to consider a plan: Maybe he'd go home. Maybe he'd leave.

Bird said later that he told no one about his intentions. Said he kept his doubts and his darkness to himself. But folks on campus that September saw through him. At least one person sensed Bird's frustration during the final pickup game that Bird played that month. The guys were in the locker room after a scrimmage. People were showering and Bird was angry, recalled team manager Larry Sherfick. He was angry because he wasn't playing or because people weren't passing him the ball.

As Bird stewed over these slights, Sherfick said, one of the players in the locker room made a comment loud enough for everyone to hear: "Tell us again, Larry—where are you from?" The implication, Sherfick said, was clear. Bird was a nobody from nowhere. And at this point, Sherfick recalled, Bird turned to him for help. "He looks at me," Sherfick said. "He's pointing at me, and he says, 'He knows where I'm from. Tell him where I'm from.'"

It was getting late by then and Sherfick was annoyed by the shenanigans. "Frankly, I don't want to get into this," Sherfick recalled thinking. "I'm just trying to get my job done and get back before the dinner line." So, he stayed out of it. He said nothing. He didn't come to Bird's defense—a choice he's thought about from time to time over the years. "I've felt some remorse that I didn't stick up for him," Sherfick said, especially after he heard about what happened next. On the second Friday of September 1974, about three weeks after

Bird's uncle had dropped him off in Bloomington, Dave Bliss said that Bird walked into his office and made a simple announcement: He was leaving.

Outside, it was starting to feel like autumn. Cool weather was moving in and kids on campus had big plans for the weekend. The Hoosiers were playing the Illinois Fighting Illini the next day in their first football game of the season. The soccer team was playing that night against Notre Dame under the lights on campus, and students at Willkie Quad, a dorm about a mile from McNutt, were planning the big party of the weekend. Beer would be served in more than a dozen different rooms. But Bird wasn't going to be there.

Bliss could tell he was serious about leaving. His mind was made up. And Bliss, who believed in Bird, maybe as much as Bird believed in himself, began to search for a way to pull him away from the brink. Bliss knew that if Bird walked out the door, he'd probably never return. "I was panicked," Bliss said. "Bird was going to be so important for us."

But there was nothing Bliss could do. Knight was out of town that Friday. He was making an appearance at a coaching clinic at a Marriott Hotel up in Fort Wayne. People were putting down $25 at the door to meet the great coach of the Indiana Hoosiers, to hear him talk about basketball, and to laugh at his inappropriate jokes, and by the time Bliss reached Knight by phone sometime later, Bird was long gone.

He had packed his things, walked out to Highway 37, and hitchhiked home. A trucker got him as far as Mitchell, and Larry Bird figured out the rest from there.

10

GEORGIA BIRD WAS FURIOUS when she learned that Larry was back in French Lick. She thought her son was squandering his one chance in life, and she told him as much.

"You disappoint me," she said.

Larry didn't seem to understand why she was so upset. He didn't see how he was squandering anything. He had no dreams, at that point, of being a professional basketball player, and didn't know why his mother—or anyone else—would want him to stay in Bloomington if he was unhappy there, which he was.

He moved in with his grandmother, Granny Kerns, in her little house in town, a couple blocks from his mother. He had his uncle Amon send word to Bloomington that his decision was final; he wasn't coming back. And Bobby Knight just shrugged. "We have accepted it," he told a reporter for the *Bloomington Daily Herald-Telephone* that weekend. Knight was moving on, and so was Bird. The young man believed he was taking control of his life, maybe for the first time ever. Then he used that control to make a curious choice. He enrolled at a small technical school in West Baden and joined the college basketball team there. He had left Indiana University—one of the best basketball schools in the country, run by one of the most successful coaches in America, in a town that bled Hoosier red for its team—to play for Northwood Institute.

Northwood was located just south of the old water plant and about a thousand feet from the Jubil Bar—and it was exactly as small as it sounded. It had a total enrollment of about 250 students, and a strange and singular campus. Northwood's dorm rooms, classrooms, and offices all existed inside an old domed hotel.

This hotel, unlike the school, had once been great. In the early part of the 20th century, it had been a hub for socialites, mobsters, vacationers, and health nuts who believed that the hotel's spring water had healing properties. People came to French Lick from across the Midwest to stay at the hotel, drink the water, play golf next to the water plant, meet the circus animals that wintered on the grounds, enjoy the card games that went all night, and attend the dances held inside the hotel's grand atrium beneath its domed roof. It was, objectively, a stunning room. Sometimes, people came to the hotel just to see the atrium and walk on its floor—a floor said to have been hand-laid with 12 million individual pieces of Italian marble.

But that was a long time ago now. The only thing stunning about the place in the autumn of 1974 was how far it had fallen. The circus was gone, and the golf course was, too. The old fairways were overrun with weeds, flooded in parts, and wild. The upper floors of the hotel were completely vacant; there weren't enough students enrolled at Northwood Institute to fill them. The kids ran amok up there because they could, and they did the same thing in the grand atrium beneath the dome. In place of the elegant dances that had once filled the room on Saturday nights in the 1920s, there were now co-eds streaking across the floor, naked at four in the morning—a scene that moneyed visitors could not have imagined decades earlier.

For all of these reasons and more, members of the Northwood team were shocked when their head coach informed them that Larry Bird was joining the roster. Glen Tow, a five-foot-five guard and the captain of the team, was coming off of a summer job laying pipe for a construction company. He would have given almost anything to have had the talent to play for Bobby Knight in Bloomington, and he had just one question when he got the news that Bird was coming to Northwood.

"Really?"

It didn't make sense to Tow. He almost felt bad for Bird, and his teammates felt the same way. They had enrolled at Northwood because they didn't have another option to play basketball. The team's center, Dave Earley, might have been working in the timber business with his father over in Seymour if he hadn't come to Northwood. One of the team's forwards, Kent Hutchinson, might have enrolled at a little school in Franklin, Indiana, if Northwood's track coach hadn't reached out to him. In fact, basketball wasn't even the primary sport for many of the guys on the team. They were there to run track or play baseball. And now they were sitting in the windows of their rooms upstairs, watching Larry Bird walk across the atrium and wondering what he was doing there.

Bird seemed to be asking himself the same question. At one point shortly after he showed up, Northwood's head coach asked Tow to help Bird get the books he'd need for class. "So I got the list and everything and took the list to Larry," Tow recalled, "and Larry just looked at me and said, 'I'm not going to need these books.'" Tow wasn't sure what to make of the comment; all the other guys were hoping to get a degree.

But for all the doubts they might have had about Bird's academic commitment, no one had questions about his work ethic in the basketball practices held that fall in an old gymnasium across the boulevard from Northwood Institute.

The little gym, called Sprudel Hall, was the last remaining relic of long-defunct West Baden High School, and it was showing its age. At places on the floor, the ball wouldn't bounce much at all. Bird's new teammates couldn't wait for practices to be over. Northwood's culinary students were always churning out great food—lasagna, chicken cordon bleu, and Cornish hens served in little nests of baked bread—and no one wanted to miss the meals. But Bird didn't care. While everyone left for dinner, he'd stay at Sprudel Hall and keep shooting. Sometimes, Dave Earley, the team's best player, would drive by hours later and find the lights still on and Bird still inside, playing games against himself. He'd bounce the ball off the bleachers, retrieve the off-kilter carom, and throw up off-balance shots from 35 feet out. Or he'd drop-kick the ball off the wall, chase it down, and shoot from wherever he scooped it up again. It didn't matter if he was 10 feet from the basket or 50, Earley recalled. Bird would just turn and shoot, preparing himself for some future moment in some future game, when it really mattered.

The Northwood guys had never seen anything like it, and Earley began to ask himself: *Who is this Larry Bird?* He'd heard stories that Bird's father drank too much and couldn't hold down a job, and because there was nothing to do in town, Earley and a couple of other guys went out one night that fall to investigate the situation for themselves. They piled into Earley's 1968 Oldsmobile, followed the railroad tracks behind the high school, found Georgia Bird's house in the dark, and idled in front of it on the street.

They probably weren't there for more than 10 seconds, but Earley would never forget the silence that filled the car—"dead silence," he said—as everyone eyed Bird's house. It was small, crooked in places, and not just poor. It sort of felt sad, Earley said. He realized in that moment why Bird stayed in the gym and never seemed to go home.

"There wasn't really anything to go home to."

Sometime that November, just before Northwood's first game and a couple of weeks before Bird's 18th birthday, Bird stopped coming to practice. He quit the team and dropped out of school again—developments that surprised almost no one at Northwood. Tow had wondered from the start if Bird would stay, and the next time Tow saw him, Bird wasn't playing basketball at all. He was working for the city street department, riding on a garbage truck, collecting trash.

Tow didn't say anything to Bird that day; he might have just waved, he thought later, as the garbage truck rolled by. He certainly didn't say what he was thinking at the time: that Bird was wasting his talents, that Bird was wasting his life. It disappointed Tow, and lots of other people in town felt the same way. They'd see Bird that winter shoveling snow, fixing streets, or picking up the trash and wonder why.

But Bird liked working for the city. The job put money in his pockets and helped him buy his first car, a used Chevy. It also gave him something to do while his father unraveled even further. That December, in the county courthouse, Georgia Bird asked the court to hold Larry's father in contempt—for failure to pay child support—and according to Larry, his father went dark. By Christmas, Larry was worried about him, and by the first week of February 1975, the local police were looking for him, knocking on the door of Joey Bird's parents' house in West Baden.

It was a Monday, right in the middle of Springs Valley basketball season, and folks in town had moved on by then. No one was talking about last year's team. No one was talking about Larry Bird. The boy had made his choices and the father was about to make his choice, too. When the police came calling, Joey Bird grabbed a shotgun, turned the barrel around on himself, placed it against his head, and pulled the trigger.

In an instant, he was dead, and Larry Bird slipped farther and farther away.

Part II

THE MOST NOWHERE PLACE

11

ON THE DAY THAT they buried Joey Bird in February 1975, laying him to rest in a cemetery on a hill outside of French Lick on the road to Dubois, Bill Hodges was facing his own sort of crisis.

His career as an assistant coach was moving in the wrong direction. He had left a perfectly good job at Tennessee Tech because he wasn't getting along with the head coach there. The players on the floor could feel the tension between the two men—at least one said he felt sorry for Hodges—and Hodges had finally decided to move on. But his new job at Armstrong State in Savannah, Georgia, was a full step below Tennessee Tech. Hodges was now mired in the wastelands of Division II, with a meager salary, a wife who felt isolated in her new town, a young daughter to raise, a résumé that might be hard to explain to a future employer, and almost no budget to do the thing he did best: recruiting, door to door. His new boss at Armstrong State didn't even like him using the phone, one colleague said, and by February 1975, this boss was whispering about Hodges behind his back, threatening to fire him at season's end.

Like Larry Bird, Bill Hodges was drifting to the edges of the basketball map. He was almost gone. But Hodges had been living on the edge his whole life. He had been raised on a dead-end road in rural Rosston, Indiana, about twenty miles north of Indianapolis and nine miles from the nearest town, Zionsville. Here, Hodges was assigned daily chores, namely milking his family's cows, but he only had one dream: He wanted to play basketball, and he practiced whenever he could on a wooden backboard nailed between two trees.

By the late 1950s, Hodges was good enough to make the team at Zionsville High, and he became something of a star there, with his hawkbill nose, slender frame, and sandy-brown hair tinged with hints of auburn. As a senior in 1961, Hodges scored 24 points against Benjamin Davis High School, 21 against Warren Central, and 17 against Whiteland. But he was only five foot ten, too small and too slow to be great at basketball, and even when he was playing, Hodges was best known as a fighter. If wronged, Hodges would fight just about anyone—on or off the floor. Kids in Zionsville would remember a few of these epic brawls long after they had forgotten Hodges's best basketball performances. They'd recall him taking down bullies, much larger kids, in the headlights of parked cars, and they'd know one other detail for a fact: No college recruiters came calling for Hodges in 1961 at his parents' farmhouse in Rosston.

Bill's father figured that was just as well. Wilson Hodges believed basketball was a frivolous pastime and a waste of human resources. He thought Bill should be farming instead of shooting on that backboard nailed into the trees, or working, like him, at the Rock Island oil refinery in Indianapolis. And after graduation, Bill made the sort of pragmatic decision that young men with limited options made in rural Indiana at the time and still make today.

He enlisted in the air force.

Bill Hodges's basketball career might have ended then, but he couldn't shake the dream. If he couldn't *play* basketball, he wanted to coach it. And in the summer of 1966, out of the air force and back home in Indiana, he got a lucky break. Hugh Thimlar, a longtime Indiana high school basketball coach, spotted Hodges playing in an outdoor league in Zionsville and took an interest.

Thimlar wasn't just any coach. He was a basketball raconteur known across the Midwest for his gap-toothed smile, his giant personality, his fondness for Scotch and water, his winning record, and his annual coaching clinics in Indianapolis—clinics that drew hundreds of coaches each spring. Now Thimlar was transitioning into the college ranks. He was the head coach at a newly opened junior college in Fort Myers, Florida, and he had a modest offer for Hodges. Thimlar would give Hodges a roster spot as long as Hodges agreed to drive the team bus and look after the young guys living in the dorm, an old firehouse in Fort Myers.

Hodges would have accepted this position from almost anyone, but doing it for Thimlar was an easy choice. He would be learning at the feet of a legend; living in Florida; spending warm afternoons on Thimlar's houseboat, the *Buccaneer*; cruising down the coast as Thimlar knocked back another Scotch and water; and driving Thimlar's bus across the state. "*Hodgo!*" Thimlar called him as he navigated through traffic. Then, around 1967, Thimlar gave Hodges another job. He asked him to run the hospitality room at his annual clinic in Indianapolis, serving cold cuts and beer to the coaches.

It was another menial position that would have earned the disapproval of Bill's father. But in that hospitality room, Hodges met coaches from Indiana, Kentucky, and three other states. He began to forge relationships with them over white-bread sandwiches and cold cans of Budweiser. Hodges soon had contacts at every little gym in Indiana. And around this time, he worked another job that helped: Hodges spent a summer selling Electrolux vacuum cleaners door to door.

Every morning, he'd leave his parents' farmhouse in Rosston, throw the vacuums into his car, and head out across the county, practicing the company's pitch in his mind. Electrolux had it all written out, but Hodges learned that his delivery mattered. And if he managed to get in the front door, Hodges went to work. He dumped dirt on the carpets, scattered heavy silver balls on the floor, and then displayed the elite performance of the Electrolux by cleaning up the mess.

If Hodges got into the living room, he was closing the deal.

In 1970, at the age of 27, Hodges finally parlayed his tenacity, his connections, and his ability to sell anything into his first meaningful basketball job, that job at Tennessee Tech.

He moved south with his young wife, Connie; coached the freshman team; returned home to recruit in Indiana; lived with his parents in Rosston as he scouted high school games, scouring the state for talent; brought Connie with him at times, turning high school games into dates; and developed his own philosophy as he traveled across the Midwest, drinking Tab soda and eating Snickers candy bars at the wheel of his car. Hodges was looking for kids with good hands, quick feet, and timing. He wanted players who could see the future on the court, who knew where the ball was going before it got there, and he was willing to do almost anything to find them. For long stretches in the 1970s, Hodges would leave Connie, and soon their daughter, Zoie, and live on the road in the name of basketball.

Like lots of young coaches with big dreams, Hodges believed that the hard work would pay off with a bigger job at a better school. Now here he was at Armstrong State, working in a shared office, driving an orange Plymouth van on the few recruiting trips he did make, and fighting for scraps at the bottom of the basketball food chain. Hodges was turning 32 that March, three years younger than Bobby Knight and the same age as Dave Bliss, with almost nothing to show for his years of sacrifices. At the time, Bill and Connie didn't even have much money for new clothes, forcing Connie to sew and tailor his sports coats. Maybe he should have listened to his father, taken that job at the oil refinery, and stopped chasing his basketball dreams long ago.

But Hodges still had one man in his corner: the good-time guy of Indiana basketball, Hugh Thimlar, and Thimlar was busy that February, working all the angles as usual. In addition to coaching his junior college team, teaching driver's ed in Fort Myers, and drinking Scotch on his boat, Thimlar was preparing for a meeting.

The new head coach at Indiana State University was flying down to Florida, and he was going to be leaning hard on Thimlar, because Indiana State was starting over. The head coach was building a staff out of nothing, and he was looking to hire the kind of people that Thimlar knew well: young assistants with nothing to lose.

12

BOB KING STEPPED OFF the plane and into the Florida sunshine in late February 1975, looking like every other snowbird who flew south in the winter: old.

King had thinning white hair, chunky black glasses, surgically repaired knees that made it hard for him to move, and a troubled heart that doctors had been warning him about since he was a teenager in rural Iowa. The problem back then was rheumatic fever; it had kept him bedridden for months on his parents' farm and scarred the valves of his heart. Now the issue was mostly stress. King, the athletic director at Indiana State, had fired his basketball coach that month and made a bold decision: He was hiring himself for the job.

The idea wasn't as crazy as it sounded. Once, a few years earlier, King had been a great coach at the University of New Mexico, building a program out of nothing in the desert. The key, King believed, was defense. "A certain type of defense," he said. He wanted his players to cover opponents man-to-man, apply relentless pressure, and stay in front of them with fundamental footwork. He taught them how to *step* and *slide* and *run* and *glide* in full-court one-on-one drills, and he never wanted to let anyone into the lane. King called this general area "the house," and sometimes he even used tape to mark it out on the floor during practice. No opponent, King said, was to run through the house without getting checked, followed, elbowed, or blocked.

But the job at Indiana State came with challenges that King had never faced in New Mexico. The school was in Terre Haute, just 50 miles west of Bobby Knight's turf in Bloomington. Knight was always going to have first dibs on any player in King's backyard, and after Knight came Digger Phelps at Notre Dame and Fred Schaus at Purdue—big-name coaches at big-name schools. This wasn't the desert; this was basketball country. Great programs were everywhere. And in truth, King wasn't even fourth in line. No high school basketball player grew up dreaming of playing for Indiana State.

For starters, the city of Terre Haute was a punch line. In the 1970s, comedian Steve Martin didn't hesitate when *Playboy* magazine asked him to name "the most nowhere place in America." "Terre Haute, Indiana," Martin replied simply. "There was nothing of anything you'd want." He told *Playboy* that he knew he was "nowhere" when he came to Terre Haute for a stand-up gig and started seeing commercials for high-quality manure on his hotel television. That seemed right to him. "Because," Martin said, "what do you do in Podunk for a night?"

The mayor of Terre Haute used the comments to his advantage. He invited Martin to return to Terre Haute and give the town a second chance—an invitation that Martin accepted, much to the mayor's surprise. Martin landed in Terre Haute, flanked by two Playboy bunnies, and by the end of this trip, he admitted he might have been wrong when he named Terre Haute "the most nowhere place in America." "I should have said Abilene." But none of this did much to help the image of Indiana State, the little school in downtown Terre Haute.

Until the 1960s, the school had been known as the Indiana State Teachers College, a name that didn't excite anyone, except perhaps aspiring educators. In an effort to modernize and diversify, officials agreed to drop the "Teachers College" moniker and seized upon a mascot to represent its nickname, the Sycamore. In 1969, a one-man committee working at the behest of the athletic department suggested that an Indian in full headdress would work best, and thus was born Chief Oubachi, and his female counterpart, the Indian Princess.

But the rebranding and reinvention couldn't change Indiana State's core identity. With a tuition of just $600 a year, the university was the most affordable college in the state. As a result, the students often came from working-class homes. Many were trying to become the first in their families to graduate from college. The presence of Chief Oubachi and his Indian Princess didn't do much to put fans in the seats at basketball games. In the 1970s, the school's new 10,000-seat arena, the Hulman Center, sat at least half-empty on most winter nights. The students didn't want to be there when they could be slugging back cheap beers at the Ballyhoo Tavern instead. Some high schools in Indiana drew larger crowds than the Sycamores.

These circumstances would have been difficult to overcome for any coach, but maybe especially Bob King. He was 51 years old that winter and hadn't coached a game in three years. He needed to find young assistants who could help him navigate the junior college ranks—a murky world where the best Division I basketball coaches circled like sharks in shallow water. In order to succeed in the mid-1970s, a coach needed to know how to sign junior college talent, bending NCAA rules when necessary. To win at Indiana State specifically, King was going to have to discover players who had been overlooked by Indiana, Notre Dame, and Purdue. He'd need to find the meat amid the leftovers. And to do that, King couldn't just turn to junior colleges; he was going to have to *live* in Indiana high school gymnasiums—or hire someone who would.

Hugh Thimlar understood, of course. He was part of that world—deals went down all the time at his coaching clinic in Indianapolis—and he had lots of ideas when King showed up at his house in Fort Myers in late February 1975. To start, Thimlar suggested that King hire Stan Evans to be his first assistant.

Evans was 30 years old that winter and would add instant credibility to King's bench. He was a head coach at a junior college in Miami. He knew how to run a program. He could show up on day one and impress boosters in Terre Haute, with his nice suits, polished shoes, and confidence. And perhaps most important, Evans knew how to play the game off the court. He wouldn't come to Terre Haute empty-handed, Thimlar assured King. He'd bring junior college talent with him, namely one player from his roster in Miami: a six-foot-eleven forward named DeCarsta Webster.

DeCarsta was a walking NCAA investigation in size 17 shoes. In the span of about nine months, DeCarsta had failed to graduate from his Philadelphia high school; resurfaced 500 miles away in Knoxville, Tennessee, for reasons no one could fully explain; started taking evening classes there to try to become eligible; and sparked an NCAA probe involving the University of Tennessee. The investigation found no evidence of rules violations, but DeCarsta was declared ineligible for an athletic scholarship, due to his grades. He then disappeared and reappeared one more time, landing on Evans's junior college roster in Miami.

Even Stan Evans had to admit that the DeCarsta story was suspect. "It's got everything in it that's wrong with recruiting," he told reporters. But Evans was not taking a Division I coaching job without bringing DeCarsta with him. They were a two-for-one deal, and King closed it that winter in Florida with an understanding, if not a promise, that Evans would replace King as head coach one day, whenever he retired.

Evans prepared to move north as he tried to keep DeCarsta a secret—he didn't want a bigger school swooping in to steal him away. Meanwhile, King stayed in Florida to find the second item on his shopping list: a recruiter who knew Indiana. The good news, for King, was that Hugh Thimlar had an idea for that job, too.

He suggested that King meet his old friend Bill Hodges.

13

HODGES DROVE DOWN TO Florida at the end of February 1975 to attend a junior college tournament and take the meeting with King. He thought it went well. The two men even had dinner together that night with Thimlar and a handful of others. But King hesitated to make the hire. He was considering another recruiter with Indiana roots, and he seemed to need reassurance that Hodges was the right choice. Sometime that March, in order to learn more, King placed a call to an unusual reference: a mustachioed forward on Indiana State's roster, Geoff Shuck.

Shuck was surprised to pick up the phone in his off-campus house in Terre Haute and hear the flat Iowa accent of his new coach, Bob King, on the other end of the line. But Shuck soon realized why King was calling. Before Shuck had transferred to Indiana State in 1973, he had played two seasons at Tennessee Tech. Bill Hodges had recruited him to go there, and King had a simple question for Shuck: What did he think of Hodges?

Shuck's mind drifted back to two places in time. He pictured Bill Hodges in the gym at Tennessee Tech in the winter of 1971, trying—and,

Shuck thought, failing—to coach Tech's freshman squad. Hodges was inexperienced, and it showed on the floor. He wasn't a great strategic coach, Shuck thought. But then Shuck pictured Hodges in a different place: in Shuck's living room in Kokomo, Indiana, in the spring of that same year.

At the time, Shuck was averaging 18 points and 17 rebounds a game for Kokomo Haworth High School and getting looks from NC State, Maryland, and Kentucky. UK's famous head coach, Adolph Rupp, even visited the Shuck house that year and did something that the family would talk about forever: Rupp, with 855 career wins to his name, got down on his hands and knees in the living room to help fix the family television with a repairman who just happened to be there at the time. It was funny to the Shucks, but also revealing. If Rupp was willing to help fix the family television on his visit, Bill Hodges was wasting his energy coming to the Shucks' house. Geoff wouldn't be playing basketball at Tennessee Tech.

But once Geoff's father, Gene, let Hodges in the door, everything changed. Gene Shuck had been raised in a tiny Indiana town, just like Hodges, and he had grown up poor, also like Hodges. Over the years, Gene Shuck had toiled in an egg hatchery, farmed, sold equipment, and worked construction jobs—anything to scrape and claw his way to a better life, just like Hodges once had. He and Hodges were soon talking about all the people they knew in common, and in the conversation that followed, Hodges landed on what Gene really wanted: a place where *both* his boys could play college basketball—not just Geoff, but his older brother Rick. It was an opening that Hodges could exploit, and he did. In an effort to land Geoff Shuck, Hodges offered a scholarship to Rick, too, and it was done.

Geoff wasn't going to Maryland or Kentucky anymore.

"Bill Hodges showed up," Geoff recalled later, "and by the end of that conversation, my dad says, 'You're going to Tennessee Tech.'"

Bob King listened to Shuck's story, hung up the phone, and soon made a decision of his own. He gave Bill Hodges the job. Hodges was headed back home to Indiana with Connie and their daughter, and in early April

1975, he moved into an office next to Stan Evans in the old practice arena that housed the athletic offices on the west side of campus. Hodges and Evans each had their own desk and their own phone, but the two offices were connected by a door. They were in this together, and King couldn't wait to introduce his new staff to the power brokers in Terre Haute.

The occasion that week was a luncheon. The location was the Varsity Club. The new coaches wore sports coats, steamed and clean, and the mood that day was upbeat. King promised to reverse years of mediocrity in Terre Haute by signing players who were physical and aggressive and wanted to be there. These players, King said, would play a brand of basketball that people wanted to see. He predicted that more people would start coming to games, and he vowed to deliver a winning program that would make locals proud.

"Within three years," King said that day, "we're going to have something here."

It sounded great, smiles all around. But by the end of that week, Hodges and Evans were already at odds over one player. Hodges wanted to drive down to French Lick—and live there if he had to—in order to recruit Larry Bird, and Evans wasn't so sure.

14

THE CORONER HAD NO trouble determining Joey Bird's cause of death in February 1975. It was a gunshot wound to the head, and Joey hadn't missed. He died instantly inside his parents' house in West Baden.

But the *why* of the matter—*why* had Joey done it?—was up for debate and discussion. The coroner blamed Joey's death on "progressive psychosis." The townsfolk whispered about the drinking. Larry's relatives liked to link it to his time in Korea, to whatever he had seen in the war. Larry came up with his own theory. He believed his father killed himself so that his mother could collect his Social Security check. By this theory, Larry's father wasn't crazy, or clouded by alcohol, or haunted by nightmares. He was a stubborn man, making good. If Joey couldn't pay child support to Georgia, he'd help her by going away.

Whatever the cause, there was no moving on from something like this. People in French Lick and West Baden talked about Joey Bird's suicide for weeks. It was gossip at the high school, rumors at the Jubil Bar, whispers in the gym, and chatter in the old domed hotel where Bird had played basketball for a short time the previous fall. In a small town, this was big news, and there was seemingly only one place Bird could go to avoid it. In late February, just two weeks after his father's death, he returned to the basketball court and began playing for a new team: Hancock Construction.

The team was out of Mitchell, 20 miles north, and it was exactly what it sounded like: glorified pickup basketball. Hancock Construction was a small group of men in their late 20s and early 30s with wives and day jobs. One of them worked as a dispatcher for a concrete company in Jeffersonville. Another was a high school teacher in Bedford. And while each of them had been good basketball players once, maybe even great, they were in the industrial league now—a collection of teams sponsored by tool companies, restaurants, taverns, and liquor stores.

The men who suited up for Hancock Construction approached their competition accordingly. They didn't practice much or even wear complete uniforms. They would play in mismatched shorts, and no one seemed to care that Larry Bird was on the roster. The small-town newspapers that covered the industrial league couldn't even spell his name. He was Larry *Baird* at times that winter. Not a star, just another has-been, lacing up his sneakers in an empty gym on a Wednesday night. In early games with the Hancock squad, Bird wasn't even the leading scorer.

But the two men who ran the team—Monk Clemons, a portly Black man, and Jerry Hancock, the white mayor of Mitchell and the owner of the construction outfit that sponsored the squad—took the games seriously. They thought Bird would help Hancock win, and they were right. In their first tournament with Bird on the floor—a statewide competition held in Mitchell in late February—Hancock beat everyone and earned an invite to a regional tournament in Des Moines, Iowa. With Bird, Hancock was good enough to travel, and the workaday guys on the roster were thrilled about the notion of the road trip to Des Moines in early March.

But a couple of key players weren't able to get away for the trip. The team drew a horrible slot for its opening game—10 o'clock on a Friday night. It was almost Saturday morning by the time it was over, and it didn't end well. The Hancock Construction guys had driven eight hours to lose, 113–95, to a team from Detroit.

The moment had come and gone for them, but it had mattered for Bird. In that late-night game in Des Moines, Bird put up his best numbers in more than a year—34 points and 25 rebounds—and college recruiters took notice. They had been coming to French Lick for months, trying to find and sign Bird, and they stepped up their efforts again now. Sometimes, they didn't even wait for Bird to get out of the showers after his Hancock Construction games, recalled Bird's teammate, Gary McCooe. They stood there in their sports coats and their ties, McCooe said, falling over themselves to be the first one to hand him a towel, or they showed up unannounced at Georgia Bird's house. In this little window of time, Georgia figured at least 200 coaches tried to entice her son back to school.

But all of their efforts failed. Bird would dress in silence and leave the gym, McCooe said, and any recruiter who had the guts to show up on Georgia's doorstep in French Lick that winter got the same treatment. Larry had told his mother to run everybody off because he knew what he was doing with his life. He wasn't going back to college. He was staying in French Lick. He was keeping that job with the street department. He liked working with his crew, and he didn't care what anybody thought about it.

15

THERE WAS NO EASY way for Bill Hodges and Stan Evans to get from Terre Haute to French Lick.

No interstates connected the two towns in the far reaches of Indiana. Anyone looking to make the trip would have to take state highways or winding country roads the whole way. These roads could be treacherous at times, especially in the dark. Cars crashed in the countryside all the time, crossing the double yellow line headlong into each other, running into deer, or plowing off the road into ditches. Under the best-case scenario, Hodges and Evans were signing up for at least four and a half hours of driving, round trip, and once they reached French Lick, there was no guarantee that they'd even find Larry Bird. This wasn't a recruiting visit. This was a wild goose chase, and the hunters were blindfolded.

But Hodges, in particular, was willing to sacrifice the day. He had seen Bird play twice for Springs Valley in 1973 and 1974 while he was up north recruiting for Tennessee Tech and working at Hugh Thimlar's clinic, and had reached the same conclusion as Dave Bliss. Bird, Hodges thought, was the best player on the floor. Hodges didn't understand why everyone didn't see it, or why Bobby Knight had let him walk away. And Hodges didn't care if Stan Evans or others thought it was a waste of time to spend a day down in French Lick. He knew it wasn't. And so, they went. In April 1975, shortly after arriving in Terre Haute, Hodges and Evans borrowed a vehicle, drove south, and rolled up about two hours later at Springs Valley High School in French Lick to pop in on Bird's former coach Gary Holland.

Holland was still young that spring, just 28 years old. But he was no longer the wide-eyed innocent he had been 18 months earlier, at the start of Bird's senior year. Since that time, Holland felt like he'd met every college coach in the Midwest—slick recruiters coming through, always asking about Bird. He had long ago learned to dodge their advances, and he continued to protect Bird, as he had during high school. Holland wasn't serving Bird up on a platter to anyone, especially not out-of-towners with their own agendas. And he had other reasons to ignore Hodges and Evans when they showed up at his office unannounced that day in April. Holland's first child, a son, had been born recently, 10 weeks premature. The baby boy was at a neonatal intensive care unit up in Indianapolis, and Holland had been going there every day after the last bell. He didn't have time for a visit from a couple of Indiana State coaches near the end of his school day. He was in a hurry to visit his son, driving north.

But for all his reservations, Holland immediately connected with Hodges. Holland felt like Hodges was on his level: a country boy, comfortable in his own skin, and not too pushy. Hodges just wanted to meet Bird, he said, and minutes later, Holland found himself driving Hodges and Evans over to Larry's mother's house—a quick detour on his way to the hospital.

Hodges was going to get his chance to knock on that door, and he was ready for it. But on the stoop of Georgia Bird's little house, it went about as well for Hodges as it did for everyone else who had come knocking. She told Hodges to go away and slammed the door in his face.

Holland could only shrug. There wasn't much more he could do. He got on the road for the hospital while Hodges and Evans got back into their car. They were on their own now, marooned in French Lick.

The two assistants, Hodges and Evans, might have been new on King's staff, but they weren't new to each other. They had briefly overlapped at Tennessee Tech a few years earlier, before Evans left for an assistant coaching job at the Citadel and then that head coaching post at the junior college in Miami. Their wives were friends. Connie couldn't wait to reunite in Terre Haute with Stan's wife, Dee, and at that moment, due to budget constraints at Indiana State, the two men were sharing a hotel room in Terre Haute while they looked for permanent places to live in their new town. They knew each other well enough to live together, at least briefly.

But Hodges and Evans were different people—too different probably to ever be close. Hodges had grown up without indoor plumbing on that dead-end street in rural Rosston, and Evans had grown up in Cincinnati, in a neighborhood called Deer Park. Hodges's father had never attended his basketball games. Evans's father had always been right there—at the scorer's table in Cincinnati, invested and involved. Hodges chewed tobacco, keeping a brown pouch of Levi Garrett leaves at the ready and spitting the juices into a plastic cup, while Evans showed up to work in pressed slacks and starched shirts, on a schedule and on time. And the two men were different in other ways that everyone noticed. While Hodges lived for basketball, Evans lived for lots of things. He enjoyed discussing politics and movies. He liked *dancing*, and in an act bordering on heresy, Evans might have preferred baseball to basketball. Unlike Hodges, Evans had possessed real talent in high school—as a catcher for the baseball team at Deer Park High School.

In 1966—the same year that Hugh Thimlar offered Bill Hodges the gig driving the team bus for the junior college in Fort Myers—the Atlanta Braves had drafted Stan Evans, assigning him to the Gulf Coast League. And even though Evans flamed out a year later—batting just .203 in A-ball—big-city Stan still managed to surpass small-town Bill in every stop of their parallel coaching careers. Evans had the job at Tennessee Tech before Hodges, and that head coaching post before Hodges, too. He was a winner in that position in Miami—going 37–22 in two junior college seasons—and Evans carried himself like he knew he was good. At one point, in Miami, Evans said he could violate any NCAA rule and get away with it. "If I wanted to," he claimed at the time, "I could get a kid in here who didn't even graduate from high school."

The problem was, Evans didn't seem to like everything about coaching—and he really didn't like being an assistant. He called it "one of the worst jobs anyone can have." He didn't want to scout games. He didn't want to recruit, either. He openly complained about the tasks that Bill Hodges loved. Sometimes, Evans even complained about the kids he was recruiting. Once, in 1974, while he was still in Miami, Evans admitted to a reporter that some kids, from tougher backgrounds, scared him. "It crosses my mind every once in a while," he said, "that if I cut a kid, I might have to look over my shoulder going out to my car." Evans even complained about the prized—and controversial—recruit he had brought with him to Terre Haute in 1975: DeCarsta Webster. Shortly after Evans had accepted the coaching position at Indiana State, a reporter called him to write a feature story about DeCarsta, and Evans shut it all down.

"Why do you want to talk to him?" he asked the reporter. "He doesn't deserve it." Evans believed that DeCarsta's publicity outweighed his actual ability, and he told the reporter that day that he wasn't even sure DeCarsta was joining him in Terre Haute for the right reasons. "He's insecure," Evans said, "and needs a friend."

This was maybe not the man to bring to French Lick to chat with a fragile, sensitive, and wounded teenager who didn't like to talk, didn't trust strangers, and didn't want to be found. Yet there they were, Hodges and Evans, cruising up and down the boulevard between French Lick and West Baden—on a loop. They drove past the pool hall, the Shell station, the JayC food mart, the Jubil Bar, and the basketball court where Bird liked to play. They drove and kept driving because Hodges had come too far to leave without finding his man. In a community this small, he figured, there weren't many boys who were six foot nine with blond hair. They'd find him sooner or later, he believed.

Hodges was right about that. On the next trip down the boulevard, there was Larry Bird, walking out of the laundromat.

Bird had spent the past eight months running: from Bobby Knight and the big campus in Bloomington; from Glen Tow, Dave Earley, and the basketball team at Northwood Institute; from the college coaches at his Hancock Construction games; from the recruiters knocking on his mother's door; from the people in town talking about his father's death; and maybe even from the pain he felt. When Bird had received the news that his father had killed himself, he couldn't decide if he should cry or not.

Now, according to Hodges, Bird tried to run again. He wanted nothing to do with these two coaches from Indiana State standing outside the laundromat on the boulevard. But Bird was there with his grandmother, Granny Kerns. She didn't think it was right to turn away these nice men who had come down to see him, and soon they were all back at Granny's house in French Lick, making awkward conversation—about Bird's job with the city, his work collecting trash, his fondness for the job, and his plans for the future, if he had any. Hodges would remember later that Bird wouldn't even look at him, and he would also remember how Evans nearly screwed it all up with his impatience and sarcasm. "What are you going to do?" Hodges remembered Evans asking Bird. "Work on a garbage truck for the rest of your life?"

Hodges grew worried. He thought he needed to get Evans out of there before he made Bird angry. But he salvaged the conversation by boxing out his fellow coach and establishing a tenuous connection with Bird over their shared experience in rural Indiana. Hodges had never lived in French Lick, but he had put up hay before, back home in Rosston. Hodges had never driven a garbage truck, but like Bird, he had worked odd jobs in hard times, selling those Electrolux vacuum cleaners door to door. They had things in common. And maybe most importantly, Bird understood the product that Hodges was selling. A year earlier, while Indiana and Louisville were recruiting him hard, Bird had considered playing basketball at Indiana State and had even made a visit there in February 1974 with Jim Jones.

Now, with Hodges in his granny's living room, Bird began to open up just a little. He started talking about Kevin Carnes, a former Springs Valley guard and the older brother of Bird's high school teammate Beezer. Kevin, Bird explained, still played basketball in French Lick; he had even made an all-star team in the local men's league that winter. If Indiana State was looking for someone, Bird suggested, maybe Hodges and Evans could go find him. Kevin lived in town, worked as a maintenance man at the Sheraton hotel, had a wife with a kid on the way, and was easy to spot in the men's league games with his long hair, mustache, and talent. In Bird's opinion, if Kevin Carnes had left French Lick and gone to college, everyone in Indiana would have known his name by now.

It was an opening, and Hodges took it.

"Larry," Hodges said, "someday they're going to say the same thing about you."

Back in the car, a little while later, Hodges and Evans drove north on the boulevard, headed home to Terre Haute. It had been a long day. They had a tough drive ahead of them. And while they had found Bird, the two assistant coaches weren't returning to campus with anything solid, or anything at all, really. They couldn't even agree on whether the trip had been worth it. In Hodges's memory, Evans believed that any player who would choose a job on a garbage truck over a college basketball scholarship at Indiana was a player not worth recruiting.

But Hodges saw it differently. He knew he'd be back in French Lick soon, and this time, he would come alone. On the ride home to Terre Haute that day, Hodges vowed to never again make a recruiting trip with Stan Evans.

16

KEVIN CARNES WASN'T SURE why Bird mentioned his name to the two recruiters from Terre Haute.

"I'm working at the Sheraton," Carnes said. "My wife's pregnant. I'm not going to Indiana State."

But Hodges kept coming around that spring. Carnes would see him at the Shell station, on the boulevard, with Bird or looking for Bird. Hodges became a fixture where the young men hung out. Bird felt like he was always there. Every time he turned around, there was Hodges. "Every night," Bird said. "Every day." He wouldn't let Bird go. Along the way, Hodges began to understand Bird's character and his needs.

Bird didn't mention his father's suicide to Hodges, or almost anyone else, but Hodges learned the news from Holland and others in town and took pains to make Bird feel comfortable—safe, even. In the spring of 1975, Kevin Carnes wasn't the only name that Bird mentioned to Hodges; he also mentioned Danny King—another former Springs Valley guard who had spent two years in junior college and played with the Bird brothers in high school. Danny was now looking to catch on with a Division I school, so Hodges began to recruit him, too, and signed him in early June 1975. If Bird came to Indiana State, he wouldn't have to bunk up with a stranger, like Jim Wisman; he could room with Danny. Hodges was building a de facto support system around Bird. And with each visit, he was building trust. Sometimes, they didn't even talk about basketball. On a trip to French Lick in late June, about three weeks after signing Danny King, Hodges and Bird talked about baling hay—Bird's job that afternoon. Bird was out there, working in the heat.

By that point, Hodges felt confident that he had Bird, but he remained concerned that another coach, from a bigger basketball school, could steal him. And his worries were validated that very night, as he drove back to Terre Haute, skipping Bird's Hancock Construction game against the Indiana high school all-stars. The all-star team that year was loaded, as usual. The roster included a prospect signed by Bobby Knight, two players going to Purdue, a seven-footer bound for NC State, and Bird's old nemesis from Loogootee, Bill Butcher. This team should have beaten Hancock Construction, and almost any other industrial league squad. But the game was just a scrimmage for the all-stars—a tune-up for an overseas trip that they were making that year. Their coach was distracted with questions about passports and paperwork. And once the game began that night in Mitchell, everyone in attendance realized that there was no stopping Bird. Straight out of the fields, baling hay, he scored 39 points and led Hancock over the all-stars, 122–121.

Hancock's coach, Monk Clemens, went striding into newspaper offices the next morning to gloat, and Bird's former coach Jim Jones could only shake his head. College coaches were bound to start peppering Bird with phone calls and visits now, Jones thought. Hodges had to close the deal, and around this time, he decided to do so by listening to Bird. He invited Bird to come visit Indiana State; play in a summer pickup game with the Sycamores, in their gym; stay overnight in a hotel; bring his brother Mark if he wanted; and bring the friend he had mentioned in that first conversation back in April, Kevin Carnes.

After weeks of gentle persistence, Hodges had finally broken through.

"I'll come up," Bird said.

The summer pickup games were supposed to be informal affairs, casual and not required of the team. By NCAA rule, a coach couldn't have a hand in the games at all. But coaches didn't obey these rules—no one was monitoring them anyway—and on the day that Larry Bird came to visit Terre Haute, Bob King couldn't resist getting involved. Before the scrimmage, he called a private meeting in his office with the team's two best players, Geoff Shuck and Rick Williams, to let them know what was happening and ask them to do him a favor.

Shuck and Williams were heading into their senior years and had battled some good college players by that point in their careers, including an imposing big man at Centenary named Robert Parish, who would find fame with the Boston Celtics in the 1980s. As a result, King wanted Shuck and Williams to guard Bird, study him, compare him to others, and report back to his office after the scrimmages to let him know what they thought.

"We'll have a good conversation," Shuck recalled King saying.

As Shuck and Williams got dressed to play, their teammates began to trickle in, and Johnny Nelson was among them. Unlike Shuck and Williams, Nelson was not an important piece of the Sycamores puzzle. He hadn't been made aware that Larry Bird and his French Lick boys were going to be there and hadn't been summoned for any sort of meeting in King's office. Nelson had just arrived, pulling up in his blue Mustang from his afternoon shift as a lifeguard in Rockville, 30 miles north, for what he imagined was another evening of pickup basketball with his teammates.

The stakes, for Nelson, could hardly have been any lower. He wasn't thinking much about basketball that summer, and he wasn't playing much, either, because he knew his place on this team. Nelson was an undersized senior, about five foot eight, who had made a grand total of six shots the previous season and was playing out the string on his basketball career. He felt lucky that King hadn't cut him that spring after taking over as head coach—but not lucky enough that he was working harder to secure his spot. In Nelson's own estimation, he had spent the summer of 1975 playing golf, flirting with women, and drinking beer— and not necessarily in that order. He was there that night in Terre Haute to work up a sweat, have a little fun, and go home. The presence of the three guys from French Lick—Larry Bird, his brother Mark, and Kevin Carnes—didn't change any of that. How important could they be if they weren't even willing to change into Indiana State's usual practice garb— blue-and-white jerseys? The French Lick boys didn't want them.

"We're fine," Larry said. They were going to play in their blue jeans and T-shirts instead.

Hodges didn't get it, and Nelson didn't, either. But Nelson didn't spend another minute thinking about it. He didn't know these boys from French Lick and he was never going to see them again. He shrugged, got dressed, hit the floor, and promptly lost his first game. Which was why he was sitting courtside a short time later when Bird, his brother, and Carnes emerged from the locker room in their street clothes and sneakers.

The French Lick boys were finally ready to play.

What happened next would alter the course of basketball history, shape life in western Indiana for decades to come, change Larry Bird—save him, possibly—help write one of the greatest underdog stories of the 20th century, and forever alter the lives of countless people, including the coaches in the arena that day and the players who would be there soon.

But at the time, the moment didn't feel significant at all. It was just summer basketball, with a few strangers on the floor in their blue jeans. Hodges gave Bird a fourth player—a backup point guard named Jimmy Smith—and Bird filled out his team by pointing to Johnny Nelson.

"I'll take that little itty-bitty guy," he said.

Bird didn't know Nelson's name—not then and not later. For decades, whenever Bird told this story, he would continue to refer to Nelson as "some itty-bitty guy." Nelson didn't care, though. For the next hour or so, no one could beat him and his team. "We never left the floor," Nelson recalled. "We just mopped up against the regulars. We were amazing. And I distinctly remember saying to myself, 'All I've done is drink beer and chase girls this summer—and I'm *better*.'"

Even Shuck and Williams had to agree that Bird was impressive. He was agile for a big man, Shuck noticed, and ambidextrous, too. Bird could score with either hand, just like Jim Jones had taught him back in French Lick, and he was seemingly unafraid. At one point that day, Shuck recalled, Bird intercepted a pass at midcourt while Shuck's team was on a fast break. Bird was now headed in the other direction, Shuck said, all alone and dribbling straight at Shuck's teammate DeCarsta Webster, who had been late in getting up the floor and was still standing beneath his own basket.

DeCarsta—the coveted recruit who claimed to have had college offers from 250 schools and who had come north with Stan Evans that summer as the centerpiece of Bob King's two-for-one deal—was poised to do now to Bird what he had done to others many times before. DeCarsta was going to block Bird's shot and prove why he was worth all the attention he was getting.

But DeCarsta was flat-footed, Shuck said. Bird was moving with speed right at him, and he seemed to know just what to do. In Shuck's memory, Bird lobbed the ball over DeCarsta's head, kissed it off the backboard, caught the ball in midair with one hand—"the left hand, by the way," Shuck recalled—and then stuffed it.

A thundering dunk in the summer night.

A short time later, Shuck exited the game for a water break and slid into a seat next to Bob King in the arena.

"Do I still need to come to your office later?" Shuck asked.

"No," King replied.

Larry Bird was enrolling at Indiana State.

Part III

THE HARRY AND LARRY SHOW

17

DR. RICHARD LANDINI—DICK, to friends—needed to pull off the impossible in the late summer of 1975.

The new president at Indiana State University had to command the room, sound capable, and impress faculty members with his intellectual heft and soaring vocabulary. But he also needed to connect with the modern student in a way that was authentic, fresh, and hip. Landini was expected to be a "liberal thinker." He needed to be like John F. Kennedy—in a state that Richard Nixon carried three times. And Landini had to do all of these things while saving Indiana State from financial ruin, growing irrelevance, and academic oblivion.

Enrollment had been stagnant or declining at Indiana State for years. The university wasn't anywhere close to the growth it had projected for itself a decade earlier, and evidence of that decline was apparent on campus. Two new dormitory towers, which had opened with great fanfare just a few years earlier, sat empty and would soon have to be shuttered and converted to other uses due to a lack of students. It was an "enrollment famine," Landini said, and he had to find a way out of it or face his own sort of oblivion: forced resignation and public shame.

Landini—a former English professor who considered the great American poet Ezra Pound to be a friend—believed he was ready to tackle the job. "I do not shrink from such demands," he told the faculty in the summer of 1975. "I welcome them." But he also knew what would happen if he fell short, because he had failed publicly before. In his first role in administration, several years earlier at Arizona State University, Landini had been put in charge of opening a new 500-acre satellite campus in the suburbs of Phoenix, and he had decided to go big. The new campus, he said at the time, was going to be a shining example of what modern education could be. He was going to have libraries in every dormitory, student-led discussions in class, a roster of liberal arts professors stimulating young minds, a plan to sacrifice history in favor of present-day issues, and a radical shift involving the three R's of education. Instead of focusing on reading, 'riting, and 'rithmetic, Landini said, he wanted students to ponder "relevance, reintegration, and reassessment."

It was a squishy curriculum that might have upset conservative lawmakers in Arizona under any circumstance, but Landini ensured their opposition when he joined a silent vigil on campus in 1968 to protest the war in Vietnam. One Arizona Republican accused Landini of agitating for three different R's: "rebellion, reaction, and revolution." Others didn't like the way he spoke to them: over their heads, as though he were better than them. The more Landini talked, in fact, the worse it seemed to get for him, and lawmakers in Phoenix ultimately took great pleasure in canceling both Landini and his celebrated campus. "Anything that has to do with Dr. Landini," one lawmaker said, "I don't want to be part of." Two years of work evaporated in two weeks. The satellite campus was dead, and Landini was soon looking for a new job.

Today, such political gamesmanship would sink an academic's career, probably forever. But Landini overcame it. He moved on to a high-level post at the University of Montana and used that job to become president at Indiana State in early 1975 at almost the exact moment that Bill Hodges and Stan Evans were interviewing with Bob King. He satisfied Indiana State trustees, who had concerns about his Vietnam scandal, and he won over skeptics with his ability to think creatively to solve the university's many problems. If 18-year-olds weren't coming to the school, Landini said, then maybe they needed to target 24-year-olds. If faculty morale was low, he said, then the president needed to be on campus to listen. And if students were upset, the new president needed to think like a student.

Landini realized that this last part would be difficult. He was turning 46 that year and noted that his blood flowed "with a more tepid fervidity" than the average co-ed's—a phrase that most students would have met with tepid fervidity as well. Lots of people needed a dictionary when Landini was speaking—even at sporting events. "At the football games, he wouldn't yell, 'Go . . . fight . . . win!'" recalled John Newton, the university's associate director of alumni affairs in the 1970s, who often sat next to Landini at games. "He yelled, '*Attrition! Attrition!*'"

But at least Landini had a plan. He pledged to move into a house in the heart of campus. He was going to live right there, with his wife and kids, among the college students every day, and he vowed to attend as many sporting events as he could, chain-smoking his unfiltered Camel cigarettes in the crowd and cheering on the Sycamores to win until the bitter ends of games—"until the last dog died," he said—because Landini knew something in 1975 that other university presidents hadn't yet fully grasped. Landini knew that sports mattered to a modern university.

If he needed proof of that, Landini didn't need to look far. In the fall of 1975, Bobby Knight's Hoosiers—the team Larry Bird had abandoned one year earlier to hitchhike home to French Lick—were coming off a 31-1 season and Indiana University was reporting record enrollment. It was a detail that surely didn't escape Landini's notice, in part because he admired Knight. He found him agreeable, forthright, and honest.

"The fact is," Landini said, "I like him."

Even later, when most fans had soured on Knight's antics, Landini would write Knight warm letters, telling the embattled coach to ignore the naysayers and pay no heed to the baseless criticism that Knight was facing—"the undeserved contumely," Landini called it in one note.

Knight probably reached for his own dictionary in that moment, or shouted at someone to help him understand what the hell Dick Landini was saying. Other advice Landini offered to Knight was easier to decipher. At one point, he dismissed Knight's critics as hypocrites and reminded Knight of the special place reserved in Dante's *Inferno* for such people. The hypocrites lived in the eighth circle of hell, wearing golden cloaks of gilded lead.

Landini's sentiment seemed to be clear. Win, and it didn't matter if a coach yanked a kid by his jersey. Win, and let university administrators like him deal with the "contumely." Win and forget the rest. It could be, Landini suggested, a good problem to have.

But Landini's problem in the summer of 1975 was different than Knight's.

He needed his basketball team to win at all, and it didn't seem likely to happen that year, despite the new coaches and their new recruit, Larry Bird. By NCAA rules, Bird was a transfer player, and transfers had to pay a price for their indecision. It didn't matter who he was, where he had come from, how much he loved basketball, or how much he needed it.

Bird had to sit out the entire season.

18

IT WAS A STEEP price for any kid to pay, but maybe especially Bird.

It had been less than six months since the death of his father, and he still wasn't talking about it with almost anyone: not Mike Cox, one of his oldest friends; not Jim Jones, his longtime coach and mentor; and not the man who recruited him to Indiana State, Bill Hodges. In all the hours that Bird and Hodges had spent together that spring and summer, he hadn't mentioned his father's death even once. He seemed intent on swallowing his pain whole, and Hodges decided to take his cues from Bird. If Bird wasn't going to talk about what had happened with his father, neither would Hodges. They could ignore it forever, walking past the darkness. But that didn't mean Hodges was going to let Bird suffer alone. He decided to support him, doing things that Bobby Knight had never done.

Bird needed a place to live that summer, so Hodges got him set up in Terre Haute. First, Hodges moved him in with John Newton, the school's associate director of alumni affairs, who sometimes sat next to Landini at ball games. Newton was in his late 20s and had a house on South 22nd Street with four bedrooms that Newton and his wife could not fill. Bob King's athletic department sometimes leveraged those empty rooms for new recruits. DeCarsta Webster lived there. A kicker on the football team lived there. And, for a brief time in the summer of 1975, Bird lived there, too.

The Newtons were good people; Bill Hodges loved them. But for Bird, someone not keen on strangers, it was probably a nightmare arrangement, and he spent his short time in the Newtons' house in almost total silence.

John Newton recalled that Bird lived in an upstairs bedroom, said little, and seemed intimidated by the basics, like dinner. "We didn't do anything fancy," Newton recalled, "but he was more used to white bread and baloney."

Hodges needed to get Bird out of there quickly, and he did. As soon as Bill and Connie got set up in an old house on Ohio Street, Hodges moved Bird into the basement and found him a roommate who could make Bird feel at home. Danny King moved into the basement with him. The two French Lick boys, who had known each other for years, didn't have much in the way of amenities downstairs, outside of a couple of beds and a secondhand refrigerator that Hodges had picked up. But it was a place to sleep. The rent was cheap—five dollars a week, Hodges said—and Bird wasn't going to have to figure out how to make the payments on his own, because Hodges had this covered, too.

From the moment Bob King had landed in town from New Mexico, he had been working to build an infrastructure of local business leaders who could help support the team. By the summer of 1975, when Bird and Danny King were living in Hodges's basement, this network was in place and ready to go to work. Indiana State had a banker who would employ the players' girlfriends or wives; a sandblasting executive who would summon his airplane at King's request; car dealers who would outfit the coaches with new vehicles; a retail leader, Lucien "Lu" Meis, who believed that putting fans in the seats at the basketball arena would help bring shoppers back downtown; and a local entrepreneur who had made his money in coal, trucking, and waste management and had more pull in Terre Haute than almost anyone: Max Gibson.

Hodges was on the phone with the banker first and Gibson second. While Danny King had to work that summer in a local plastics factory, melting down scraps over a blazing-hot furnace, Bird got a job as a groundskeeper in a private, bank-owned park. He was doing what he loved, working outside. He was making a little cash. And he was soon booked for a dinner date that most people in Terre Haute did not get. Not long after he landed in town, Bird was invited to share a meal with Max Gibson at his house.

Gibson was in his mid-30s at the time, and he was country, like Bird.

He had spent most of his childhood in rural Fontanet, about 10 miles outside of Terre Haute, and had a family story that connected him to everyday people. Max's father had started the Gibson Coal Company in the 1930s with just one truck. That truck had helped build a fortune. Max now oversaw much of that fortune, and his house in Fontanet was unlike anything Bird had ever seen in French Lick or West Baden. It sat on about 500 acres of farmland, had a tennis court out back, and felt a little like a country club, only with cattle—Gibson had cows, too.

Almost any teenager would have been out of place in this situation, and Larry Bird certainly seemed to be on the night he came to dinner. Max Gibson's oldest son, Greg, 13 years old at the time, would always remember Bird's first visit. Bird wore overalls and was painfully quiet while Max tried to pry words out of him at the dinner table. Bird didn't seem like an all-time great—"I thought, *Man, who is this dude?*" Greg recalled.

He wasn't making decisions like an all-time great, either. That fall, shortly before the basketball season began—the season Bird would have to sit out—he married Janet Condra, his girlfriend from Springs Valley High. He was still a few weeks shy of his 19th birthday, and now he was a husband, moving into married-student housing, a complex of squat buildings south of campus. The buildings had the look and feel of old communist bloc apartments. Bird would admit later that he wasn't sure why he was there with Janet. He knew he was too young to be married. And now he was living almost a mile away from the place he liked best: the practice gym.

It didn't go well at the gym that fall. On the floor, in front of the basket, Bob King taped out "the house." He taught the players to *step* and *slide* and *run* and *glide* in his full-court one-on-one drills, and he ran them until they got the fundamentals right. But the Sycamores didn't win.

The stars from the previous year's squad, Geoff Shuck and Rick Williams, began to wonder if King cared about this season, the last one of their college careers. Meanwhile, Bird grew frustrated with the way King was using him in practice. One night, he threatened to quit—*again*. Bird said later that King wasn't playing him against the first-teamers because he was dominating them and destroying their confidence. Shuck and Williams disagreed with that premise; they believed they challenged Bird every night. And amid all the changes and drama, Indiana State limped to the finish in March 1976. The team was mediocre, as usual, ending the year one game over .500.

However, something was building in Terre Haute. Bird spent countless hours that year just shooting—first in the practice gym, and later at the Boys' Club in town. Sometimes, Hodges would return home late from a recruiting trip, see the lights on at the club, walk inside, and find Bird on the floor with a basketball in his hands. It was midnight, it was one o'clock in the morning. It was time for him to be home with Janet, Hodges said, and there was Larry, shooting. The long nights in the gym seemed to fill Bird with an almost unshakable belief in himself. At one point that season, Bird turned to Rick Williams as they peeled off their practice jerseys in the locker room and made a pronouncement that Williams never forgot.

"One day," Bird said, "I'll be making a million dollars doing this."

Williams laughed. He thought it was a joke. But Bird was serious. And while he was working on his game, Hodges was, too. Hodges lived on the road that year, drinking his Tab sodas, eating his Snickers bars, sacrificing time with Connie and his daughter for Indiana State, and searching for players who could fit with Larry Bird.

19

THE FIRST TIME BILL Hodges saw Carl Nicks—in a high school gymnasium on the South Side of Chicago in early 1976—he didn't even know the player's name. Hodges had come there to scout a six-footnine forward on the opposing team who had an older brother playing at Michigan—proven Division I genes. But once the game started, Hodges found himself fixated on Nicks. The left-handed guard for Englewood

High School was built more like a running back than a basketball player. He was compact and muscular. And he was using his speed—and above all, his grit—to dart around the forward that Hodges had come to see. Nicks just kept scoring, and by the end of the game, Hodges didn't even want to talk to the other player. He only wanted to see Carl Nicks.

Nicks wasn't used to talking to recruiters, and he was wary of Hodges specifically. He had spotted Hodges in the stands before the game and convinced himself that the assistant coach had to be an undercover cop. In the 1970s, white men didn't show up unannounced at Englewood High, an almost entirely Black school in the city's tough Public League, about 10 miles south of downtown, three "L" stops past Comiskey Park, and deeper into the South Side than most people were comfortable venturing at the time. Unemployment in Nicks's neighborhood hovered around 20 percent. Rival gangs fought over the turf. Innocent people often got caught in the crossfire, and kids like Nicks had their own problems at home. Carl's father, the Reverend O. C. Nicks, was a prominent Black preacher who was hard on Carl and his brothers, and Carl's mother had taken to drinking, perhaps in an effort to escape.

Nothing good could come of a conversation with a strange white man, Nicks thought, and Hodges's opening remarks, introducing himself after the game, didn't do much to change Nicks's mind. He had never heard of Terre Haute, Indiana. But the more Hodges talked, the more Nicks liked him. Hodges didn't make promises he couldn't keep, and he kept the one promise that he did make. He said he'd be back soon to see Nicks again.

While Hodges began to work his way into Nicks's life—and his parents' house near the corner of Eggleston Avenue and 63rd Street on the South Side—Stan Evans drove 100 miles east from Terre Haute, to Rushville, Indiana. The little town, population 6,700, was surrounded by farmland and had never been known for basketball greatness. But that was changing in 1976, thanks to Brad Miley.

The Rushville senior had terrible shooting form. He'd pull the ball back over his head and release it with two hands, almost like a soccer player executing a throw-in. But Hodges wasn't interested in Miley for the beauty of his shot; he was drawn to his six-foot-eight frame, his defense, his willingness to work, just like Nicks, and his one basketball superpower: rebounding. In March 1976, Miley powered tiny Rushville to the brink of a state title by pulling down 29 rebounds in the state semifinal game—a new record. In a place where basketball mattered, where thousands of kids had collected millions of rebounds, no one had ever grabbed more in a single game than Brad Miley.

He was a basketball unicorn. A flawed unicorn that could not shoot, but a unicorn all the same. Hodges had to have Miley on the roster that fall, and he wanted one more player—a player who would come to define the next two years almost as much as Bird.

Hodges wanted Harry Morgan.

Morgan had been on Hodges's radar since at least 1974, when Morgan was a senior at Madison Heights High School in Anderson, a factory town about 15 miles outside of Muncie. That year, Morgan set the school scoring record, averaging 24 points a game. More importantly, perhaps, Morgan did it with flash and style. He swaggered onto the court with his tall Afro and big smile and liked to entertain the fans by leaping into the air and throwing down dunks. "I can do it all," he said. "My offense is just *there*."

The comments—and the leaping displays—sometimes earned Morgan side-eye looks; no one seemed to work harder at promoting Harry Morgan than Harry Morgan himself. But opposing players had no idea what he had overcome. His parents had left their homes in rural South Carolina and moved to Anderson for those factory jobs, only to learn that the racial problems in Anderson were worse than the ones down south. The Ku Klux Klan ran thick in Anderson. Hundreds of white-hooded men had once paraded through town. And while the hoods were harder to find now, the Klan's messages were not. In the 1970s, racial fights shut down Harry's high school. Black parents walked out of a school board meeting when they couldn't get answers. White families cheered as the Black families left. One Easter weekend, crosses burned in people's yards, and in

1976 the Klan marched again in Anderson, no hoods necessary this time. They walked down the street, proudly showing their faces.

It was as if the Morgans couldn't catch a break. They had found the good work they had dreamed of, but they were still fighting for everything they got. And in some ways, Harry internalized this fight every time he stepped on a basketball court. He was playing for a leg up, a better life, a fresh start, and for his family. Like Bird, Harry was married. He and his wife, Rita, had a young son to support. Morgan thought about them every time he stepped on the floor as a junior college player in 1976, and he was thinking about them again that April when he drove down to Evansville to showcase his skills at an event that he thought had a chance to change his life, the annual tri-state AAU tournament.

This plan could have sounded like more bluster and folly from Morgan. The tri-state tournament games in Evansville typically drew small crowds—maybe 75 people.

But there was nothing typical about this night. Morgan's team, Sun Oil, was playing Red Geranium, and the Red Geranium squad included a handful of retired Indiana Pacers and former college stars. Rick Williams, Indiana State's graduating senior, was playing for Red Geranium that night. Four-time ABA all-star Bob Netolicky was going to be on the court, too. And Red Geranium's biggest name was one of the most famous Pacers of them all: six-foot, nine-inch Mel Daniels. In the 1960s, Daniels had been a standout for Bob King at the University of New Mexico. In the early 1970s, Daniels led the Pacers to three ABA titles. Along the way, he won two MVP awards, and he burned with an intensity that fans in Indiana loved. Daniels once used his formidable elbow to open a gash on a defender's head that required 30 stitches.

This was something to see; even Larry Bird was coming. Bird caught a ride with Williams to watch Daniels play that night in Evansville. But there was a reason why Daniels was playing for Red Geranium in April 1976, and not the Pacers. He was washed up at age 31, overweight, out of shape, and past his prime. He also lacked the motivation of a Harry Morgan. While Daniels was playing for gas money and a hotel room in Evansville, Morgan was playing for everything. And in front of a crowd of about 600 people—an enormous audience for an AAU game—Morgan took it to Daniels that night. He went over and around him. He scored 33 points for the game, and he made a play that people who were there would never forget—Harry Morgan perhaps most of all. Fifty years later, Morgan could still see it in his mind: how Bob Netolicky tried to put the ball into the hoop with an underhanded lay-up, how Harry blocked the shot against the backboard and went streaking down the court the other way, how Rick Williams tried to get back in time to stop him, how Harry ran right past Williams, cupping the ball in one hand, and how he slammed it through the hoop for a show-stopping dunk.

Red Geranium won the game in the end, thanks in part to some friendly refereeing. With the revenue that tournament organizers were making at the gate, they didn't want Daniels's team to lose. But the story that night was Harry Morgan.

"Couldn't nobody stop me," Morgan said afterward. "I did it all."

On the ride home to Terre Haute, Rick Williams and Larry Bird found themselves agreeing. They stopped on the road, Williams recalled, bought a six-pack of beer, drank it in the front seat of Williams's car as they drove, and talked about Morgan. And the next day, everything that Bill Hodges had been working for started to fall into place.

Carl Nicks signed with Indiana State. Two weeks later, Harry Morgan joined him. And in early May 1976, Brad Miley decided to come to Terre Haute, too. Miley wanted to stay close to family in Indiana, but mostly he wanted to play with Larry Bird.

20

BOB KING COULD HARDLY believe his good fortune. He had the star he needed and the team he wanted. He had Harry and Larry. And as he pondered his new lineup before the season began, King made a prediction—to himself at first, and then to others, out loud. He believed that reporters would be coming to Terre Haute from across the country to cover this basketball team.

It was an absurd statement, full of hubris, and no one knew that better than Ed McKee, the school's sports information director. McKee had been in Terre Haute since 1971, long before Bob King and Dick Landini, his new bosses with their big dreams. So McKee knew the dark reality of Indiana State sports in those years. He had logged long miles on Sycamore road trips in the midst of seasons that no one cared about. He had called reporters and never heard back. He knew what it was like to ask for media coverage and get none, and he had learned long ago that he had little control over any of it.

A few years back, McKee had been in the front seat of a team bus headed to a game at Western Illinois when the steering wheel jammed on a two-lane highway and the bus careened off the road, through a fence, and into a farmhouse. The athletes on board that day walked away uninjured—a miracle. But the final moments before impact felt a little bit like McKee's life every day. He had the wheel in his hands, he was driving, but there was only so much he could do. The steering wheel on this bus was jammed, and the farmhouse was coming at him through the windshield.

McKee could at least understand why King was hopeful about his prospect from French Lick. Not that long ago, McKee had been a basketball player himself, at a small college in Kansas. He had been good enough that the Indiana Pacers took him in the same draft as Mel Daniels. And when it didn't work out with the Pacers, McKee played for a few years with one of the most famous industrial league teams in the country—the Goodyear Wingnuts, out of Akron.

It was hard to imagine McKee battling under the basket for a rebound or using his elbow to slash open another man's head, as Mel Daniels had once done. Unlike Daniels, McKee had a gentle Midwestern way about him. But that basketball player was still somewhere inside of his six-foot, seven-inch frame. McKee knew Larry Bird was good—maybe even great. And so he decided to humor Bob King's dreams about national media coverage. Before the 1976–77 season began, McKee created a new position at King's request, effectively doubling the size of the sports information office. He would be taking on a student intern as an assistant, and he found a candidate who would be agreeable to King.

His name was Craig McKee (no relation to Ed). He was about to enter his sophomore year at Indiana State. He was living at home with his parents in Terre Haute, and King liked him right away. Craig had a father working with Landini in administration, the maturity of a much older man, the ability to write press releases, and the poise to handle whatever question Bob King threw at him.

"Do you know Larry Bird?" King asked during Craig's job interview.

"No," Craig replied.

King nodded. That was fine. Most people hadn't heard of Bird at that point. He hadn't played a single college game. But that was about to change, King said. And when it did, he predicted, Craig would realize why Ed was going to need his help.

"Larry Bird," King said, "has the potential to change everything."

Hodges understood why King was so excited, but he hated it when King talked this way about Bird in public. Hodges didn't want King putting too much pressure on Bird or overhyping the situation. After all, Bird hadn't played a real basketball game since March 1974, when Springs Valley lost in the regional final to Bedford with Jim Pentzer pinching his legs. It had been a year and a half—and it felt like a *lifetime*. Since Bird had last played, he had weathered an odyssey of challenges. He had signed with Bobby Knight, abandoned Bobby Knight, worked on that garbage truck, learned of his father's death, attended his father's funeral, and married Janet. And things were changing even still, in ways that would impact them all. Around September 1976, Hodges got a call from a tipster in town that Bird was in trouble: Janet had filed for divorce, citing "an irretrievable breakdown of the marriage." Bird needed to get a lawyer and get himself into Vigo County Superior Court.

On the last Friday of the month, Janet and Larry appeared there together, represented by counsel, and dissolved their 10 months of matrimony in a matter of minutes. With a stroke of a judge's pen, it was over. Janet would be taking back her name, and assuming the court costs, and Larry would be moving on without her. He could stay in married-student housing if he wanted, but he wasn't married anymore. He was 19 years old, newly divorced, saddled with the dreams of others, and about to prove if he was worthy of them.

In the locker room before the first game of the fall of 1976—a scrimmage against the Brazilian national team—Bird was nervous. It showed on the floor. The play was sloppy in the early goings. There were miscues and turnovers. Harry Morgan quickly got himself into foul trouble, and Bird started cold. In the opening minutes, he couldn't hit a shot, and neither could anyone else. But with about seven minutes to go in the half, Bird did something that marked the start of a new era. For the first time since 1967, NCAA players were allowed to dunk in games, and Bird took advantage of that rule change, slamming one home.

This wasn't going to be close. The Sycamores beat the Brazilians by 20, and Bird put up a stat line that folks in Terre Haute couldn't recall ever seeing before. He had 7 steals, 8 assists, 15 rebounds, and 31 points.

It was just a scrimmage, yes. But it wasn't an anomaly. Bird produced almost the exact same stat line in his first regular-season game against Chicago State later that month: 31 points with 18 rebounds and 10 assists. He led Indiana State to victory over St. Ambrose College, even as the St. Ambrose coaches rolled out a defense just to stop him. He scored 33 on Robert Morris, and then he led Indiana State to yet another victory over the University of Denver.

At this point, Bird was averaging 27.5 points a game and reporters at small papers in western and southern Indiana began to place their first interview requests with the Indiana State sports information office. Bird—who had barely uttered a word while staying in John Newton's upstairs bedroom, who had hardly spoken while living in Bill Hodges's basement, and who had struggled to engage while having dinner at Max Gibson's sprawling estate in Fontanet—now had to speak to the press. Craig McKee, Ed's newly hired student assistant, knew that it was a fraught situation. "It was just well known," Craig said later, "that there was subject matter with Bird that was out of bounds. Anything about family. Anything about his father's death. Even leaving IU and going home." These were pages that Bird seemed to want to tear from his diary, Craig recalled. And there was one other potential problem: Bird's manner of speaking when he *did* open his mouth. To the consternation of some locals, it wasn't proper English. Bird sprinkled conversation with *ain'ts*, *cain'ts*, and double negatives.

The good news was, reporters at the small papers seemed more than willing to clean up his quotes. And topics considered "out of bounds" didn't have to be topics at all. The stories could run as if the two McKees, Ed and Craig, had written the pieces themselves, and Bird participated without complaint. In late November and early December 1976, he gave interviews discussing everything related to his favorite subject: basketball.

He discussed how he was learning to play Bob King's defense; how he wanted to pull down more rebounds than DeCarsta Webster in every game; and how he had identified right away what St. Ambrose had been trying to do to him the other night and had adapted accordingly. St. Ambrose had employed a box-and-one to stop him, he said. Man-to-man defense on him and zone defense everywhere else. So Bird passed the ball to Morgan. Morgan led all scorers that night with 24, and Bird was fine with that. "If I get the shot, I'll take it," he said. "But if I don't, if the defense is worried about me too much, I'll hit Harry."

It was a great start—better than even King had imagined—and the Sycamores kept it rolling. They lost to Purdue on the road in early December, as everyone expected, but proceeded to win the next 12 after that. Bird kept putting up points. He was on track to finish the year as a top five scorer in the country—a rising and legitimate star, just as he and Hodges had believed. Morgan was happy with how things were going, too. "I think I'm getting better every game," he told the press. Brad Miley, the new recruit from tiny Rushville, had established himself as the team's best defensive player, coming in off the bench, and reporters coined a nickname for the team—a catchy one that was easy for the two McKees, Ed and Craig, to use in marketing material.

They started calling them "The Harry and Larry Show."

Morgan loved the name and certainly deserved the marquee billing. He was averaging almost 17 points a game that season. But Bird was in a different class. He was scoring almost 33 points per game. In the era before the shot clock and the three-point shot—two changes that would increase scoring in college basketball—Bird was a one-man scoring machine. And at some point, reporters started flipping the order of the two players' names in their stories. The Sycamores became "The Larry and Harry Show," a change that made Morgan bristle.

"I'm not taking nothing from Larry," he said later, "because Larry? He's doing Larry. He's doing great." There was just too much on the line for Harry and his wife, Rita, to allow the media to erase him or belittle what he was doing. The Morgans were living in married-student housing with their young son, and they were dreaming, as a family, of one day going pro. Harry needed the attention. The nickname helped. He didn't understand why reporters felt empowered to change the order of their names in their stories and their headlines. "You can't change history," Harry protested. "See what I'm saying?"

As this tiny fissure began to grow, burrowing into the foundation of Bob King's team—unnoticeable at first, then a crack, spreading and plain for all to see—Carl Nicks sat at the end of the bench, stewing. Unlike Miley, Nicks was hardly playing at all as a freshman. It felt as though Hodges had recruited Nicks to leave the South Side of Chicago and come to Terre Haute—the whitest place Nicks had ever seen—to *attend* basketball games, not play in them. Nicks poured his unspent energy into partying with DeCarsta—a little too hard, Nicks admitted later. They'd start the night at the fraternity parties, and they'd end the night there, too, with Nicks singing Earth, Wind & Fire songs as they walked home in the dark. And within hours of Indiana State breaking into UPI's vaunted poll of the top 20 teams in the nation at the end of January 1977—a watershed moment for Bob King, Terre Haute, and Indiana State—the Sycamores blew it. They lost a game to Illinois State, an average team, and fell out of the top 20.

It didn't even matter that they rallied to win their last nine games and finish the regular season 25–2. This squad wasn't getting an invite to the NCAA tournament. They weren't considered one of the top 32 teams in the country—the number of teams that received an invite in those days. They were overlooked and forgotten and headed to the NIT instead, the lesser of the two tournaments. And, to Bob King's frustration, they weren't even getting a home game out of the deal—a gift that the best NIT teams typically received. Officials dismissed the Sycamores again and shipped them off to the hinterlands.

They were headed south to play the Houston Cougars.

21

THE TEAM FLEW CHARTER down to Houston on a little twin-engine DC-3 propeller plane that the players hated. It was loud and small. There was no room on board for the big men. On the runway, it pitched back with its nose pointed up and its tail riding lower. In the sky, it bounced around, and to the guys, it just felt old, because it was. It had been built decades ago, around World War II.

But no one complained about the DC-3 around team manager Rick Shaw, a sophomore from Plainfield, Indiana, who was wide and heavy at 260 pounds. There was no room on the plane for Shaw. If he wanted to come to Houston—and he did—he was going to have to hitch a ride. While the team flew south on the DC-3, Shaw piled into a small car with a few fraternity brothers he didn't know, squeezed his round frame into the back seat, because he was the extra guy, and then chipped in for gas all the way down.

Still, it didn't matter. Shaw was going because everyone was going: the local radio and television broadcasters from WTHI; the sports editor from *The Indianapolis News*; one of the school's two mascots, the Indian Princess, wearing her full feather headdress; the cheerleaders; Dick Landini; Stan Evans; Bill Hodges and his wife, Connie. She was nine months pregnant with their second child, a son due any day, but Connie was still coming. NIT or not, this was the biggest game that Indiana State had played in years, maybe ever. Houston had the second-highest-scoring offense in the nation and one of the best players in college basketball in Otis Birdsong. The six-foot-four guard from Florida was about to finish his college career as the fourth-highest scorer in NCAA history. Birdsong was on a list just behind Pete Maravich, Oscar Robertson, and Elvin Hayes. He was about to be selected with the No. 2 pick in the 1977 NBA draft, and without question, he was the superior "Bird" in this game.

Until that week, Houston coach Guy Lewis had never even heard of Larry Bird.

The game was on a Wednesday night, and Houston came out ready. The university had imported live cougars to walk on the floor. The Houston band was there, playing loud, and the Cougar cheer squad had made a sign for the team to run through as they appeared on the court for the first time. ON TO THE GARDEN, it said—a reference to the next destination on the NIT bracket. The winner of this game was headed to the tournament semifinals at Madison Square Garden in New York City, and Birdsong walked onto the floor like he knew he was going there.

"I'm ready, man," he said.

King tried to downplay the importance of the moment—and of New York, specifically. NIT games weren't drawing fans like they once had. In recent years, the Garden sat mostly empty during the semifinals. Sometimes, there were just 4,000 fans scattered throughout the arena, like flotsam on an endless sea. But the furthest east that Harry and Larry had ever played was Cleveland. It would have been huge for the young duo to hit the East Coast together, and it would have been big for Landini, too—a reality that King knew well.

"A victory here," he admitted on the trip down, "would be a big jump for our image."

The DC-3 arrived late after being forced to make a stop in Little Rock—an unexpected landing, for unknown reasons. Rick Shaw pulled up with the fraternity boys after 17 hours in the car. Everyone met at a Ramada Inn not far from the Astrodome. The coaches discussed a strategy to stop Houston, then got dressed on game day, with Stan Evans subtly upstaging King and everybody else. While King donned denim-colored slacks and a black button-down shirt, open at the collar, for a game to be televised back home on WTHI, Evans went corporate. He appeared in the lobby of the Ramada in a snappy three-piece suit. It was as though Evans were auditioning for a new job, while they still had a job in front of them: beating Houston. And King knew it wasn't going to be easy. In order to compete against the Cougars, the Sycamores were going to have to take care of the ball, rebound well, and hold Birdsong to 30 points or fewer—an assignment King was officially giving to Harry Morgan, but maybe not for long. In the lobby of the Ramada Inn, just before the Sycamores boarded the bus to head to the game, King pulled Brad Miley aside to tell him to be ready. Just in case.

Early on that night, much to King's frustration, Morgan didn't do anything on offense *or* defense. He came out running and gunning, over-hyped for the moment. He took bad shots, and King got tired of the Harry Show early. When Morgan took his fourth ill-advised shot—and then followed it up by failing to play defense on Birdsong, who scored at the other end—King inserted Miley into the lineup, almost pushing him off the bench and into the game. Still, the problems continued. The Sycamores struggled to adjust to Houston's speed, and a single play in the middle of the first half seemed to encapsulate that issue.

Bird was inbounding the ball from underneath his own basket. He saw Morgan streaking down the court. He threw a perfect pass, 80 feet down the floor, and hit Morgan in stride going to the hoop. Two steps, and Morgan was off his feet and about to score. But Houston's center, Mike Schultz—Guy Lewis's toughest player, his *meanest* player, Lewis said—caught up to Morgan and swatted his lay-up off the backboard. No good. The Houston crowd shrieked, and the Cougars quickly went up by 13.

Only Larry Bird was keeping Indiana State in the game now. He scored every possible way in the first half: baseline jumpers, lay-ups off the glass, tip-ins, dunks. While Birdsong scored 20, Bird scored 24. And Bird continued scoring into the second half, until the sports editor of *The Indianapolis News* made an announcement on press row: Bird was better than Birdsong. It wasn't close. The only trouble was, Bird was losing the game. With 5:58 left, Indiana State was trailing, 80–70, and Morgan couldn't help anymore. He had fouled out.

On the bench, Carl Nicks desperately wanted to play. But King ignored him, inserting Miley back into the game, and the comeback began. DeCarsta hit a 15-footer—a shot he typically missed. Junior guard Jimmy Smith drained a jumper from the left wing. Miley's defense led to a Houston turnover, and his passing led to an easy basket for Bird. And Bird did the rest. In the last five minutes, Bird did almost everything. He took a charge to induce a Houston turnover; he blocked a shot off the backboard, pinning it against the glass; he dove on the floor for a loose ball, cradling it in his arms; he dove two other times, throwing his body everywhere; and he led the Sycamores all the way back. With 55 seconds to go, he tied the game with a turnaround jumper, and when a Houston player missed a free throw moments later, it was Bird who speared the rebound out of the air. Time-out, Indiana State. Down one now, with 26 seconds to go.

Everyone knew what was coming next: a final shot from Larry Bird. In the Houston huddle, Guy Lewis called up a double-team to stop him, while in the Indiana State huddle, Bob King designed a play with Stan Evans that they thought would work. Bird was to inbound the ball to point guard Jimmy Smith. Then he was to park himself in the left corner and wait until the clock was ticking down. At that point, Smith would drive to the hoop, drawing the defense, and Bird would move, running across the baseline to the other side of the basket. While the defense crashed on Smith, Smith would be able to dish the ball to Bird, who should have a decent look. A good shot. A chance.

Out of the time-out, King got exactly what he wanted. Bird inbounded the ball and disappeared for 20 seconds into the left corner while Jimmy Smith and others passed it around. Then Smith went to work. He sliced toward the basket and jumped into the air, as if he was going to shoot. And at this point, some of his teammates thought he should have. Smith was only being guarded by one man, and Bird was late in getting to his spot on the baseline. But how could Smith *not* get the ball to Bird? He made the pass that King wanted, and Bird collected the ball just outside the paint on the right side of the basket with about three seconds to go.

On the bench now, the Indiana State players had their hands in the air. Bird was spinning around to shoot only four feet from the basket—a shot he'd made all night. But Birdsong was in his face, and a second Cougar was there, too, flashing over on the double-team that Guy Lewis had called. And Bird's shot was a little long. It sailed over the cylinder, clanged off the back of the rim, and bounced out.

Houston 83, Indiana State 82.

Larry Bird had scored 44 points, 14 more than Birdsong, but he had missed the shot that mattered the most—a reality that Bird's teammates couldn't process in the moment.

They had been sure he was going to make it.

After the game, Guy Lewis apologized for not knowing Larry Bird's name a few days earlier. "He's the best I've ever seen," he said. "I don't know how he missed All-American; he should be All-World." Otis Birdsong agreed. In four years of college basketball, Birdsong said, he had never faced a player as good as Larry Bird. But that was little consolation to Bob King. The white-haired coach looked even older than usual as he stood on the floor waiting for his postgame interview. He was pale, and tired, and could barely talk to WTHI's play-by-play man, Bob Forbes.

Forbes wanted to discuss the courage the team had displayed coming back in the final minutes, and King conceded it was true. His guys had shown a lot of toughness. But King couldn't stop himself from going dark. He couldn't believe they had been snubbed by the NCAA tournament. He didn't understand why they had to play on the road in Houston—"the boonies," he called it. He felt sure that the Sycamores could have "beaten the heck out of these people anywhere but here." He argued that Bird had been fouled on that last shot—"We had the foul," King said. "They didn't call it."—and he appeared to be staring into a personal abyss: several months without basketball.

"You hate to face not playing," King said.

Forbes was a team-friendly reporter, like every other journalist in Terre Haute. He wasn't there to dig deep, to push King. But in the moment, Forbes felt like he had to ask one question.

"You're going to be back next year, aren't you?" Forbes said.

"Yeah," King answered.

"You're not going to fire yourself, are you?"

"No," King said, "I guess not."

King appeared stunned by the exchange, and more than a little confused. His team hadn't lost a home game since February 1976 and had just finished the season 25–3. Both Harry Morgan and Larry Bird were returning the following year, and Hodges was out there on the road, recruiting more talent. *Of course* he was returning as coach; King was not the problem here. But there were issues that threatened the delicate balance of the team.

For starters, the coaches had difficult news to break to Carl Nicks: He wasn't ready to play Division I basketball. Nicks had struggled in the classroom during his freshman year at Indiana State, and he had struggled on the court, too. His greatest strength—his hustle—had become his greatest weakness. Nicks played too fast, too hard, out of control at times. King kept him on the bench in every meaningful game, including the game at Houston. Nicks didn't play a single minute there, and now Hodges was letting him go. He was demoting Nicks to a school where hopefully he could grow up a little, mature, earn some playing time, and get the experience he needed to save his basketball career.

"We're going to send you down south," Hodges informed Nicks not long after the Houston game, "to Gulf Coast Community College."

The school, in Panama City, Florida, was about a thousand miles from Nicks's home in Chicago, and the last place he wanted to go. In fact, maybe he wouldn't go at all. Nicks didn't like the plan and was determined to weigh his options. But Hodges figured that Nicks would come around—he didn't *have* other options. And besides, Hodges couldn't spend too much time worrying about Nicks because he had other problems.

With the game against Houston, "The Harry and Larry Show" had been officially canceled. This was going to be "The Larry and Harry Show" from now on—a reality that everyone recognized, maybe especially Bird. On the Houston trip, he seemed to flex his confidence in new ways.

At the Ramada Inn, Bird came up with a plan to call Morgan in his room, disguise his voice, pretend to be a reporter, and get his teammate talking. Morgan, a trustful man by nature, fell for the trick. "I didn't know who it was," he said later. He was soon telling Bird all the ways he had been overlooked that season—not complaining, just speaking his truth—while Miley and others leaned over Bird's shoulder, straining to hear the conversation through the telephone and stifling their laughter. Bird couldn't believe how well the prank worked; he'd talk about it for years. "We was all laughin' to bust a gut," he said once, when recounting the prank. Laughing, it seemed, at the expense of Harry Morgan. He also wasn't finished joking around. On the flight home to Terre Haute on the DC-3, Bird offered to deliver the child that Connie Hodges was carrying. Just think of the publicity, he told Connie, if he delivered her baby on a plane. And when they landed back in Indiana, and the players stepped out onto the tarmac to find a small crowd of die-hard fans waiting for them, Bird didn't mind speaking to the people—in jest.

"We don't want no applause," he told the crowd. "We want money."

The quiet kid from French Lick was settling into his new role as a college star, revealing little pieces of himself, for better or for worse. But around that time, Hodges got news that threatened to upset the new order—or at least Bird's state of mind. Bird's ex-wife, Janet, was pregnant, and she said the baby was Larry's in a meeting that Hodges said happened at his house on Ohio Street. If true, this wasn't a problem that Hodges could help make go away by calling lawyers, or by enlisting the help of Bob King's benefactors or anyone else. Bird was going to have to deal with it himself, and he was going to have to do so at a time when his profile was growing even bigger.

In June 1977, Bird began working directly for the most important man in town, Max Gibson, tending to his property in Fontanet and growing closer with his son Greg. The two young men bonded as they mowed the grass on the sprawling piece of land, went swimming in the family's lake, borrowed Max's cars, drove around town with Bird at the wheel, or played tennis on the court behind the Gibson house with visitors, including Bill Hodges.

Then, in July, Denny Crum—Louisville's head coach and Bird's old H-O-R-S-E opponent in French Lick—invited Bird to try out for a team of college basketball stars who were going to spend a month in Europe playing for a world title. Only the 12 best players in the country would make the cut, but with Bird's amazing season and his incredible game against Houston, he was in the conversation.

Larry Bird had a chance.

22

JEFF JUDKINS, A GUARD at the University of Utah, reported to Louisville that July to compete against the best college players in America for a spot on Denny Crum's all-star team, and as he landed in town, Judkins knew his competition well.

He had heard of Phil Hubbard, the Michigan forward who had won an Olympic gold medal the previous summer. He was familiar with the Louisville stars who were trying out, Darrell Griffith and Ricky Gallon.

He was aware that at least two other white players were coming, Dave Corzine from DePaul and Roger Phegley from Bradley. And everybody coming to Louisville knew the big names: Sidney Moncrief at Arkansas; Freeman Williams, one of the nation's top scorers, at Portland State; and "Jammin'" James Bailey, a six-foot-nine forward from Roxbury, Massachusetts, who had helped lead Rutgers to its first—and only—NCAA Final Four one year earlier, in 1976.

Larry Bird, however, was a mystery. Judkins had never seen him on television, or even in a photograph. Indiana State didn't make the newspapers in Utah, and even after flirting with the top 20 in UPI's polls that winter, the Sycamores never made the national magazines. All Judkins knew about Bird was that he was a scorer. Bird had averaged 32.8 points per game in 1976–77, good enough for third best in the nation. And so, when Judkins arrived in Louisville and learned that he was rooming with Bird, he formed a picture of him in his mind: "I'm thinking, *OK, I'm rooming with a guy from Indiana who's African-American.*" Then Judkins opened the door to his dorm room and saw Bird splayed out on one of the two beds. "He's a white guy," Judkins said. "It was kind of shocking."

The dorm room was standard college fare. It was small, Judkins recalled, and stripped down to the basics. It had two twin beds, an air conditioner, and a preponderance of flies. Judkins only remembered the flies later because Bird liked to entertain himself by catching them in his bare hands—a feat that Judkins had never seen anyone pull off before, but one that Bird turned into a personal hobby that week, plucking flies out of the air with ease. His hands were fast and his dreams were big. At night in the dark of their dorm room, with the air conditioner thrumming, the two young basketball players talked about maybe one day playing in the NBA.

Judkins liked Bird right away. He was humble and easygoing, and he showed respect for Judkins, which was notable at the time, at least to Jud. He was a practicing Mormon who didn't drink or smoke, tried not to curse, and was engaged to be married that summer. Jud was, put simply, unlike anybody Bird had ever met before, and Bird was cool with that. Bird was good with Jud drinking Cokes, not beer, if they went out at night.

Bird's only problem that week would come on the basketball court, in Denny Crum's practices and scrimmages. Everyone was trying to make this team, and no one wanted to lose their spot to a white player from some school in Terre Haute—wherever that was.

As the practices began, Tom Apke, the head coach at Creighton, a Jesuit school in Omaha, Nebraska, settled into a seat in the arena to watch. He was there to support his younger brother, Rick, who was going to be a senior at Creighton in the fall and was trying out for the team with everyone else. Tom figured it couldn't hurt to show his face, mingle with Denny a little, be in the gym. But pretty soon, Tom Apke was only watching Larry Bird.

It didn't matter that he wasn't a big name from a big school; Bird dominated during the tryout. If the other players bodied him up inside and wouldn't allow him to get close to the hoop, Bird took them outside and scored. If they pressed him outside, he passed off to someone else or put the ball on the floor and went around his defender to the basket. Jammin' James Bailey, the Rutgers star, realized shortly after the tryouts began that Bird was different. He could pass, shoot, post up, rebound, or never touch the ball and change a possession by setting a pick.

"He was just a total player," Moncrief said.

"By far the best player," Judkins agreed.

Perhaps most importantly, Bird proved to everyone that he was willing to fight for the ball, for the team, and for himself. Rick Apke recalled that he was guarding Bird at one point during the tryouts, and both of them came down with a rebound together, but Apke couldn't hold on to it. Bird was too strong and snatched it right out of Apke's hands. At another point, gold medalist Phil Hubbard recalled that Bird did the same thing to Calvin Natt, a six-foot-six forward from Northeast Louisiana—or at least Bird tried to do the same thing to Natt. Unlike Apke, Natt wouldn't let go of the ball, Hubbard said, and neither would Bird, and the two men began to tussle over it. "And that's when you kind of knew," Hubbard said. "He was here to show that he deserved to be on this team—and that he could play."

Tom Apke, watching from the stands, logged it all away—if not for his brother, then at least for himself. In the following season, both Creighton and Indiana State would be joining the Missouri Valley Conference for the first time. At some point, Apke was going to have to create a plan to stop Bird. Then he logged something else away—something that perhaps only a coach would notice. In the second half of the tryout sessions, Denny Crum would split the guys into teams and let them play, full-court, up and down. No one ever stayed with the same group of five. Crum was always mixing and matching, and that's when Apke started counting and realized that Bird's teams never lost. "They were all the best college basketball players in the country," Apke said. "And yet, when it came time to win games, his team won every time."

At the end of the week, Crum had to let one player go due to injury, and he cut six others, including Tom's brother, Rick. But Bird made the team. Judkins did, too, and on the last Saturday of July 1977, the two new friends stepped onto a plane with Bailey, Moncrief, and the other collegiate stars to make the trip of a lifetime. They were flying from Louisville to New York to Rome for a month of basketball in Europe.

Crum was worried. He didn't think his young players were ready. They'd only had five days to practice together as a unit. Not enough time to insert systems. "We will just have to run," Crum said, "and play it wide open." And they would have to do it jet-lagged, on no rest. "We'll be playing," Crum said, "from the minute we get off the plane."

But that was just fine with Bird. He didn't want to go to Europe for any other reason.

23

THE EARLY GAMES, IN Italy and Yugoslavia, were a bit of a struggle for the team, just as Crum had feared. The college kids were playing grown men, 10 years older than them at times, on outdoor courts with foreign referees and different rules. European players were allowed to set moving picks. One outdoor game started after 10 o'clock at night—so late that fog had set in and dew was bubbling up on the playing surface. Players slipped on the condensation, risking injury. Moncrief called the conditions the worst he had ever faced in a real game.

But at least Moncrief and the other guys were still eating then. As soon as they crossed over into Eastern Europe, that stopped. Unwilling to consume the local offerings, which consisted of peas, carrots, and some sort of stringy meat, many of them chose to live on hard bread, cold butter, and white rice. "Dear Mom," Larry wrote home in one postcard. "Just a note to tell you that I'm never leaving the US again."

The American team lost as often as it won in the early exhibition games. But as Crum's college stars landed in Bulgaria for the main event—the 1977 World University Games in Sofia—they found their footing. They moved into a dormitory not far from the arena. They made friends at the US embassy. They fortified themselves with a hot-dog cookout that Crum's wife organized with the help of the US Marines. They passed long hours away from the basketball court playing Ping-Pong. They watched Bird dominate in that sport, too, playing left-handed or right-handed, taking on all comers, even the Marines. And the team itself crushed the weaker competition it faced in the early rounds at the University Games. The US college stars opened the tournament by beating Belgium by 79 points, Kuwait by 86, and Poland by 28, then prepared to face the Soviets.

By this point, Bird had worked his way into Crum's starting lineup. He took the floor that night in Sofia with James Bailey, Darrell Griffith, Freeman Williams, and Phil Hubbard, while outside the arena, chaos reigned. The game was sold out, and local authorities nearly lost control of a surging crowd at the gates. People tried to rush inside, forcing police to respond. But the near stampede was the biggest drama of the night. The Americans won easily again, beating the Soviets, 129–95, and moved on to the next round to face their toughest opponent yet: Cuba.

Once more, Crum was worried. The Cubans were fast. They rebounded well. The two countries had a history of physical battles on the court, dating back to an epic fight in the 1973 games. And the US victory over the

Soviets had come at a cost: Hubbard had hurt his knee. The Michigan star was going to miss the Cuba game, while other players were showing signs of exhaustion. They had been gone for three weeks, and many of them weren't sleeping well in their dormitory. Their little bunks sagged under the weight of their bodies, and efforts to modify the beds—by placing chairs beneath the mattresses—had failed. With their backs aching and their legs tired, the players limped into the Cuba game, fell behind early, and found the score tied, 46–46, early in the second half when the ball squirted out of bounds near the US bench and the referees awarded possession to Cuba.

Crum, at this point, was growing ornery. He hated the moving picks that foreign players set. He hated that his players got whistled for fouls anytime they slapped the ball out of their opponents' hands—even if the swat was clean—and he especially hated that there was no consistency with the referees from game to game. Now Crum wanted a word about the out-of-bounds call. He objected to it and rose from his seat on the bench to approach an official.

What happened next, witnesses said, took only a couple of seconds. As Crum was talking to the ref, a Cuban player bumped into Crum with a shoulder. Crum pushed the Cuban in retaliation. The Cuban bench cleared, as if the players had been waiting for a reason to fight all day, and the Americans were caught off guard. The Cubans were suddenly on them, throwing punches and swinging the only weapon they could find on the bench: glass water bottles.

Moncrief recalled later that some of his American teammates shrank from the moment. "We had a couple of guys under the bench, frightened," Moncrief said. "They did not want any part of it." But Bird reacted differently. He realized that his team was outnumbered and began fighting like he was back home in West Baden, in the parking lot outside the Jubil Bar.

"No one's swinging at me," Judkins said. "They're all swinging at Larry." And Bird didn't care. "Larry's just punching guys, right and left," Judkins said. "He's just clocking guys."

It was a melee. An international incident. But it was also inspiring. "That's when I had a different level of respect for Larry Bird," Moncrief said. "He was in the neighborhood, all out, protecting myself, protecting my teammates, protecting the honor of this country." Moncrief wanted to fight just watching Bird, and other guys did, too. Darrell Griffith jumped into the fray to defend Crum and found himself fighting not just Cuban players, but a Cuban photographer as well. The photographer took his gear and whacked Griffith across the head with it. Meanwhile, James Bailey moved in to protect Bird. At one point, Bailey said, a Cuban player tried to attack Bird from behind with one of those glass bottles, and Bailey grabbed the would-be assailant and threw him to the floor. But then someone pushed Bailey down and someone else was swinging a bottle at him. This bottle was broken. And as Bailey held up his left arm to protect himself, the jagged teeth of the bottle ripped open the skin around his elbow.

In the moment, Bailey didn't feel much pain; he just felt the air breathing in the open wound. But the Rutgers star knew he was hit, and he knew he was hurt.

"How bad is it?" Bailey recalled asking Bird.

Bird just looked at him. "Oh, it's bad."

It took at least 10 minutes to restore order in the arena—too long, Crum believed. Then he and everyone else began to assess the damage.

Bailey's left arm required 17 stitches and his right hand another three; his tournament was over. Cuba seemed spent after the fight and couldn't compete the rest of the evening. The Americans won, 94–78. They moved on to claim gold a few days later, and the college stars all flew home at the end of August, telling wild stories of their epic conquest overseas. Some of the players had grown up in tough American neighborhoods. But nothing had ever happened to them, they joked, until they went to play basketball in Sofia.

"We had to go all the way to Bulgaria . . . ," Bailey laughed.

Bailey's parents came down from Massachusetts to meet him at the airport in New York when the team landed back on US soil. But by the time Bailey found his family in the terminal, his new friends had scattered. Judkins went home to Utah, Moncrief to Arkansas, and Bird continued on to Terre Haute.

Bob King collected Bird at the airport back in Indiana, and Bird asked King to promise not to tell anyone he was home for at least a day. Bird said he had lost 20 pounds in Europe. He wanted to sleep, and he might have needed to reacclimate for other reasons, too. While Larry was in Europe, his ex-wife, Janet, had given birth to their child—a baby girl.

King agreed to Bird's terms, but there was bad news coming. The two McKees—Ed and Craig in the sports information department—were planning a big press conference for a few days later. Ed McKee was to be the master of ceremonies, showcasing Bird. Reporters were going to have questions for him about Europe, and King remained certain that more reporters would be coming to Terre Haute soon, given the work that Bill Hodges was doing in living rooms across the country that spring and summer.

For starters, Carl Nicks finally came around and agreed to report to Gulf Coast Community College down in Florida. He still wasn't happy about the reassignment, and he wasn't excited about one of his new teammates there: Roger Maris Jr., the son of the former New York Yankees slugger. Maris's wealth was off-putting to Nicks, a kid from the South Side of Chicago. But Hodges had read the situation right: Nicks didn't have other options. He could either report to Florida or stay in Chicago. And when Nicks thought about it that way, the choice was clear. He flew south and moved into a barracks-style dorm near the beach.

To replace Nicks, Hodges recruited his polar opposite: Steve Reed, from Warsaw, Indiana. Reed was white, could handle the ball, liked to study, and was named the Warsaw Exchange Club's Student of the Year—a set of characteristics that attracted the interest of a coach whose name would become notable later. Mike Krzyzewski, a man on his way to a 47-year head coaching career and a record 1,202 NCAA victories, tried to recruit Reed to play for him at Army in 1977. But Reed chose Indiana State after spending a night with Bird and Miley at an off-campus party in Terre Haute. Miley called Hodges in the wee hours of the morning to let him know it had been decided: Reed was coming.

Miley wasn't the only one calling Hodges at odd times that year about recruits. At some point, Hugh Thimlar phoned Hodges—"*Hodgo!*"—to let him know he needed to get down to Florida to see Leroy Staley, a junior college player who had Harry Morgan's leaping ability and no ego whatsoever. Hodges met with Leroy's adoptive parents—his aunt Eula and uncle Moses—in a little house near the foot of the runways at Tampa International Airport and sold everybody on Indiana State. Staley cried when he saw his powder-blue Sycamores jersey for the first time. And when it was time to move into the dorms late that summer, Hodges placed Staley in a room with potentially the most important new recruit of all: a six-foot-eleven, 250-pound giant from Detroit named Richard Johnson.

This was a different team, a better team, a scarier team, and that meant one thing.

Bird wasn't going to be able to hide for much longer.

24

AT HIS HOUSE IN the heart of campus, Dick Landini was excited about all of it.

Thanks in part to the success of the basketball team the previous year, Indiana State's freshman enrollment was up 20 percent in the fall of 1977. It was a spike that the college hadn't seen in years, and Landini touted the latest numbers whenever he spoke, which was often. But increased enrollment wasn't the only way Indiana State was lining its coffers that fall.

The school was selling tickets to basketball games at an unprecedented rate. Season-ticket sales set a new record. Total sales were up 250 percent. The phone was ringing in the sports information office. The two McKees were busier than ever before, printing off a new press guide and preparing for their first-ever Missouri Valley Conference media day in Omaha. Bob King was going to attend with his two stars: Harry and Larry, or Larry and Harry—reporters could pick the order of their choosing. And local businesses were capitalizing on the craze. That fall, a drugstore in downtown Terre Haute was selling a new T-shirt for $4.99. "I'm a Bird Watcher," the shirt said.

The drugstore owners believed the shirt could one day become a collector's item. But if that was true, Bird wasn't going to receive a dime in royalties or licensing fees. There was no name, image, and likeness money in those days, no profit sharing to be had. People were just cashing in on Larry Bird, and the national media was about to take a slice out of him, too. Sometime in September 1977, the phone rang in Ed McKee's office inside the practice arena on campus. *Sports Illustrated* was on the line, and an offer was on the table.

The magazine wanted to fly Bird to New York to be photographed for its 1977 college basketball preview issue.

It's hard to overstate how important *Sports Illustrated* was—to the world of athletics and to pop culture more broadly—in 1977. The magazine had a weekly readership of roughly two million people, an unwavering popularity among young men, and a deep roster of writers who could go anywhere and write anything, traveling the country on generous expense accounts. Their stories were treated like the gospel. Their subjects became prophets and gods and the magazine itself was the Bible—the sports Bible. To appear in it was to be someone, a reality that even reclusive stars understood in those days. They'd throw their arms around *Sports Illustrated* reporters, welcome them into the clubhouse, take them home, introduce them to their wives and mothers, and sit them down on new living room furniture that had been purchased just for this moment, because *Sports Illustrated* was there, in the house. "*Sports-fucking-Illustrated*," one staffer said, reflecting on the magazine's place in the national conversation. "Everybody, EVERYBODY, loves *Sports Illustrated*."

But Larry Bird was different. He wasn't so sure about sitting down for a photo shoot with the magazine. He had just returned home from Bulgaria a month earlier. He didn't seem to want to leave Indiana again, and he definitely wasn't excited about getting attention from a bunch of people in New York. Bob King had to talk sense to him. Bird *had* to agree to this plan, King said. For the good of the university, Terre Haute, Landini, Hodges, the team, everybody. And with King begging and pleading, Bird finally bent to King's wishes. In early October, he flew east with Ed McKee to meet with *SI*.

It was an amazing week to be in New York City. The sun was shining. President Jimmy Carter was there, landing by helicopter on Wall Street and speaking at the United Nations. Secret Service agents fanned out across the city, following the president's motorcade wherever it went. Traffic jams stretched into Brooklyn, with people lining up to catch a glimpse of Carter. And the president's visit wasn't even the biggest story of the week. The New York Yankees were hosting the Kansas City Royals at home in the Bronx in the first two games of the American League Championship Series. The city was alive.

Ed McKee, a Royals fan, was happy just to be close to the action. *Sports Illustrated* had them set up in a nice hotel, not far from the Time Inc. offices in Midtown Manhattan. And Ed didn't even have to be stressed about the *SI* meeting the next day. Bird wouldn't be sitting down for a long interview, full of questions about his personal life or moments where he might slip up and say the wrong thing. He was just posing for a series of strobe-lit photos in a studio made to look like a basketball court, with a handful of other top players, including Freeman Williams, Bird's high-scoring teammate from the World University Games in Bulgaria. These photos were going to appear in a package publicizing the best basketball players in the country, and its headline was going to be the stuff of a sports information director's dreams. *Sports Illustrated* was calling the story THE HOTTEST OF THE HOTSHOTS. This wasn't hard-hitting journalism; it was great PR for Bird and Indiana State. And it came with a perk. At the end of the photo session, Kent Hannon, the lead reporter on the preview issue, invited Bird and McKee to attend the Yankees game that night as guests of the magazine.

McKee, a calm man by nature, nearly hopped out of his size 16 shoes. He had never been to Yankee Stadium before, and now he had a chance to see the Royals and the great George Brett face off against Billy Martin and Reggie Jackson in a playoff game. But Bird declined Hannon's invitation—no, thanks. He had a new girlfriend by then, Dinah Mattingly, who was two years older than him, the daughter of an FBI agent in Terre Haute, a former high school honor roll student, and different from Larry's first wife, Janet, in other ways. Dinah would rebound for Larry when he wanted to shoot. She took an interest in basketball.

Bird said he wanted to get home. He wanted to get back to Indiana. And if Bird was leaving, Ed McKee had to leave, too. He wasn't going to Yankee Stadium, free tickets or not. He was returning to Terre Haute—though McKee wasn't finished wrangling Bird that fall. He was just getting started.

Shortly after they arrived back on campus, McKee learned from Hannon that *Sports Illustrated* wanted Bird for a second photo shoot. This one would be in Chicago. It would be with two Indiana State cheerleaders, if Ed could make that happen, and it would be a bigger deal than the shoot in New York. This session, if it went well, was for the magazine cover.

Bob King broke the news to Bird, begging and pleading for his cooperation again, and once more Bird reluctantly agreed. Meanwhile, Ed McKee worked on the second element: the cheerleaders. He walked across campus, talked to the cheer coach, and secured the participation of Marcia Staub, that year's Indian Princess, and Sharon Senefeld, the happiest, bubbliest cheerleader at Indiana State. The two women packed what little they needed for their trip: makeup, lipstick, and their cheerleading outfits, shimmering blue with a frilly white fringe. And on the last Sunday of October 1977, this unlikely group of traveling companions—McKee, Bird, Staub, and Senefeld—met at the airport in Terre Haute to fly to Chicago.

The skies were foggy that morning over Indiana, and the flight north wasn't nearly as glamorous as it sounded when Staub and Senefeld had agreed to the photo shoot. The little plane was crowded. The two cheerleaders sat in the back with Bird, crammed shoulder to shoulder three across while McKee rode in the front seat with the pilot. Despite Senefeld's chatty nature, the former homecoming queen from Connersville, Indiana, failed to get much out of Bird. He didn't seem to know why he was there, why he was bothering to go to Chicago. As usual, he didn't feel much like talking. Years later, Staub would recall only one conversational detail from their plane ride. Bird briefly discussed one of his hobbies: squirrel hunting.

But as the little plane approached Chicago and prepared to land at Meigs Field, an airstrip right downtown, it was hard not to feel the weight of the moment. The city was out one window. Lake Michigan was out the other. The fog had lifted to reveal a beautiful fall morning, and their *Sports Illustrated* photographer was waiting in a studio near Michigan Avenue with some props, a plan, and a purpose.

H. Lane Stewart was there to make them famous.

25

THE *H* STOOD FOR Homer, Lane's father's name, but it had never worked for Lane. In the first half of his life, it conjured up *The Odyssey*, and in the second half, it made people think of *The Simpsons*. So, no, he was just Lane—though there was no "just" with Lane Stewart. In an era of large and colorful media personalities, Lane fit right in, with his long, disheveled hair, his unique fashion sense—part uptown Gucci and part 1970s hippy—his booming voice, prone to storytelling, and his specific preferences when it came to photo assignments.

Lane didn't like covering games. He didn't want to attend the Olympics, and he didn't want a credential for a seat that was ringside or courtside. He wanted to photograph people—humans who had done something great. And when Lane took on these assignments, he wanted to do more than just capture an image. He wanted to capture the *essence* of his subjects. He wanted to illustrate their lives in one frame. And to make this happen, Lane was willing to take chances that other photographers wouldn't.

In late 1975, he turned a *Sports Illustrated* cover shoot of Pete Rose into a garish representation of the man himself. Lane draped a backdrop with red, white, and blue bunting, strung red, white, and blue streamers over the bunting, wrapped Pete in a sash of roses, sprinkled him with confetti, and had Pete open a bottle of champagne as the shutter fired on Lane's Hasselblad camera. It was madness. It worked, and Lane's approach worked again in the spring of 1977 with another cover subject: Mark "The Bird" Fidrych.

Fidrych, a pitcher for the Detroit Tigers, was coming off a 19–9 rookie season with 24 complete games and a massive following that transcended baseball. People loved Fidrych because he talked to the ball on the mound, pranced around the infield with a mop of golden curls spilling out from under his cap, and exuded so much joy that it gave Lane an idea. He decided to pair Fidrych with Big Bird from *Sesame Street* and photographed the two Birds pitching together in a New York studio, with Fidrych in full windup and the yellow, feathered children's character smiling over his shoulder.

Now, less than five months later, the editors at *Sports Illustrated* tasked Lane with shooting a different bird—Larry Bird—and as usual, they didn't give Lane much in the way of direction. In a meeting in New York before he flew to Chicago, Lane recalled that the editors wanted to "spring" Bird on the nation with this cover, and they only had one suggestion for how he might do that. Maybe, they said, Bird could jump out of a large magician's hat.

Lane Stewart wasn't excited about the magician idea, but he humored his editors. He hired a local magician to join him in Chicago in late October 1977. He had the man bring his magician's box, two top hats, and a couple of wands. Lane flew into Chicago from New York two days early to meet the man, survey his wares, and set everything up in a studio just off Michigan Avenue, and along the way, Lane made sketches, noodling on what he really wanted to do.

Lane decided he wanted to photograph Bird and the cheerleaders whispering with their index fingers pressed to their lips—as if Bird were a secret—and he really wanted to capture Bird *springing* onto the scene by having him jump through a hole punched into a backdrop. The trouble was, Lane had never met Bird. He didn't know him at all until Bird walked into the studio that Sunday morning with McKee, Staub, and Senefeld, and upon meeting him, Lane realized that his job that day was going to be difficult. Most young athletes on their way to becoming multimillionaires had a presence about them, Lane said. They understood who they were. They knew where they were going and they recognized that Lane's cameras were an all-expenses-paid ticket to that destination: fame.

But Bird didn't seem to care. He didn't engage with Lane in the studio. He didn't flirt with Staub and Senefeld. He didn't chat with McKee, and he didn't joke around with the magician, either. "He was detached," Lane said. He was also trapped. For the next four hours and 45 minutes, Larry Bird and the cheerleaders posed for Lane Stewart. A marathon of photography. All day.

First, Lane did the magician thing. He shot Staub and Senefeld wearing top hats and waving wands as they flanked Bird. Next, Lane did the whisper setup, with the cheerleaders crouching down in front of Bird and pressing their fingers to their lips. Finally, when Lane was confident he didn't need his backdrop anymore, he destroyed it, carefully cutting a large hole in the seamless double-wide paper through which Bird could jump. Then Lane stood back, grabbed his Hasselblad camera, and prepared to capture the image he really wanted, the image he had come to Chicago to create. He asked Bird to jump through the hole.

"Jump *throooooough!*" Lane said.

It was something to be done with joie de vivre. It was something to be done with reckless abandon. It was something to be done with one's arms spread wide and a big smile, and almost everyone in the studio tried it that day, even Lane himself. They had fun, he said, jumping *throoooooough*. "Everybody got their Christmas card out of it," Lane said. "Everybody but Larry."

He couldn't smile. There was no joie de vivre here. Bird had no idea what Lane wanted—or he knew and would not give it. Bird jumped through the hole again and again with no joy on his face whatsoever.

Around 5:45 that evening, Lane Stewart finally called it: They were done here. The college kids got changed out of their uniforms. Lane said his goodbyes—he would never meet Bird again—and McKee ushered his charges out onto the streets of Chicago. Night had almost fallen by then, and they were all tired after their long day in the studio. But their little plane was waiting at Meigs Field, and they were wheels up in no time, flying back to Terre Haute in the dark.

The flight home was quiet. Bird, Staub, and Senefeld didn't say much in the second row of the plane, leaving McKee to stew in silence in the passenger seat up front. He hoped that Lane had captured enough for the cover and he wondered when he might hear for sure. McKee knew that a *Sports Illustrated* cover would change all of their lives, Bird's most of all.

Somewhere south of Chicago, flying through the night, McKee believed then—and later—that he got an answer to his questions in a sign from the gods. He spotted a shooting star out the windows of the cockpit, he said, and turned around to point it out to the college kids, but they had fallen asleep by then. They missed it. Bird, Staub, and Senefeld would have to wait until McKee got the news about the *Sports Illustrated* cover in a more tangible way: in a letter, in mid-November, from the preview issue's lead writer, Kent Hannon.

The note was typed on magazine stationery. It was paper-clipped to a black-and-white mockup of the cover. It was addressed to three parties— Ed McKee, Larry Bird, and "The Ladies in Fringe"—and Hannon got straight to the point.

"Barring some catastrophe such as Reggie Jackson gunning down Billy Martin in an East Side bar," Hannon wrote to Ed, "this is what the Nov. 28 issue of the magazine will look like."

McKee held the mockup in his hands and recognized the image right away. It was the photo of the women crouched down in front of Bird, holding their index fingers to their lips as Bird smiled. Hannon assured

McKee that it was beautiful. "You'll like it better in color," he wrote. Then Hannon ended his note with a directive for Bird, Staub, and Senefeld.

"Those persons in the picture," Hannon wrote, "are hereby forbidden to break any bones or withdraw from school until at least Thanksgiving."

Sports Illustrated had placed a bet on Larry Bird—COLLEGE BASKETBALL'S SECRET WEAPON, the cover headline said—and *Sports Illustrated* didn't like to lose.

In some ways, these days in November—between the photo shoot, Hannon's note, and the actual publication of the magazine—were the last anonymous days that Larry Bird would ever know.

He went to Omaha with Bob King and Harry Morgan for Missouri Valley Conference media day. He wore faded jeans and a white T-shirt to the event, as if it were no big deal. He tried to deflect attention when he could, calling Morgan the best player on the team, and he did other things that Bob King asked of him. In Omaha, he helped run a basketball clinic for kids.

But already, things were changing for Bird. Coaches and reporters in Omaha picked Indiana State to win the Valley conference title, turning up the wattage on the spotlight already trained in Bird's direction. There were expectations now—to win. And, also, new demands on Bird's time. Reporters at small Midwestern papers wanted interviews with him, and at least one other national magazine wanted a photo shoot, forcing King to prostrate himself before Bird yet again.

Then, right before Thanksgiving 1977, the *Sports Illustrated* issue hit the newsstands, selling out in Terre Haute within minutes and spilling the Larry Bird secret to two million people nationwide.

The cover minted Bird as a star. It put Terre Haute on the map. It made Indiana State a contender and it gave Marcia Staub and Sharon Senefeld a measure of fame that they, too, would never shake. Much to their dismay, male readers were soon writing letters to the Time Inc. offices in New York, asking questions about them.

"Forget Larry Bird," one man wrote. "Who are those beautiful cheerleaders?"

It was the biggest thing to happen in Terre Haute in years. Maybe ever. But Bird didn't want to discuss it. Not with his teammates and not with reporters, either. By then, he was only talking about Purdue. The Boilermakers were the second opponent on Indiana State's schedule that year, and Bird wasn't shy about making a prediction for the game.

This year, he said, the Sycamores were going to win.

26

IN CASE ANYONE HAD forgotten Harry Morgan, he announced his presence with authority, starting the season in a Saturday-night home opener against tiny Westmont in late November 1977. Morgan scored the first basket of the year with one of his trademark high-flying dunks.

Morgan didn't mind that Bird had made the cover of *Sports Illustrated*. In his opinion, Bird deserved the cover and more. But Morgan's primary interest—understandably—remained his wife, Rita, and his growing family. That fall, the same week that Bird flew to New York with Ed McKee for the first meeting with *Sports Illustrated*, Rita gave birth to their second child, another son. If Morgan had to choose between supporting Larry Bird and supporting his family, he was choosing his family every time. It wasn't like he and Bird talked much anyway.

"You can't tell him nothing," Morgan said that year. "He's got a head like a brick wall."

Also, this was it for Morgan. It was his senior year, his last chance to make an impression on NBA scouts. Morgan had to show up if he was going to realize his dream of one day playing in the league, and he was willing to get creative to help claim a small sliver of Bird's ever-growing spotlight. One of Morgan's brothers had started coming to games wearing a full-length, custom-made cape stitched with the following message: "ISU PRESENTS THE HARRY AND LARRY SHOW."

And Morgan had given himself a nickname, too: "Wild Dunk." He hoped it would stick.

The season opener, against Westmont, was never close. The Sycamores won, 88–55, with Bird scoring 29, Morgan adding 16, and Leroy Staley making a strong debut as King's fifth starter, with 15 points of his own. But Westmont was a cupcake. The opponent that really mattered was the next one on the schedule, and Bob King worked around the clock that week to pretend his guys had no chance against them: the Purdue Boilermakers.

Sure, King said, Indiana State was ranked in most preseason polls: UPI (No. 16), *Sports Illustrated* (No. 17), and *Playboy* (No. 19). But the Associated Press poll, the most prestigious one in the country, had ignored Indiana State altogether. King pointed out that the Boilermakers were ranked higher than the Sycamores on every single list, and he wanted everyone to know that the Purdue game did not matter. He said the only date he had circled on the schedule was January 4, the first game of the Valley conference schedule. He said that all he cared about was intensity—defensive intensity. He said he wasn't going to measure the team's progress by wins. He pointed out that Purdue *had* to be favored over Indiana State—in 24 previous meetings, the Sycamores had only beaten the Boilermakers once. He said his guys would struggle to match Purdue's speed. He said he was worried about covering their guards man-to-man. And in general, he complained a lot. At a media dinner in late November 1977 hosted by Bob King, Stan Evans, and Bill Hodges—and friendly enough that all three coaches brought their wives—King claimed to be disappointed with the team's practices of late. "We have not looked as sharp as I would like," he groaned.

Up in West Lafayette, Fred Schaus, the Boilermakers' head coach, wasn't buying King's act. Unlike other coaches, Schaus wasn't flying blind into Larry Bird. He had seen him play the year before in West Lafayette. He considered Bird one of the best players in the country, "pro or college," Schaus said, and he had players on the roster who agreed. Purdue's two six-foot-seven senior forwards, Wayne Walls and Walter Jordan, had known Bird for years. They had played with him on the Indiana high school all-star team back in 1974. They had played against him the previous year in West Lafayette. And Jordan had seen Bird up close all summer as a teammate of his in Bulgaria. In fact, Jordan had been listening to Bird talk about this game for months.

At the time, Bird was typically quiet during basketball games, even polite. He rarely trash-talked other players. This was a skill he would sharpen, hone, and use like a carving knife later, gutting opponents on the floor. But with Jordan, Bird was different. He wasn't quiet—probably because the two young men had spent long hours together in Indiana gymnasiums, on transatlantic planes, in Denny Crum's practices in Louisville, and inside those barracks in Bulgaria furnished with flimsy beds. They had won together, lost together, fought the Cubans together. And perhaps because of this familiarity, Walter Jordan may have been one of the first recipients of Bird's epic trash-talk, outside of Bird's older brothers or his crew of French Lick boys back home. Bird gave it to Jordan all summer.

Jordan was going down, Bird said. The Sycamores were going to "whip him," Bird said. And Jordan seemed to know it. The day before the Purdue–Indiana State game in late November 1977, Jordan revealed a shocking plan to the press in West Lafayette. The Boilermakers, he said, hoped to hold Bird to less than 50 points. *Fifty.*

"The Bird," Jordan said, "can do it all."

The season's first winter storm hit Terre Haute before the game, bringing four inches of snow in one squall, another inch several hours later, and then a steady dose of freezing rain that coated the town in a thick layer of ice.

Cars spun out on the Wabash River bridge. Tractor-trailers jackknifed on rural highways. Police scrambled to respond to motorists trapped in ditches, and none of it dissuaded fans from coming to the game that Monday night. Students gathered outside the Hulman Center four hours before tip-off. They rushed to claim seats near the court when the doors finally opened and the townsfolk filled in around them until every seat in the arena was taken and the university had to post an announcement on the marquee outside: ISU VS. PURDUE—SOLD OUT.

At least the game was going to be televised. People would be tuning in that night on WTHI out of Terre Haute, WTTV out of Indianapolis, and a host of newfangled cable television channels beaming the video feed into six other states: Illinois, Iowa, Kentucky, Ohio, West Virginia, and Wisconsin. The estimated television audience—three and a half million people—was 50 times the size of Terre Haute itself. More people were about to see Larry Bird than ever before. The two McKees—Ed and Craig—ran around before the game, checking on the camera operators posted in four locations, while down in the locker room, Bird rolled a dangerous thought over in his mind: *This is the biggest game of our lives.*

But King continued to perform his act, pretending the game didn't matter, and the guys took the floor loose and ready. Bird, Morgan, and Miley had never lost in Terre Haute. They didn't intend to start now, and Bird opened the game that night with one of the most electrifying plays ever seen inside the Hulman Center.

Just 20 seconds in, senior guard Jimmy Smith had the ball at the top of the key while Wayne Walls covered Bird on the right wing. Walls seemed to be trying to establish dominance early, but Bird sensed that about Walls and took advantage of his enthusiasm. Bird popped out, as if he was going toward the sideline for a pass, and when Walls followed, fast on his feet, Bird immediately stopped and turned back toward the hoop. Smith hit Bird with a perfect backdoor bounce pass and Bird, wide open now, threw down a one-handed dunk right over Walter Jordan.

The rim barely moved; there was no showboating here. But the dunk resonated like thunder across the Midwest. From Davenport, Iowa, to Huntington, West Virginia, cable viewers had just seen something different, something noteworthy and rare.

Larry Bird was taking it to the rack and scoring at will.

Purdue settled down and Walls's relentless defense neutralized Bird for a while. At one point in the first half, he missed 10 shots in a row. But Bird didn't panic. Instead, he began to pass, finding open teammates all over the floor. Morgan had easy baskets, as the defense keyed on Bird. Miley did, too. Staley went off, having the best night of his life. And just when it looked like Purdue was creeping back into the game late in the first half, Richard Johnson asserted himself under the hoop. Indiana State's new 250-pound center from Detroit blocked a shot from Walter Jordan as the crowd roared. By halftime, the Sycamores were up 12, and by the early minutes of the second half, it was already over. Indiana State was crushing its interstate rival, a Big Ten power and one of the best teams in the country.

In the waning minutes of the game, Schaus sat on the Purdue bench, grim-faced and fuming about everything: the score, the refs, the calls that didn't go his way, and the fact that Larry Bird was still playing in a blowout. The Sycamores were up by more than 30 points, and Bird was still out there on the floor. But King wasn't leaving anything to chance. He didn't pull his starters until there was 1:28 left on the clock—and that's when the celebration began for real in Terre Haute. Fans started to chant—"*We're No. 1! We're No. 1!*"—and downtown business owners hurried to change their signs in the snowy darkness, broadcasting the unlikely news to the frozen world of western Indiana. The new sign outside the pizzeria said it all.

ISU 91, PURDUE 63.

The Sycamores had just handed the Boilermakers their worst loss in years.

27

THE INDIANA STATE LOCKER room bubbled over with euphoria after the game like a shaken bottle of champagne. It was loud and crowded with boosters and benefactors. King gave a short speech that finally acknowledged the truth about the game that he had been downplaying—"This one," he conceded, "was for national recognition"—and, uncharacteristically, Bird couldn't wait to talk about all of it. He made himself available to the throng of reporters who had come to Terre Haute from across the state.

Bird spoke to the press that night about taunting Walter Jordan all summer. He made predictions. Said Indiana State wouldn't lose a single home game all year. He praised his teammates, especially Jimmy Smith, who had made crisp passes against Purdue, and Staley, who had scored 22 points in just his second Division I basketball game. Without Smith and Staley, Bird said, Indiana State wouldn't have won. And Bird ignored the reporter who dared to suggest that he had struggled against Purdue, only scoring 26 points as he missed shot after shot with Wayne Walls chasing him all over the floor. Bird just looked at the reporter.

"I thought we hit real good," he said. "We won by 30."

The two McKees worked in the press box until after midnight, making sure writers from out-of-town papers had what they needed to make their deadlines. But everyone else went out to celebrate. Students filled the Ballyhoo Tavern on the east side of campus and nearly jumped through the ceiling that night when Bird walked through the door. Everyone was happy, even Harry Morgan.

Morgan had been in foul trouble for most of the Purdue game and saw just 16 minutes of action as a result. While Bird had played too much, according to Fred Schaus, Morgan had played barely at all. But not long after the game, Morgan learned that his name would appear on ballots nationwide for a chance to play in the 1978 Pizza Hut All-American showcase, an annual event held in Las Vegas for college basketball's best seniors. Bird's spotlight *was* big enough to include him. Morgan could feel its tantalizing warmth. And he was even more excited when the owner of the local Pizza Hut threw his full weight behind Morgan's candidacy, taking out advertisements in the newspapers, calling on fans to vote for Morgan, and organizing ballot-casting parties on campus. VOTE AS MANY TIMES AS YOU WANT, the ads said.

The Sycamores, feeling like a team, proceeded to win their next six games. They closed the calendar year undefeated at 8–0. They stayed together over Christmas break, bunking up at the Sheraton Hotel, up the street from married-student housing. They partied on New Year's Eve, counting down the seconds to 1978. They ran the steps in the arena the next morning—up and down every aisle, all the way around the oval, like Bird used to do for Jim Jones back at Springs Valley. And the Sycamores continued to win when their conference schedule began in January, until they were 10–0 and Bird was overflowing with confidence that he didn't mind sharing out loud.

"If I get the ball," he said, "there's no way they can stop me."

At this point, John Newton, the alumni director who had once taken Bird into his home, couldn't help himself any longer: He picked up the phone in his office, not far from Landini's house, and booked a block of hotel rooms in St. Louis, the site of that year's NCAA Final Four. Newton figured it was worth the risk, given the Sycamores' hot start and their rising profile in the national polls. By early January 1978, even the Associated Press couldn't ignore them anymore. The latest AP poll ranked them No. 6 in the country. Newton wanted to make sure the university would be ready to entertain guests and alumni if they made it that far. But the polls didn't capture what was really happening in Terre Haute. Behind the scenes, things weren't nearly as smooth as they seemed.

For starters, less than two weeks after the Purdue game, the team suffered what can only be described as a near-death experience. On a Saturday night in mid-December, the Sycamores faced the Evansville Purple Aces at home in Terre Haute and dismantled them, 102–76, in front of another near-sellout crowd. Larry and Harry combined that night for 61 points, overwhelming the Aces' best player, Mike Duff, a high-scoring freshman from rural Illinois that Bill Hodges had tried—and failed—to sign the previous spring. Duff led the Aces with 23 points, but he seemed to know that he had made a mistake in choosing Evansville and seemed to be questioning his life choices in general. At one point during the beat-down, Hodges recalled, Duff locked eyes with him on the bench and just shook his head in dismay.

The two teams now had some travel coming up, and it was the kind they liked the least. Evansville and Indiana State were each scheduled to fly charter that week on the same small twin-engine DC-3 propeller plane. The Evansville team would be using the charter service that Tuesday afternoon to fly south to Middle Tennessee, and Indiana State was scheduled to be on the plane three days later to head north for a game at Eastern Michigan. In between now and then, King said, he was planning some rigorous practices. "We will work hard," he promised, "all week." Then, late Tuesday night, word began to spread across campus in Terre Haute that Evansville's plane had gone down on takeoff.

The DC-3 had been late arriving into Evansville due to bad weather in Indianapolis. Instead of flying out in the daylight, the Purple Aces were now going out in the dark, three and a half hours behind schedule. The small flight crew rushed the departure, loading the players and their luggage onto the plane in just seven minutes. According to witnesses, the luggage was loaded haphazardly, and almost exclusively into the tail of the plane. Upon takeoff, the DC-3 struggled to climb into the air—maybe because of the weight of the luggage and maybe for reasons unknown. The pilot banked hard to the left, trying to get back to the runway, but he came up short, plowing into a wooded ridge and cartwheeling across the landscape in the night. Mike Duff was dead, and so was everybody else on board—29 people in all.

Steve Reed, the guard who had once been recruited by Mike Krzyzewski, knew there was something wrong when he saw classmates crying that night in his dorm. The world of western and southern Indiana was small; everyone seemed to know a young man on that plane—from high school, a friend of a friend, basketball camps, or basketball games. Reed couldn't stop himself from asking a question that had no answer: "Why wasn't it our team?"

But if Reed was seeking empathy from Bob King that week, he didn't get it. King seemed strangely out of touch with the tragedy and failed to acknowledge it in any meaningful way—a miscalculation, Craig McKee thought. While the students were permitted to mourn, the players had to keep going, burying their feelings and their fears. They practiced all week, boarded a different plane for Eastern Michigan that Friday, kept traveling by air that winter as though nothing had happened in Evansville. And on these trips, it was soon clear that something else had changed: The coaches weren't getting along anymore.

King no longer trusted Stan Evans. He believed Evans was trying to get him forced back into retirement at the end of the year—that Evans was trying to take his job—and that he had met with Landini in an effort to make it happen. No one knew if it was true, though if it was, not everyone blamed Evans. He was well liked in the athletic office. Several people—including the two McKees; the team's athletic trainer, Bob "Doc" Behnke; and the team manager, Rick Shaw—were close with him. Behnke and Evans were doubles partners in a local tennis league. They were friends away from the gym, and the small crew of staffers often had lunch together or scouted high school games together, talking about the future. Everyone knew that Evans was poised to take over as head coach one day, whenever King retired. It had been promised to him, he told everybody. From the moment he had taken the job in 1975, Evans expected to be head coach. And many people were excited about that future.

Now this plan, long in place, had frozen over like the streets of Terre Haute themselves. Evans was still sitting next to King on the bench during games, wearing his nice suits and always in King's ear. But King wasn't inclined to listen to him anymore. Instead, he complained about Evans in his office and in the halls of the practice arena. He said that his protégé had betrayed him. And the stress of the fractured relationship seemed to be affecting King. He popped aspirin like breath mints that year; he seemed especially anxious before games, suffering coughing fits in the locker room; he complained about a stiff neck; and he sometimes turned to Behnke for help, asking the trainer to run him through a series of stretches to work his neck up, down, and around. "I think it's just the tension," Behnke recalled King saying. "I'm so tense, so wound up."

Meanwhile, there were the usual problems, on and off the court. Morgan seemed to want the ball more than he could have it and was disappointed that nobody would call him Wild Dunk. "I guess it just don't turn nobody on," he sighed. Leroy Staley, the star of the Purdue game, lost his confidence after the victory, and then lost his playing time. He was now languishing on the bench for reasons he didn't understand, like Carl Nicks had the year before. Richard Johnson, the team's imposing big man from Detroit, was right there on the bench with Staley, with a foot injury and, seemingly, other issues. Sometime that winter, local police visited the locker room, asking questions about Johnson. Miley had never seen so many police officers at one time—and Johnson wasn't the only distraction in the building. As reporters showed up with increasing regularity to write stories about Larry Bird, Bird had made an upsetting discovery: He couldn't control his own narrative.

He wanted to talk about basketball, that night's result, his teammates, Harry Morgan, and what had happened on the floor. But reporters wanted to talk about his past, French Lick, Bloomington, Bobby Knight, why Bird had left the Hoosiers, the *Sports Illustrated* cover, the cheerleaders, his relationship status—*Did he have a girlfriend?*—and whether he might leave college and jump to the NBA in June.

The questions drove him crazy.

"I don't want to talk about the past or the future," Bird said. "I just want to talk about right now."

But that's not what reporters wanted. And in mid-January 1978, a reporter flew in from New York City, determined to get answers to the questions that Bird was most reluctant to touch.

28

THE REPORTER'S NAME WAS Larry Keith. He was one of *Sports Illustrated*'s lead college basketball writers. And unlike Kent Hannon the previous fall, Keith wasn't there to put together a short capsule on Larry

Bird for a preview issue. He was going deep and he had an expense account that would allow him to travel with the team until he had what he needed for his story.

It was Landini's dream and Bird's nightmare, and Larry Keith walked right into it. Shortly after arriving in Terre Haute and meeting with Ed McKee, Keith explained to Bird what he was there to do. He said he wanted to show readers that Bird was more than just a basketball player, more than just statistics and his achievements on the court, and Bird immediately shut down. He went dark, Keith recalled, as if he'd been powered off by a switch.

Keith was surprised. By 1978, he was used to getting access to players by just mentioning the name of his employer. "All *Sports Illustrated* had to do," Keith said, "was just walk in the door." But if anything, in this instance, the name of the magazine only made Keith's job harder. For the rest of the week, he almost had to write around Bird. The subject of his story had become the obstacle. Keith began by interviewing the people closest to him, starting with King, Hodges, and Morgan. Then Keith made a phone call to French Lick in hopes of landing an interview with a key source who would know almost everything: Larry's mother, Georgia Bird.

Keith had never met Georgia, but he guessed how she might react to such a call. "She would be polite," Keith figured. "She would want to be helpful. She would offer as much as she could. And there would be a sense of pride in what her son was doing." He picked up the phone and dialed, and Georgia answered on the other end, sounding exactly like the woman Keith had imagined. She was all too happy to talk to this nice man at *Sports Illustrated* about her son.

Georgia didn't share everything. Keith didn't learn, for example, about Bird's father, his suicide, or that Bird had a daughter, now five months old. Some details people held close, even Georgia. But Keith learned about almost everything else: about Bird's time on the garbage truck in French Lick, about Hodges finding him there, and about Georgia slamming the door in Hodges's face. He learned about Janet and the failed marriage.

And long before the article even came out, he learned that Bird was upset—with him.

At one point that week, Keith recalled, Bird stopped him and informed him that it was wrong that Keith had called his mother. "I knew where he was coming from," Keith said later. Bird didn't want people discussing his private life. "And what can be more private than your mother?" But Keith had a job to do and a story to write. He was going to do it, even if it upset one of the best college basketball players in the country. He stayed with the team for days—as the Sycamores defeated Tulsa and Drake—and flew home to New York just before Indiana State won again, for the 13th time in a row.

The guys by then were feeling good. The Associated Press had moved the Sycamores up two spots to No. 4 in the country. Bird thought they would keep winning. "I honestly don't think we'll get beat," he bragged. Bob King wasn't worried about Keith's magazine article. He wasn't even sure if the *Sports Illustrated* story would ever come out. To King, it felt like Larry Keith had been working on it forever.

Then more snow hit Terre Haute: a blizzard. The Sycamores could barely make it to their next game against Southern Illinois. The team bus left a day early to get to frozen Carbondale, where there was two feet of snow on the ground, and the players were sleeping in their hotel rooms the next morning when Craig McKee picked up the new issue of *Sports Illustrated* in Terre Haute, found Keith's lengthy article inside, and called Ed's room to read it to him.

By any objective measure, Keith's article was great—positive for Bird and positive for the university. Landini was going to love it. *Sports Illustrated* had given the Sycamores four pages of free advertising with color photos under a perfect headline: BIRD HAS THOSE TREES AT THE TOP. But the two McKees read it with different eyes. They knew they had a problem.

Keith had gone into "the stuff" from back home, spilling some of Bird's long-held French Lick secrets. He had mentioned Bird's marriage and his divorce. He had quoted Bird's mother at length. They worried that Bird wouldn't like it—and they were right. Bird was soon blaming Ed McKee for the *Sports Illustrated* article, Craig thought, as if Ed had been the one to write it. And at that point, something changed. Something subtle, but real.

That night, in Carbondale, the Sycamores began to lose.

29

SOUTHERN ILLINOIS CAME OUT on fire that Thursday in front of a wild sellout crowd.

They took an early 29–16 lead, kept their fans in the game, rowdy and excited, and forced Bob King into a series of poor decisions. Just when Indiana State closed the gap around halftime, King switched from a man-to-man defense to a zone, outthinking himself. The Salukis started slicing through the new defense and straight to the hoop. King was forced to call time-out after time-out in the second half, seething with frustration. The Sycamores lost by three—"Welcome to the league," the Salukis' coach wanted to tell King as they left the floor—and Bird refused to speak to reporters afterward, sending Ed McKee out with a canned message for the waiting media.

"I don't really want to talk," Bird said. "We lost."

It would have been nice to go back to Terre Haute at that point, but the schedule didn't allow it. The team woke up the next morning, practiced in the gym in Carbondale, got on the bus again, drove north to Normal, Illinois, and got ready play the Illinois State Redbirds—a game that got ugly in a hurry. The referees called 50 fouls between the two teams. Indiana State committed 16 turnovers. Bird missed almost 60 percent of his shots, even as he scored 37. King, at times, seemed lost on the bench. Players wondered if maybe he was thinking about the team's next opponent: Valley conference rival Wichita State. And the last few minutes of the game were the ugliest of the night by far.

Down by a basket with 3:02 to go, Bird stole the ball on the Sycamores' end and ran down the court for a dunk and, he thought, the tie. But the refs whistled Bird for a foul on the steal and then assessed him with a technical for taking a dead ball down the floor for that dunk. A two-point deficit ballooned to five points. Indiana State couldn't get back in it. A fight broke out between the players in the last 10 seconds. Morgan was ejected, and for the second game in a row, Bird refused to talk to reporters afterward. Stan Evans and Ed McKee barred the door to the visitors' locker room.

This time, at least, the Sycamores got to go home. They drove back to Terre Haute in the dark. But new problems were looming. A blizzard was moving in on Wednesday—the same day the Sycamores were scheduled to fly to their next game, in Wichita. The National Weather Service called it "a very dangerous storm." Meteorologists discouraged people from venturing outside, and the team moved up its flight in order to get in the air at all. The plane left so early that day that Ed McKee missed it—a boon, perhaps, for Bird. No one was going to be at the Wichita State game prodding Bird to talk to reporters.

But instead of dodging the storm, the Sycamores' little plane was now flying right into it, nose first. A three-hour trip became an absurd 10-hour odyssey. Weather diverted the plane no fewer than three times. Players had to endure rough landings in Chicago, St. Louis, and Kansas City—"layovers everywhere," King complained—before they could even make an approach in Wichita. Doc Behnke, the team's athletic trainer, sat up front near the pilots that night, thinking that they weren't even moving. The headwinds had them standing still or rattling up and down, everything shaking in the turbulence. Tom Crowder, a walk-on track star now in his second season with the team, called it "the worst evening of my life." He and backup guard Howie Johnson kept exchanging glances—they shouldn't be in the air. Steve Reed was in full agreement—this was all wrong—and the entire team white-knuckled it into Wichita, thinking about losing, Evansville, the Evansville plane, the Purple Aces star Mike Duff, and the fickle nature of fate.

It was four o'clock in the morning by the time they landed in godforsaken Kansas, safe on the ground, but cold. King canceled the morning shootaround so everyone could sleep, and he probably should have just canceled the game, too. That night, Indiana State lost again, its third in a row, and then proceeded to drop the next two games as well.

Their losing streak was now at five.

King, at this point, had lots of excuses to explain what was happening. They were playing too many games; they were traveling too much; they weren't used to the Valley schedule; they weren't getting the calls; they weren't supporting Larry and Harry enough; they weren't playing fundamental defense; they needed to start Steve Reed instead of Leroy Staley; they needed to get Richard Johnson back from his foot injury; they were tired.

That week, over the course of just a few days, King tested every one of these theories with the media, almost as if workshopping his best answer. But in King's mind, Stan Evans was at least part of the problem. King seemed uneasy around Evans, and for the next road trip, in early February 1978, King installed a new coach on the bench. He called Bill Hodges in off the recruiting trail and asked him to start coming to every game, home and away.

The road trip—to Texas and then New Mexico—was awkward at best. Evans seemed to understand why Hodges was there, and Hodges's presence proved to be no buffer at all. There was now tension between three men instead of just two. Hodges, who sat next to Evans, wasn't even sure if any coaching advice he spoke into Evans's ear during games made it down the bench to King. They were at odds with themselves.

But in spite of it all, the Sycamores finally got a win that Saturday night, against the West Texas Buffaloes, and the next day, they flew south to El Paso, boarded a bus for Las Cruces, and prepared to face an opponent that was about to become their greatest rival.

The Sycamores were taking on the New Mexico State Aggies.

30

THE AGGIES WERE EVERYTHING the Sycamores wanted to be. They had won seven of their last eight games. They had the best record in the Missouri Valley Conference. They were trending toward a spot in the

NCAA tournament, and their players not only liked each other; they adored their coach, Ken Hayes. Hayes was chatty and personable, with dark hair, sleepy eyes, and roots in the Sand Hills of Oklahoma. He wrote letters home to the parents of his players, keeping them up to date on how their boys were doing in Las Cruces, and he carried himself like a friendly cowboy in a Saturday matinee. Hayes proudly wore Western shirts, while his players were just proud. Hayes's four Black stars, in particular, were unafraid of Larry Bird.

Albert "Slab" Jones, once the most coveted high school recruit in the state of Texas, controlled the block down low for Hayes. Robert Gunn, a transfer from a junior college in Oklahoma, was a natural scorer, automatic from almost anywhere on the floor. Cyrus Cormier, the player who would be assigned to cover Bird, had learned toughness by unloading cargo ships in the port of Houston, a hard job that attracted hard men. And then there was Greg Webb, Gunn's roommate. Webb, the son of a retired army sergeant, could have played basketball at lots of places, but he chose to play for Hayes, so that his parents could attend the games, driving north from El Paso.

These young men didn't care what *Sports Illustrated* had written about Larry Bird. As Webb put it, "Can't no white guy be that good." Cormier thought Bird looked goofy in his old-school canvas Converse shoes. He was confident he could guard him, and the other Aggies agreed. To them, Bird didn't appear to be a real ballplayer.

But walking onto the court that night in Las Cruces, Webb began to rethink his position on Bird. In the Aggies' home arena, the Pan American Center, the two opposing teams had to come down the same set of stairs to reach the floor. And heading out for warm-ups, Webb was right behind Bird on the staircase, making observations that he would never forget.

Bird was a legitimate six foot nine—Ed McKee had not embellished his size in the program—and he was dribbling a ball between his legs as he walked *down* the stairs. In his two years at New Mexico State, Webb had never seen anyone do that before. When Webb tried to replicate the feat himself, he couldn't. Everyone watched Bird during warm-ups that night—one eye on him—and before tip-off, Hayes told the players that they should aim to hold him to fewer than 40 points.

If they could do that, Hayes said, they could win.

The crowds at the Pan American Center were known for their fervor and fanaticism. Within a few years, people would be calling the arena the "Pandemonium Center," and the fans would become the "Panamaniacs." But as the game unfolded on this night, the locals didn't have much reason to cheer.

The Sycamores controlled the game early. Harry and Larry looked great. Richard Johnson was back on the floor, menacing and strong. Leroy Staley was, too—at least for a while. Indiana State led for most of the night, sometimes by as much as 12. And with about three minutes to go, the Sycamores had the ball and a four-point lead. They also had Larry Bird, the best player in the entire time zone.

At this point, Bob King should have gone in for the kill. Harry and Larry were about to combine for 58 points on the night, almost unstoppable together. King should have let his stallions run. But instead, he put them in the barn and directed them to go into a four-corners stall. In this primitive era before the shot clock and the three-pointer, King was using Larry Bird's talent to burn time—a strategy that the guys hated, Bird especially. Instead of trying to score, they were just passing the ball around, and it cost them immediately.

Slab Jones stole the ball and threw down a dunk, cutting the lead to two. Then the Sycamores turned it over again, and Slab ran down the court for an easy lay-up. With the game now tied, Bird and Gunn exchanged shots, blow for blow. But Bird made two mistakes in the final moments of the game. He missed a free throw with 1:28 to play, and he took his last shot too early. Bird scored with 31 seconds left.

The Aggies were now trailing, 82–81, but they had the ball and a chance to win it, and they knew where they wanted to go: back to Slab. With 20 seconds on the clock, and the Panamaniacs on their feet, Slab worked the ball down the right side to a shot he knew he could make, and he fired it up while Greg Webb slipped down the other side of the court to put himself in position for a rebound. Webb had been outworking Indiana State all night, but no rebound was going to be more important than this one. When Slab missed his shot, Webb grabbed the ball out of the air, and then Harry Morgan made a mistake of his own: He fouled Webb, putting him on the line for two shots with 10 seconds to go.

Webb's father, the army sergeant, was so nervous that he couldn't watch his son take his foul shots. But Webb felt good as he stepped up to the line. He was only thinking about the net, 15 feet away. He drained his first free throw to tie the game. He hit his next the shot, too. And when Bird's last-second desperation heave rimmed out—*no good*—pandemonium reigned in the Pan American Center over a result that no one had expected outside of Ken Hayes's team.

Bird had scored 38 points. But the Aggies had won, 83–82.

Bob King could barely contain his grief afterward. Just three weeks earlier, the team had been undefeated. Bird was still talking to reporters, and he had been boasting that the Sycamores might never lose again. Now the guys had blown six of their last seven. Bird had missed the potential game-winner in Las Cruces. The Sycamores had been outmatched on the boards—"murdered," King said—and there was no time for anyone to rest. In the morning, they would be back on the bus for El Paso and heading home to Terre Haute via multiple connections and possibly another bus—their longest road trip of the year in the thick of their Valley conference schedule.

"I tried to tell everyone," King said, "that we weren't going to waltz through the Valley."

But in a sign of what this team was—or could have been—Indiana State recovered in the days ahead, fought off a flu epidemic that swept through the locker room back home, went 8-1 down the stretch, beat New Mexico State twice in that window of time, and advanced all the way to the championship game of the Missouri Valley Conference tournament in early March 1978. With just one more victory—over the Creighton Blue Jays in Omaha that Sunday—the Sycamores had a chance to wash away all of their problems and earn an automatic bid to the competition that had eluded them the year before: the NCAA tournament.

Bird, for one, liked their chances. That week, the Associated Press named him a first-team All-American—an accolade he had earned by averaging 30 points and 11 rebounds a game. When he stepped on the floor in Omaha, he would once again be the best player in the time zone. And Ken Hayes, who had now faced Bird three times that season, winning once and losing twice, believed that description failed to accurately capture what Bird had become.

"Larry Bird," Hayes said that March, "is the best basketball player I've ever seen."

But with the conference championship, the Sycamores were playing their fifth game in nine days, and the morning of the game in Omaha, Bird woke up with debilitating back pain that had him in tears. Bob King summoned Doc Behnke to examine him. Behnke invited Creighton's team physician to help, and soon a third official was at Bird's bedside. Dick Landini wanted to examine Bird, too, or at least be part of the discussions, because by then Bird was no longer just a prized player for Indiana State; he was a public commodity about to be sold to the highest bidder on the open market. In less than three months, an NBA team was probably going to draft Bird—almost certainly with a high pick—and Landini wanted to make sure that Bird was being protected, potentially from himself.

"We don't want to do anything to jeopardize Larry's future," Landini said.

The Creighton doctor understood. But since it was clear to him that Bird wanted to play—the tears were at least partly out of frustration—the doctor pledged to do whatever he could for Bird. He drove him to a local hospital for a heat massage and other treatments, and about 45 minutes before game time, Bird walked into the visitors' locker room to get ready. He appeared stiff, and he almost shuffled through warm-ups, like a statue in short pants, but he didn't complain and he wasn't crying anymore.

Bird was playing.

"If he finishes the game with 35 points and 20 rebounds," the Creighton doctor told a reporter from *The Terre Haute Tribune* as the game began, "I may have to ride back to Terre Haute with you."

That afternoon, Morgan carried the team in the early goings. Then Bird put together one of the best stretches of basketball in his life. To start the second half that afternoon, he scored 18 points in a row, and the Sycamores settled into a comfortable lead. They were up by 10.

But once again, Bob King couldn't stop himself from stalling, from killing the clock, and this time he directed his players to go into the stall offense with a stunning 15 minutes left to play. It wasn't just unorthodox; it was almost inexplicable. And Creighton's coach, Tom Apke, who had watched Bird compete at Denny Crum's tryouts the previous summer in Louisville, took advantage of King's conservative approach. The Blue Jays came roaring back to tie the game, and with 21 seconds to go, Tom Apke had the ball and a plan. The Creighton coach called a time-out to draw up a play for his younger brother, Rick.

Rick Apke had failed to make the World University Games team the year before and was now considering career choices outside of basketball. He was interested in attending medical school in the fall. But he was still a player when he took the floor out of the time-out and still competing when he prepared to execute the play that his older brother had called. Rick Apke set up in the high post with his back to the basket, received the ball with about six seconds to go, dribbled once, spun on his heels, turned around, and let his shot fly from about 17 feet away.

As the ball left's Apke's hand, it felt like the air had been sucked out of the arena. Spectators in Omaha could only stand and watch as the ball sailed over the outstretched arm of DeCarsta Webster, arced over the lane, fell from the rafters on a line, and found its target, straight and true. *All net.*

Creighton fans stormed the floor moments later and carried the future Dr. Rick Apke off on their shoulders as he held his arms in the air.

He and his older brother, Tom, had beaten Larry Bird and were headed to the NCAA tournament, while Bird and the Sycamores were headed home with nothing. For the second year in a row, there would be no love from tournament officials and no at-large invite for Indiana State.

They were banished to the NIT. Again.

31

AT THE START OF the 1970s, a school like Indiana State would have been ecstatic to play in the NIT in back-to-back years. It was the oldest basketball tournament in America. It was played, for the most part, at Madison Square Garden in New York City. Its location, at the epicenter of the East Coast media, gave college players a stage that could propel them to personal fame and professional greatness, and people tuned in to watch the NIT games on CBS. Television writers called the NIT "the most brilliant gem in collegiate basketball." But since 1973, rival network NBC, and executives at the NCAA, had buried the once-great tournament in a grave from which it would never emerge.

It began with a business decision: NBC decided to expand its coverage of the NCAA tournament. In addition to carrying the semifinal games and the final itself in March 1973, the network planned to televise the two early rounds of the tournament in full color. Then executives took an even bigger risk. They worked with the NCAA to rip up the entire format and try something radical. Instead of broadcasting the semifinal games on a Thursday night and the finals on a Saturday afternoon, they moved the two semifinal games to Saturday and placed the championship game in a slot it had never owned before: Monday night, at nine o'clock Eastern. Prime time.

The move was built on a precedent. ABC's new runaway hit, *Monday Night Football*, had proven that fans would tune in during this previously dead slot on the television sports calendar. But football was already the most popular sport in America, having eclipsed baseball a few years earlier. No one knew if people would want to watch a college basketball game on a Monday night. And by making the move, NBC was messing with a good thing. In 1972, about 32 million people had tuned in to watch the NCAA championship game between UCLA and Florida State—a game that tipped off at five o'clock Eastern and two o'clock Pacific on a Saturday. NBC could have been making a horrible mistake by tinkering with this formula, and to complicate matters, the network drew a bad matchup for the championship in late March 1973: UCLA vs. Memphis State, a game everyone knew UCLA would win. John Wooden's unstoppable Bruins, led by the great Bill Walton, hadn't lost a game in more than two years and were favored over Memphis by 13½ points. Sportswriters joked that there were only three inevitabilities in this world: death, taxes, and UCLA. No one was tuning in on Monday night to watch this game.

Still, NBC believed in its product. For the game that Monday in St. Louis, the network set up nine color cameras around the court, installed two devices with slow-motion capabilities, and had a pair of videotape machines on hand to process the slo-mo recordings in real time and convert them into instant replays for viewers watching at home. UCLA won, as predicted, blowing out Memphis by 21 as Walton set a championship game scoring record with 44 points. But the lopsided victory didn't hurt the audience at all. An estimated 37 million Americans saw the game that night—15 percent audience growth. NBC had just aired the most-watched game in basketball history, college or pro, and the NCAA quickly moved to capitalize on the moment.

In 1975, the tournament expanded from 25 to 32 teams. Under the new format, colleges no longer had to win their conference title to get an invite to the tournament; NCAA officials had about a dozen at-large bids to hand out. More excitement that spring led immediately to more viewers—and yet another record audience in late March 1975. This time, about 42 million people tuned in to watch the Monday-night NCAA championship game, and a new tradition was born. In just a few years, the game had become one of the nation's most popular television shows. And like the best TV shows of the era—*The Six Million Dollar Man*, say, or *Starsky and Hutch*—the tournament gave viewers a cast of characters to root for and against.

John Wooden, a good guy, won his last championship in 1975 and rode off into that great basketball sunset at age 64 with 10 NCAA titles to his name and with three standing ovations from the crowd. Bobby Knight, a bad guy, won in 1976 with an undefeated Hoosiers team that could have included Larry Bird, if Bird hadn't hitchhiked home from Bloomington a year and a half earlier. In celebration that night, Knight hugged Bird's old roommate Jim Wisman—instead of grabbing Wisman by his jersey and throwing him to the bench. Al McGuire, a former bartender from Brooklyn, won with Marquette in 1977, drinking with journalists well after midnight that week and weeping with joy in the waning moments of the championship game. Then McGuire, the life of the party, parlayed his likable nature into a job that lots of coaches would soon be seeking: a television gig with NBC. And as the fans watched this show—Al McGuire's show—they stopped caring about the NIT at all.

Television ratings for the once-great NIT cratered. CBS dropped the tournament entirely. A new network called Mizlou Television, most famous for broadcasting the Tangerine Bowl and the Birmingham International Indoor Tennis Tournament, picked up the NIT contract. Mizlou couldn't compete with NBC, and the NIT continued to flounder. Sportswriters began to joke that the letters didn't stand for National Invitational Tournament anymore; they stood for "Not Important Tournament." And that's where Indiana State was headed in March 1978.

The Sycamores had effectively received an invitation to play on the edge of oblivion.

32

BOB KING DID HIS best to hide his disappointment. The NIT was still better than nothing, and this year, at least, the Sycamores got a first-round home game—a financial boon for Landini, the athletic department, and Indiana State.

The arena in Terre Haute that Friday night in March was just a few hundred tickets short of a sellout. Ten thousand people were going to flood into downtown, and the press box was going to be packed, too. Eighty reporters were coming—a media horde that the two McKees had never accommodated before, not even at the Purdue game three months earlier. And with everyone in the building, Landini wanted the university to look good. He wore his anxiety that night like a second sports coat, pacing the arena before the game. He stood beneath the Sycamores' basket, as if he were coaching the team himself, and cheered on the Sycamores to win along with 10,149 others because no one could bear the thought of losing to the Illinois State Redbirds—a team that had beaten them before.

The game was close the whole way. But with 11 minutes to go, Richard Johnson put his significant shoulder into the chest of one of Illinois State's top shooters, knocking him out of the game. Brad Miley scored 12 points, one of his best outings of the year. A pair of Sycamore role players came through in the final two possessions, hitting shots while the Illinois State defense keyed on Harry and Larry, and then Indiana State got lucky. The Redbirds missed a shot at the buzzer. The Sycamores escaped, 73–71, and moved on. They might have missed the NCAA tournament, but they still had a chance to make it to Madison Square Garden.

However, there was no published bracket here, no formula. NIT officials were winging it, deciding the sites for the games on the fly, and almost arbitrarily they sent Indiana State to play Rutgers in New Jersey for round two, because, according to the NIT officials, an East Coast site "would go well" for both teams.

It made no sense to the Sycamores, who now had to travel 700 miles for their next game, but there was nothing they could do about it. That Monday, the team, the cheerleaders, Bob King, Stan Evans, Bill Hodges, Ed McKee, and Dick Landini all flew east to Newark.

For all the grumbling in Terre Haute over the game taking place in New Jersey, the NIT officials had probably made the right choice by putting Indiana State on the road.

East Coast sportswriters had never had a chance to see Bird up close, unless they had traveled to Terre Haute, like Larry Keith at *Sports Illustrated*. The game at Rutgers would change all that. The Scarlet Knights' arena in Piscataway was just 25 miles from lower Manhattan. Even Mizlou Television, the production company broadcasting the game, couldn't screw this up. About four million people were expected to watch the Indiana State–Rutgers game on local channels and cable TV. Win or lose, it was going to be one of the biggest audiences that the Sycamores—and Bird—had ever drawn.

The problem was, Bird still wasn't talking to reporters. Since Larry Keith had written about his failed marriage to Janet back in January, almost no one in the media could get access to him. Basketball beat writers who showed up in Piscataway the day before the game, including one from the *New York Daily News*, weren't going to get to interview Bird, or even Morgan. Bob King had shut it all down, closing the locker room as the Sycamores prepared. To write their feature stories on Bird, reporters would have to work the fringes the way Keith once had, interviewing King, Landini, and a player in the Rutgers locker room who knew Bird well, Jammin' James Bailey, from the World University Games team the previous summer.

Bailey's arms—sliced up by that glass bottle in the fight against Cuba—had healed long ago, and Bailey had managed to put together a great year. He led the Eastern Athletic Association in scoring, besting players from Villanova, Pitt, and UMass. He led the Scarlet Knights in dunks, blocks, and steals. He had established himself as one of the best players on the East Coast and he happily spoke to the press about Bird. More importantly, Bailey shared a scouting report with his teammates and his coach, Tom Young. And with Bailey's input, Young crafted the rough outline of a plan to stop Bird. Rutgers would cover him with Hollis Copeland, the son of a Trenton autoworker about to be drafted by the Denver Nuggets; Abdel Anderson, a tough forward raised by his grandmother in nearby Belleville; or Steve Hefele, a guard from Long Island. But Copeland, Anderson, and Hefele would never be covering Bird alone, because Young was also implementing a disguise zone on Bird. Anytime Bird got the ball, the Rutgers defense would shift his way, covering him with not just a man, but a man and a half.

In preparation for the game—and the assignment covering Bird—Young worked his players hard that week in practice, to the point that Anderson was angry at his own coach. But Young wasn't changing anything else to prepare for Indiana State. He didn't see the need to do anything exotic. By mid-March 1978, the Sycamores had become two-dimensional, Young believed. They had Larry and Harry and nothing else. All the Scarlet Knights had to do was shut down one of the two stars from Indiana State, and they would win.

Early on, it didn't look like the Knights would be stopping Bird. In the opening minutes of the game, Abdel Anderson was all over him, just like Young wanted, and still Bird drained a 20-footer right over him, banking it in off the glass. Anderson couldn't believe it. He shook his head in disgust while Bill Hodges sat on the Sycamores bench, feeling good. He had scouted Rutgers for Bob King. He believed that Indiana State had the better team, and he felt even better after Bailey got into foul trouble, picking up his fourth foul just 30 seconds into the second half.

The Rutgers leader was heading to the bench. But even without Bailey, the Scarlet Knights hung around as Bird struggled to hit his shots after that opening bucket over Anderson. He couldn't operate against Rutgers's man-and-a-half zone defense, and he was so inconsistent that East Coast reporters complained. They were unimpressed. They hadn't been able to interview Bird the day before; now they wondered why they had even bothered to try. Larry Bird wasn't great, they said. He was "rather slow" and "somewhat awkward"—"less than all American," noted a reporter at the *Daily News*. Even Tom Young wondered why he had been so concerned about Bird. He wasn't taking outside shots and he was missing half of his shots inside. At one point in the second half, Bird didn't score for seven minutes. Almost every other Sycamore disappeared, too. Brad Miley had three points. Steve Reed only scored two. Leroy Staley didn't get on the floor at all. And DeCarsta Webster and Richard Johnson couldn't stay out there, as they got into foul trouble of their own.

Only Morgan was keeping Indiana State in the game now, getting his usual 18 points. But Morgan couldn't do it alone, and with 3:19 left to play, Bob King made the same mistake he had made many times in recent weeks. As his players clung to a three-point lead in the hostile arena filled with Rutgers fans, King directed them to hold the ball, to stall. Again.

Indiana State proceeded to turn the ball over three times in a row. Bailey, who was back on the floor, hit two shots—*bang, bang*—and Rutgers took a one-point lead with 17 seconds left. At this point, King called a time-out and drew up a play for either Larry or Harry, but off the inbounds pass, Larry never touched the ball. Instead, it went to Harry, who never gave it up. He dribbled, tried to get around Hollis Copeland, failed to do so, and with the time ticking down, threw up a 35-footer over Copeland's outstretched arms. It was a prayer with no answer. And when it missed—and missed badly—the final two seconds of the game devolved into chaos.

Harry fouled Rutgers's best shooter to stop the clock. The Rutgers player proceeded to intentionally miss a free throw to create havoc for the Sycamores. DeCarsta pulled down the rebound and flung the ball up the court to Bird with one second to go. And the last thing anyone saw in Piscataway was Steve Hefele and Larry Bird tumbling to the court in a tangle of arms and legs.

Bird wanted a foul to be called. But there was no whistle. Just the buzzer. It was over.

Rutgers had won, 57–56.

The arguments began immediately on the floor. Bird, who was held to just 23 points in the game, got in a referee's face, arguing that Hefele had pushed him to the ground. King joined him, shouting and pleading. The referee tried to pull himself away; he needed to get out of there. Then the Rutgers fans stormed the floor in a wild stampede.

James Bailey said later that it felt like the Cuba fight all over again. The refs were gone, security had lost control, and the players were running to the locker rooms to save themselves. But not Bird. "We're shaking hands," Copeland recalled. "He and I are shaking hands. We disengage hands and start to walk away, but what caught my eye is a fan comes out of the stands."

According to two witnesses, this fan jumped on Bird's back. According to other witnesses, he just taunted Bird with his call of "Birdshit!" The only thing people can agree on is what happened next: Bird popped him. "Bird lets him have it—*pow!*" Copeland said. "And before I knew it, the guy is on the floor. Blood was everywhere. His glasses split . . . And you think this guy is dead, to tell you quite frankly, because he's not moving."

In an instant, Bailey moved in to get Bird off the court. "Because you know how Larry is," Bailey said later. "Larry? He'll go." Bailey escorted him into the tunnel, trying to save Bird the way Bird had saved him the previous summer in Bulgaria. But the Indiana State locker room was hardly a refuge for anyone. In the aftermath, Stan Evans and Bill Hodges argued openly with each other, weeks of tension finally rising to the surface. Ed McKee had no chance of getting the players to speak to reporters, especially not Bird. Bob King barred the doors again. Steve Reed blamed King for the loss, believing he should have been handling the ball during the final minutes instead of senior Jimmy Smith. Staley blamed King, too, wondering why he hadn't played at all, and the East Coast media circled like vultures around the carcass of Larry Bird, shouting questions at him about the incident on the floor when Bird finally emerged from the locker room to make his way to the Indiana State bus.

"What happened?" the press hollered.

"Huh?" Bird replied.

"You were there—what happened in the end?"

"I don't know."

A couple of East Coast newspapers had a field day with the fight, putting it in their headlines and their ledes, but Hollis Copeland, who is Black, was stunned that it wasn't a bigger story, a sensational news story, and he came to believe later that Bird's race mattered in how the altercation was handled in the press. Bird wasn't just a white star by the spring of 1978, Copeland said. He was "a white superstar . . . the Great White Hope." Newspapers were happy to bury the details about what happened with the fan in an effort to protect Bird, especially back home in Indiana.

The Terre Haute Star didn't mention the incident until the last paragraph of its game story, reporting that "Bird or someone among the Sycamores" had struck a fan "in the postgame confusion." And *The Terre Haute Tribune* dodged the issue entirely, not mentioning the altercation in its game story at all, leaving it to a columnist to break the news in an ambiguous way. The columnist wrote that Bird "might have been involved in a ruckus."

No one in Terre Haute wanted to know the truth: The team had come unglued, its star was recoiling from the spotlight, its coach felt older by the day, and its roster was going to be radically different by the fall. Harry Morgan, DeCarsta Webster, and Jimmy Smith were all graduating, or due to graduate. And they weren't the only ones who had just played their last games for Indiana State. Shortly after returning to campus, Staley informed King that he was quitting. If King wasn't going to play him, Staley was out, returning to his home at the foot of the runways in Tampa. In early May, right about the time that Staley made his decision, authorities arrested Richard Johnson and charged him with robbing two students in a dorm. The charge was later dismissed, but Johnson was gone, too, returning home to Detroit. The same week that police came for Johnson, King met with Landini inside his office on back-to-back days—possibly to discuss Johnson's arrest and maybe to discuss Stan Evans. People speculated that Evans could be fired for his alleged insubordination.

And while all of these questions were swirling over the program, Larry Bird's future was in doubt, too. In a matter of weeks, Bird could leave for the NBA. In fact, by April 1978, just a few weeks after the loss at Rutgers, he was already practicing with future NBA stars down in Kentucky, including a man who would alter the course of Bird's career more than any other.

Bird was playing that spring with Earvin "Magic" Johnson.

Part IV
CINDERELLA IN MIDDLE AMERICA

33

AROUND THE HOUSE ON Middle Street in Lansing, Michigan, no one called the boy "Magic."

To his parents, he was Earvin or Junior; to his friends, he was E or E.J.; and to old-timers in the neighborhood, he was "June Bug"—as in, "There goes that crazy June Bug, hoopin' all day." Young Earvin was always bouncing his basketball somewhere on the little grid of urban streets hemmed in between the interstate and the river on the west side of Lansing. And he felt fortunate later that the last of these names, June Bug, had fallen out of favor by his ninth-grade year at Dwight Rich Junior High. Because if the name had still been around then, it would have been in the papers. At age 14, Earvin Johnson was already a star in Lansing.

He held multiple junior high records: most points in a season, most rebounds in a season, and most points in a game—48. The day that he recorded his 48 points, he could have beaten the opposing team by himself. Earvin's school won that afternoon, 89–25. With these accolades preceding him, he walked in the doors of Everett High School in the fall of 1974 as a bona fide college prospect. Scouts across the Midwest already knew his name, and the basketball writer at *The Lansing State Journal* did, too. Fred Stabley Jr.—a young reporter and the son of the longtime sports information director at Michigan State—couldn't wait to write about Earvin. Stabley was so excited, in fact, that he approached Earvin in December 1974 after one of his first high school games to inform him that he needed a nickname.

"Dr. J" had been taken by Julius Erving, Stabley informed Earvin, and "Big E" had been claimed by Elvin Hayes. But Stabley had an idea that he thought might work for the kid.

He wanted to call him Magic.

Earvin was embarrassed by the conversation—which he said took place in the locker room in front of his new teammates—and Earvin's parents, Christine and Earvin Sr., hated the name. His mother wanted her son to know that his talents "came from God," not magic, and his father, an autoworker, didn't like that the flashy nickname might motivate opposing defenses to play hard against his son. But the Johnsons didn't have a say here.

On a Friday night in late January 1975, Earvin scored 36 points and grabbed 18 rebounds in his 11th high school game, leading the previously woebegone Everett Vikings to victory over a crosstown rival inside a gym packed with 3,000 screaming fans, and Fred Stabley had seen enough. In the next day's *State Journal*, Stabley called him Earvin "Magic" Johnson. He put it in the lede. The editors stripped the story across the top of the sports page, and the name stuck, in part because it was such a perfect fit.

Magic had a way about him, even then. Stabley noted how he smiled, exuded positivity, celebrated with his teammates, lifted them up, and played to the crowd, holding his fist over his head in victory. He was so good—and so mature—that college coaches said he could play for them right then, at age 15. People in Lansing questioned whether he was really that young, and Everett's head coach, George Fox, sometimes turned team huddles over to Magic. Everybody wanted to hear what he had to say, even Fox. "Earvin," the coach conceded, "is a once in a lifetime thrill."

By the first week of February 1975—the same week that Bird's father killed himself in West Baden—tickets for Magic's high school games were being scalped on the streets of Lansing. People were willing to pay more than double the asking price for a chance to see him play. He drew 2,000 people, 4,000 people, and then 10,000 people. By 1977, Magic's senior year, he was selling out games across town at Michigan State's arena, Jenison Field House, while still playing in high school. A reporter said they should hold his playoff games that March in the Pontiac Silverdome, the home of the Detroit Lions with seats for 80,000 fans. Local television stations were paying for the right to broadcast his games *live*. The stations sometimes even covered scrimmages. And print reporters covered everything Magic did, especially the debate over which college he would choose: Michigan, in Ann Arbor, or Michigan State, three miles away. In April 1977, one reporter made 132 phone calls in a single day, trying to chase down the answer. And the next day, one month after leading Everett to a Class A state title, Magic convened yet another crowd at his high school to reveal his choice.

He walked into an auditorium through a side door with his parents and a family friend, soon to be his agent; he sat down at a table in front of 10 microphones, including one wired directly into every classroom in the school; he looked out on his teammates, the faculty, the administration, and the gathered media; and he smiled his electric smile and made his much-anticipated announcement, with his voice echoing down the halls of the school.

"Next year," he said, "I'll be attending Michigan State University."

34

THE SCHOOL ROARED IN approval and Magic settled in to answer questions from reporters, happy to engage with them all. He said he'd made his choice the day before while listening to soft music. "That's the only time I can think sometimes." He said the green leather jacket he was wearing on the day of the announcement didn't carry any special significance. "But I think I look pretty good in it." He said he would play center, guard, or forward for the Spartans. "Whatever it takes to win." He oozed confidence, speaking of himself in the third person. "I'm going to MSU for Earvin Johnson," he said, "not for the community." And he admitted he would leave school when it was right for Earvin Johnson, too. He wasn't committing to stay at Michigan State for four years. "A lot of pro teams have been looking at me," he said. "If something comes up, I might have to take it."

He was, in short, the opposite of Larry Bird in almost every single way. Magic was coveted and comfortable, personable and prepared, a fully formed star at age 17 and an open book. He had no secrets, nothing to hide. There was, it seemed, only one hole in Magic's game: He struggled to shoot from the outside. To score, Magic usually had to drive to the basket.

A glaring flaw like this—a weak jump shot—typically would have upset Magic's new head coach, Jud Heathcote at Michigan State.

Heathcote didn't think basketball was supposed to be fun. He believed it was work. Any fun the players derived from the game needed to come from growth or victory. If players didn't achieve these things, Heathcote raged on the sidelines, and he didn't reserve his rage for games alone. Once, while the Spartan players ran drills during a clinic for high school coaches at Jenison Field House, Heathcote criticized them in real time over the public address system—like a broadcaster calling the action, only with biting sarcasm. His patience was about as thin as his hairline, and Heathcote was sorry to report that his hairline was almost gone.

But on the day of Magic's signing, Heathcote wasn't worried about the young star's limitations. The Spartans coach was a master strategist, capable of identifying his opponents' flaws and exploiting them for his gain. He figured that Magic, who was about six foot eight, could account for 40 points a game with his passing and floor vision alone, even if he only scored 15 points himself. And anyway, Heathcote already had shooters on his roster. He had a plethora of young guards, a future NBA first-rounder in forward Greg Kelser, and he had just signed the second-best player in the state: Jay Vincent, also from Lansing. Under normal circumstances, Vincent on his own would have been reason for excitement. Now Heathcote had Vincent *and* Magic. He had it all, and he seemed to know it.

On the morning of Magic's press conference at Everett High, the Michigan State coach had his feet propped up on his desk at Jenison Field House and a bottle of champagne on hand—a bottle he very nearly opened one year later, at the end of Magic's freshman year. While Larry Bird made the cover of *Sports Illustrated* in 1977 and then failed to even make the NCAA tournament in March 1978, Magic led Michigan State to a Big Ten championship. The Spartans entered the tournament that March ranked No. 6 in the country and then came achingly close to beating the nation's best team, Joe B. Hall's Kentucky Wildcats. On the cusp of the Final Four, the Spartans lost to Kentucky, 52–49.

It was a devastating outcome for Magic in particular. He struggled to shoot the entire tournament that March, and went 2-for-10 against Kentucky, missing badly. "Missing by feet," one reporter said afterward, "not inches."

But Magic didn't run from the media after the loss, and Heathcote didn't have to bar the locker room door, as Ed McKee and others were doing in Terre Haute. Magic gave his interviews as usual. He admitted that he was terrible that day. He confessed that his missed shots against Kentucky got in his head. He conceded that he began to doubt himself during the game, and then he pivoted, ending his interview on a positive note. He said he still planned to hang out with friends that night in East Lansing, dancing and listening to music. Because it was Saturday night and there was nothing to worry about.

"We'll be back," Magic smiled.

He had blown the game and he still looked happy, looked like himself. Maybe it was because Magic's season wasn't technically over.

Within days of losing to Kentucky in March 1978, Magic reported down to Lexington to suit up with a team of college all-stars. Several Kentucky players were going to be there, and a handful of others would be, too, including three notable names: James Bailey, Sidney Moncrief, and an All-American who had never played in the NCAA tournament, Larry Bird.

It was like the World University Games from the year before, but different. There were only four games, for one thing—against Cuba, Yugoslavia, the Soviet Union, and a team sponsored by Marathon Oil. Magic skipped the Marathon Oil game to attend a year-end Spartans banquet back in Lansing. Other guys came and went, too, dipping in and out. And the person in charge seemed to lack the objectivity he needed to lead. The coach of this year's college all-star squad was Kentucky's Joe B. Hall, the man who had passed on Bird three years earlier.

The decision was already haunting Hall and would continue to do so for the rest of his life. In some ways, Hall never stopped answering questions about Larry Bird. But that spring, as the college all-stars assembled in Lexington, Hall had earned a brief moment of peace. His Wildcats hadn't just beaten Magic Johnson to advance to the Final Four. They had gone on to win the national title and returned to Lexington flush with cash. Just three years earlier, in 1975, a Final Four appearance would have earned Kentucky about $49,000—a nice chunk of money. Now the prize had ballooned to $240,000. And according to a *Lexington Leader* analysis, the team had earned more than $1 million through season-ticket sales and gate receipts—enough money to float almost every other sport at the school. Athletic directors across the country wanted a slice of this pie, and the NCAA was about to accommodate them. By summer that year, the tournament would expand from 32 to 40 teams. With more teams, and more games, and a new seeding system to help ensure that the top teams would advance farther, officials predicted still more revenue in 1979. And all of these developments gave Joe B. Hall a certain amount of leeway when it came to his all-star team. He decided to put Bird and Magic on his bench and start a lineup of Moncrief, Bailey, and three Kentucky players, including the Louisiana high school star who had taken the scholarship that could have gone to Bird back in 1974, Rick Robey.

Robey and Bird hit it off right away. They were both country boys with a fondness for straight talk and beer, and Bird didn't mind telling Robey what he thought of Hall's lineup. "What the hell is your coach thinking?" he asked. In four games, Bird averaged 3.5 points, and in three games, Magic averaged 5. They were barely playing. But the abbreviated week on the exhibition circuit mattered for three reasons.

First, Larry Bird met Magic Johnson. They didn't speak a lot. Sidney Moncrief, Magic's roommate that week, doesn't remember seeing Bird much, and Jay Shidler, a Kentucky guard who roomed with Bird, agreed. The two future stars were together, but apart. While Magic was listening to his slow grooves in Moncrief's room—Moncrief said that Magic played the same song over and over again in the hotel—Bird was off drinking beer or eating pizza with Shidler. But Bird and Magic did bond over at least one thing: Joe B. Hall's curious lineup choices. They spent a lot of time wasting away on the bench together. Above all, they had crossed paths, a meeting that would matter later.

Second, Bird and Magic shared one moment of greatness together. In the final game in Lexington against the Soviet Union, Magic dribbled up the court on a fast break in the second half, drove into the lane, and leaped into the air in front of a Soviet defender. But instead of shooting, Magic dropped the ball off to Bird, who was trailing behind him. Bird, at this point, went up like he was going to take the shot, but as the Soviet crashed on him, Bird flicked the ball back to Magic across the lane for an easy two—"a dizzying display of back-and-forth passing," one reporter called it. Fans almost felt bad for the Soviets.

Lastly, and most importantly, NBA scouts were at the exhibition games, taking notes in advance of the draft in June, and one of those scouts was Red Auerbach, the cigar-smoking general manager of the Boston Celtics and the architect of one of the greatest dynasties in NBA history. Auerbach typically didn't have much need to scout the best college players. The Celtics rarely drafted in the top 10 in the 1970s. But they were coming off a dismal year. Auerbach had been selling his team off for parts—and draft picks—since December. He now had two picks in the top 10, and after returning to Boston from the exhibition games, Auerbach knew what he wanted to do with the first of those picks. He was taking Larry Bird with the sixth choice overall, if the five teams in front of him—the Pacers, Kings, Trail Blazers, Knicks, and Warriors—made a mistake and passed on him.

35

FOR A WHILE IN April and May 1978, it seemed unlikely that five NBA franchises might fail to select Larry Bird. In truth, it didn't seem possible that he could get past the team picking first, the Indiana Pacers.

They were in financial disarray and had been in danger of folding for months. To stave off disaster and save the team, ownership had organized a 16½-hour telethon the previous summer, rallying local fans to buy tickets. Head coach Bobby "Slick" Leonard, a former Hoosier star, conceded that the telethon was an act of desperation. He himself answered the phones that day, taking ticket orders and donations from locals, and now he was hearing from these people again. Polls showed that four out of five Pacer fans wanted Leonard to draft the Indiana boy from French Lick, Larry Bird. There was just one problem. In a meeting that spring with Bird and his escort for the evening, a Terre Haute banker named Ed Jukes, Leonard learned that Bird wasn't leaving school. He would be staying at Indiana State for his senior year.

Under NBA rules at the time, Leonard didn't have to care about this choice. A team drafting a player in 1978 owned the player's rights for a full year—whether he left college or not. As long as the Pacers signed Bird before the NBA draft one year later in 1979, Bird could have stayed home in Indiana and been a Pacer, maybe forever. Leonard just needed to be patient.

But no one was sure that Bird was worth waiting for—and Leonard, in particular, couldn't afford to squander the No. 1 pick in the draft on a player who wasn't going to step on the court for some 16 months. The Pacers might not *exist* by the fall of 1979. So, Leonard traded the pick to the Trail Blazers, who also failed to convince Bird to leave school, and the top five picks in the 1978 draft played out like this: The Blazers took Mychal Thompson. The Kings took Phil Ford. Leonard and the Pacers drafted Bird's new friend Rick Robey. Micheal Ray Richardson went to the Knicks. Purvis Short went to the Warriors. And there was Red Auerbach, puffing away on his cigar. He had the chance to select Larry Bird with the No. 6 pick just like he had dreamed.

The draft in those days wasn't nearly what it would be later, and neither was the league. The NBA Finals had ended two days earlier, and most Americans had not watched a single minute of a single game. Fans didn't care about a series involving the Washington Bullets and the Seattle SuperSonics, even when the series went seven games. The deciding Game Seven—usually a big deal in sports—ranked 442nd in shows watched that year, roughly as popular as *Country Night of the Stars*. CBS executives, who had recently inked a new $74 million deal to broadcast NBA games through 1982, blamed the poor ratings on the bad matchup. But Kevin O'Malley—a young vice president at CBS Sports, moving up the corporate ladder quickly, two rungs at a time—knew that the problem went far deeper than the Bullets and the SuperSonics.

By 1978, lots of television programs outperformed NBA games: reruns of *Baretta*, amateur boxing, tennis, auto racing, pro bowling, and a show called *Superstars*, where athletes from different sports competed against each other in feats of strength. Every week, when the ratings came in, O'Malley would pore over the numbers in his office at CBS, trying to identify trends, strengths, weaknesses, and curiosities. He was 32 at the time, a graduate of Boston College, fully dialed in to pop culture, and keen on basketball in particular. O'Malley had been raised in the birthplace of the sport—Springfield, Massachusetts. And he had started to believe there was a disconnect between viewers and the NBA. CBS was the network of middle America, O'Malley said, giving the people stars like Walter Cronkite, Mary Tyler Moore, and Valerie Bertinelli; shows like *The Waltons*, *The Jeffersons*, and *The Incredible Hulk*; characters like Archie Bunker in *All in the Family*, Hawkeye Pierce in *M*A*S*H*, and Johnny Fever in *WKRP in Cincinnati*; and perhaps the most American show of them all: NFL football, on Sundays in the fall.

The NBA, on the other hand, didn't feel middle American at all. It was an "urban game," O'Malley said. "By far, the most urban of games." Or, to put it another way, it was seen by millions of Americans as a Black game. NBA rosters were 70 percent Black in 1978. Half the teams in the league barely had any white players at all. And while NBA commissioner Larry O'Brien claimed that fans didn't care about such things—"By God," O'Brien said, "color is meaningless"—Black players in the NBA disagreed. They knew that race mattered, especially as racial slurs rained down on them in arenas across the league. They believed that teams sometimes signed white players just to be "more white." They couldn't begrudge teams this practice, knowing in the end that fans paid their salaries. Drug scandals around this time involving Black players, including Bernard King, one of the league's most promising rookies, only exacerbated the NBA's image problems. And two incidents during the 1977–78 season made it all worse: fights between Black and white players on the court.

In the opening minutes of the first game of the season that year, Black star Kareem Abdul-Jabbar punched white rookie Kent Benson—the player who had briefly played with Bird during his short time in Bloomington. Kareem's punch left Benson reeling with headaches for months. And eight weeks later, a different Black player on the Lakers, Kermit Washington, leveled Rudy Tomjanovich, a white forward with the Houston Rockets, with a punch that fractured his nose, jaw, and skull, and put Tomjanovich in intensive care. In addition to its race problem, the league now had a violence problem, exemplified by the lawsuit that the Rockets were filing against the Lakers for ending Tomjanovich's season. It was a moment of crisis, a turbulent year, and Larry Bird emerged from this storm like a beacon of light on a rocky shore. It apparently didn't matter that Bird had his own history of fighting on the court. At least he was white—an important reality that some NBA executives, including Red Auerbach, publicly acknowledged.

Auerbach had been the first NBA coach to draft a Black player, the first to roll out a starting five that was all Black, and the first NBA executive to hire a Black coach. He was, by the standards of the era, an enlightened man, even as he chomped on that cigar. But he was also keenly aware of what Boston fans wanted—or rather, didn't want. The city was hard on Black players in the 1970s. "My job," Auerbach said around this time, "is to get a ballclub out there the town will like." Larry Bird fit this bill. He was, one NBA executive said, "an unusual commodity in our business." He was a white star in an era when such a thing mattered and people didn't mind saying it out loud.

"White people have to have white heroes," said Ted Stepien, a white advertising executive who owned a piece of the Cleveland Indians in 1978 and was about to purchase the Cleveland Cavaliers, too. "I myself can't relate to Black heroes. I'll be truthful—I respect them. But I need white people."

On draft day in early June 1978, Auerbach monitored the other teams' picks by phone as he sat in a club bar in the Boston Garden. He didn't have a detailed scouting report on Bird. He had seen him play in person only once and admitted later that he wasn't sure what Bird would turn out to be. Auerbach just knew he couldn't pass on him.

"How many times do you get the chance to sit at this table," Auerbach said that day, "and get the player with the No. 1 ability in the country?"

He didn't care if he had to wait a year. A year goes fast, Auerbach said. He believed executives would be kicking themselves later for not taking Bird when they had the chance. He selected Bird No. 6 overall, just as he had planned. He picked Bird's roommate from the World University Games one round later. Jeff Judkins was a Celtic now, too. And as Auerbach lit up a celebratory cigar at the Garden, the San Antonio Spurs moved in to take Bird's teammate Harry Morgan, making it one of the best days in the history of Indiana State basketball.

Morgan was working at a basketball camp the day of the draft and was overjoyed when he got the news that the Spurs had selected him with the 129th pick near the end of the sixth round. "I was hoping to be drafted by San Antonio," he said in celebration. But his warm feelings about the Spurs—and his own future—quickly faded as the cold reality of professional sports set in. The Spurs were inviting 20 prospects to camp that summer and only planning to keep five. Morgan didn't make the cut, and in the fall of 1978, he came up short yet again. He failed to earn a spot with the Tucson Gunners of the Western Basketball Association. With nowhere left to play in America, Morgan caught on with a team in Aalst, Belgium. "I was a real scoring *machine* over there," he boasted at the time. Yet this, too, didn't last, and soon he had run out of options entirely. Harry Morgan—a man who had scored more than a thousand points at Indiana State, playing with Larry Bird—wasn't headed for NBA greatness. He was headed home to Anderson with Rita and their boys, and he felt fortunate when he later landed a steady job working for the state highway department. Harry Morgan's dreams of playing professional basketball were over.

Meanwhile, Bird didn't want to talk about his dreams at all, not even with his teammates. That summer, Steve Reed lived with Bird in his apartment in married-student housing, and Reed never once heard him talk about the Celtics, Boston, Red Auerbach, or his future. Bird had Ed McKee send out a press release on draft day, announcing that he was grateful for the Celtics' interest but he was staying in Terre Haute, and he never mentioned it again. He was busy cutting Max Gibson's grass in Fontanet with Max's son Greg; driving Max's Lincoln to a bar called Rafters; sneaking the underage Greg inside; training at the Boys' Club, shooting baskets; or hanging out with pals and not thinking about basketball at all.

That summer, Bird played for a softball team sponsored by an oil company, 500 Platolene, and probably had more fun with the Platolene crew than he did with Magic Johnson and Joe B. Hall's all-stars. Larry's older brother, Mike, was on the team. His former teammates Howie Johnson and Danny King were, too, and in August 1978, they all piled into cars and drove to South Bend to compete in a state championship tournament.

Huge crowds came out to the ballpark that weekend to watch the softball games, in part because Bird wasn't the only college star competing. A local quarterback named Joe Montana was playing for the South Bend softball team. But Bird's team was better than Montana's. Bird hit six home runs that weekend—tied for most in the tournament. 500 Platolene won the title with a walk-off win in the bottom of the seventh inning that Sunday evening, and Bird was so happy afterward that he allowed his coach to take a photo of him on the infield dirt.

In the snapshot, the summer sun is setting. The brim of his ball cap is creased down the middle. Bird holds his trophy and his glove. He looks at the camera, eyes squinting beneath the folded brim of the cap, and he is almost smiling.

36

BOB KING AND BILL Hodges didn't worry about Bird disappearing that summer. He had given them his word that he was going to return to Indiana State for his senior year, and they knew Bird well enough at that point to know that Bird kept his promises. The Pacers and the Trail Blazers could call Bird all they wanted, and Red Auerbach could take him with the sixth pick in the draft if he believed in his talent. It wasn't going to change Bird's mind.

"He'll be playing for me next season," King told reporters whenever they called. "He's committed to that."

The problem, for King and Hodges, was everything else. King had opted not to fire Stan Evans, despite all the tension the year before, and Evans had chosen not to leave. The three men—King, Evans, and Hodges—were reupping for another season together, a recipe for dysfunction, if not disaster. And Hodges had lots of questions about his own future. He figured King would retire in a year, leaving his head coaching post when Bird graduated in 1979. Hodges had little faith that Landini would hire him to be King's replacement. As a result, Hodges had started to apply for head coaching jobs elsewhere, quietly testing the market. But Bill and Connie had two kids by then. It was going to be difficult to leave

Terre Haute for the unknown, and the one job offer that Hodges received that summer wasn't going to work for them. It was at a small school in rural Texas, about 200 miles from El Paso, Hodges said. A hard sell at home and a hard pass for Hodges. Like Bird, he was staying with King in Terre Haute and doing what he could to rebuild the Sycamores—a team gutted by the loss of three starters, both centers, and roughly 40 points a game in scoring.

To begin, Hodges flew down to Tampa to meet with Leroy Staley and convince him to return to college. Hodges understood why Staley had been frustrated the previous spring. In the second half of the season, as the team unraveled and King searched for answers, Staley hadn't played much at all. But quitting the team and leaving school—Staley's second school in two years—wasn't going to help him. In the meeting at Staley's house in Tampa not far from the airport, Hodges explained to Staley and his aunt Eula all the reasons why he needed to return to Terre Haute in the fall, and by the time Hodges left the house, he had closed the deal, as usual. Staley was coming back.

As Hodges worked to smooth things over with Staley, he asked the players to work on another teammate who felt he had been snubbed: Carl Nicks. Nicks had reported to Gulf Coast Community College down in Panama City the previous fall and, once there, had decided to apply himself, working as if Gulf Coast might be his last shot. Off the court, Nicks studied hard. He utilized the help of tutors offered by the school and he ran wind sprints every day in an open field near the beach. Then, with his legs weary, Nicks would go to the gym to shoot on his own, a habit he had picked up from Bird. It was important, Bird believed, for players to practice shooting while they were tired, replicating how they would feel in the final minutes of a game.

Nicks started to see results right away. That year, he averaged 22 points a game at Gulf Coast, and more importantly, he grew up a little. Nicks boosted his grade point average. He learned patience. He realized that playing fast was sometimes just playing badly. He earned the respect of his Gulf Coast teammates—they made him the captain—and he finished the year with something he didn't have before: interest from a few Division I schools.

But Hodges had made a key decision months earlier. He didn't assume Nicks would return and chose to recruit him as if he were any other new player. Hodges flew Nicks back to Terre Haute for a visit. He called him on a regular basis, checking in, invested, and then he asked an important player to make calls on his behalf. Larry Bird was soon on the phone, ringing Nicks up in Florida, and there was no way that Nicks was ignoring Bird. Like Staley, he agreed to return to Terre Haute in the fall of 1978, and he felt good about his choice. If Bird wanted him, Nicks was coming.

Hodges now had two pieces in place, Staley and Nicks, but he needed more talent, and to find it, he was going to have to leave Connie and the kids yet again. First, he went to Wabash Valley, a little junior college in southern Illinois, and recruited two players who also happened to be best friends: Eric Curry from Chicago and Rich Nemcek, a descendant of Slovakian immigrants who had taken a year off from basketball to work at a steel mill in northern Indiana. Curry and Nemcek had options to play elsewhere, just like Nicks. But Curry was insistent that if they had an opportunity to play with Larry Bird, they had to seize it. The two friends signed with Hodges, and then Hodges set out to land one more player. He wanted Alex Gilbert, the son of a stockyard worker in a Black enclave of East St. Louis known as Goose Hill.

As a boy in Goose Hill, Gilbert had watched construction crews build the Gateway Arch across the Mississippi River in St. Louis itself. He could see its two legs rising into the sky—an engineering marvel and a symbol of American greatness. But greatness had proven to be more elusive for Gilbert. Out of high school in 1976, almost no one had recruited him, and as a result, he enrolled in a small junior college in rural Kansas, 60 miles from nowhere.

Gilbert could have easily disappeared out there on the Kansas prairie. But in 1976, college basketball changed its rules, allowing players to dunk the ball for the first time in a decade. Gilbert, at six foot seven, with a 40-inch vertical leap, found himself unleashed. In two years in rural Kansas, he scored a thousand points, many of them via the dunk. The stats earned him a junior college All-American honorable mention, and suddenly lots of schools were interested in him, including the University of Missouri.

Gilbert was excited about playing there. If he went to Missouri, he would compete against the Kansas Jayhawks and one day step on the floor at Allen Fieldhouse—Kansas's home floor and sacred basketball ground that Gilbert wanted to touch. But Bill Hodges was persistent in his pursuit of Gilbert. At some point that year, he sat with Alex's parents in their house in East St. Louis and managed to convince their son to at least make a visit to Terre Haute.

The trip didn't go well. Gilbert found the city drab, the weather cold, and the entertainment options thin. *I do not like this place at all*, he thought. Also, dangling Larry Bird in front of Gilbert wasn't going to help. Gilbert had never heard of Bird. But when Gilbert returned to his junior college in Kansas, he received a package in the mail from sports information director Ed McKee. Among the materials, McKee was sure to include a copy of Larry Bird's *Sports Illustrated* cover. Gilbert's teammates were impressed, and his older brother, Lindell, couldn't stop talking about Bird and what it would mean for Alex to play with him.

"You go there," Lindell told him, "and you play with this guy."

Lindell was a lot like Alex. He was tall and athletic, with a welcoming smile, and he had a certain power over his brother. Alex always listened to Lindell, and so he listened to him again in the spring of 1978. Despite his misgivings, Alex signed with Indiana State. He moved to Terre Haute a few weeks later. He spent the summer working alongside Brad Miley—on jobs that Max Gibson helped arrange—and Gilbert and Miley quickly became the best of friends. One was tall and white and from the country, the other was tall and Black and from the city, and they were inseparable, drinking beers that summer in the off-campus bars.

By chance—by sheer accident—Hodges had added glue to the locker room. The other dab of glue just walked in the door of his own volition. He showed up one day out of nowhere, set down his duffel bag, laced up his shoes, and asked if he could play. His name was Bob Heaton. He was from Cory, Indiana, and like everybody else in the locker room, he was looking for a second chance.

Actually, in Bob Heaton's case, it was more like a third.

37

HEATON'S ANCESTORS ON HIS mother's side had been farming in Cory, population 200, for at least five generations, since before the Civil War. Over the years, they might have driven trucks, mined coal, fought for the Union, traveled the country, tested life in Illinois, and gone as far west as California seeking their fortune, but they always came back to Cory and they were always farming—soybeans and corn, mostly.

In this way, Bob Heaton's parents, Forrest and Betty, were like those who came before them. They lived in Cory, and farmed in Cory, and Forrest helped make ends meet for the family by working in a railyard on the Wabash River. There was just one difference. In 1966, when Bob Heaton was 10 years old, his father made an improvement to the land. He poured a concrete slab next to the farmhouse, about 30 feet long and 20 feet wide, so that Bob and his three siblings could have a proper basketball court. His oldest brother, John, seemed especially bound for greatness. But young Bob was showing promise, too—at least until Christmas 1967.

Two days after the Heatons opened presents that year, Bob Heaton, then 11, tumbled out of the house to help his grandpa Everett put up the last of the year's harvest into the corn crib next to the concrete slab. Everett fired up the corn hiker, a narrow chute that worked like a conveyor belt. The power takeoff shaft beneath the hiker began to churn, spinning around, hot and steady, powering the belt along. And while his grandfather dumped corn into the chute, and his brother John assisted, Bob handled his part of the work. He picked up the ears of corn that spilled off the side and tossed them onto the belt.

It was cold that day. Bob was wearing his father's winter jacket to stay warm. The sleeves of the jacket hung off his wrists, and as he stood up one time, with the corn in his hands, the left sleeve of his father's coat brushed up against the churning rod. Suddenly, there was no time to think. There wasn't even time to scream. The shaft caught Bob's sleeve, sucked him in, and began to spin him around, snapping his left arm above the elbow.

The appendage just hung there, broken clean through.

It was the kind of thing that took arms entirely—or worse. In farm country every year, people died in power takeoff shaft incidents, ripped apart by the spinning rod. And it easily could have happened to Bob Heaton, if his family hadn't acted quickly.

His grandpa Everett shut off the power to the shaft. His mother ran out of the house. His brother John gathered towels to try to stanch the bleeding. His sister, Marcia, 12 that winter, hurried up from the pond behind the corn crib, where she had been ice skating, to hold the towels on Bob's arm. Then, together, the Heatons carefully laid Bob in the back of the family station wagon. Marcia tried to position her brother's useless arm to keep it from flopping off his chest, and everybody stood back and watched as their mother drove away, headed to Clay County Hospital, 30 minutes north.

En route, Bob didn't cry and he said he didn't feel pain anymore, either. Just a sensation, he recalled. *It burns*, he told his mother from the back of the station wagon. *It burns*. Perhaps it was shock setting in—not a good sign. And that night, across the county, word spread in hushed and urgent tones about what had happened to Forrest and Betty's son. People prayed for Bob, rallying around the Heatons, and from the moment his fifth-grade classmates returned to school after Christmas break, they wrote letters to him, asking with innocence for the impossible.

"I hope you can play on the basketball team," they wrote.

"I hope you are back with us soon and can play . . ."

"I hope you are all right."

That week, with the whole county waiting and watching, doctors performed the first miracle of Bob Heaton's life. They saved him, and his left arm. Heaton wouldn't be able to attend school for almost two months, and in some ways, his arm would never be the same. For the rest of his life, it would be covered with jagged scars and marked with a deep indentation between his left elbow and his shoulder at the place where his humerus bone plunged through his skin on that cold winter day in Cory. But he was alive and he was going to make a full recovery.

By summer, Heaton was shooting baskets again on the concrete slab next to his house. By the end of his freshman year, he was in Clay City High School's starting five. By his junior year, he was a star in western Indiana, all-state honorable mention, just like Larry Bird. And by the spring of his senior year, 1975, Bob King wanted Heaton to attend Indiana State. That spring, while Hodges was down in French Lick chasing Bird, King was in Cory, trying to convince Heaton to come to Terre Haute.

But Heaton chose to play at the University of Denver instead—a choice he came to regret as that program imploded. By the spring of 1977, he was back in Indiana, standing on Bob King's porch like a lost dog. King agreed to take him on as a transfer, if Heaton was willing to sit out the year, as Bird once had. Now Heaton had finished his year in NCAA-mandated exile. He was finally cleared to play, and Bird approached him on the streets of Terre Haute with a question. Bird was finally moving out of married-student housing in the summer of 1978. He was looking to rent a place off campus and he wondered if Heaton, the kid from Cory with the scars on his arm, might want to live with him.

Heaton had felt detached from the basketball team up until that moment—he was the new guy and the outsider, unable to play—and he hadn't felt particularly close to Bird, either. Now Bird and Heaton were moving into a small house on South 11th Street and hanging out all the time. Bird was still dating his girlfriend, Dinah, and Heaton had a girlfriend, too—Jane Ann, a bank teller from just outside the city. On any given night, the four of them might all be at the house—or Bird and Heaton might be at the Boys' Club, shooting and shooting.

There was no catchy name for this duo, as there had been for Harry and Larry. Bird and Heaton weren't a "show"; they were just friends. And with everything that was happening with Stan Evans that year, Bob King needed a friend, too. In July 1978, King reached out to Mel Daniels, the one-time Pacer great who had played for King at New Mexico and who had once faced off against Harry Morgan in that AAU game down in Evansville. King wanted to ask Daniels if he would leave his horse ranch near Indianapolis, stop playing in AAU tournaments, and get closer to the game in a more meaningful way. He wanted Daniels to be the Sycamores' third assistant coach, joining Hodges and Evans on the bench.

Daniels had turned down coaching offers in the past. He was only 34, and as recently as a year earlier, he had still been trying to catch on with an NBA team. But by the summer of 1978, Daniels knew his playing days were over, and he was beginning to warm up to the idea of coaching, especially if he could do it with King. Daniels figured that he could learn from him while working with the team's big men: Gilbert, Miley, and Bird. He accepted King's offer and made a plan for the season. Daniels would coach part-time while still living on his ranch.

In a matter of just a few months, an entirely new team had taken shape in the practice arena on campus. But Hodges remained concerned about his own career, his own future, and sometime that summer, he aired these concerns to a former player: Johnny Nelson, the little guard from Rockville who had played in that first scrimmage with Bird and his French Lick boys way back in 1975.

Nelson was living in Florida by then, working for Wilson Sporting Goods and selling golf equipment in Wilson's most fertile territory, the Southeast. It was a lucrative job. Nelson was making far more than he'd thought he could in his early 20s. He told Hodges about it over a round of golf one day that summer and, as they played, Hodges turned to him with a question: Could Nelson help *him* get a job at Wilson, too?

Nelson was stunned by the request. He knew how much Hodges loved basketball, and didn't understand why he was thinking about walking away. But between the pressures at home, the stresses at work, and the uncertainties of the upcoming year, Hodges said he needed to consider every opportunity—even a job selling sporting goods.

Nelson said that he would do what he could for Hodges. He would put in a word for him. But he never got that chance. Within days of the golf outing—and the uncomfortable discussion about Bill Hodges's future—news broke that changed everything.

38

THE PAIN CAME ON while Bob King was on the road in Algona, Iowa, visiting old friends on his way to a coaching clinic in Minnesota. He had played his own round of golf that day. He was taking a shower at a friend's house, getting ready to go out for dinner, and suddenly he was clutching his chest as the water ran down the drain. It felt like someone was standing on his sternum, only no one was.

Within 10 minutes, he was on his way to a small medical facility in Algona, and by the end of the night, he was inside an ambulance driving 55 miles east to St. Joseph Mercy Hospital in Mason City, red lights flickering in the dark and cardiologists waiting at the door. King was admitted into intensive care at St. Joe's for a heart attack, while his wife, Sharel, hurried to catch a plane out of Terre Haute to be at her husband's side. The King children—ages eight, five, and three that summer—would awake in the morning to find both of their parents out of town and family friends in the kitchen telling white lies about why their mom had left in a rush.

For the next few days, King's heart attack was the best-kept secret in

Terre Haute. Hodges knew what had happened, and at some point the team's radio and television man, Bob Forbes, learned about the medical situation unfolding in Mason City. But Forbes sat on the story, protecting King and keeping everyone else in the dark. Stan Evans didn't know what was happening, and Ed McKee didn't, either. McKee flew to a Valley conference meeting in Tulsa that weekend, rested and tanned—and uninformed about King's health crisis. Perhaps most troubling, Dick Landini didn't learn about the heart attack until Friday—roughly 36 hours after the fact. Finally, the next day, a Saturday, Landini looped everyone else in. He had a university official call *The Terre Haute Tribune* to break the news.

Craig McKee, who was about to enter his senior year, was working as an intern at the newspaper that summer, and like every reporter, he hated working the Saturday shifts. The newsroom was quiet. Almost everyone had the day off and nothing good ever happened. Craig would pass the long hours looking at the clock and reading the news of the world off the wire. Now a reporter was on the phone and waving at Craig from across the room, and Craig was walking up to his desk to read the note the reporter was scrawling on a piece of paper.

Bob King . . . St. Joseph Mercy Hospital . . . Mason City . . . heart attack.

The problem was said to be an acute myocardial infarction, a blocked coronary artery—a "minor" problem, according to the hospital. But Craig's father, who worked with Landini in administration, suggested to Craig after his shift was over that King's health was worse than officials were letting on. Doctors kept King in the Mason City intensive care unit for five days—an unusual treatment plan for a "minor" heart ailment—and then moved him to a rehabilitative wing at St. Joe's for almost two weeks after that. King wasn't going home to loom on the fringes of the team's off-season workouts and summer pickup games. He was staying in Mason City for half the month of August—a delay that concerned lots of people, even King.

Doctors had warned him long ago that he could face heart trouble down the line, due to the rheumatic fever he had suffered as a boy; now it was here. King was trapped in Mason City, 400 miles from his family and his team, and he was already morphing into someone else. He said he'd be back for the season, and he maintained that he would resume all of his usual duties. He would coach again, he said. But in the same breath, King admitted that he needed to slow down. He felt compelled to listen to his doctors and his body. He had to change. King was shaken by what had happened—"kind of concerned," he said—and he needed to forget about basketball, at least for a while.

Bird called from Terre Haute to tell King not to worry. He would run the pickup games and off-season workouts now. He would stay on the players. "I'll keep 'em in shape," Bird told King, "until you get back." And, of course, Hodges and Evans were there, too, burying their disagreements in the moment to get through the crisis.

But even after King returned to western Indiana, on a plane in mid-August 1978, he didn't come back to the practice arena. He wasn't even coming to the office anymore. He was holed up at his house, in the suburbs south of town, with Sharel and the kids. If anyone wanted to meet with him, the meetings happened there. It was as though King was too weak to venture out or too afraid to push it. Then, on Labor Day, Sharel summoned Doc Behnke to the house to examine her husband, this time for chronic neck pain.

King believed it was the usual stiffness—the kind that sometimes ailed him during times of stress in the basketball season. He wanted Behnke to run him through those neck stretches that they did after practices and games, and Behnke did as King requested. He lived about three blocks from King and was soon inside his house, placing his hands on King's head to apply resistance while the coach worked his neck around.

But something felt different to Behnke about this pain. It wasn't just in his neck this time; it was in his head, too. King was having headaches, and Sharel seemed to sense that something was seriously wrong with her husband.

"Is he all right?" Behnke recalled Sharel asking after he was finished working on King.

In Behnke's memory, they were sitting in the backyard by then. King was out of earshot, and Behnke leveled with Sharel. Bob's pain didn't seem to be muscular, he said. This wasn't tension or stress like before, and a visit from an athletic trainer who lived down the street wasn't going to be enough.

King needed to see a doctor.

39

DICK LANDINI WAS ONE of the highest-paid public officials in the state of Indiana that fall, and he had big plans for the year—Bird's last at Indiana State.

Landini hoped to build on the successes of 1978, continue to grow enrollment at the school, and send Bird off the following spring with a celebration built strictly around him. In a matter of weeks, the so-called Larry Bird Committee would start meeting twice a month, with Bird's friend Max Gibson presiding and all the other local power brokers at the table. The banker Ed Jukes, who had accompanied Bird to his meeting with the Pacers, would be there. The department store tycoon Lu Meis would be there, too. The sandblasting executive who regularly donated his plane for the basketball team to use was going to head up the decorations subcommittee for the celebration, and of course Landini would be sure to attend as many meetings as possible in order to weigh in on the plans.

But King's health posed a problem that none of them had anticipated. By the Thursday after Labor Day—three days after Behnke's visit to the house—King was back in the hospital. By the following night, at least a few players had heard about it. Word began to spread around campus of King's "strange headaches." People speculated that the coach had suffered a stroke. Bird came out to the house to visit him personally. The other players debated among themselves who should take over the team, if King couldn't coach that fall, and there didn't seem to be a consensus. While most supported Hodges, some backed Evans.

In short, it wasn't clear what Landini should do if he had to make a head coaching change, but it was increasingly obvious that he was going to have to do something. By early October 1978, King still wasn't able to play any real role with the team. On Tuesday, October 10, five days before basketball practices officially began, King finally realized why. Doctors found a ballooning blood vessel in his brain—an aneurysm that needed to be repaired with emergency surgery before it could burst and potentially kill him.

The news came at a terrible time for both the basketball team and Landini. It was homecoming week in Terre Haute, and Landini was swamped with appointments, photographs, trips, and dinners. That Tuesday evening, Landini was scheduled to crown the homecoming queen and her male escort, the college's "bachelor of the year." Then, the following morning, Landini was supposed to fly to Washington, DC, for two days of gatherings with alumni. And when he landed back in Terre Haute that Friday, he was booked solid through the weekend. He was personally hosting three separate banquets, including one at his house on campus. He had to attend the homecoming parade on Saturday morning. He needed to be at the football game that afternoon and was supposed to be at the basketball arena that Saturday night for a special sold-out show featuring a musician who was popular with the kids and the adults alike. Bob Dylan was in town.

Landini didn't have time for urgent conversations about replacing Bob King. But that's what he got. With the news of King's aneurysm swirling, Landini hastily arranged a 5:15 meeting that Tuesday evening with the school's assistant athletic director and three other high-ranking university officials. What they discussed in the room isn't exactly clear. But it centered on a question that Landini had been rolling over in his mind for weeks: "Is Bill Hodges the man we want for the job?"

On the one hand, the answer had to be no. Hodges had no head coaching experience at any level, outside of his limited work with the freshman team at Tennessee Tech years earlier. Who was he to run a program? And how could he leap in front of Stan Evans? As Evans liked to remind people, he had real head coaching experience, from his years in Miami, and had been promised this job from the start.

But on the other hand, Landini thought, the answer had to be yes, because Hodges had everything else that mattered. He knew the game, was dedicated to the players, had been in their houses, had met their parents, had found Larry Bird in French Lick, had befriended him from the start, and had the backing of both King *and* Bird. Evans had been falling out of King's favor for months already; and if a change had to be made, Bird wanted Landini to choose the man who had chosen him back in 1975: Hodges.

The next morning, while Sharel drove Bob to a hospital in Indianapolis, worried that the aneurysm could burst on the way, Hodges kept his usual routine, having coffee at a downtown café where prominent locals liked to gather for breakfast. At some point shortly after he arrived at work, a university official called Hodges and asked him to report to Landini's office. Hodges didn't fully believe the news was coming until he walked across campus to meet with Landini and heard it from the president himself: Hodges was taking over as acting head coach, effective immediately.

"We pray for Bob King's speedy recovery," Landini said that day. But until then, Hodges had the job. Landini was even writing the press release himself, as he ran out the door for his flight to Washington.

It was 9:40 that morning when Craig McKee first learned what was happening. It was 10 o'clock when university officials ran around the building, looking for his boss, Ed, in the sports information office. It was 10:15 when Landini, Hodges, Ed McKee, and several others met in a room to discuss the unfolding situation and the new regime. And it was shortly after this meeting that Stan Evans announced a decision of his own.

He wasn't sticking around to work for Bill Hodges. He wasn't even staying for a three o'clock meeting with the team. Stan Evans was out, leaving Hodges to face the team alone.

40

STAN EVANS'S FRIENDS IN the athletic office were stunned. They had been talking for years about what it would be like one day when Evans was head coach. Now, just a few days before practices were set to begin in mid-October 1978, he wasn't even in the building.

Evans vacated his office right after Hodges's meeting with Landini, moving into the sports information office with the two McKees. He was apparently so frustrated that he didn't even want to be near Hodges—a feeling that blew down the halls of the practice arena that morning like the bitter winds of January, until everyone knew how Evans felt. He didn't consider the hiring of Hodges to be a "credible move." He hadn't left Miami three years earlier to work—even temporarily—for Hodges, a good recruiter who had no coaching experience. "I didn't give up a head job," Evans said around this time, "to remain an assistant at Indiana State." The whole situation was insulting to him, and even the promise of Larry Bird's final year—with Landini, Max Gibson, and the Larry Bird Committee planning galas for the springtime—wasn't enough to change Evans's mind. Indiana State's window for success had closed, in Evans's opinion. He thought the team would go 14–12 in the upcoming season, especially with King headed to the hospital in Indianapolis.

This view was, no doubt, colored by Evans's feelings over how things were ending for him in Terre Haute, but that didn't mean he was wrong. Plenty of experts agreed with him. In preseason polls that fall, reporters picked Indiana State to finish third in the Missouri Valley Conference, behind Southern Illinois and New Mexico State. Coaches in the conference had even less faith in Larry Bird's team; they picked the Sycamores to finish fourth. And the writers at *Sports Illustrated*—the magazine that had celebrated Bird just 12 months earlier, springing him onto the nation with that famous cover—had moved on as well. Just as Indiana State coaches were turning on each other, *Sports Illustrated* selected a new cover boy for its college basketball preview issue—Earvin "Magic" Johnson—and dispatched Lane Stewart back to the Midwest to take the photos.

In East Lansing, the day of the shoot, Lane walked into Jenison Field House at Michigan State, set his eyes on one of the basketball hoops, and made it his studio for the day. He strung up a massive white backdrop behind the hoop. He tested the lighting for hours, and once he thought he was ready, he walked into the Spartans locker room with a black tuxedo for Magic, and some instructions. Lane wanted Magic to come out onto the floor in the tuxedo, complete with dress shoes and a top hat. He wanted him to dunk the ball in front of that white backdrop with his coattails flying, and he wanted him to do it while he looked into the lens of Lane's Hasselblad camera and conveyed the feeling that had been missing with Bird the year before in Chicago.

"Joie de vivre," Lane said.

A short time later, Magic emerged in his tuxedo, as instructed, and made it easy for Lane, while his teammates watched. Magic smiled his smile, dunked his dunk, and created a cover that Lane Stewart loved—and fans did, too. In November 1978, when the magazine hit newsstands, people in Lansing snapped up all 3,000 copies in two hours, enjoying Lane's photos and perusing the content that mattered most: the magazine's preseason poll.

Duke, an emerging powerhouse, was ranked No. 1. Notre Dame, a team led by media-friendly head coach Digger Phelps and six future NBA players, came in at No. 2. UCLA, the best college program of the past two decades, with seven future NBA players on its roster, was inserted at No. 3. And then came Magic Johnson's team, Michigan State.

The Sycamores weren't mentioned at all.

The poll seemed to support Stan Evans's view of the team. Maybe he wasn't crazy to quit. But that didn't make it any less sad for Craig McKee when Evans finally moved out of the athletic offices for good one night about two weeks after Hodges took over. McKee helped Evans carry his stuff out to his car, and as Evans drove off, McKee went back inside to erase the final traces of Stan Evans. He took his posters off the walls and his calendar off his desk. If they were starting over, McKee thought, at least they were starting fresh.

41

BILL HODGES DIDN'T UNDERSTAND why there needed to be so much drama. As far as he was concerned, his position as acting head coach was only temporary. Bob King would be back soon, he believed, and King's surgery that Friday confirmed his feeling. Going in through one of his temples, doctors clipped and sealed the bulging blood vessels inside King's brain and defused the aneurysm—a delicate process that took almost five hours, but was successful. Within days, King was well enough to meet with Hodges and Mel Daniels in his hospital room in Indianapolis. The following week, King was able to give a short interview by phone to a reporter calling to write a story about him. "I'm just looking forward to getting out of here," he told the reporter that day. And on the last Friday of the month, exactly two weeks after his surgery, King did just that. He returned to Terre Haute, walking through the door of his house to find his three children waiting for him and a handmade sign on the walls of the foyer.

WELCOME HOME, DAD, it said.

In Hodges's mind, he was just tending to the store while the shopkeeper was away. He thought King would be back by the middle of the winter at the latest. But by that time, the season would be half over and the Sycamores would be well into their Valley conference schedule, a set of unusual circumstances that placed Hodges in a difficult position. It was his team, but it wasn't. He was in charge, but for how long, no one knew. The only assistant with any head coaching experience, Stan Evans, had just quit, electing to take a job in the personnel office across campus instead of staying to work with Hodges. Evans's departure left Hodges with one of the thinnest and least experienced coaching staffs in America. Hodges had Daniels, a part-time coach with no bench experience whatsoever. He had Danny King, Bird's former roommate and high school teammate, now serving as a graduate assistant. And there was no time to make new hires. Basketball season was starting now. Anyone who knew how to coach already had a job, forcing Hodges to call on an old friend for help: Hugh Thimlar, down in Florida. Hodges wanted to know if Hugh's son, Terry, was available to assist.

Terry Thimlar was just 25 years old that fall and walked with a limp from a bout of polio that had struck him in 1954, months before his first birthday and right around the time that Dr. Jonas Salk was rolling out the first tests of his polio vaccine. Terry's left leg grew shorter than his right; his left foot turned out smaller, too. He would need to have medical interventions at age nine and a significant surgery at age 14 just to get around.

And still, Terry found a way to play basketball—first at Pike High School in Indianapolis, and later at his father's junior college in Fort Myers. Perhaps more importantly, Terry had more coaching experience than anyone else working with Hodges that October. He had served two years as a student assistant at Indiana State and one year as an assistant at the University of Florida. He knew how to scout, thanks to his father, and he knew Bill Hodges personally, thanks to the hours the two men had spent together at Hugh Thimlar's basketball clinics in the late 1960s. Terry and Bill had grown close in the hospitality room, serving up cold cuts to high school coaches. Now Terry Thimlar was driving north to claim Stan Evans's office.

It wasn't a flashy hire, it was simply the best that Hodges could do. Terry's arrival in town around the start of November did nothing to change anyone's impression of the team. But Hodges liked his coaching staff, and from his bedroom at home, Bob King liked it, too. He believed that Hodges had a special connection with the players, and Hodges quickly proved this to be true. In early November 1978, he convinced Larry Bird to talk to reporters again, after almost a year of media silence.

The site was the Savery Hotel in Des Moines, Iowa. The occasion was Missouri Valley Conference media day. The date was the first Sunday of November. Bird agreed to be there—with stipulations. Unlike Steve Reed, Carl Nicks, and 15 other Valley conference players, he wasn't going to sit at a table in the ballroom at the Savery and answer questions from reporters all afternoon. He was going do it just once, in front of everybody.

In this controlled environment, the reporters in the room—from the *Des Moines Register*, the *Tulsa World*, the *Wichita Beacon*, the *Omaha World-Herald*, and a handful of other small outlets—didn't go deep, asking questions about Bloomington, Bobby Knight, French Lick, Bird's childhood, his father, his failed marriage, or his daughter with Janet. They kept it light, and Bird briefly shone in the spotlight, hitting their questions out of the park like the softballs he had hammered over the wall for 500 Platolene that summer.

When the reporters asked Bird if he studied shooting, Bird shook his head no. "I don't even study my lessons," he deadpanned. When they asked him why he never fouled out, he said it was because he didn't play any defense. When they asked him if he would be signing with Red Auerbach and the Boston Celtics the following spring, he refused to commit. He would sign, he said, with the team that offered him the biggest contract. And he happily answered all their little questions about Missouri Valley basketball. Bird called Creighton's Tom Apke the best coach in the conference, New Mexico State's Robert Gunn the best shooter, Southern Illinois the best team, and in front of everybody, he pulled off one of Bob King's favorite party tricks. Bird lowered expectations for Indiana State to the floor.

"We'll be respectable," Bird said. "We'll do all right."

It wasn't the interview Magic Johnson would have given. Magic would have smiled, laughed, told stories, sat at his table all day, and probably still would have been there that night for the $12.50-a-head Valley conference dinner. But Bird's performance was better than reporters were expecting. They left wondering why he didn't talk more—a question that would bite Bird soon enough—while Hodges left eager to get back to Terre Haute. Inexperienced or not, he was molding this team in his own image.

They were still going to *step* and *slide* and *run* and *glide*, just as they had under Bob King, winning games with relentless defense. As Hodges reminded the team that fall, "We are on offense when our opponent has the ball." But this team wasn't going to be holding the ball at the ends of games in Bob King's conservative four-corners stall; they were going to keep scoring. Hodges tweaked the offense to run it through Bird, like his old coach back in Zionsville would have done. Hodges wanted Bird to touch the ball 75 percent of the time. He designed specific plays for Bird, and one for Carl Nicks, too. And he introduced a new, aggressive press to use against bigger, faster opponents. In this press, Hodges gave his players permission to gamble. "Don't be afraid," he told them. He also gave them permission to fight, like Hodges had back in high school and Mel Daniels had in the ABA. "Play hard, hard, *hard*," Hodges said.

In one practice that fall, this intensity led to an actual scuffle between two of the team's top players. Bird and Staley squabbled on the court, with Bird going so far as to throw a punch. It was the sort of moment that could tear a team apart. But not this one. By design, this team was fighting in practice every day. In one drill that Mel Daniels liked to run, no fouls were called whatsoever. Brad Miley and Alex Gilbert would have to outwork each other for a rebound beneath the basket and try to score in the lane, no matter what the other guy did. The two friends would leave practice with bruises up and down their arms, and Bird would leave stronger after going one-on-one with Daniels after practice was over. The former ABA great was teaching Bird how to get his shot through contact, and also teaching him how to talk trash as he pushed Bird up and down the court.

Sometimes, the guys would linger after practice to watch Daniels and Bird go at it. Then they would bring the same energy to the practice arena the next day. Even the bench players were working hard. In the first Blue vs. White scrimmage that fall, the week after media day in Des Moines, the White team—led by Tom Crowder, the walk-on track star; Eric Curry and Rich Nemcek, the two friends from Wabash Valley; Bob "Tex" Ritter, a coach's son from Indianapolis; Rod McNelly, an all-state punter from Speedway; and Scott Turner, a freshman from Bedford, Indiana—scored again and again on the team's top seven, wearing blue. Bird, Nicks, Staley, Miley, Gilbert, Reed, and Heaton couldn't stop the bench players that day.

But Hodges liked that the White team was making his starters work, and he loved that no one was picking Indiana State to win anything. With Reed and Nicks at guard, Hodges believed defenses wouldn't be able to double-team Bird as they had in the past. With Miley and Gilbert down low, Hodges thought they would be able to rebound against anyone. And with Staley and Heaton coming off the bench, Hodges knew this team was deeper than before. He was looking forward to their first real test—an exhibition game against the Soviet national team on a Sunday near the end of the month—and he kept his only real concern to himself: Bob King's health. By mid-November, it was clear to Hodges that King wasn't recovering at the pace that he expected.

King was living in his bedroom in his house in the suburbs. Many days, especially early on, he didn't even leave the room or change out of his pajamas, his kids recalled. Once hard-charging, he was now quiet. Once in control, he was now lost. On visits to the house that month to discuss the team, Hodges realized that King often couldn't remember something they had discussed just 10 minutes earlier. His long-term memory was still there—he could talk at length about a game from last season—but his short-term memory was riddled with holes, and King seemed to know that he had lost something more than his mind. One day that fall, his daughter Dianne, a third-grader, just eight years old, remembers watching her father cry as he stood near the fireplace in the living room.

Dianne went to her mother with questions, she said, and her mother explained that Daddy simply couldn't do all the things he wanted to do anymore. Specifically, he wasn't going to be able to coach his team—a realization that Hodges made for himself after one of his visits to the house that fall. King wasn't coming back midseason. King wasn't coming back at all. Hodges was the coach now, whether people realized it or not, and with Larry Bird on his roster, he knew that he was working under the worst kind of pressure.

"If we win," Hodges said that month, "we're supposed to. If we don't, I botched it."

42

THE SOVIETS ARRIVED IN Terre Haute the Saturday night before Thanksgiving looking like white giants from the frozen north.

They had several players who were six foot ten or taller. They had two players over seven feet tall. One of those two, Vladimir Tkachenko, was seven foot four and loomed like a mustachioed behemoth over everyone. Tkachenko could box people out with his dark brown mullet alone; his mustache probably averaged more rebounds per game than most American players. And while Tkachenko was still young—just 21 years old—many of the Soviets were grown men in their mid-20s or early 30s. They had won gold at the Olympics in 1972 and bronze at the Olympics in 1976. They landed in Terre Haute with bags full of purchases they had already made on their tour, requested by their wives and children. They were going to be flying home with blue jeans from JCPenney, warm boots from Sears, and the hottest new records from Western pop stars.

But while they were still here in America, they were working. This was a business trip for the Soviets, intended to prepare them for the 1980 Olympics in Moscow. In order to do that, they were playing against American colleges for three weeks. And if they lost sight of their primary purpose—their reason for being here—their white-haired coach, Alexander Gomelsky, or their 33-year-old captain, Ivan Edeshko, could no doubt remind them with a comment or a stern look. Both Gomelsky and Edeshko were officers in the Soviet Red Army.

This was not a team that could be easily beaten, especially since the American college players hadn't even started their seasons yet. They were just getting up to game speed and would now have to face the Soviets under their rules—international rules. In games played that November on college campuses, there would be a 30-second shot clock and little need for referees to handle the ball before inbounds passes. Under these adjustments, there would be quicker transitions and more running, and US basketball officials tried to prepare fans for what they were about to see: American college kids losing to the bigger, stronger, tougher Soviets. "We're showing the American people we've got our hands full," said one high-ranking US basketball official, "that we can no longer walk onto the floor with five days' practice and beat anyone."

In their first two weeks in America, the Soviets rolled over their collegiate competition. They beat a team of touring Christian athletes. They blew out Kent State and New Mexico. They defeated three Big Ten powers—Purdue, Illinois, and Bobby Knight's Indiana Hoosiers. They took down the No. 2–ranked team in the nation in Notre Dame. They only lost three times, and Gomelsky didn't really count two of those three losses. Against Oregon State and Iowa, the Soviet coach believed his team had been jobbed by the referees to the point that he finally snapped, ran out onto the court, stood at the foul line, grabbed the basketball, and stopped play to stage a one-man protest—a spectacle that American fans found hilarious. No, in Gomelsky's mind, he had only lost once—to a squad that could almost match the Soviets in size, to a team that could beat them with their speed, to a coach who had a perfect zone defense to neutralize Tkachenko, and to a player who created his own mismatches by being a six-foot-eight point guard, handling the basketball and running the offense: Magic Johnson.

"This Johnson," Gomelsky said, "is a very good player."

Michigan State beat the Soviets by 16—a victory so definitive that even Gomelsky couldn't make excuses afterward. Instead, he and his team retired to the home of Michigan State's athletic director, where they drank vodka and socialized all night, with Magic's teammate Mike Brkovich making conversation possible with his ability to speak some Serbian.

It was, one Soviet player said later, the best night of their American tour, perhaps because they weren't talking about basketball at all. But even if they had discussed basketball, they wouldn't have discussed Indiana State, the Soviets' opponent five days later. They had already beaten every other team in the state of Indiana, and Hodges's approach to the exhibition game seemed to ensure a communist sweep of the heartland. Unlike Jud Heathcote at Michigan State, Hodges wasn't going to employ a zone defense against the Soviets. The Sycamores were going to do what they always did: play man-to-man and see what happened.

"We aren't changing anything," Hodges said.

Hodges wasn't just being stubborn; he had scouted the Soviets in their game against Purdue. He believed that his guys could match up well against the bigger foreigners. The Indiana State players could feel his confidence before the game started that Sunday. Hodges didn't seem nervous at all. And the players knew for a fact that Bird was ready. Bird had faced Tkachenko, Gomelsky, and most of this Soviet squad the previous April, in the college all-star game down in Lexington. In his brief time on the floor that day, Bird had tangled up the Soviets with his passing, and this time he wouldn't be riding the bench, as he and Magic had before. He was going to be out on the court, and Nicks thought the Sycamores could beat anyone as long as Bird was out there.

It was a belief that, for Nicks, was almost unshakable. But even he felt a twinge of doubt when they stepped on the floor that Sunday afternoon. The Soviets, dressed in ragged red uniforms, were the biggest team the Sycamores had ever seen. Tkachenko looked even larger than seven foot four. If the game programs had listed him at eight feet tall, the Indiana State players wouldn't have questioned it. He stood like a small office building in downtown Terre Haute, and the Sycamores struggled for most of the afternoon, falling behind by seven points in the first half and by eight to start the second. With 17 minutes left to play, the Soviets were up 45–37.

But Hodges had been right about something: They did match up well. Even as the Sycamores were trailing, they were outrebounding the bigger, taller Soviets. And in a quick two-minute burst in the second half, they finally went on a run. They tied the game, 48–48, and then pulled away with a total team effort in the minutes to follow—as Nicks, Gilbert, Reed, Miley, and Bird all made shots. An eight-point deficit became a nine-point lead, and that's when trouble struck. With nine minutes to go, for the first time in his college career, Larry Bird fouled out of the game.

It was a moment that the team wouldn't have survived a year earlier, when Bird was on the cover of *Sports Illustrated* and Indiana State was ranked in most preseason polls. That Sycamores squad, though undoubtedly more talented, never meshed as a team, didn't seem to trust one another, didn't pass as much as Bird wanted, likely would have folded without Bird on the floor. And Hodges wondered if they might fold now. But Heaton came in off the bench. The offense kept rolling. Gilbert filled the void underneath the basket. Nicks refused to lose, leading all scorers with 24 points. Staley closed out the game with a breakaway basket. The Sycamores beat the Soviets by four—without Larry Bird—and Gomelsky returned to his excuse-making, blaming exhaustion this time.

"This was our 11th game in 18 days," the Soviet coach said afterward. "My boys were a little tired."

But the Soviets' leading scorer, Anatoly Myshkin, knew what he had just seen. He called Indiana State the best team they had played on their American tour. Gomelsky gathered himself to congratulate Hodges. "Your team is very good," he said in broken English. "Not big boys. But you did good job on organization—nice offense, nice defense, a good combination."

Hodges couldn't wait for the next game: the regular-season opener against tiny Lawrence College at the end of the week. "We want to go on to the next one right now," Hodges said after beating the Soviets. Six nights later, Indiana State destroyed Lawrence, with Nicks leading all scorers again. In the first two games, Nicks was averaging more points than Bird, and Bird didn't care. They were winning—that was all that mattered—and now they were heading north by bus to take on a team that wanted revenge: the Purdue Boilermakers.

The game in West Lafayette was a sellout, to be broadcast on television statewide on WLFI out of Lafayette and WTTV out of Indianapolis. More than 14,000 fans were packed into the arena. Almost all of them were rooting for Purdue, and for most of the second half, the locals were poised to get what they wanted: a victory over the little Indiana college that had beaten the Boilermakers by 28 points the year before. But in the final seven minutes, Nicks, Reed, and Heaton combined for 13 points. Bill Hodges's defense held the Boilermakers to just two buckets, and with

47 seconds left, Bird and Reed locked eyes, nodded at each other, and executed a play that silenced the crowd and iced the game for good.

Purdue's best player, Joe Barry Carroll, was at the foul line with a chance to cut the Indiana State lead to one. But Carroll, the future No. 1–overall pick in the 1980 NBA draft, missed the front of his one-and-one. Bird pulled down the rebound and Steve Reed released, racing up the court. Bird threw another one of his perfect passes to Reed—50 feet down the floor—hitting Reed in stride. Reed dribbled once as he sprinted to the basket. Purdue ran him down from behind, and everyone watched as a Purdue player plowed into Reed at the exact moment that Reed left his feet, going up to score.

In the collision that followed, Reed's body slammed to the floor and came to a rest at the base of the basket. But he popped right up, and within a moment, Nicks, Heaton, and Bird were there to greet him, because a whistle had blown, a foul had been called against Purdue, Reed's shot had gone in, and this game was effectively over.

Bird only scored two points down the stretch, and it didn't matter. Indiana State still beat Purdue by 10.

43

THE TELEVISION BROADCASTERS WERE surprised by what they had just witnessed. They noted that Steve Reed had carried Indiana State in the final minutes of the game. They praised Alex Gilbert for his rebounding and his defense, and they dared to suggest that Larry Bird might not have been the most important player on the floor in West Lafayette. "I think the difference has been Carl Nicks," the WTTV play-by-play man said late in the game, as Indiana State took the lead. It was not what anyone had expected when the season had started just days earlier. And when the team bus rolled into Terre Haute late that night, a crowd was waiting in the dark outside the arena to let the Sycamores know they were appreciated. It was well after midnight—Tuesday-morning classes would begin in just a few hours—and still, about 200 students were there, chanting and cheering as the bus pulled to a stop.

But the Sycamores' early victories over the Soviets, Lawrence College, and Purdue didn't earn Bill Hodges any respect from reporters across the state. Basketball beat writers pointed out that the Sycamores only shot 36 percent from the floor in West Lafayette and turned the ball over 17 times, dreadful metrics for any team. Newspapers in Indiana ran insulting headlines—ISU DOESN'T DO MUCH or INDIANA STATE LESS THAN IMPRESSIVE—and voters in the national polls continued to ignore the Sycamores at the end of the first week of play. The spotlight remained trained on Duke, Notre Dame, UCLA, and Michigan State—the top four teams in the country. No one cared about what was happening in Terre Haute. And Indiana State's next opponent, the Evansville Purple Aces, didn't seem to care, either. The Evansville coaches had scouted the game in West Lafayette and had gone home that night fully believing that their brand-new team—rebuilt and reconstituted after the previous year's devastating plane crash—could defeat Bill Hodges's squad.

In interviews that week, the new coaches for the Purple Aces said they weren't going to make the same mistakes that Purdue had. Among other things, they said, they weren't going to double-team Bird or play a box-and-one to stop him. Hodges found himself on the defensive as reporters asked him what was wrong with his team, and Hodges had to admit: He didn't get it. All they had done was win, and people were acting like the Sycamores were losing—a narrative that Hodges refused to accept. His team was still learning, Hodges acknowledged that week, and he conceded that he was inexperienced as a coach. "I'm kind of a rookie," he shrugged. But they didn't have any problems, not until that Thursday morning, anyway, when the phone rang at Hodges's house on Ohio Street with bad news.

Alex Gilbert's older brother, Lindell, was dead.

Gilbert knew that his brother was struggling in East St. Louis. He had started using drugs and was hanging with the wrong people. That Wednesday—about 48 hours after Indiana State's victory over Purdue—Lindell made a visit to the Gompers Homes, a cluster of low-slung, redbrick public housing units near the banks of the Mississippi River. While there, he got into an argument with a friend he had known for most of his life. The friend pulled out a gun, shooting Lindell, and now Bill Hodges was walking across campus to Alex's dorm room to let him know that his brother was gone.

At the sight of Hodges in his doorway, Gilbert assumed he was in trouble and figured it was because he was late for class. But Hodges told Gilbert that he wasn't there to discuss classes. He broke the news in the best way he could. Hodges sat with Gilbert while he cried, and then Brad Miley showed up to sit with Gilbert, too. Miley was there for what felt to Gilbert like hours.

Miley didn't know what to say, but Gilbert didn't mind. Later, he would just remember that his friend was at his side. And his coaches were there for him, too. By NCAA rules, Indiana State couldn't do much to help him. They couldn't bankroll his trip home or advance him cash for his travels. Gilbert was on his own—even now in the face of a family tragedy. But no one was following NCAA rules in a moment that begged for humanity. As Miley sat with Gilbert, Terry Thimlar made arrangements to get him to East St. Louis. Terry drove him there himself that night, delivering Gilbert to his parents' house. And when Gilbert decided that Saturday that he wanted to rejoin the team—he wanted to play against Evansville—benefactors in Terre Haute scrambled to send one of their planes to get him there in time.

As it turned out, the Sycamores would need everybody that night. In front of a sold-out crowd in Evansville, the all-new Purple Aces, starting over with nothing, nearly beat Indiana State. Bird had to score 40—and had to stay on the floor for the entire game—just to keep his team in it. The Sycamores eked out a narrow four-point victory, struggling to shoot yet again. The struggles continued that Monday against a foe that always caused problems for them: the Illinois State Redbirds. With 10 minutes

Dave Bliss, far right, and Bobby Knight, far left, recruited Larry Bird to play at Indiana University in 1974. But Bird lasted less than a month in Bloomington and never stepped on the floor with Knight's Indiana Hoosiers.

Bob King, right, the athletic director at Indiana State, hired himself to be the head coach of the Sycamore basketball team in 1975, and then brought in two young assistants: Stan Evans, center, and Bill Hodges, left. For a while, everyone got along.

Harry Morgan, shooting, and Bird, foreground, both played their first games for Indiana State in the fall of 1976 and briefly became a sensation. The press called them the Harry and Larry Show.

The team traveled a lot on an old aircraft, a DC-3. In December 1977, the Evansville basketball team went down in that same model of airplane, flown by the same charter—an event that rattled the young players at Indiana State.

Ed McKee, the sports information director at Indiana State, pictured here with his wife, Linda, and Larry Bird, initially had success in getting Bird to talk to local reporters. That ended once the national press started showing up in Terre Haute.

| THE TOP 20 | AL McGUIRE SPEAKS OUT | THE HOT SHOTS |

Sports Illustrated

NOVEMBER 28, 1977 ONE DOLLAR

COLLEGE BASKETBALL'S SECRET WEAPON

Explosive Larry Bird

Bird was reluctant to appear on the cover of *Sports Illustrated* in late 1977. The two Indiana State cheerleaders who joined Bird for the photo shoot—Sharon Senefeld, left, and Marcia Staub, right—said Bird hardly spoke that day and didn't seem to know why he was there.

Bob King and Larry Bird argued with the referees after losing at Rutgers in March 1978, as Rutgers star James Bailey (number 20) looked on. Moments later, Bird struck a Rutgers fan with an elbow or a fist, bloodying him on the basketball court.

Bill Hodges, pictured here with his wife, Connie, was selected to take over as head coach of the team in October 1978, thanks to his personal connection with the players—especially Larry Bird.

During a pivotal game against New Mexico State in Las Cruces in February 1979, Bird once again struck a fan—an incident that incited the crowd. Student photographer José Lopez captured the moment, and his photos went out on the AP wire.

After the game at New Mexico State in February 1979, Bird, left, and Bob Heaton, right, could hardly stay at their home on South 11th Street in Terre Haute. The phone was ringing off the hook.

Bird, center, resisted speaking to the press, forcing teammates like Carl Nicks, right, to step up. Nicks didn't mind talking, but as the attention on Indiana State intensified, Bird's silence became the story.

In defense of Bird, Bill Hodges lashed out at the media and others. "The pressure," one opposing coach said, "must be eating him up alive." Then, in March 1979, it got worse: Bird broke his thumb.

In the waning seconds against Arkansas in March 1979, Bob Heaton (number 30) threw up a prayer with his left arm, the arm he nearly lost 12 years earlier in a farm accident at his home in Cory, Indiana.

After defeating Arkansas, Alex Gilbert wept on the floor with his family, thinking about his brother, who had died that winter.

The win over Arkansas sent Indiana State to the Final Four, sparked Sycamore fever across the Midwest, and led to signs like this one in Terre Haute.

At the Final Four in Salt Lake City, Bird and Magic appeared together at a press conference before the title game. Magic was thrilled to talk. Bird was not. And the next day, the media punished him for it. National publications called him a "hayseed" and a "low-rent slob."

After the loss to Michigan State, Bird couldn't hide his emotions. He sobbed beneath a towel on the bench, as team manager Rick Shaw tried to hold back the media.

From left to right, Brad Miley, Eric Curry, Larry Bird, Leroy Staley, Bill Hodges, and Carl Nicks walked off the floor in Salt Lake City with the second-place trophy.

Back at the Hotel Utah that night, Dinah Mattingly, Bird's girlfriend and future wife, center, tried to comfort Bird at a party held to celebrate the season.

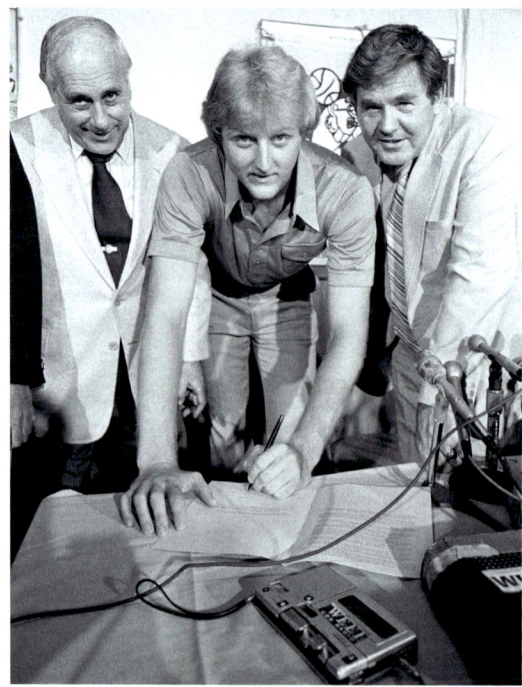

Weeks later in June 1979, Bird signed a contract with the Boston Celtics, flanked by team president Red Auerbach (left) and head coach Bill Fitch (right), ending one journey for Bird and beginning another.

to go in that game, Indiana State was trailing by nine. Then Bird missed an easy basket from point-blank range. The Redbirds scored at the other end to go up by 11 and Hodges called a time-out while the local television broadcasters complained.

"Indiana State can't hit a thing," said WTHI's Bob Forbes. "Even Larry's having a poor night. Larry is 8 of 19. Can you believe that?" Forbes said. "*Eight of 19.*"

During the time-out, Hodges decided to do something different, something radical even. He benched Bird to give him a short rest and sent the team out in a full-court press to slow down Illinois State. Heaton promptly scored four points to cut the gap to seven. Bird checked back into the game and immediately stole the ball in the press, feeding Heaton for yet another basket, and the Indiana State comeback was on. In the final two minutes of the game, Bird scored seven points, as Steve Reed did his job, passing the ball to Bird down low on the block. Then Nicks stepped up to hit the game-winner in the end. As the Illinois State defense keyed on Bird in the Sycamores' final possession that night, Nicks drained a 20-footer from the right side to give the Sycamores the victory, 78–76.

Indiana State, despite all its early-season troubles, was suddenly undefeated at 4–0, and no one was questioning Bill Hodges anymore. He wasn't just making the right substitutions during the games; he was making the right choices off the floor. He kept it loose in the locker room, joking that the team needed to make him look good. He kept it loose on the long bus rides, too. If Bird wanted to chew tobacco, spitting into a soda can or a plastic cup, Hodges didn't care. Hodges also chewed tobacco, stuffing a pinch of Levi Garrett into his mouth. "We're both country," Hodges said. And it wasn't like a little tobacco juice was hurting the team. They won their next three games to go 7–0, before turning to Bob King for help winning their eighth.

Hodges invited King to watch practice—his first since his brain surgery in October. King pointed out that Reed and Nicks weren't applying enough pressure when the ball crossed the midline. It was a detail so small—"so minute," Hodges said that week—that he couldn't see it from the bench. And King's coaching tip made an impact that Saturday night, when Butler came to Terre Haute. In one of the last games before King took over in 1975, Butler had beaten Indiana State in the Hulman Center by 13 points. This time, the Sycamores won by 38 as they dropped 109 points on Butler—two points shy of the school record—and flirted with history in other ways. Bird came within a basket of scoring 50.

The Butler coach, Joe Sexson, just shook his head after the game. "We couldn't have stopped him with a cannon," he said. "But it's not only Bird," he pointed out. "They've got a fine team." And unlike previous years, this team smiled a lot together. They loved it when the backups got on the floor during blowouts. They cheered as Tom Crowder, the sparingly used high jumper, got a chance to dunk the ball at the ends of games, and they laughed at a new tradition started by Rich Nemcek's friend Eric Curry. Before each game, Curry would write the team's record on the chalkboard in the locker room—and he did so in his own quirky fashion. Curry insisted on including the Soviet victory, even though that game didn't count, and also insisted on including that night's victory, even though they hadn't played the game yet.

"That's not the way you're supposed to do it," Hodges informed Curry.

But there was no changing it now. That would be bad luck, Curry explained, given the team's undefeated record. They were 8–0, officially.

The Sycamores were still considered inconsequential compared to the nation's top programs—Notre Dame and Michigan State most of all. Notre Dame was undefeated, just like Indiana State, and had just beaten UCLA on the road in California, while Michigan State was drawing unprecedented attention. That weekend in the suburbs of Detroit, the second-largest crowd to ever watch a college basketball game—31,683 fans—filled the Pontiac Silverdome to see Magic Johnson play against Cincinnati. Larry Bird wouldn't draw that sort of crowd in the next three games *combined*. But at least the Sycamores had finally cracked the national polls. The AP had them ranked 15th overall, the UPI slotted them at No. 16, and the guys rolled into the holidays feeling good about themselves.

Once again, they bunked up at the Sheraton south of campus. They celebrated on New Year's Eve, sneaking beers into the hotel and counting down the seconds to 1979. Again, they ran the steps in the arena the following day, up and down and all the way around. And they hung out together away from Terre Haute, too. Many of them took a field trip out to Bob Heaton's farm in Cory, where they spent an afternoon riding tractors, shooting guns, and goofing around on the fallow fields of winter.

At one point that day, amid the laughter in the cold, the tractor ferrying Larry Bird and backup guard Tex Ritter nearly toppled over as it skidded backward down an embankment with its front wheels suspended in the air. In this moment, Ritter saw his future. He and Larry were dead or maimed, crushed beneath the tractor, and Ritter was going to be a footnote of history. He could see the headline as he clung to the sliding vehicle: ALL-AMERICAN LARRY BIRD AND UNIDENTIFIED PLAYER INJURED IN FARM ACCIDENT.

But the tractor's rear wheels dug into the hard Indiana ground. The machine stopped skidding and righted itself on its axles. Larry Bird was safe; Tex Ritter was, too. The young men exchanged a look of relief, Ritter said. And the team kept winning—undefeated to start 1979, 9–0 on the year, and moving up in the polls. By early January, they had cracked the top 10.

44

RED AUERBACH HAD KEPT his distance—and his promise—since drafting Bird the previous June. He hadn't meddled with Bob King's or Bill Hodges's team. He hadn't tried to convince Bird to leave school and join the Celtics. He hadn't even made a visit to Terre Haute. Now that was about to change. With Indiana State undefeated—and Bird leading the nation in scoring, averaging 33 points per game—Auerbach flew to Indiana for the first week of January 1979 to watch the Sycamores play the Tulsa Golden Hurricane and check in on his long-term investment.

Tulsa was not a good team. It was bound for its fourth losing season in a row and was a joke to reporters in the press box that night in Terre

Haute. One compared Tulsa to a Division II outfit. But the game marked an important turning point in the season. Indiana State's conference schedule was beginning. And this schedule was only thing that mattered to Hodges. He didn't care what people thought of him, where pollsters ranked Indiana State, or how badly his guys beat teams like Purdue or Evansville, as long as they finally won the conference title and earned that elusive bid to the NCAA tournament.

"Everything we do," Hodges said, "is pointed in that direction."

Consequently, the Tulsa game was of interest to people outside of Terre Haute. Home Box Office had signed up to air the game. The cable channel, better known later as HBO, only had about two million subscribers nationwide at the time. It wasn't going to be covering mainstream sports like college basketball for very long, and it wasn't going to be airing this game live. The Tulsa–Indiana State contest would go out on tape delay; HBO viewers wouldn't be able to watch it until it was over. Still, it was the first time that people in most parts of the country would ever see Larry Bird in their living rooms, and HBO's play-by-play man, Len Berman, and color analyst Tommy Heinsohn, the former coach of the Boston Celtics, made a big deal out of this moment in their intro that night.

"This is the state bird of Indiana," Berman said as Bird warmed up in slow motion. "*Larry* Bird . . . No. 1 in the nation in scoring . . . the most complete player in college basketball today. We are in Terre Haute, Indiana, tonight to do some . . . Bird watching."

Auerbach found his seat with the help of the two McKees, Ed and Craig, while the game got off to a sputtering start. Bird missed several easy baskets at the rim. At one point, he even missed a dunk. And early in the game, an incident on the floor nearly stole the headlines from Bird and Auerbach both. Staley came down with a rebound. A Tulsa defender tied him up. The two players briefly scuffled under the basket. Mel Daniels came off the Sycamores' bench to step into the fray, and Tulsa's coach ran onto the floor to intervene, pushing Daniels. For a moment, players on both benches had to hold back *their coaches*.

But everyone soon settled down. Indiana State won easily. Bird scored

27 points and grabbed 19 rebounds. Auerbach loomed over the Indiana State student who was collecting the game stats in the press box. The Celtics executive seemed to want updates in real time, and Bird made a handful of plays that got Auerbach's attention. On the first play of the game, Reed passed to Bird on the right wing. Bird swung around into the lane, and as the Tulsa defense swarmed around him, he threw a left-handed no-look pass over his head to Gilbert, who scored from seven feet away. Later, Bird threw long outlet passes to both Staley and Reed, like a quarterback in high-top sneakers. Then, late in the first half, Bird made a play that brought everyone to their feet.

Tulsa had made a 60-foot pass down the floor to a wide-open six-foot-nine freshman rumbling toward the basket for an uncontested dunk. But Bird caught up to him from behind, and as the Tulsa freshman leaped into the air, Bird blocked his dunk cleanly. The Tulsa kid never saw him coming. Auerbach cheered with the rest of the crowd and, at some point, lit up one of his signature cigars.

The Celtics general manager stayed until the end of the game, gave interviews afterward, and even visited the Indiana State locker room, where he took direction from team manager Rick Shaw. Auerbach would have to wait in the trainer's room, Shaw said, if he wanted to talk to Bird. Bird would come to Auerbach—not the other way around.

But Auerbach didn't seem to mind. And he didn't care that Bird hardly spoke when he finally showed up in the trainer's room that night. Auerbach didn't need Bird to talk. He just wanted him to play next season in Celtic green.

"He's a damn good player," Auerbach told reporters after the game.

"The kind of player that the Celtics need?" one reporter asked.

"Pal," Auerbach replied, "he's the kind of player anybody needs."

The Sycamores won their next three games to move to 13–0 and then prepared to face their toughest opponent of the season, a team that knew them well, a team that was unafraid of Larry Bird, and a team that had beaten most of this crew the year before.

The New Mexico State Aggies were coming back to Terre Haute.

Hodges wasn't superstitious, but he didn't like being 13–0. That had been the Sycamores' record the previous January, right before Larry Keith wrote his *Sports Illustrated* story about Bird and they lost five in a row, then seven of ten. That had been the Sycamores' record, right before everything unraveled on Bob King.

"That No. 13," Hodges said that week. "It was unlucky for us last year."

But the Aggies didn't feel like they had luck on their side, either. The team—including Slab Jones, Robert Gunn, Cyrus Cormier, Greg Webb, and coach Ken Hayes—hated going to western Indiana under almost any circumstance. The trip from Las Cruces to Terre Haute often required two connections and a full day of travel. The weather seemed to be cold every time they landed in town, and it certainly was on this visit. Temperatures hovered around zero degrees, with snow piled up on the ground. And the Aggies' reception inside the Hulman Center wasn't any warmer. Amid the win streak, students had embraced a new tradition. They cleared out the dormitory bathrooms of toilet paper, ripped the paper into small squares, tossed the squares into the air like confetti at exciting moments during the games, hurled entire rolls onto the court at times, and sometimes threw other items, too. As Ken Hayes took the floor for the game in mid-January 1979, he said someone threw a pocketknife at him.

The game that night was a battle, as usual. Hayes and Hodges argued on the sideline over calls, non-calls, and seemingly everything else, jawing at one another again and again. The Aggies jumped out to an early lead and held it for most of the game. But the Sycamores came back late, after Slab Jones got into foul trouble, and with less than a minute to go, the score was tied, 69–69.

At this point, Bill Hodges broke his own rule. He had the Sycamores hold the ball for a final shot, killing the game clock like Bob King used to do. But Hodges wouldn't get a chance to call a time-out and set up a final play. With 19 seconds left, the Aggies opted to foul Bob Heaton, sending him to the line with a chance to win the game—or blow it.

Heaton understood what was at stake here: the undefeated season, most of all. But as he toed the line, he tried to clear these thoughts from his head. He wasn't shooting foul shots in front of ten thousand people inside the sold-out arena, he told himself, and he definitely wasn't shooting them in front of a million viewers watching on statewide television. Heaton was back on his farm in Cory, shooting on the concrete slab that his father had poured behind the corn crib, not long before the farm accident that had nearly claimed his arm. He wasn't a star; he was just a kid playing basketball in Indiana.

"If I miss," Heaton told himself, "I miss."

He dribbled five times, slowly and methodically, and drained the first shot. Then Bob Heaton did it again: all net. The Sycamores went up 71–69 and the Aggies were finally spent. On their final, manic possession, with the clock ticking down, they tried to work the ball in down low, but Miley tipped the entry pass and Bird stole it, immediately flicking the ball to Staley, who churned down the court like one of Bob Heaton's tractors and found Nicks standing alone underneath the Aggies' basket. Nicks scored at the buzzer—just for fun. The Indiana State students thew their toilet paper in the air and the Sycamores escaped with yet another win, 73–69.

Ken Hayes was furious afterward. He walked off the court that night ready to file an official complaint with the conference over the referees—the terrible referees who had put Slab in foul trouble and cost him the game—while the Indiana State students ran out into the cold to celebrate. They marched across campus to Landini's house. They roused the president in the dark and asked him to join them. And for a brief moment that night, Landini allowed the students to carry him on their shoulders down the snow-covered streets of Terre Haute. He didn't even seem to mind when they dumped him into a snowbank, because the seemingly impossible had happened.

The Sycamores were the last unbeaten team in the country. By the next morning, they would be ranked No. 5 in the nation, and later that same day, Red Auerbach made a move that seemed designed to get Bird's attention. He traded with the Indiana Pacers to bring one of Bird's friends to Boston: Rick Robey, his all-star roommate from the previous spring. Between Robey and Judkins, the Celtics now had two players in their locker room who were close with Bird. Bird might sign with Boston just because his friends were there, Hodges speculated. Meanwhile, the Sycamores kept rising in the polls as they remained undefeated. The following week, they moved up to No. 3—just behind Notre Dame and just in front of Magic Johnson and Michigan State.

This was a story that the national basketball writers couldn't ignore any longer, and they were about to descend on Terre Haute in droves—an exciting development for Landini, the students, the team, and the townsfolk.

Exciting for everyone but Larry Bird.

45

SINCE MEDIA DAY IN Des Moines in early November, and his brief moment of preseason chattiness at the Savery Hotel, Bird had again stopped talking to reporters.

He wouldn't speak to sportswriters at either *The Terre Haute Star* or *The Terre Haute Tribune*. It didn't matter that neither paper had ever written a cross word about Bird or even once published a story digging into his failed marriage, his daughter's existence, or his father's death. The two local papers were getting nothing from him, and out-of-town reporters had no chance at all. They could fly hundreds of miles to Terre Haute, drive in from Indianapolis, call the two McKees in advance, put in their requests to interview Bird, and still fail to land any quotes from him. Ed McKee wasn't even coming out of the locker room anymore with manufactured comments to hand out to the media, as he had done the previous winter—perhaps because Bird wasn't talking to McKee much anymore, either. The best college basketball player in America was holing up in the trainer's room with Doc Behnke and manager Rick Shaw after his games, resting his achy joints in a whirlpool and dodging reporters at all costs.

"They all want to talk to Larry Bird," McKee mourned in his office that month, as the phone rang and rang. "And Larry's not talking."

Bird said it wasn't personal, but it sort of was. He claimed to have been misquoted at media day in Des Moines by a reporter at *The Terre Haute Tribune*. The quote that angered Bird was about how Hodges's role had changed since Bob King had fallen ill. "Used to be," Bird had said of Hodges, "he was the guy you'd see if you had problems, like if you wanted to get out of a test or something." Bird meant that Hodges was the assistant who helped players *reschedule* tests around road trips. But it didn't read like that; it sounded like Bird had used Hodges to get out of his academic obligations. And the alleged misquote—the *Tribune* never ran a correction—gave Bird the cover to do what he wanted to do from the start anyway: decline to speak to reporters. Especially a certain kind of reporter.

"People that try to push you," Bird said at the time. "People that try to get things out of you. Things that don't even pertain to basketball. Them are the type of people that I like to stay away from."

Now Bird's personal feelings had become unofficial school policy—a policy handed down to the two McKees from above. Reporters could talk to Hodges and interview players after games. They just couldn't interview Bird.

The silence troubled lots of people, including NBA executives. One general manager wondered how Bird could ever adapt to life in Boston, or another NBA city, if he had been too "terrified" to make it in Bloomington and now couldn't handle the attention in little Terre Haute. "He's a country boy," the general manager said. "How's he going to relate to a big-city situation?" His mother, Georgia, was concerned that Larry's effort to dodge publicity was just delaying the inevitable. "It'll hit him one of these days," she said. "It may hit him so hard it'll knock him down." Carl Nicks wished that Bird would speak, too. "Mainly because when the press comes to me," Nicks complained that winter, "they want to talk about Larry." And, of course, the entire situation infuriated the media for all the obvious reasons.

Then, starting around mid-December, Bird made things worse. He agreed to speak with *some* television reporters, under *certain* circumstances, apparently believing that the TV reporters wouldn't be able to twist his words since he was being recorded, and maybe believing that they wouldn't dare ask him the personal questions that the print reporters seemed to love. The result was this: The two McKees, already under pressure, now sometimes had to hand out awkward announcements informing the press that the players would be available for interviews that night—"excluding Larry Bird, who will give television interviews only." The sportswriters almost revolted, and it seemed to take a toll on Ed McKee most of all.

Ed, always thin, appeared to be losing weight as the tension closed in from all sides. One reporter joked that by the end of the season, Ed wouldn't be a man anymore; he'd be "vapor," a mist. Sometimes that winter, Ed didn't even travel with the team. He drove separately, feeling unwelcome with his own people. Worst of all, in Indiana State's greatest moment, the sports information director barely had access to the player who mattered most. "He's afraid I'm going to give away some deep, dark secrets," Ed complained about Bird that winter.

It left Bird seemingly unprepared for what was coming: a day when he wouldn't be able to choose silence. But no one at Indiana State could change Bird's mind or intervene in a way to make him see the flaws in his approach.

Bob King had failed to get Bird to talk for most of the previous year, and he couldn't be of much help now. Three days after the Sycamores' win against New Mexico State in mid-January 1979, King set up an afternoon meeting in Landini's office to break some news.

He was done coaching.

"The doctors just . . ."

King's voice trailed off.

"They feel it would be a very bad decision."

With King's announcement, Hodges was now officially in the running to be hired as head coach. It didn't seem like a great career move for him to require Bird to do the thing that he didn't want to do most. "Whether he's right or wrong," Hodges said that month, "I have to honor his feelings." And that left just one person who could have interceded to broker a deal between Bird, McKee, and the media: Dick Landini.

But Landini, at this point, had his own reasons not to rankle his star player. He was using Bird that winter as a bargaining chip in negotiations with state lawmakers over the university budget, and he was making sure that the lawmakers got a chance to bump into Bird—Indiana's biggest celebrity—when they made a visit to campus. Landini joked later that the politicians had brought their "first team" to Terre Haute. So, Landini said, "We just thought you should meet ours."

He was also honest with himself about the power that Bird possessed. "I can knock on 100 doors, which I have," Landini said that month, "and give 95 speeches to service clubs throughout the state of Indiana, and go to 115 alumni meetings, which I have in my four years here." Yet Bird could do more for the university's reputation, and he could do it, Landini said, "in a three-game road trip."

For all of these reasons, Bird could talk or not talk, engage or disappear, make life easy for the two McKees or make it hard. No one was going to tell him what to do. But Bird couldn't insulate himself from the deluge of national beat writers who were about to show up in Terre Haute after the latest win over New Mexico State. The *Chicago Tribune* was coming. The *Philadelphia Daily News* would be there. The *New York Post* and *The New York Times* were both flying into Terre Haute, and *The Boston Globe* was sending its best investigative sportswriter to finally tell the full Larry Bird story, whether Bird wanted it told or not.

Mike Madden, a blue-collar son of Irish immigrants, was known for chain-smoking cigarettes at his desk in Boston and pursuing the truth, wherever it led. In the 1980s, he would pen an exposé revealing that the Boston Red Sox had been partnering for years with an Elks Club in Florida that refused to admit Black players during spring training. To report it, Madden would wade into the Elks Club himself, ask questions in the face of angry white segregationists, listen as they accused him of "fighting the Civil War all over again," leave only after they started to threaten him with their guns, and write his story anyway—an embarrassment for both the Red Sox and the Elks.

This was not a man who was going to cower in the face of a college basketball star or listen to Ed McKee's directives about where he could go and whom he could talk to. From the moment that Madden landed in Terre Haute on a cold and snowy day in late January 1979, he went his own way. He talked to seemingly everyone. And his story, published in *The Boston Globe* that Sunday, just hours after Indiana State's 18th victory in a row, broke news about Bird's father's death, telling the full story for the first time. "A suicide," Madden called it.

Madden handled the tragedy respectfully; he wasn't there to hurt Bird. But the information was out there now. Another detail that didn't pertain to basketball—maybe the most important detail—had been found and revealed to the world. And the following day, editors at *The Terre Haute Tribune* got a sneak peek at the next big story that was coming. This one was from *Sports Illustrated*, and the writer, Bruce Newman, had used his local connections as a native Indianan, raised nearby in Evansville, to tell the last of Bird's well-kept secrets. Newman reported that Bird didn't just have an ex-wife, Janet, but a daughter with her, and a paternity suit was pending in a Vigo County court.

In just a few days, everything had come spilling out, and Hodges was livid. He soon lashed out at *Sports Illustrated*, calling the magazine "second rate." In defense of Larry Bird, Hodges was now picking his own fight with the media, and he was doing it at a moment when he should have been celebrating—or at least saying nothing. The top college teams in the nation all lost that week. Notre Dame fell to Maryland and Michigan State blew a game at Northwestern that left Jud Heathcote so angry he could barely speak afterward. The Sycamores, 18–0, were now moving up to No. 2 in the polls. More reporters would be coming soon, and one day after the *Sports Illustrated* story leaked to the local press, Hodges's team set out on its longest road trip of the season.

They bused three hours to St. Louis, flew west to Dallas, changed planes to get to El Paso, and then took yet another bus to Las Cruces for a Thursday night rematch in the desert against a team that desperately wanted to end the Sycamores' undefeated season: the New Mexico State Aggies.

46

KEN HAYES COULDN'T STAND the thought of losing to Indiana State again, and neither could his players. Greg Webb, the hero from New Mexico State's lone victory over Bird the year before, wanted to get out to a fast start that night. Robert Gunn, Webb's roommate, hoped the Aggies would stay out of foul trouble this time, and Cyrus Cormier, the Aggies' defensive specialist, hoped to be able to win and have fun afterward. His mother had flown in from Houston and had made a gumbo for a gathering in Cyrus's apartment. With a win, the plan was to feast on her meal and maybe head out to the Las Cruces dance club that the players liked best, the Rain Forrest.

A record crowd of Panamaniacs—13,684 people—filled the Pan American Center for the game. On the floor beforehand, the television broadcasters could barely hear themselves speaking, and in the locker rooms both teams felt the weight of the moment. In addition to the sell-out crowd inside the arena, millions of people would be watching that night on KOB-TV out of Albuquerque and multiple stations in Indiana. Cormier could barely breathe before tip-off, and Bob Heaton felt a similar sort of pressure.

Indiana State had traveled to New Mexico with a large contingent that included Connie Hodges, Max Gibson, and Bob King, who was back with the team for his first road trip as a spectator. Distractions were everywhere; Bill Hodges was even wearing one—a new, special-edition powder-blue sports coat that Lu Meis's department store had introduced back home. It would be devastating to come this far and climb this high, Heaton thought, only to lose now, and he sought solace before the game in the only place he knew.

He read the Bible, Heaton recalled, and asked God to grant him peace.

The Lord gaveth in the early goings that night. With the fans on their feet, the Aggies came out tight while the Sycamores took the floor looking like a finely tuned powder-blue machine. Nicks, Gilbert, Reed, and Miley all scored in the opening minutes. Bird hit shots from the deep corners and made passes that no one else could, including a behind-the-back no-look pass that hit Nicks in stride 60 feet down the court for an easy basket. The Sycamores went up by eight. The lead would grow to 14, and Hayes had to call a time-out to prevent his team from getting run out of its own gym in front of that record crowd.

But Slab Jones and Robert Gunn kept the Aggies in it. In the first half, Slab matched Bird point for point while Gunn abused Bird on the offensive end of the floor. Three times that night, Gunn popped out as though he was going to collect a pass near the sideline. Then, as Bird followed him, Gunn cut to the basket, received a perfect backdoor pass, and slammed the ball through the cylinder with one hand. The Aggies weren't going to fold, and the Sycamores hurt themselves again and again with mistakes.

Nicks played like the younger version of himself for much of the evening: out of control. He picked up three fouls in the first 10 minutes and had to grab a seat on the bench. Gilbert was soon in foul trouble, too, with three of his own, and had to join Nicks on the sideline. With two starters out, Hodges had to give significant minutes to Rich Nemcek, the descendant of Slovakian immigrants who had quit the sport a couple years earlier to work in that steel mill. This wasn't how Hodges had scripted it. Then, with 7:30 to go in the first half, Bird accidentally incited the crowd in a way that conjured up memories of his incident at Rutgers 10 months earlier.

Bird tumbled into the stands beneath Indiana State's basket as he tried to score on a fast break, and before Bob Heaton and Brad Miley knew what was happening, a fight had broken out between Bird and the fans. Heaton and Miley were almost 100 feet away when it started—too far away to help or even see what was going on. But Mel Daniels saw it. The fans obstructed Bird as he tried to get back on the court and into the game. In the scuffle that followed, one fan threw a game program at Bird. Bird began to fight back and Daniels came running. Daniels wanted to protect Bird—or get in the fight, if necessary, throwing elbows the way he had during his playing career. Greg Webb wanted to protect Bird, too. The New Mexico State guard pulled Bird back with two hands, worried.

But the damage here was already done. In the altercation in the stands, Bird had apparently drawn blood, just as he had at Rutgers. According to one account—later confirmed by a series of photographs, captured by a student photographer working that night for the AP—Bird threw a "quick left hook" that caught a student in the forehead. This student was now bleeding above one of his eyes, a trickle of blood bubbling up on his skin, and Aggies fans were upset. As New Mexico State officials walked the injured student over to the bench for medical treatment, boos rained down from the rafters and the game started to turn.

A 14-point Sycamore lead evaporated in a matter of minutes. The arena became so loud that the players could no longer hear the referees' whistles—"Everybody's standing at the Pan American Center in Las Cruces, New Mexico!" KOB's play-by-play man cried—and down the stretch, late in the game, everything that could go wrong for Indiana State did.

With 2:12 to go, the Aggies claimed their first lead of the night. Thirty seconds later, Bird picked up his fourth foul on a suspect call. Not long after that, Nicks fouled out, reckless again. Bird then blew a chance to tie the game, missing the front end of a one-and-one with 14 seconds to go. At that point, he fouled out, too, seemingly out of frustration, and without him, the Sycamores looked discombobulated on the next play. Only four players took the floor out of a time-out—an oversight that no one caught in the moment, not even the referees. So, when the Aggies missed their own free throw and Miley pulled down the rebound with about 10 seconds to go, the Sycamores were playing four on five, down a player and down two points, 83–81.

In the mayhem that followed, Reed took a panicked shot and missed. Gilbert fouled out in the shorthanded scrum for the rebound. Greg Webb was now heading to the foul line for New Mexico State, and it probably didn't matter whether he made his free throws or not. With just three seconds left on the clock, and New Mexico State up two, this game was surely over—a result so obvious that the KOB color analyst decided to say it out loud on live TV.

"It don't make a whole lot of difference," he said. "I believe this game belongs to the New Mexico State Aggies."

On the Aggies bench, Cormier was thinking about his mother's gumbo and the party they were about to have. Webb was thinking about dancing at the Rain Forrest. Gunn had total confidence in his roommate to make the first foul shot and end the game, and so did Ken Hayes. But if Webb didn't make it, Hayes had a plan for that, too. He didn't want anyone to try to get a rebound or play any defense whatsoever. "It's kind of hard to get the ball," Hayes said that night, "dribble, and get off a shot in three seconds." The Aggies would be fine, he believed, as long as they didn't commit a foul.

About 50 feet away on the Indiana State bench, Sycamores team manager Rick Shaw agreed. From the moment that Bird had fouled out, Shaw started packing up the gear for the team's next destination: Tulsa. He didn't want to be out there when thousands of fans stormed the court to celebrate one of the greatest wins in New Mexico State history.

But Hodges was still coaching. He worried that a single defeat could gut his team and break the spell, as it had the year before. So he directed Shaw to bring him his chalkboard, even if it had been put away. Shaw dug it out in a hurry to please Hodges, and Hodges utilized the board to draw up a play—something that could plausibly work if, and only if, Webb missed the front end of his one-and-one.

Hodges wanted three rebounders in the lane: Miley, Staley, and Curry. He wanted Reed and Heaton up near midcourt, one on the left side and the other on the right, and he wanted whoever got the rebound—if Webb missed and there *was* a rebound—to fling it to Reed or Heaton, who by then would only have time to heave the ball at the basket.

"You just have to turn around," Hodges said, "and shoot it up there."

Hodges was serious, even if almost no one else believed. Heaton wasn't even really listening to Hodges. All Heaton heard in the moment was the crowd: 13,000 people cheering and then chanting—chanting two numbers.

"18–1."

"18–1."

"18–1 . . ."

Heaton stood up in a daze, not knowing what Hodges wanted from him or where he was supposed to stand on the floor. He was a ghost in powder blue. But as he walked away from the bench, Bird's onetime roommate in Hodges's basement, Danny King, almost grabbed Heaton and shook him and said something that neither man would ever forget.

"Don't give up," King told him. "Don't give up."

Greg Webb had felt great just moments before, clapping his hands, flexing, and thinking about the Rain Forrest. But the time-out had altered his mindset. He didn't like that his own coach had made him sit there and ponder what he was about to do. He walked to the line not feeling like himself, out of sorts—or at least out of his typical mindset. Unlike the year before, Webb wasn't just thinking about the net 15 feet away. He was thinking about lots of things—not good.

He missed the front end of the one-and-one, as the ball rattled off the rim to the right. Miley grabbed the rebound, and at that point, the clock started to tick down.

Three . . .

Webb wanted to play defense, and for a moment he almost did. He started to move his body in front of Miley. Then he remembered Hayes's instructions in the huddle—*don't foul*—so he pulled back, just standing there. Miley had a free path to do what he wanted. But he made a mistake.

Miley dribbled the basketball, wasting time.

Two . . .

The dribble cost the Sycamores a full second. But Miley used the dribble, and his long legs, to gain almost 10 feet of ground. He had closed the gap between him and Bob Heaton or him and Steve Reed, who were each standing at midcourt, awaiting the pass, and Miley had made his choice.

He threw the ball to Heaton.

One . . .

The pass, traveling 30 feet in the air, landed in Heaton's hands, soft and true, and Heaton turned to face the basket in one fluid motion. Then he planted his sneakers into the court just behind the midline, jumped into the air, and released the ball into the desert night, leaning into the shot. He was giving it everything he had. Maybe too much.

As Heaton let it go, he was certain that he had just taken the worst shot of his life. He believed the ball was going to clear everything—the rim, the backboard, the student section, the arena—and land somewhere out there in the scrub brush of the Mesilla Valley. Hodges said a quiet prayer, and about a thousand miles away in Terre Haute, Craig McKee, watching the game on television inside his parents' house, picked up the phone to do his job. He was ready to call in the final score to all the Indiana news stations and newspapers, and he knew what the score was going to be: Sycamores were going to lose by two.

But the arc of Heaton's shot began to bend toward the basket. Hayes, standing directly behind Heaton on the sideline, realized with horror that the ball wasn't long. It was on target. Hayes couldn't believe it—this shot had a chance—and Landini couldn't believe it, either. Back inside his house on campus, Landini stood in front of his television and began to shout.

"*IT'S GOING IN!*"

The ball ricocheted off the backboard, caromed off the front of the rim, circled the cylinder one time, and danced around before falling through—*good*.

Heaton had tied the game at the buzzer. Aggies cheerleaders dropped to the floor, and Greg Webb did, too, while Daniels found Heaton and wrapped him in a bear hug. They were going to overtime, and in order to win, Hodges was going to have to play his most unusual lineup of the season: Reed, Heaton, Miley, Staley, and Nemcek. But this game was already over. Everybody knew it. Even the Aggies. Maybe especially the

Aggies. And when the Sycamores won in the extra period, 91–89, the guys hoisted Hodges on their shoulders and carried him off the floor.

That night, Greg Webb was almost inconsolable. He didn't go to Cormier's apartment for gumbo. No one went dancing at the Rain Forrest. And Ken Hayes barely slept at all, as he replayed the final the moments of the game in his mind. He couldn't believe he had decided to pull his players back, when just a little defense would have won them the game. It was, he admitted later, the worst mistake he ever made, and he never let it go. "It's still in my craw," he said nearly five decades later, "and I'll die with it in my heart."

The Sycamores, meanwhile, were the ones who went out on the town. Max Gibson secured a restaurant in Las Cruces to stay open late. Everyone piled into shuttle vans and drove there, laughing. Heaton sat in the front of one of the vans, and as his vehicle pulled into the parking lot, there was Larry Bird, standing in the headlights, pointing his fingers at Heaton through the windshield. They stuffed themselves with chili rellenos, artichokes, and steaks, and the next morning they drove to El Paso.

The itinerary that day called for the team to fly on to Tulsa, but there was time to kill on the border. So, with Hodges's permission, the guys drifted into Juárez and purchased cowboy hats. Heaton picked out a black one. By the time they got on the plane for Tulsa, they weren't just basketball players anymore, they were gunslingers in the Old West, and Hodges decided to test out their sharpshooting later that afternoon. At the end of the shootaround that day in Tulsa, Hodges lined his team up at the spot on the floor where Heaton had made his miracle shot and asked everybody to give it a try.

The players missed. Most of them, badly. Heaton threw up an airball. But one player managed to make it: Larry Bird.

"That wasn't so hard," Bird said, walking away.

They beat Tulsa, of course, and flew home to Terre Haute still undefeated.

20–0.

47

TERRE HAUTE WAS STILL buzzing from the miracle shot when the team arrived back on campus, this time with about 2,000 students deciding to greet them with an impromptu pep rally.

Bird wanted none of it and slipped away with his old pal Danny King. In King's memory, they went to Bird's favorite bar, Rafters, and drank a beer. But it didn't really matter because the person the students wanted to see was Bob Heaton, and Heaton was willing to please. He gave a short speech in his new black cowboy hat, and the crowd gave him a new nickname: "The Miracle Man." The student government then voted to declare February 12 as Bob Heaton Day, cementing his hero status. Though, by then, the students didn't need an official piece of legislation to celebrate Heaton, Bird, or the team. They were celebrating them almost every day at the rented house that Bird and Heaton shared on South 11th Street.

Before the road trip out west, not many people came by the place, outside of Bird and Heaton's teammates, the players' two girlfriends, Dinah and Jane Ann, Bird's French Lick boys, and an elderly neighbor whom Bird and Heaton called "Smitty." It wasn't unusual for Heaton to come home and find Smitty and Bird sitting in the living room, splitting a six-pack of Stroh's. Now, on some nights, Bird and Heaton couldn't even stay home as their phone rang again and again. They were getting 10 or 20 phone calls a night from strangers, reporters, and fans—everybody wanting something. And they weren't the only ones who found that their lives had changed.

Lu Meis invited players to come down to his department store and pick out cowboy hats to wear, if they hadn't already purchased one in Juárez. Miley, Gilbert, Nicks, Crowder, and others began wearing them, too. Meis featured some of them in advertisements, using the players to sell his hats, just as he had used Hodges to sell sports coats, and the whole team walked with a different sort of confidence, even Hodges.

Just three weeks earlier, Hodges had thought of himself as a placeholder for Bob King. "I'm still King's assistant," he told the reporters who came to Terre Haute, "and when he gets well, he'll be the head coach again." Now, with King's announcement that he could never return, the team's 20–0 start, and Heaton's miracle in the desert, Hodges wasn't talking like that anymore, and Landini decided to end his abbreviated search for King's long-term replacement. Before the team landed back in Terre Haute, he announced that he was hiring Hodges as head coach.

In just six months, Hodges had gone from inquiring about selling golf equipment with Johnny Nelson in Florida to landing a coaching position with the second-best team in the country. His whole world had changed. The parties at Bill and Connie's house that winter reflected the moment—everyone who mattered was there—and most importantly, Hodges's team continued to beat up on opponents.

One coach that winter, Joe Gottfried at Southern Illinois, admitted that his team didn't really have a chance against Larry Bird and Indiana State. He told reporters that his Salukis would do their best. "Then," he said, "we pray." It sounded desperate, but not to Bob Ortegel, the coach at Drake. Ortegel said there was only one way to stop Bird: "Take away his basketball shoes." In a game in Peoria, Illinois, on a Saturday night in mid-February 1979, Bradley head coach Dick Versace basically tried to do just that. Bradley, the worst team in the Valley conference, rolled out the "Bird Cage Defense"—a triangle and two, where two Bradley players sandwiched Bird wherever he went on the court and the other three players fell back into a zone. In this defense, one player stood in front of Bird—face-to-face with him, not even looking at the basketball. The other bodied him from behind. Bird could hardly shuffle his feet without running into someone, and at halftime Bradley was only down by five. The Bird Cage was working.

But Bird never got frustrated. He urged his teammates to shoot anytime they were open, which was most of the night. Nicks and Reed carried the Sycamores, scoring 50 points between them. It didn't even matter that Versace's radical defense held Bird to just four points—his lowest total since his junior year of high school. The Sycamores still won, cruising to victory.

Two days later, Red Auerbach dispatched three Celtics players to check in on Bird. Auerbach was sending the former league MVP and current player-coach of the Celtics, Dave Cowens, and Bird's two friends from the team, Rick Robey and Jeff Judkins. Auerbach figured some familiar faces couldn't hurt—"They know him," he said—and that night in Terre Haute, this illustrious group, along with Bob Heaton and Rich Nemcek, went out drinking at Rafters.

Crowds mobbed them as they tried to order beer or play pool, and in this moment, Nemcek almost felt sorry for Bird. He was no longer a college student living in a poorly furnished house south of campus; he was the sun in a universe, everything revolving around him. And the craze was only beginning. Games sold out that entire month—both at home and on the road. In Terre Haute, students slept in front of the Hulman Center, skipping classes and meals to make sure they got a good seat in the general-admission section reserved for them. The Larry Bird Committee, led by Max Gibson, started selling tables for its postseason celebration at $400, and the tables quickly sold out, too, as the undefeated season rolled on. The Sycamores were now 25–0.

At this point, almost any other team in the country would have been the consensus No. 1 in both the AP and UPI polls. But somehow UCLA, with a record of 20–3, had leapfrogged Indiana State and jumped into the top position. And two other programs, Notre Dame and Michigan State, continued to overshadow the Sycamores in the Midwest. The Irish and the Spartans had both played that winter on national TV, on NBC. Notre Dame's head coach, Digger Phelps, was working the room with a green carnation in the lapel of his suit coat—"You've got to play to the crowd," he said. "It's show biz, it's entertainment"—and Magic Johnson innately understood that about college basketball, too. That winter, the same week that Bird skipped the impromptu pep rally in Terre Haute, forcing Heaton to face the students alone, Magic played on national TV in NBC's game of the week, defeated Kansas by 24, recorded his typically strong stat line— 12 points, 11 assists, 10 rebounds—gave interviews afterward, praised his talented teammates Greg Kelser and Jay Vincent, both bound for the NBA with him, and then sat down with a reporter from the *Los Angeles Times* and answered the same questions all over again.

"The question I tire of the most," Magic said that day, "is whether or not I'll turn pro at the end of the year."

Still, he answered it. Again. Without objection and all smiles.

"The truth is," he said, "I just don't know."

Indiana State students, feeling disrespected, underestimated, and overlooked, finally resorted to a drastic measure. In late February 1979, the student body government voted unanimously to call for a congressional investigation into the basketball polls themselves. But by that point, NBC had already made a decision that would give the students what they wanted.

Network executives announced they were moving the Sycamores' last regular-season home game, against Wichita State, from a Saturday night to a Sunday afternoon, so that NBC could beam Bird into living rooms nationwide on network TV.

For the first time in his life, Larry Bird would be everywhere.

48

NBC WAS HAVING A moment that winter, thanks in part to something new: a two-man color analyst team in Billy Packer and Al McGuire.

Packer—a former player and assistant coach at Wake Forest, known at birth as Bill Paczkowski—played the role of the straight man in this duo. At every opportunity, the 39-year-old Packer wanted to teach viewers about basketball, going deep on detail. McGuire, on the other hand, was freewheeling and fun. The former coach at Marquette wore every emotion on the sleeve of his red NBC sports coat, spoke in a thick Brooklyn accent, had a cheery gap between his two front teeth, and had no formal television training whatsoever. But that's what made it work. McGuire was genuine. His authenticity oozed through American television screens, and his chemistry with Packer created an atmosphere that network producers would be chasing for the next 50 years.

They worked well together in part because Packer and McGuire liked to argue with each other, on air. As they sparred, ratings skyrocketed, and advertising rates did, too. By mid-February 1979, a 60-second commercial during NBC's college basketball coverage cost $45,000—about $200,000 in today's money. And corporations happily paid the premium, because Packer and McGuire drew larger audiences than NBA games, much to the consternation of CBS and its young, number-crunching vice president, Kevin O'Malley. Companies looking to sell products to basketball fans wanted to do it while Packer and McGuire were talking, or arguing, or both. And the two NBC analysts didn't disappoint when it came time to discuss the big story of the season: Indiana State.

McGuire loved everything about the Sycamores—their working-class school, their overlooked city, their accidental head coach, and Larry Bird—while Packer threw cold water on all of it. Packer questioned the strength of Indiana State's schedule. He didn't believe the Sycamores were worthy of being ranked No. 2, much less No. 1. And while he praised Bird's instincts and skills—"some high school," Packer said, "really did a good job teaching him the fundamentals"—he doubted that Bird would become an NBA star like Bill Walton or Kareem Abdul-Jabbar. In one interview that winter, Packer compared Bird to Bailey Howell—a great player from the 1960s who was already mostly forgotten.

These comments made Packer the least popular person in western Indiana and turned McGuire into a Midwestern folk hero. Students held up signs inside the Hulman Center that said, AL MCGUIRE FOR PRESIDENT. And the quietest of those students, Larry Bird, broke his media silence that winter to talk to McGuire for an NBC interview in February 1979, covering material he'd never addressed publicly before.

Bird spoke that day about his year collecting garbage in French Lick. "I learned how to do lots of things, not only that," he said of the job, a bit defensive. "But that's what they stick to. That's what people stick me as." He talked about his three weeks in Bloomington with Bobby Knight. "I had just turned 17 years old in December," he said. "I didn't know what I was doing." He discussed his refusal to meet with the media. "I like to be with people I like to be with, and I like to stay away from people I don't like." And he shared his thoughts on McGuire's broadcasting partner. "Billy better not come to Terre Haute," Bird said, "for a long time."

Locals couldn't wait to see McGuire, up close and in person, and everyone in the locker room was excited for the opportunity to play in front of the NBC audience. In the era before widespread cable, broadband internet, social media, and viral moments, nothing had the impact of national network television. It had the power to turn ordinary people into stars, and stars into icons. But at times that February in Terre Haute, it felt like the team might not even make it to its one nationally televised appearance. With each win that month, the pressure seemed to build.

In the game after Heaton's miracle shot, Hodges had argued with Tulsa coach Jim King because officials had shut off the lights in the arena while the Sycamores were finishing their pregame warm-up. It happened while the public address announcer was introducing the Tulsa starters, and the lights were only off for a short time, maybe 30 seconds. Still, Hodges vented his frustration, shouting on the floor. "He called me all kinds of names," Jim King said after the game. "The pressure must be eating him up alive."

A week later, in Peoria, Hodges started an argument again—this time with the referees over Dick Versace's Bird Cage Defense. Hodges didn't think it was legal. "The rulebook states that a man must be allowed room to maneuver," he protested that night. The refs ignored him, and Versace bristled at the notion he was breaking the rules.

About a week later, at a road game in Des Moines, Drake head coach Bob Ortegel had a physical altercation with Hodges on the floor near the end of the first half. The issue on this night was Drake's organist, a middle-aged musician. Hodges didn't like that he was playing the organ while Brad Miley was shooting a free throw, and Hodges walked all the way down the sideline to complain to Ortegel about it. Ortegel didn't notice that Hodges was there until he was almost on top of him, and the two men began to bump and push each other, forcing referees and police officers to get involved. Ortegel hadn't even heard the organ. And either way, he didn't know why Hodges was complaining to him. "No. 1," Ortegel said, "I don't play the organ. And No. 2, the organist is part of the tradition at Drake University."

The entire affair once again raised questions about what was happening to Indiana State—or Hodges specifically—in the midst of the winning streak. But Hodges shrugged it all off. No, he wasn't feeling any pressure, he claimed. He was just pointing out wrongs, and he vowed to keep doing so. He was going to fight for his team as he had once fought in high school back in Zionsville. "If I step on someone's toes, too bad," Hodges said. "That's the way I am."

But the biggest fight was still to come. The morning after the argument at Drake, David Israel, a nationally syndicated writer for the *Chicago Tribune,* banged out a column attacking Hodges for protecting Bird, Indiana State for coddling Bird, and Bird for being Bird. Israel, a provocateur by nature, called Bird "a pretty good player from some place called Indiana State" and proceeded to fill his column with a litany of questions posed to Bird himself.

"Has anyone ever suggested to you that part of a college education is learning how to cope with outsiders, learning how to converse with people who might be a little different from you?" Israel asked. "Is it true that when Bill Hodges, your coach, was recently asked a question, he responded, 'I have no comment because Larry and I have a good relationship, and I wouldn't want anything he reads in the paper to change that'?" Then Israel asked, "Don't you think it is sad and inappropriate that your friends are so afraid of speaking their mind on the subject of Larry Bird because it might alienate you?"

The column managed to upset everyone—Hodges, Landini, Bird, his teammates, and the two McKees. In their opinion, Israel had gone too far. But whether Indiana State officials wanted to admit it or not, Israel had managed to raise a few valid concerns. In the column, he wondered if a

Black star would be able to get away with the silent routine that Bird was pulling off in Terre Haute. He raised doubts about how Bird would perform if the Sycamores made it to the NCAA tournament, where players were required by rule to speak to the media. And, like others before him, Israel questioned how Bird would survive in the NBA, where the locker rooms were open and reporters would have lots of questions about everything.

"Do you know you're going to be asked about being the Great White Hope?

"Do you understand the implications?

"Can you answer the question intelligently?"

The day the column came out, bad weather moved in across the Midwest—torrential rains this time, followed by a dense and unrelenting fog. Then the temperatures dropped. The fog lifted, the rain froze, and a blizzard hit Terre Haute, closing the highway south of the city and many other roads, too. Amid the chaos, NBC's production team barely made it into town for the game, and the roof of the Hulman Center began to leak. Maintenance crews now had to scramble to stop cold water from dripping onto the basketball court and Ed McKee had to skip NBC's preproduction meeting at the Sheraton to assess the failing rooftop.

But there was no canceling the game. The Sycamores weren't just 25–0, ranked No. 2 in the country, and about to appear on NBC for the first time; it was Larry Bird Week in French Lick. Local businesses were decorated in his honor. Many shops were offering Larry Bird specials. The Springs Valley Church of the Nazarene was inviting Granny Kerns to accept an award on her grandson's behalf. State lawmakers were lobbying to pass a resolution celebrating Georgia Bird as the Hoosier Mother of the Year, and local officials in French Lick were renaming a street in his honor not far from the old laundromat where Hodges had found Bird four years earlier.

LARRY BIRD BOULEVARD, the new sign said.

The roof at the Hulman Center *had* to hold. The maintenance crews had to do whatever it took to mop up the water and plug the leak. And Bill Hodges's team, at 25–0, had to win its one game on national network TV.

"A defeat," Hodges said, "might knock the wind out of us."

49

IN THE HISTORY OF Indiana State basketball, Terre Haute, western Indiana, and maybe the entire state, no arena was ever louder than the Hulman Center in the moments before NBC went live on national TV that Sunday afternoon at three o'clock.

It didn't matter that the snowstorm prevented about 700 people from making it downtown for the game. Everyone who counted was there: Max Gibson, Dick Landini, Bob King, and Georgia Bird. Wichita State's head coach, Gene Smithson, had managed to get his Shockers to Terre Haute amid the snow, employing his personal mantra: "Mental Toughness, Extra Effort"—or as Smithson liked to say, more succinctly, MTXE. NBC's play-by-play man, Jim Simpson, stood on the floor with his buttery voice ready to go, his microphone in his hand. Al McGuire stood next to him in his red NBC sports coat, and perhaps appropriately, Billy Packer was nowhere to be found. The network had sent him to Louisville for the day to spare him the verbal abuse he would have endured in the arena.

But the NBC producers didn't paper over Packer's absence; they embraced it, putting the conflict between him and Indiana State at the center of the TV show they were making that day. In the opening remarks that afternoon, Simpson and McGuire talked about Bird's national network debut. "Welcome to Larry's world," McGuire said, nodding to the raucous crowd. Then the two broadcasters pivoted to discuss their colleague Packer, displaying for viewers the lyrics to a new jingle that students were singing all over campus:

Here's to Billy Packer,
Billy Packer, Billy Packer.
Here's to Billy Packer,
Don't come to our state.
We'll haunt you.
We'll taunt you.
We'll make you a fool.
Here's to Billy Packer,
Don't come to our school!

Simpson and McGuire had a good chuckle at Packer's expense. Then Alex Gilbert won the opening tip, and Indiana State came out like a team eager to prove the skeptics wrong. On the first play, Bird passed the ball to Nicks without even putting the ball on the floor, and Nicks scored an easy lay-up, flying to the hoop. But over the next several minutes, the Sycamores were almost too eager. They made ill-advised passes. They turned the ball over. Bird didn't hit a single shot until about the 13-minute mark. Smithson's boys were in it, and McGuire diagnosed the Sycamores' problem. "I personally think they're a little sloppy," he said, "because they're trying to impress a national audience."

Hodges agreed. The team, in his opinion, was running too hot. And at halftime, with the Sycamores only up by six, Hodges emphasized the importance of taking care of the ball in the final 20 minutes of the game. It was going to be the key to victory, he said. Still, early in the second half, the turnovers continued. Reed coughed it up while trying to make a pass. On the next trip down the floor, Nicks fumbled the ball in the lane. The Shockers converted Nicks's mistake into points, and suddenly, the Sycamores were clinging to a narrow lead, 52–50.

It was the nightmare that Hodges had held at bay all week. He didn't want to lose *any* game. "That's like chopping a finger off," he told reporters. "You lose something you can never get back." But he especially didn't want to lose this one, with millions watching at home, Simpson and McGuire sitting courtside, and Packer ready to gloat from Louisville.

Hodges called a time-out to settle his guys. Reed threw down the ball in disgust and Bird couldn't get to the bench fast enough. As usual, he had played every minute of the game.

It wasn't as if Bird were playing poorly. He had already logged 26 points and 12 rebounds on the afternoon—a stat line that a great player might have in an entire game. And he definitely wasn't doing it alone. Nicks had 13 points, and the other regulars had combined for 13 more. They just needed to play better defense and go on a run, and out of the time-out, they finally did. Reed drained a 20-footer from the left wing, wide open as the Shockers worried about Bird. Wichita State missed three shots in a row; Bird got the rebound every time. Nicks hit two baskets. Then Bird took over, nailing shots from the outside and the inside—11 points in three and a half minutes, and nine points in a row. Even when Wichita State had him blocked out, Bird found ways to get the rebound and score as Jim Simpson gushed about him on national TV.

"Guess who's there?" Simpson cried, after yet another unlikely rebound. It was Larry Bird.

In the span of just 10 minutes, a two-point nail-biter became a 20-point blowout, leaving fans in the Hulman Center with only a few reasons to stay in their seats. They wanted to be there for the postgame ceremony honoring the team's seniors, to watch Bird embrace his mother in the stands, and to see if he could make history. Bird had a chance to pass his all-time scoring record of 48 points and maybe get to 50.

But with six minutes left, Bird was still passing, and one of those passes nearly shook the Hulman Center off its foundation and into the snowbanks outside. Wichita State had missed another shot. Bird had pulled down another rebound. He was standing beneath his own basket, with the backboard over his head, and from his hip, he unleashed a rainbow—an 80-foot pass to Steve Reed running down the court.

From the moment Bird let it go, it appeared to be a busted play. The pass was a little short and a Shockers guard, Ronnie Ryer, was there to defend it, chasing Reed down. Ryer should have stolen the pass at least twice. But he couldn't collect the ball. It bounced off his hands and fell to the floor. And when it did, Reed scooped it up, threw it high off the glass, scored, and punched the air with his fist as the crowd shrieked with glee. A couple minutes later, Bird notched his 49th point, a new record. Indiana State won the game, 109–84. Smithson walked off the court, sniping at Hodges for keeping Bird on the floor until the final minute, and Al McGuire had another opinion that he wanted to share with viewers at home.

"Red Auerbach better live down here the next couple of months," McGuire said. Because Bird wasn't just great; he was, McGuire believed, the best player in the country. And if Auerbach wasn't careful, he could lose him. "How many guys, 22 years of age, have a street named after them in their hometown?"

In celebration, someone went out to Larry Bird Boulevard down in French Lick and stole the street signs. They were gone by Wednesday.

Meanwhile, after the game, everyone wanted a piece of Bird as usual—*The New York Times*, the *Chicago Tribune*, the local papers, the Indianapolis papers, and Al McGuire. But it didn't happen. Bird was only sticking around for the postgame ceremony honoring the seniors. He went into the stands to hug his mother when Hodges introduced him to the crowd. Then, when prompted by Staley, the whole team went back into the stands, put Bob King on their shoulders, and carried their old coach out onto the floor. "Bob King is responsible for each one of these players," Hodges announced, "and he deserves credit for all of this."

People in Terre Haute wept openly as King sat on the shoulders of his players, and the next day, their emotions spilled over again as they heard the news on their televisions and radios. For the first time in Indiana State history, voters in both major polls, the AP and the UPI, had named the Sycamores the No. 1 team in the country—ahead of Notre Dame, UCLA, and Michigan State. A journey that had begun in a remote Indiana valley four years earlier, with Bill Hodges and Stan Evans driving down to French Lick, had reached a sort of mountaintop. And the view from this vista mattered. With Indiana State's No. 1 ranking—and the NCAA tournament's newly expanded 40-team field—the conference tournament, to be hosted that week at the Hulman Center, was just a formality now. The Sycamores didn't even have to win in order to make the NCAA bracket.

But as the new No. 1 team in the country, undefeated at 26–0, the guys couldn't bear to lose now. Hodges couldn't, either. He chose not to rest anybody, and the team kept its streak going that week in three tough conference battles.

In the sold-out arena in Terre Haute, the Sycamores beat West Texas, Southern Illinois, and their rival, New Mexico State, for the third time that season and the fifth time in a row. The players presented the conference tournament trophy to Bob King, with Staley and Miley walking it over to him, and then they moved in to carry Bill Hodges off the floor as he tried to give a postgame interview.

"I'll see ya!" Hodges told the live television audience as the team picked him up and carried him away.

In the locker room moments later, they celebrated by throwing Hodges into the showers. Then they tossed in Max Gibson and Dick Landini. Then they threw in some guy who just happened to be there at Landini's invitation: US senator Birch Bayh. The Terre Haute native— and one of the most powerful men in Washington—was now drenched like everyone else, but he didn't care. No one did. Bayh was just happy to be part of the moment. Indiana State was 29–0 and headed to the NCAA tournament with the biggest names in basketball—Digger Phelps's Fighting Irish; Sidney Moncrief's Arkansas Razorbacks; Bird's old H-O-R-S-E opponent Denny Crum, still coaching at Louisville; Magic Johnson's Michigan State Spartans; and the most successful college basketball program of the decade, UCLA.

50

HODGES WAS ALMOST NUMB in the celebration after the game. But as he and the players laughed in the showers, the water running off their faces, Indiana State was already facing new problems, and it wasn't just that the water had ruined Hodges's wool suit. In the NCAA tournament, Bird was going to have to talk to the media. Even print reporters. Even people he didn't like. And he was going to have to answer questions about a new and irksome topic: his left thumb.

In an effort to defeat New Mexico State and remain perfect, Bird had injured the thumb early in the second half of the conference championship game. It happened as he tried to slap the ball away from Robert Gunn, and it was immediately clear to everyone in the building that there was a problem. Bird came off the floor, grimacing and clutching his left hand. Doc Behnke went to work on his thumb with the help of Rick Shaw and others. As they poked and prodded, Bird missed six minutes of game time—his longest stretch on the bench in any game that season. Behnke needed time to assess the damage, see if Bird could play, and wrap the thumb, if he could. And while Bird ultimately returned to the game, leading all scorers with 20 points, he wasn't the same. On the floor, after the injury, he didn't pull down a single rebound, and in the celebration afterward, he seemed distracted by the pain. Bird held his left thumb close to his chest and caressed it with his right hand. Later that evening, at the student health center, he learned why it was bothering him so much. The thumb was broken.

Doctors described it as a T-fracture, a cracked bone at the tip with no displacement—that was the good news. Bird could still play. But the injury typically required the patient to wear a splint, and a splint wasn't going to work for a basketball player. Behnke was going to have to get creative in order to get Bird on the floor again, and he was going to have to do it on a deadline. Indiana State was headed to Lawrence, Kansas, the following weekend to play the winner of Virginia Tech vs. Jacksonville in historic Allen Fieldhouse.

In the meantime, Hodges and Bird were getting on a plane and traveling in the other direction. The morning after winning the Valley conference tournament, the head coach and his star player flew down to Atlanta so that Bird could accept the James Naismith Trophy—the award given to the best college basketball player in the country.

Hodges was not excited about the media scrutiny that he and Bird were about to face in the NCAA tournament. By rule, Hodges was going to have to open the locker room 10 minutes after each game, win or lose, and players were going to have talk to reporters, even Bird. It felt wrong to Hodges—"kinda like letting someone into your bedroom," he complained at the time—and he was inclined not to follow the rule. But at the Naismith awards ceremony in Atlanta, Hodges dropped his guard for a moment.

The luncheon crowd was warm and festive. Many high school basketball players were in the room to collect their own awards. Hodges joked about his own relative anonymity, saying that when it came time for people to vote for Coach of the Year, the ballots would say "Bob Hodges, Tom Hodges, Joe Hodges, the Coach Who Replaced Bob King, and Bird's Coach." Bird opened up a little, too. He confirmed the reports that his thumb was broken—big news—but vowed that it wouldn't stop him. "I know I can shoot," Bird said.

Then, since everyone was in a good mood, Bird decided to grant interviews to the small gathering of television and radio reporters at the luncheon and didn't bother to banish two writers from the local papers, as he normally would have. The two Atlanta writers stood in the scrum with everyone else and Bird answered everything, just like he had that winter in his NBC interview with Al McGuire. He said he liked the Celtics. "I like the organization and the way they do things." He reminded the reporters not to forget his teammates. "We are not a one-man team," he said. He predicted that Indiana State would go far in the tournament. "Right now, we don't think anybody can beat us." He didn't even blink when one of the two Atlanta writers asked him why he hadn't been talking to print reporters all year.

"You really want to know?" Bird replied.

He spit out a curse word insulting newspaper and magazine reporters in general—a word that the Atlanta newspapers declined to print. Then, more congenially, Bird added, "The writers around Terre Haute wouldn't leave me alone."

Bird's comments hit the wires, making headlines across the country, especially in Boston, where Celtics fans were looking for clues about whether he might sign with Red Auerbach. But by the time Bird landed in Kansas that weekend, with the most notable broken thumb in the country, he had gone dark again.

It didn't matter that the Valley conference commissioner was there in Lawrence to remind Bird of the rules; that reporters would be in the locker room; that this was show biz, to quote Digger Phelps, this was entertainment; and that he was expected to talk this time.

Bird wasn't having it.

It was the scenario that NBA general managers, reporters like David Israel, and sports information intern Craig McKee had been discussing—or worrying about—for weeks. What would Bird do now that he was forced to speak? No one knew. But Hodges had more pressing concerns. He was thinking about their first NCAA tournament opponent, the game, and the stakes.

Landini had canceled classes that Friday, so that people could drive over to Lawrence or stand in line for a chance at earning a seat on a bus. Some people waited in the queue for 12 hours. Eleven buses, packed full of fans wearing powder blue, headed west in a caravan. Thousands more went by car. Bob Heaton's girlfriend, Jane Ann, was among them, driving over with Heaton's parents. Interstate 70 turned into one big rolling party, and Allen Fieldhouse that weekend took on a similar feel. Almost everyone in the building was there for Indiana State.

But the Sycamores' opponent was ready. The Virginia Tech Gobblers had played a first-round game and won while Indiana State sat at home on a bye. Terry Thimlar had scouted them and reported to Hodges that the Gobblers were not to be taken lightly. They had athleticism inside and shooting ability outside. They would be coming into the game relaxed, having already secured a successful season by winning their first-round matchup, and no one knew how effective Bird would be with his busted thumb. Doc Behnke wasn't even sure how Bird was practicing.

Behnke had crafted a modified splint out of foam and rubber and then taped it around the top of the thumb to give Bird the ability to move the digit and feel the ball. But even with the padding, Bird wasn't supposed to bend his thumb. That sort of movement could exacerbate the fracture, Behnke said. Any movement could set Bird back. And the makeshift splint didn't do anything to stop the pain. Bird cringed in practice anytime he touched the ball. Miley wondered how his friend would play against real contact. Reed was worried, too. In the moments before they left the locker room that Sunday afternoon to play their first NCAA tournament game, Reed checked in with Bird to see if he wanted him to pass the ball to him differently—to his right side, say, or his right hand only. But Bird just shook him off. No, he said. He didn't want Reed changing anything.

They headed out onto the floor at Allen. Fifteen thousand fans stood up and cheered. NBC fired up its national feed, putting Indiana State in living rooms across the country yet again. Billy Packer sat courtside—there was no hiding the Sycamores' critic this time—and Virginia Tech made it clear right away that it wasn't afraid. The Gobblers went right at Larry Bird, who was struggling.

Packer pointed out the problems again and again. Bird didn't want to dribble with his left hand. Sometimes, he didn't even want to touch the ball with that hand. When he did, he'd hold his thumb away from the ball, cradling it with just four fingers on that side. The Gobblers took an 18–14 lead about midway through the first half, and Alex Gilbert knew the Sycamores were in trouble when a Virginia Tech player did something that opponents rarely did that season: He started talking trash.

Gilbert had been living in a haze since the death of his brother, Lindell, back in November. He was also drinking too much, trying to make the pain go away. Later, he'd remember almost nothing about this season—it was like it never happened. But the game against Virginia Tech was different, because Gilbert had dreamed of this. He had longed to play in Allen Fieldhouse in Kansas, and he had shared that dream with Lindell.

Now Gilbert was out there. And with Bird hobbled, it was Gilbert who was about to change the course of the game. Reed and Staley hit back-to-back shots to even the score, 18–18. Then, after a defensive stop,

Staley fired up another shot, but this time he missed. The ball caromed hard off the back of the rim, bouncing high into the air. Virginia Tech failed to box out and Gilbert took advantage of the mistake. He moved unfettered into the lane, grabbed the rebound, palmed the ball with his left hand, and slammed it home in one smooth, violent motion.

The dunk only counted for two points, of course. But the play felt much bigger and the rout was now on. Over the next few minutes, the Sycamores reeled off 14 unanswered points. Bird threw dazzling passes to Reed and Nicks that led to buckets, and he made three plays in a row that had Billy Packer screaming into his microphone.

On the first of those plays, Bird had the ball in the right corner. He head-faked to get his defender in the air and then moved around him for an open jumper. But instead of taking the shot—the play that Virginia Tech expected—he fired a dart to Miley, who was standing beneath the basket, and Miley scored an easy two. Next, Bird stole the ball with his right hand—no left hand necessary. Then, at the other end of the floor, he made a play that perhaps only a few other people in the country could have executed. He hit Nicks with a no-look pass as Nicks ran through the lane at speed. The ball had to get around four Virginia Tech defenders to reach Nicks—there was no chance—and yet Bird's pass still found him.

Nicks scored at the rim as Virginia Tech fouled him, and Bird couldn't help himself.

He smiled.

51

INDIANA STATE WENT ON to beat Virginia Tech by 17—with five players scoring in double digits—and reporters flooded into the Sycamore locker room afterward with assurances from the Valley conference commissioner that, yes, Bird would talk about everything: his thumb, his teammates, the win, those passes, and Carl Nicks's great game. Nicks had scored 22, saving the Sycamores in their hour of need. If nothing else, Bird could have just talked about Nicks all evening and the reporters would have returned to their typewriters happy.

But Bird couldn't do it, policy be damned. For the longest time, he wouldn't even look at the reporters who had gathered at his locker. They finally started directing questions at the top of his head while he sat there, ignoring them. At that point, Bird got up and walked away.

"I don't talk to reporters," he said. "You know that, too."

"I didn't know that," one reporter replied. "I've never talked to you."

"Well," Bird said, "you know it now."

Indiana State was 30–0 and headed to Cincinnati in a few days for the next round of the tournament. Two more wins, and they'd be in the Final Four. But the story—the great underdog story of Indiana State—had been swamped at this point by Bird's silence. Once just Ed McKee's problem, it was now swallowing the whole team. Bird's stubborn refusal to talk had become the headline. Some reporters wrote more words about Bird's dealings with the media than they did about the Sycamores' miraculous season itself. They wanted Bird to be like Magic, who was laughing with sportswriters as Michigan State advanced that weekend, too, moving on to play in Indianapolis. And Bird's attitude in the locker room that Sunday evening, picking fights with the media in Kansas, wasn't going to solve the problem. The next morning, Bird was scheduled to appear on an even bigger stage, in downtown Chicago. He was headed to the annual Associated Press awards.

The AP awards were more prestigious than the Naismith Trophy that Bird had picked up the previous week in Atlanta, and Indiana State was about to dominate them in Chicago.

Hodges was going to collect the AP's Coach of the Year honors, having bested Digger Phelps in the balloting—enough voters must have gotten his name right. Bird was going to pick up the Player of the Year trophy, having won easily in a field of all-time great players. He had earned 328 votes compared to Sidney Moncrief's 17 and Magic's 9. He arrived in Chicago that morning with a large entourage to support him. In addition to Hodges, Landini was there, too. The three men landed on the lakefront in a little blue plane. They stepped out onto the tarmac that Bird had last visited on his trip to Chicago for the *Sports Illustrated* photo shoot in 1977. They met a handful of Terre Haute benefactors in the terminal and then they drove downtown together for the ceremony.

Landini, by this point, knew a few things about Bird. "He's no Oxford don, that's for sure," he said that spring. If Bird spoke, Landini knew to expect grammatical errors—or, as only Landini could describe them, "gross indiscretions in the agreement of his subjects and verbs." The university president had also come to expect a good bit of what Landini called "southern Indiana colloquialisms"—vulgarities and slang. And at the dais that morning in Chicago, Landini got all of that out of Bird. But at least, this time, he was speaking.

Stepping up to accept his award, Bird looked out on the crowd and asked if David Israel was there. He wanted to know if the *Chicago Tribune* columnist who had penned that negative column about him about two weeks earlier had come to see him collect this trophy. Israel had not—he was covering spring training that week down in Florida—and Bird used the opportunity to insult Israel with yet another curse word that the newspapers declined to print.

But Landini knew something else about Bird. Behind his silence, there was sincerity, and beneath the vulgarities, there was depth. For the rest of that morning, Bird stood in front of the crowd and revealed those parts of himself, too—at least a little. He thanked his teammates in an earnest and humble way; he praised the other players who could have won the AP award; he mentioned Sidney Moncrief by name; and he explained for the second time why he had spent the year freezing out the press. Bird said that he had been burned in the past by reporters. He said that reporters had hurt his family, and he hoped that by not talking, his teammates might get more attention. "If I sit out the press conferences," he said, "the writers will talk with the other players, and that helps them."

That it wasn't exactly working out this way didn't get addressed in Chicago. But Bird went into detail on almost every other matter. He said he wasn't thinking about next year at all, but if he did end up in Boston, he was willing to play any role that Auerbach wanted. "If I have to," he said, "I'll average two points a game to win." He said he understood why people were calling him the Great White Hope, and he also understood that this title put a target on his back with every Black player in the league. "I hope I can hold myself up with them," Bird said. "I know they're waiting for me." He revealed that his injured thumb was indeed affecting his performance. "It still hurts," he said. "Every time I get the thing hit, it hurts for five minutes." And he made it clear that the pain didn't matter to him. He might not practice that week, he said, but he would be on the floor for the Sycamores' next game, on Thursday night in Cincinnati, against an old friend, Dave Bliss, and his new team, the Oklahoma Sooners.

"I'll play," Bird promised.

52

LANDINI WAS THRILLED BY the appearance in Chicago. Bird hadn't been polished. There had been the usual "southern Indiana colloquialisms." And yes, there had been that opening insult to David Israel.

But Bird had also exhibited grace—"a great deal of grace," Landini thought. He had deftly handled the question of his whiteness in a way that Landini found sophisticated, and he had proven, above all, that he could talk to anyone. Bird could handle himself in a spotlight, if he wanted to. And everyone believed that the Sycamores were going to be able to handle the Oklahoma Sooners that Thursday night, back on NBC. Even Dave Bliss seemed to know it.

Bliss had long ago left Bobby Knight's side in Bloomington to become his own man: the head coach in Oklahoma. And in his fourth season there, Bliss had finally built a championship-caliber team, made possible by his recruitment of three Indiana high school stars. Whenever possible, Bliss was still out there on the road, with his chewing gum on the passenger seat, recruiting in the place he knew best. But that week in Cincinnati, reporters didn't want to talk to Bliss about the program he had built; they wanted to talk about Bird. And Bliss happily retold the whole Larry Bird saga: how he had been one of the first people to recruit him; how he had attended his high school games at Springs Valley; how he had gone mushroom hunting with him in French Lick in an effort to build a relationship; and how he had known that Bird was going to be great because of his hands—"the greatest pair of hands in basketball today."

Oddsmakers in Las Vegas established Indiana State as a 5½-point favorite. Both CBS and NBC News prepared to air features on the team. Walter Cronkite—CBS's famed anchorman, dubbed "the most trusted man in America"—looked into the cameras that week and introduced a story on Larry Bird. The piece focused almost exclusively on his whiteness. CBS joined the chorus of people calling Bird "the Great White Hope." In the CBS story, Red Auerbach called him the "Great Hope—period." Millions of people tuned in, learning about Larry Bird for the first time, and thousands of fans flocked to Riverfront Coliseum in Cincinnati for the Thursday-night NCAA games—Louisville vs. Arkansas, followed by Oklahoma vs. Indiana State. Two first-team All-Americans, Moncrief and Bird, were going to be in the building. Almost 200 reporters were going to be there to cover them. Red Auerbach and front office executives from eight other NBA teams were going to be on hand to watch. The games would draw the largest crowds to ever attend a basketball game in the state of Ohio, more than 17,000 people.

Landini was planning to stay for the entire weekend. He reserved a block of rooms at a downtown luxury hotel, ordered $250 worth of food, made arrangements for open bars to be available to Indiana State boosters, and sent out invites for a slate of parties to be held all weekend in the hotel's Bronze Room and Grand Ballroom, because in Landini's mind, there was no way that Indiana State was losing to Oklahoma.

It was an all-time jinx; Landini was courting disaster. Who was coming to a Friday-night Indiana State social hour and a Saturday-afternoon bloody mary tip-off party if the Sycamores lost their first game on Thursday? But Landini knew what he was doing. He arrived at Riverfront Coliseum early on Thursday evening, enjoyed a cocktail in his suite before the games began, watched Arkansas beat Louisville as Sidney Moncrief scored 27, and then sat back as his Sycamores prepared to take the floor against Oklahoma.

"Buy your seeds!" Oklahoma students chanted, throwing birdseed at Indiana State fans as they walked inside the arena. "Feed the Bird!"

But the joke was on Oklahoma. The Sycamores blew out the Sooners by 21 points.

It was almost midnight by the time the game was over, and Hodges apparently didn't excite the media when he showed for the postgame press conference. He didn't say much about how he intended to stop Indiana State's next opponent, the Arkansas Razorbacks. Reporters complained about him on deadline, grousing in the press box, and they couldn't help but compare Hodges to the likable Marquette coach turned NBC broadcaster, Al McGuire.

"Heck," one reporter grumbled, "Al McGuire would have danced with us tonight—win, lose, or draw. Al would tell us a bunch of stuff about devising a new zone defense for Saturday's opponent, go back to his favorite watering hole, have a couple of Black Russians or whatever, and laugh at us."

The press wondered why Hodges wasn't more like that, why he wasn't more like McGuire. And one newspaper called him out for it. ISU'S HODGES CAN'T RELAX, *The Cincinnati Post* said in a headline the next day. The story went on to ask a simple question: "When is the last time Bill Hodges laughed?"

Hodges tried to pretend that the story didn't bother him, but it did. He couldn't let it go as he prepared for Arkansas—the toughest opponent that the Sycamores had faced all year. The Razorbacks had a speedy guard in U. S. Reed. They had a confident defensive specialist in Alan Zahn. They had two big men inside, including six-foot-ten freshman Scott Hastings and six-foot-eleven senior Steve Schall. They had a winning streak that dated back to January. And, of course, they had Moncrief. The Arkansas star had helped lead the Razorbacks to the Final Four in 1978. He was on the precipice of taking them back again now, and like Magic and Bird, Moncrief was the most celebrated person in his home state.

Down in Arkansas, a newly inaugurated governor by the name of Bill Clinton was about to declare a day in Moncrief's honor and summon him to Little Rock for a banquet to be broadcast on live TV, because, Clinton acknowledged, Moncrief was far more popular than he was. Now, in Cincinnati, Moncrief wanted one more chance to prove his worth to his state, his school, and his governor. He wanted to cover Larry Bird—a player six inches taller than him—in the Saturday-afternoon regional final.

Arkansas head coach Eddie Sutton debated the plan with his assistant coaches right up until game time, and he almost agreed to it, knowing that Moncrief's quickness and tenacity could disrupt almost anything Bird wanted to do. In the end, however, Sutton assigned Zahn to cover Bird, the conservative route. Hodges, on the other hand, decided to take a risk. He told the team that they would be unleashing a full-court press on the Razorbacks, but not until the second half. Hodges didn't want to give Sutton a chance to adjust to it. So, he was holding it back like a trump card, hoping his team could contain Moncrief until then.

It was difficult to stop Moncrief in any situation, but maybe especially in this one. In addition to Bird's broken thumb, Nicks was now sick, fighting off a sore throat and exhaustion. He felt weak before the game against Arkansas, and the team itself just felt different. On the short bus ride to the Coliseum, the players didn't talk, and they were quiet in the locker room, too. No one was bantering. No one was saying a word.

53

NBC EXECUTIVES COULDN'T WAIT for tip-off in Cincinnati.

In recent years, the college basketball games that determined the participants in the Final Four had always drawn a decent audience: about 17 million viewers in all. But the four games on this weekend—Indiana State vs. Arkansas, DePaul vs. UCLA, St. John's vs. Penn, and Michigan

State vs. Notre Dame—were poised to make history. A record 23 million people would tune in. When given the choice that weekend between watching NBA games or college, viewers would choose the college games in droves. The numbers weren't even close, and it all started with NBC's Saturday-afternoon telecast from Riverfront Coliseum.

A rising star at the network named Bryant Gumbel welcomed viewers watching at home. He teed up the weekend, the game, and an easy-to-digest story line for the next two hours—Moncrief vs. Bird. Jim Simpson and Billy Packer took over from there, sitting courtside, and in the first half, Arkansas nearly ran away with the game.

Bird traveled on the first possession and missed his first two shots. Zahn's defense was effective, and Moncrief showed why he was a first-team All-American and about to be a top pick in the 1979 NBA draft. Late in the half, Moncrief grabbed a rebound from another Bird miss and threw a 70-foot pass down the court, just as Bird often did. The ball hit Zahn as he ran toward the basket. He scored at the rim, putting Arkansas up by seven, and Hodges had a difficult decision to make: Was he really waiting until the second half to use his full-court press?

While Hodges pondered this question, Bird scored to cut the lead to five, and Staley made a play that changed the trajectory of the game. On the next trip down the floor, Zahn had a chance to score in the lane, but Staley planted his feet and stood his ground. Zahn barreled into him, picking up his third foul. Sutton had to pull him from the game, and with Zahn out in the final minutes of the first half, the Sycamores clawed their way back into the contest.

At halftime, they were only down two.

In the locker room, the guys weren't quiet anymore; they were excited about what was happening. They were hanging with Arkansas. They believed they could win. And with the tip-off of the second half, the game took on the feel of a barroom brawl.

Arkansas and Indiana State exchanged baskets. Moncrief and Bird matched each other up and down the court, and just a few minutes into the half, Bird helped tie the game. With the Sycamores trailing, 45–41, Reed passed it to Bird on the right side. Bird cut across the court into the lane, and the Razorback defense followed him. But Bird had no intention of shooting. Instead, with his injured left hand, he flicked the ball over his head to a wide-open Alex Gilbert. Bird couldn't see him, and it didn't matter. Gilbert scored. Then, on the Razorbacks' next possession, Bird punched the ball out of Scott Hastings's hands, dove on the floor to retrieve it before it skittered out of bounds, and threw it down the court—from his back. This time, Nicks missed the shot. But again, it didn't matter. Gilbert was there for the putback. The game was tied, 45–45. The crowd erupted. Jim Simpson and Billy Packer had to shout to be heard, and for the next 16 minutes, NBC found itself broadcasting one of the greatest college basketball games ever played.

If Moncrief scored, Bird answered. If Indiana State took the lead, Arkansas came roaring back. And when Hodges unleashed his secret plan—the full-court press, forcing the Razorbacks into turnovers—Eddie Sutton switched things up, too. He put Moncrief on Bird, covering one first-team All-American with another.

It was the opportunity that Moncrief had wanted that morning, and he did not squander it. Bird, who had scored 25 points up to that point in the game, would have just six the rest of the way. Moncrief was chasing him all over the floor and shutting him down with the help of Schall and Hastings. Both teams got buckets from unlikely players down the stretch. Nicks carried Indiana State in the final minutes as Moncrief stifled Bird, and then, with the game tied at 71–71 and 1:08 to go, Indiana State caught a break.

Arkansas had the ball and Sutton called a time-out to script the last 68 seconds of the game. "We're going to run it down," he told his team. "We're going to go for the one shot." But out of the time-out, U. S. Reed stepped on Nicks's foot as he was dribbling the ball on the left wing—an unlucky encounter that caused the Razorbacks' guard to tumble to the floor. The referees could have called tripping or maybe nothing. Instead, because he picked up the ball from his knees, they whistled him for traveling.

Arkansas had turned the ball over. Indiana State could now hold it for the final shot, and with 18 seconds to go, Hodges called his own time-out to talk it over.

In the huddle, he considered running a play that they had used many times before: a pick play that could free Bird up along the baseline. But Hodges was worried about the length of Schall and Hastings—both were taller than Bird—and was also worried that Bird wouldn't be able to break free from Moncrief. Sutton would surely have some sort of double-team scripted to stop Bird from winning this game. So, Hodges suggested a different play. He was sending the team's five best shooters out onto the floor: Bird, Nicks, Heaton, Staley, and Reed. And if the defense came to Bird, Bird was to reverse it to the other side.

Hodges wanted his best player to pass the ball, and Bird agreed.

"Be ready for the pass," he told his teammates.

Out of the time-out, things went as planned, to a point. Bird was double-teamed at first, with Moncrief squaring him up and Schall looming over his shoulder. And when Bird got the ball, he did as they had discussed in the huddle. He passed it to Heaton on the other side of the floor.

But now time was ticking down.

"Ten seconds to go," Simpson announced.

Heaton threw the ball to Nicks, who threw the ball to Reed.

"Seven seconds to go," Simpson said.

At that point, Reed had run out of both time and options. With Moncrief still covering Bird in the low post—and Schall still there, ready to help—Reed drove to the elbow of the lane, jumped into the air, and prepared to shoot.

On the bench, Hodges liked what Reed was about to do. Bird was in position for a rebound on the right post, and Staley was crashing in from the left. Even if Reed missed, Indiana State would have chances to gather the rebound, put it back up, and win the game. But once Reed left his feet, he saw the big body of Scott Hastings crashing down on him. Hastings was so close to swatting the ball away that later Hastings would swear that he could still feel the ball on his fingertips. The touch of it would linger for decades like a phantom pain. And upon seeing Hastings, Reed made a different choice—one that seemed wrong in the moment. Instead of shooting, he made an awkward bounce pass to Heaton in the lane.

Heaton was surprised to find himself with the ball. Like everyone else, he thought Reed was going to shoot, and he nearly fumbled the pass away as the Arkansas defense closed in around him. Zahn was there, and Schall was, too. Heaton was standing in a sea of red shirts. And with four seconds left, he did the only thing he could, amid the chaos and the defenders: Heaton jumped and sort of pushed the ball toward the hoop with one hand—his left hand.

Twelve years earlier, on a cold winter day in Cory, this hand had dangled off Bob Heaton's body, limp and useless, while his grandfather rushed to shut off the power to the corn hiker, while his mother laid him in the back of their station wagon, while his sister adjusted the broken limb to stop it from falling off his chest, and while young Bob described the pain to his mother. *It burns*, he had told his mother that day.

Now he felt nothing as the ball hit the rim, bounced around four times, and finally settled into the net at the buzzer—*good*.

Fans stormed the floor. Players nearly tackled Bird in the celebration. Gilbert began to cry, thinking of his late brother. And amid the madness, Bob Heaton just smiled.

"It's a miracle, I guess," he said.

Another one. Indiana State was 32–0 and headed to the Final Four in Salt Lake City.

54

HODGES HAD STASHED A bottle of champagne on the bus, Nemcek said, just in case Indiana State won. But he never got the chance to drink it.

By the time Hodges left Riverfront Coliseum, Bird, Nemcek, Tex Ritter, and others had popped the cork, passed the bottle around, finished it off, and the party continued all the way home. The players wanted beer. The bus driver pulled over. A case was acquired en route to the airport, and a short time later, the guys boarded their little plane for Terre Haute with their pockets stuffed full of cold aluminum cans.

It was against NCAA protocol, but no one cared. It was Saturday night. The players had achieved something that no one in Terre Haute would have expected a few years earlier. They had earned this moment. Even the naysayer Billy Packer had to acknowledge that the Sycamores were great—"It's destiny with these guys," he marveled after Heaton's shot fell into the net to beat Arkansas—and the student body agreed. As the plane landed in Terre Haute that evening, the players stepped outside to find a massive crowd waiting for them on the tarmac. "It's kind of like a fever," the mayor of Terre Haute said. Everyone had caught it.

Callers overwhelmed the university switchboard as people phoned loved ones and friends to share the news: The Sycamores had won. Applications for enrollment were up 15 percent, as high school seniors took a fresh interest in attending college in Terre Haute. Alumni donations were up, too, Landini noted, and NBC, the network set to broadcast the Final Four, was all but cheering from the press box for Indiana State.

Billy Packer signed autographs for Sycamore fans after the game in Cincinnati and personalized some of the notes upon request, admitting he had been wrong. "I'm sorry," he scrawled. "ISU is #1." Jim Simpson flew home, still thinking about what he had just seen, and fired off a note to Ed McKee thanking Indiana State as a whole, and the players specifically, for "the thrills and excitement." "I just want them—and you—to know," Simpson wrote, "that even 'veteran' broadcasters get a big kick out of this kind of sports 'happening.'" Al McGuire finalized a deal with Max Gibson's Larry Bird Committee to be the keynote speaker at the big Terre Haute celebration in April. For McGuire's agreed-upon fee of $2,000—"I don't do anything for nothing," he said—the popular color commentator was happy to return to Terre Haute for the party and sing the praises of Larry Bird. And McGuire's bosses were overjoyed at the possibility that Bird might face Magic in the nationally televised championship game the following Monday night.

In the other regional final games that weekend, DePaul, a private Catholic school in Chicago led by longtime head coach Ray Meyer, had upset perennial power UCLA. Penn had toppled St. John's to become the first Ivy League school to make it to the Final Four since 1944, when there were only eight teams in the tournament, and Michigan State had dismantled Notre Dame, thanks in part to Magic Johnson's mastery running the point, Greg Kelser's dominance inside, and the shrewd coaching of Jud Heathcote.

In preparation for the game, Heathcote had noticed that Digger Phelps didn't keep a defender in the backcourt on the opening tip, so Heathcote drew up a play to take advantage of Digger's aggression from the start. He wanted Kelser to outjump Notre Dame's forward, Orlando Woolridge, on the tip-off and bat the ball forward to Magic. Magic would then tip the ball to Mike Brkovich, who was supposed to release to the basket from the moment that Kelser left his feet. The Spartans were so intent on running the play that they practiced it in the days before the Notre Dame game. And Magic told Brkovich that he didn't just want him to score; he wanted Brkovich to dunk the ball—send a message.

It was just one play, but it was symbolic. When the Spartans executed it to perfection in the opening seconds of the game—Kelser-to-Magic-to-Brkovich-*slam*—Digger Phelps knew his team was in trouble.

"Not ready," Digger said afterward.

Michigan State won by 12, as Magic and Kelser combined for 53 points. The game drew a television audience about five times larger than the NBA programming on CBS that same afternoon, and by Sunday night, when the team arrived back in East Lansing, they were favorites to win it all—much to Heathcote's frustration. "We're unbeatable," he snarled, sarcastically.

Oddsmakers installed the Spartans as an eight-point favorite to defeat Penn the following weekend and reach the championship game, and the line quickly grew to 10 as money poured in on Michigan State. Everyone was backing Magic now, even Al McGuire. He joined Packer in picking the Spartans to win it all, and Magic was seemingly so confident about beating Penn and advancing to the final game that he was already talking to the press about what it would be like to play Larry Bird. "I'd love to play Larry," he said, not backing down from the question when a reporter brought it up the day after the Notre Dame victory. "That would mean we'd be in the championship . . . and I love challenges."

It was the breaking point for Heathcote. Within hours of Magic's quote appearing in the *Detroit Free Press* on Tuesday morning, he closed his practices, kicked out reporters, barred the autograph seekers that had started hounding his team—200 or 300 people at a time—and couldn't wait to leave for Salt Lake City the next day, one day earlier than all the other teams.

But Magic wasn't wrong to be talking about the potential history that could be made if he and Bird managed to make it to the finals together. Network executives were talking about it, too. "We should go over the top," one NBC official said that week, "if Indiana State is in the championship game." And across town at CBS, Kevin O'Malley, the young vice president who liked to analyze the ratings every week, understood why his counterparts at NBC would feel that way. The Sycamores didn't just have the best player in the country, O'Malley said. Their team was undefeated. Their games were filled with miracles and they were giving people a story that was both familiar and new all at once.

It was Cinderella, O'Malley said. Cinderella in middle America.

On Tuesday evening that week—the same night that Heathcote closed his practice in East Lansing to reporters and autograph seekers—the president of NBC Sports sent Landini a telegram, cordially inviting him to join network honchos at a gala that Saturday night in Salt Lake City. Powerful men would be gathering over drinks in the Grand Ballroom at the Hotel Utah, a stately 10-story hotel across the street from the famous Mormon temple in the heart of the city. The location was convenient for Landini—Indiana

State was staying at the same hotel—and it was the kind of party that Landini loved. He could put his vocabulary on display at a place like the Hotel Utah. But by that Tuesday, Landini was having trouble thinking about the weekend. He was awash with requests for tickets, demands on his time, and questions about how Indiana State was even getting to Utah.

Everyone wanted to fly west for the game: Bob King and his entire family; Larry's mother and his brothers; Larry's high school coach, Jim Jones; Bob Heaton's girlfriend, Jane Ann, and his parents, Forrest and Betty; Carl Nicks's parents, the Reverend O. C. Nicks and his wife, Carolyn; Max Gibson and Greg Gibson; Lu Meis; and every other local benefactor. The list went on forever. But Landini didn't even have a plane for the marching band, the cheerleaders, the university dance troupe, the Sparkettes, the student government leaders, or the student body at large—a source of frustration on campus and in town. Cheerleaders stopped by Landini's office unannounced that week to plead their case in person, and people called to say they were willing to donate money to get the students to Salt Lake: one dollar, five dollars, ten dollars, and five hundred dollars. Even retirees, living on Social Security checks, called Landini, offering to help.

Landini conceded that money was a concern; it was going to cost the university about $25,000 just to get the band and the Sparkettes to Salt Lake. But the real problem was transportation: It simply didn't exist. Commercial flights were already booked and charters spoken for, leaving Landini with just two planes at his disposal—a DC-10 out of Chicago and a Piedmont charter jet out of Terre Haute with seats for just 93 people. Landini didn't have enough room for everyone who wanted to go to Utah. And Hodges didn't seem to have the patience for what the press continued to crave: full and intimate access to Larry Bird, his locker room, and him.

After beating Arkansas, Hodges had blasted *The Cincinnati Post* for its story criticizing him for not smiling, not being as fun as Al McGuire, not hanging out at the bars, and not drinking Black Russians and regaling everybody with stories. "Don't expect me to be somebody I'm not," Hodges said. "I don't drink Black Russians . . . I drink Tab." Now every reporter who had ever crossed the team and wronged Larry Bird—including Mike Madden of *The Boston Globe*, Bruce Newman and Larry Keith of *Sports Illustrated*, and David Israel of the *Chicago Tribune*—was going to be waiting for the Sycamores in Salt Lake City. And NCAA officials had announced that Larry Bird wasn't going to be allowed to dodge them, as he had in the early rounds of the tournament. Bird's participation at press conferences was considered mandatory, and reporters in attendance were going to have lots of questions about Bird's future, his feelings, and his thumb.

In the celebration on the floor in Cincinnati, a fan had inadvertently grabbed and twisted the broken digit, exacerbating the injury. By Bird's own admission, he wasn't himself that week. "I'm missing a lot of shots that I usually don't miss," he said, "because I can't grip the ball right."

Hodges hated the idea that the Sycamores might lose because of Bird's thumb, an injury, bad luck. But there was no time left for fears, requests, demands, or questions. On Thursday morning, Hodges reported to the Hulman Center with his wife, Connie. The team gathered around them in their powder-blue sweatsuits and cowboy hats. They all boarded a convoy of buses headed to the airport. The buses joined a parade that stretched all the way to the river, and then this parade, led by those buses, eased down Wabash Avenue, pushing through a sea of people.

No one in Terre Haute was working that day. They were hanging out their windows, sitting on the hoods of their moving Camaros in the parade, running next to the team buses, honking their horns, holding up signs, or standing beneath marquees that had been changed overnight to wish the team well.

THIS IS BIRD COUNTRY, said the sign at the pizzeria.

WE ARE PROUD OF YOU, said the sign at the liquor store.

Then, at the Baptist church, there was this one:

GOD IS IMPARTIAL, said the sign. WE AREN'T. GO SYCAMORES.

In the hours ahead, the players laughed and joked inside the Piedmont charter plane. At one point, the pilots would even let them take over the public address system, and the guys would take turns rallying the passengers with silly comments and cheers. But on takeoff, the people were quiet, Hodges perhaps most of all. He believed in fate; he said so that week. Now, win or lose, one thing was clear: Bill Hodges was flying straight into it.

55

RAY MEYER HAD BEEN coaching the DePaul Blue Demons since 1942. He took the job five months after the Japanese bombed Pearl Harbor. He had 564 more wins to his credit than Bill Hodges. He had written a book about how to coach basketball while Hodges was still driving Hugh Thimlar's bus at the junior college down in Fort Myers. He had friends in the media. He had the support of his fellow coaches. He had the entire city of Chicago behind him. In a lot of ways, Ray Meyer *was* Chicago, gritty and good-natured with a toothy smile. And perhaps most importantly, Meyer had a star player of his own: freshman phenom Mark Aguirre.

Aguirre was, in Meyer's estimation, "the most heralded recruit in DePaul history." He was built like a cinder-block wall at six foot six and anywhere between 225 and 250 pounds, depending on the last time he had eaten his mother's cooking. But Aguirre still had speed and he could shoot. He had honed this shot as a child on the West Side of Chicago, playing on a hoop nailed into a telephone pole in an alleyway, and in his senior year of high school, he used his rare combination of size, talent, determination, and experience to make himself the best player in the state of Illinois. Aguirre averaged 33 points and 16 rebounds a game. He dominated the city's Public League, the tough courts where Carl Nicks had once played, and he had opportunities to get paid to play college basketball—a sign of the changing times.

According to Aguirre, one coach offered him $5,000 and a new car; another offered $10,000 and a trip to Hawaii; a third offered up college basketball's new full ride—clothes, money, and a wink-and-a-nod agreement that Aguirre wasn't really going to be taking classes. Several also tried to woo Aguirre by trying to buy his high school coach, mentor, and friend, Frank Lollino. The West Chicago man said he could have escaped the hardscrabble streets of the city, vacationed in the tropics, sailed on a yacht, and become a college coach—if he delivered Aguirre.

Such tactics would succeed in the years to come with many other high school players and coaches, money moving under the table and deals signed in the dark. But it didn't work with Aguirre and Lollino. Aguirre had been raised by his mother and his grandmother, God-fearing, churchgoing women intent on teaching Mark how to do the right thing. Aguirre didn't like the coaches who tried to purchase his loyalty—"They absolutely turned me off," he said at the time—and he did like Ray Meyer's son Joey, a DePaul assistant, who kept coming around.

In meetings inside Lollino's house, with Joey at first and then Ray, Aguirre came to believe that he had a lot in common with DePaul's head coach. Meyer was old and white, while Aguirre was young and Black; they were different people from different worlds and different times—all different. But they were both from Chicago. That meant something in the 1970s, and Aguirre knew instinctively that he could trust Meyer. "He never, ever lied to me," Aguirre said decades later. "On every occasion, he gave me the straight and narrow."

Sometimes that first season, the straight and narrow hurt. In just his fourth collegiate game, Aguirre scored 28 points as DePaul crushed a weaker opponent. But Meyer was upset that his star freshman had missed 11 shots on the night—too many. He worked him so hard in practice that month that Aguirre vomited. Meyer put him on a diet to help control his weight. He restricted him from going home so that Mark wouldn't eat his mother's barbecue ribs—Mark's favorite—and doled out real punishments, too. In January, after Aguirre missed the team bus for a trip to Kalamazoo, forcing Joey to drive him separately, Meyer benched Aguirre for the first six minutes of that night's game against Western Michigan—a consequence that cost them all. The Blue Demons lost the game by two.

But Aguirre understood what was happening: Meyer cared about him. "A kid like this," Meyer said that winter, "he's *gotta* work harder." That work ultimately turned into wins—22 of them in the regular season. The Blue Demons rolled through their bracket during the NCAA tournament, upsetting UCLA just a couple of hours after Bob Heaton's miracle shot in Cincinnati, and Al McGuire nearly wept with joy during his postgame interview with Ray Meyer on the floor.

"How do you feel, Ray?" McGuire asked him.

"I feel great," Meyer said. "I feel like I was born again."

"You *are* born again," McGuire said.

Chicago's beloved coach was headed to the Final Four—"I'm a young coach today," he cried—and he quickly devised a plan to slow down Larry Bird. He was going to cover Bird with Aguirre's teammate Curtis Watkins, a six-foot-six senior known for his quickness. He was going to let Bird get his points and hope to bottle up everyone else with the help of his defensive-minded guard, Gary Garland.

No matter what happened that weekend, Garland was about to be eclipsed in fame by his half-sister, a singer named Whitney Houston. But at the moment, Garland was full of confidence, and Meyer was, too. The old coach happily discussed his game strategies with everyone that week: the reporters he knew well, the reporters he didn't know at all, and David Israel. In fact, Israel knew almost everything that Meyer was thinking by the time they got to Salt Lake. Because, in addition to writing his usual columns that week, Israel was ghostwriting "Ray Meyer's Tourney Diary," a daily feature in the *Chicago Tribune*, written in Meyer's voice and penned exclusively by Israel. The man who had written that negative column about Hodges and Bird was *inside* Meyer's head.

Hodges, however, wasn't worried about what Meyer was thinking. In his opinion, DePaul had no depth and no bench. In the Demons' win against UCLA the previous weekend, their five starters had played every minute of the game but two. And Watkins—the man who was supposed to cover Bird—was entering the weekend hobbled with his own injury. He had hurt his knee with 1:33 left against UCLA when Aguirre's thick body fell into his leg as Aguirre tried to take a charge. It wasn't clear how effective Watkins was going to be, and unlike the previous weekend in Cincinnati, the Sycamore players were relaxed from the moment they landed in Salt Lake City and checked into the Hotel Utah downtown.

When Rich Nemcek and Tex Ritter ran into Red Auerbach in the lobby of the grand hotel, and Auerbach asked Nemcek to inform Bird that he was there, Nemcek smiled and told the Celtics legend that he could tell him himself—a line that felt good as it rolled off his lips. In Nemcek's memory, Auerbach was terse, abrasive, and entitled in their brief interaction in the lobby, and Nemcek wasn't having any of it.

"I'm not going pro," he remarked. "It doesn't matter what I say to him, anyway."

When the guys saw Billy Packer on the floor at their four o'clock shootaround that Friday afternoon, they all conspired to lob their basketballs at him at the same time just before they walked off the court—a joke that Packer seemed to appreciate. "I sure hope you shoot better than that during the game," Packer laughed.

Then, when Bird had to speak to the media after the shootaround, by NCAA rule and mandate, half the team went with him: Nicks, Gilbert, Reed, Miley, Heaton, Staley, and Nemcek.

They were in it together, even if all the questions were for Bird.

56

PENN NEVER HAD A chance the following afternoon against Michigan State. The Ivy Leaguers couldn't penetrate Jud Heathcote's matchup zone. They shot 17 percent from the floor in the first half. They failed to score for almost nine minutes. They fell behind 32-6 and lost by almost 40 in the end. Heathcote had hardly broken a sweat by the time he took his courtside seat to scout the second game, Indiana State vs. DePaul, and the Michigan State fans had long ago turned their attention to that game, too.

"We want Bird!" they began to chant late in the first half of the Penn blowout.

"We want Bird!"

"We want Bird!"

For a long time that day, it looked like they would get him. Watkins, with his left knee wrapped tight, couldn't stay with Bird. He picked up his fourth foul early in the second half, just trying to cover him. And when Bird drained a 23-footer moments later—staking the Sycamores to their biggest lead of the night, 55–46—Ray Meyer didn't appear to be a young coach anymore. He looked like what he was: a 65-year-old relic trying to stop one of the greatest college basketball players of all time. Bird felt so good, he was almost begging for the ball.

But over the course of the next 12 minutes, DePaul chipped away, with the sort of team effort that the Demons had been giving all year. Every starter contributed, and with five minutes left on the clock, the game flipped on its axis. Nicks missed a deep shot. Aguirre hit his second basket in a row over Miley. Bird committed a turnover in the backcourt—one of 11 he made that day, possibly because of his wounded thumb. Gary Garland made him pay for it, burying a 12-footer to give the Demons their first lead of the second half, and on the next possession, Bird missed a shot in the lane and failed to collect the rebound, giving Ray Meyer the ball again with a two-point lead and 4:33 to go.

At this point, Meyer wanted to hold the ball and kill clock, like Bob King used to do. But the DePaul players were exhausted; Meyer hadn't substituted once. The Demons turned the ball over with a bad pass that rolled off Watkins's foot. And for the next couple of minutes, the two teams battled for everything, building up to another epic finish. Heaton scored on a beautiful pass from Bird to tie the game. Garland hit one of two free throws to reclaim the lead for DePaul. Heaton scored again—this time on a dazzling feed from Nicks—and the Demons found themselves in a position that Ray Meyer would have taken any day: They had the ball, down one, 75–74, with 36 seconds to go and a chance to win it with one shot.

On that final possession, Garland got his chance early—right around the 20-second mark. He dribbled into the lane and was wide open, Meyer thought. Wide open to shoot over Steve Reed. But Garland passed it up. He dribbled back out to the point, and suddenly, it seemed, there was only one option: Aguirre on the right side, squared up to the basket with five seconds left to play.

Aguirre wanted the ball. He wasn't afraid of this moment. And when he turned to release his shot, eyeing the rim in Salt Lake the way he had once sized up the hoop nailed into that telephone pole in the alleyway on the West Side of Chicago, Aguirre liked the feel of the ball in his hands, the way it rolled off his fingertips, and how it arced toward the basket. He believed he had just taken the shot that would send his beloved coach, Ray Meyer, to the national championship game after 37 years of waiting. "Oh, goodness," Aguirre thought, as he released his shot. "That's good . . . that's good . . . that's *good*."

But Miley was on top of Aguirre, as he had been all day, and Nicks was streaking over to help. There was only a little daylight between the three of them, and there was, as it turned out, no way this shot was falling.

It was long. It bounced hard off the far end of the rim. Leroy Staley chased down the rebound and it was over.

Indiana State had escaped the Demons' clutches to remain undefeated at 33–0.

Meyer hugged his star freshman on the floor afterward, forgiving and fatherly, as Aguirre apologized to him again and again. "I just leaned on him," Aguirre recalled, "and said, 'Coach, I'm so sorry . . . Jeez, I'm so sorry.' I know I said I'm sorry probably a million times."

Neither man would ever make it back to the Final Four.

But NBC executives didn't mind, no apologies necessary, because they had the result they wanted and the game they needed in order to make history on Monday night.

Bird vs. Magic on national TV.

57

SALT LAKE CITY HAD disappointed Jud Heathcote in lots of ways. He wasn't fond of the team's hotel, a mid-century motor lodge on the north side of the city. The lodge was only about two blocks from the Hotel Utah, where Indiana State was staying and the NBC executives were hosting their parties, but it was a significant step down and quite possibly the worst place the Spartans had stayed in all year.

In his room, Heathcote's phone rang without end. He couldn't avoid distractions and he couldn't prevent Magic from talking anymore. Bound by the same NCAA rules as Bird, Magic was soon giving his interviews again, smiling and chatty and open. Heathcote also had to sit through one other indignity. At a special event arranged that weekend for the four colleges, the Mormon Tabernacle Choir sang the wrong fight song when it came time to celebrate Michigan State. The choir sang the University of Michigan fight song.

Heathcote knew he could be grumpy. He joked that week that, while Ray Meyer was headed to the Hall of Fame, Heathcote himself was probably headed to the Hall of *Fume*. But after Indiana State's victory over DePaul on Saturday, even Heathcote had to admit he was excited for the Monday-night showdown between Bird and Magic. The Spartans wanted the chance to end Indiana State's perfect season. Magic and Kelser wanted to test themselves against Larry Bird, and Heathcote, the master strategist, already had ideas on how they could stop him.

In his mind, Heathcote called it a "man-and-a-half" defense. One man would always be covering Bird in the Spartans' matchup zone, and if Bird decided to put the ball on the floor—if he tried to dribble—he'd get a man *and a half*, a fistful of Spartans. Someone would always be flashing over to disrupt him.

Bird didn't know it, but he was about to run into a defense that resembled the one that had stopped him at Rutgers in the NIT one year earlier, the defense that held him to 23 points and left him so frustrated that he bloodied that Rutgers student on the floor in the aftermath. And this time, it would be even more challenging for Bird to break free. The Spartans had length everywhere. They had three starters who were six foot seven or taller. They had two other players at six foot seven who could come in off the bench. Two of their tallest players were also All-Americans: Magic Johnson, first team, and Greg Kelser, third team. Kelser was the highest-scoring player in Michigan State history. And by Sunday morning, Heathcote had a plan for how to use one of his two All-Americans in the Spartans' shootaround that day. He was going to have Magic pretend to be Bird while the rest of the starters tried to stop him—a role that Heathcote believed would help the Spartans test their new man-and-a-half approach.

Just one thing worried Heathcote about his plan. Before the shootaround, he had to drive Magic and Kelser to a noon press conference at the Salt Lake Hilton that would be bigger than anything the two young men had ever seen before. About 200 reporters were going to be there, and every one of them, Heathcote said, was going to try to get them to say something negative—"something negative about Larry Bird."

Heathcote was concerned that Magic might take the bait and say the wrong thing. Meanwhile, about two blocks away, at the Hotel Utah, Bill Hodges had a different problem: He couldn't get Bird out of bed.

Bird's wakeup call came earlier than Magic's that morning. He was supposed to attend yet another awards ceremony—this time to accept the Eastman Award for the best college basketball player of the year—and Bird didn't feel like going.

He didn't care about this award, or any of the others, for that matter. In the weeks ahead, the various trophies and plaques that he collected sat inside his rented house on South 11th Street back in Terre Haute, like junk mail piled up on the kitchen counter. Bob Heaton marveled at how Bird didn't want to display them or even talk about them. And Bird definitely didn't care about the Eastman Award, an honor voted on by the coaches, if it meant getting up early the morning after the DePaul game. Hodges accepted it on his behalf, with apologies to the crowd. Reporters complained about Bird's absence, and Craig McKee found himself sitting in the lobby of the Hotel Utah around 11:30 that morning, anxious that Bird wouldn't appear for the next event on his schedule: the noon press conference at the Salt Lake Hilton with Magic, Kelser, and the 200 reporters. But Bird surprised McKee when he emerged from the elevator right on time, walking across the room in a T-shirt, jeans, and a powder-blue Adidas jacket, and McKee did the rest. He drove Bird across town to the Hilton in Bob King's rental car.

The drive was quiet, as usual, and McKee knew Bird well enough at this point not to fill the dead air with small talk. But in the car on the way to the Hilton, Bird did something unusual, McKee said. He broke the silence himself and started talking about something that neither of them had ever seen before: the snowcapped mountains rising above the city.

"I looked over, he says, 'Boy, this sure is a pretty town,' or as Larry would say, 'a purdy town,'" McKee recalled. "And I said, 'Yes, it is. The mountains are amazing.' And then it got quiet and I thought, *Good Lord, Larry, the places you'll see in just a few months, in the next years of your life, the cities you'll be in, the life you're going to live.*"

McKee couldn't imagine it, and he wasn't sure that Bird could, either. They pulled up at the Hilton; Bird walked inside and stood offstage for a bit, tall and awkward in his jeans. He barely spoke to Magic before the press conference began, acting like he had never met him before, and he waited around while Magic put on his usual performance, smiling in the spotlight.

"I'm loving this," Magic told the room full of reporters. "Every minute of it. I'm like a kid going to a birthday party. This is so exciting, the Final Four, getting all the attention, your name in the papers throughout the country."

What wasn't to love? Magic was about to compete for a championship on national television against Larry Bird. He was going to be leaving the press conference to go play the role of Bird at the Michigan State shootaround and he was enjoying this moment with Bird, right then.

"I'll probably dream about him tonight," Magic admitted.

It was an impossible act for Bird to follow. He wasn't Magic, not then and not later. He couldn't do what Magic had just done, and he didn't want to. But as Bird settled in to take his questions, he surprised Craig McKee for the second time that morning: He delivered the press conference of his life.

Bird talked about his choice to leave Indiana University. He admitted that Bobby Knight would have made him a better player. He conceded that there were certain things he couldn't handle—"like when I'm asked about my family"—and he took questions on everything else, displaying the deadpan humor that his teammates knew well, and doing it this time without insulting reporters like David Israel.

"How's your thumb?" one reporter asked.

"Broke," Bird said.

"For somebody who has avoided interviews, you seem to be enjoying yourself."

"That's wrong," Bird said.

Then, unlike past interviews, he cracked a smile, making it clear that he was just joking. Bird was excited for Monday night, too. He was just showing it in a different way.

Not everybody understood. In the next day's newspapers, big-city reporters from Chicago and New York called Bird "a low-rent slob" and a "hayseed," mocked him for the outfit he wore to the press conference, the T-shirt and jeans, criticized him for skipping the Sunday-morning awards ceremony, mentioned his father's suicide and Larry's divorce, even though he declined to discuss these topics, and questioned how his team could ever prevail over Michigan State, given the Spartans' superior height, size, talent, and depth.

This final point, Hodges admitted later, was a fair discussion. The matchups for his team were difficult across the board. Carl Nicks would typically cover the opponent's best guard, and Nicks desperately wanted the opportunity to cover Magic Johnson on Monday night. He believed that he could slow Magic, dogging him all over the floor in the same way he had dogged Moncrief a week earlier in Cincinnati. But Magic was almost seven inches taller than Nicks, and much bigger than Moncrief. So Hodges was leaning toward covering Magic with his best overall defender, Brad Miley—a choice that only raised other questions: If Miley was on Magic, who was covering Kelser? And did Miley have the footspeed to keep up with Magic anyway?

While Hodges went back and forth on the best approach, talking it over with Terry Thimlar and Mel Daniels, Jud Heathcote struggled to hold it together at the Michigan State shootaround that afternoon. Magic torched the Spartans' first team as he pretended to be Bird. Heathcote was soon yelling at them all—welcome back to the Hall of Fume. Assistant coach Fred Paulsen remembered going back to the team's motor lodge, asking himself a question: How would they ever cover Bird, if they couldn't cover Magic? And Heathcote had to admit that he didn't know the answer. "If we play like this tomorrow," he said, "we're going to get our asses kicked."

Night had now fallen in Salt Lake, darkness in the mountains, and no one could sleep—especially not the Indiana State players. As they tried to doze off in their rooms at the Hotel Utah, members of the Michigan State marching band were right outside their windows, drums banging and horns blaring in the dark. Hodges couldn't get them to stop, even after he went down to the front desk to complain. Hotel staffers couldn't help. They said they didn't know what to do. Nicks lay in bed, listening to the ruckus outside his windows, and the next night in the Sycamores' locker room, Bird seemed off before the game even started.

"I ain't feeling it," he said as he sat in the trainer's room.

The guys didn't understand what he meant, but they heard him right.

"I ain't feeling it."

58

IN FRENCH LICK THAT night, the streets were quiet. In West Baden, the boulevard was deserted. In Terre Haute, not a single car made its way down Wabash Avenue, and on campus at Indiana State, students were hard to find even five hours before tip-off. They had holed up in their dorms, in the fraternities, at the pizzeria, or at the Ballyhoo Tavern to make sure they had a seat to watch the game on NBC. They were not alone.

In Cleveland, on the road to play the Cavaliers, Jeff Judkins and other members of the Boston Celtics were watching, piled into a hotel room together. In Florida, Kevin O'Malley and other CBS executives were watching, sitting in a villa near a golf course. In New Mexico, Greg Webb and his roommate, Robert Gunn, were watching, wondering what might have been if the Aggies had beaten the Sycamores that year or if Bob Heaton's miracle shot hadn't fallen in early February. In Lansing, city councillors wanted to make sure they were watching. They moved their Monday-night meeting an hour ahead so that everyone could get home for the game. In Salt Lake City, fans arrived early at the arena to take their seats, including one of the most famous fans of them all. UCLA's former coach John Wooden was there, sitting next to Rich Nemcek's father. And across America, people made similar choices until NBC reached a milestone. Fifty million people tuned in that night for the NCAA championship—the biggest audience ever assembled for an American basketball game. Whether Bird was ready or not, "feeling it" or not, he knew what this was: the most important game he'd ever played.

It started badly for the Sycamores. On the Spartans' third possession of the night, Magic Johnson did something that no one had done to Indiana State that entire year. He grabbed a rebound off the defensive glass, ran it the length of the court, scored in transition in the lane, got fouled in the process, and then completed the three-point play as he sank his free throw.

Michigan State was only up 5–2, but already it felt like more. Magic was punching the air, fired up. Bird could hardly move on the offensive end, as Heathcote's man-and-a-half defense erected walls that he could not get around. Bird found himself boxed, sandwiched, pressured, and pressed. Steve Reed and Carl Nicks were going to have to start scoring to give Michigan State a reason to abandon Bird, but Reed and Nicks didn't score much early on, and over the next several minutes, the Spartans nearly buried Indiana State as they had Penn two days earlier. The Sycamores fell behind by 8 points, then 11, then 12. The only thing keeping them in the game, it seemed, was the Spartans' inability to stay out of foul trouble. Magic spent the last five minutes of the half on the bench, with three fouls, and Kelser picked up his third just seconds before the intermission, when Bird made a savvy play, forcing Kelser to run into him.

In the locker room at halftime, with Indiana State trailing, 37–28, Nicks believed it was time for a radical adjustment. At a minimum, he still wanted that chance to guard Magic. He wanted to hound Johnson, Nicks said, especially now that he had three fouls. But Hodges wasn't inclined to change the plan. The Sycamores were 33–0 and had trailed at halftime before, including just nine days earlier, against Arkansas. There was no need to panic, in his opinion—until there was. Out of the break, the Spartans scored the first seven points of the second half to go up by 16, and suddenly, it felt like the Sycamores couldn't do anything right.

The referees called fouls on Miley and Nicks that didn't seem to exist, putting the Spartans on the line again and again. When the Sycamores made it to the line themselves, they missed their foul shots, often badly. And just when it looked like they had a chance—down by only seven points, with five minutes to play—Bob Heaton ran out of miracles. As Magic drove into the lane, Heaton moved in to take a charge and appeared to have his feet set. But referees whistled Heaton for a foul—and not just any foul. They ruled that he had cut Magic's legs out from underneath him. A flagrant foul. Not only had Magic thrown down his dunk and knocked Heaton to the floor, he was going to the line for two shots. Magic's dunk became a four-point play, as Magic made both his free throws, and for once, both Billy Packer and Al McGuire were in agreement: The call felt wrong.

Maybe it wouldn't have mattered, either way. Bird made his next shot, but he missed his next three. Nicks fouled out. Heaton threw up an airball late in the game. Gilbert failed to hit a free throw all night. Staley recorded just four points. Miley went scoreless, and by the time Reed starting hitting shots, Greg Kelser was streaking down the court for a breakaway dunk to end the game.

It was never really close. Michigan State won, 75–64.

59

AFTER THE BUZZER SOUNDED, it took Magic all of 30 seconds to find the cameras. An official walked him over to NBC's Bryant Gumbel. Magic threw an arm around Gumbel like they were old friends from the neighborhood in Lansing, and as Magic prepared to give his postgame interview on national television, still hugging Gumbel, Bird tried to disappear.

Forced to stay on the floor for a ceremony in which each player would receive an engraved NCAA watch, Bird sought refuge on the bench. Rick Shaw and Terry Thimlar stood in front of him to hold NBC's cameras at bay. Bird began to cry, and when he did, Shaw protected him one last time. He covered Bird's head with a towel to conceal Bird's sobbing.

"Get your head up, man," Gilbert said, trying to console him.

Bird didn't react.

"You got nothing to be ashamed of, Larry Bird," Gilbert said, prodding him, almost desperate. "*Please* get your head up."

Still, Bird wouldn't show his face, wouldn't talk, wouldn't stand. In the moment, it felt like he was just upset about losing, like they all were. But as the guys grew older—and then old, suffering life's losses along the way—they began to realize just how much Bird had been carrying in those years: the burden of expectations, the trauma of losing his father, the pressure of the spotlight, and the questions about all of it.

Now on the bench, it seemed, Bird was letting it all go, crying beneath that towel.

They collected their watches after a while and headed to the locker room, and reporters waited around to get their interviews with Bird, per NCAA rules. But Bird wasn't talking. For the longest time, he wouldn't even leave the trainer's room, forcing Ed McKee to scramble yet again. Forty minutes after the game ended, McKee emerged from the locker room, looking stressed and tired, handing out some quotes on mimeographed paper that reporters could attribute to Bird, if they wanted. It was the best that he and Hodges could do.

They were 33–1.

That night, back at the Hotel Utah, everyone scattered. Heaton had dinner with his parents and his girlfriend, Jane Ann. Reed went out with his parents, too. Miley and Nicks had a few drinks. Gilbert went out hard, staying out till dawn, and Bird finally shook off his sorrow and made an appearance of his own. He went to Landini's postgame reception at the hotel, double-fisting cans of Coors with his left thumb heavily taped and wrapped.

Already, the critics were circling, and not all of them were reporters. One college coach found it notable that Indiana State's star only scored 19 points in the biggest game of his life. "The word is out on Larry Bird," the coach whispered to a reporter after the loss. "He chokes in the big games . . . It was Choke City."

Bird refused to use his broken thumb as an excuse for what happened that night, even when he had opportunities later. He and the guys had tried their best, he said. They had come up short, he reckoned. They had probably lost to the better team and they had the rest of their lives to think about it—starting with the long flight home the next day.

Heaton was worried about returning to Indiana; he felt like they'd let everybody down. But as the team plane landed back in Terre Haute on Tuesday afternoon, he realized he was wrong about that. In the hours after the loss on Monday night, locals had flocked downtown to celebrate the season. They weren't crying. They were cheering and singing in the dark, and the city was still celebrating as the Sycamores landed in Terre Haute. The Indiana National Guard scrambled a flyby of fighter jets, painted powder blue with a message: ISU IS STILL #1. The players stepped off the plane into a sea of 5,000 people. Thousands more lined the streets into town. And as the team buses pulled up outside the Hulman Center, and the players began to walk down the freight ramp to get inside, the guys could hear yet another crowd buzzing through the walls. Almost 10,000 people were waiting in the arena to cheer them and thank them. The Sycamores had lost the game, but they had still won.

Connie Hodges caught her breath when she first saw the crowd in the arena.

"I can't believe it," she gasped.

Heaton bounded up onto a stage in his cowboy hat, disbelieving it, too, and as the players filled in around him, the crowd showered the team with a standing ovation that lasted for three full minutes. Amid the noise, Hodges moved among the players, preparing everybody for what was going to happen next. Landini, King, and Hodges were each going to make brief remarks; King would nearly weep on the stage that day. Then Hodges was going to turn it over to the players. The fans would want to hear from each of them, and from Bird most of all, and this time, Bird didn't shy away from the assignment.

He stood before the microphone, looked out on the crowd, and steadied himself to speak.

Part V

AFTERLIFE

60

IN HIS FORCED INTERACTIONS with the media that season, Larry Bird had reluctantly revealed snippets of himself. He had displayed his sarcasm, his dry wit, his folksy demeanor, his plainspoken directness, and his penchant for the well-placed curse word. But he had never truly shown himself in public until the pep rally in Terre Haute after the loss to Michigan State.

That day, in front of the crowd in the arena, Bird didn't just speak; he took on the role of an emcee, introducing every member of the team after Hodges ceded the microphone to him. And as he spoke, Bird couldn't help but needle everyone, just a little.

He mocked Bill Hodges for his ego. "Before I got here," Bird joked, "Coach Hodges wore a 7½ hat. Now he takes a 10." He made fun of Mel Daniels for being old. "I'm sure you all remember Mel Daniels playing," Bird said. "Well, keep those memories 'cause he can't play no more." He joked about Brad Miley's poor shooting form. And when Miley gave it right back to Bird, saying he had been the one to teach Bird how to shoot, Bird admitted that it was true. "Brad did show me some shots," Bird said. "In fact, I used some last night."

He was making fun of himself. He was, he said that day, just "a hick from French Lick." But even a hick like him knew how to say thank you. As Bird closed his remarks in the arena, he held up the second-place trophy and presented it to the crowd. He said it belonged to them.

"To the community of Terre Haute," he said, "the student body, and anybody else who thought we'd be here."

Conservative Midwesterners, who had never heard Bird speak before, were troubled by the comments at the rally. Amid the jokes and the barbs, there were expletives, double negatives, and other examples of poor grammar. All of these missteps went out over the airwaves, live on statewide TV and radio. Unbeknownst to the players, everyone was watching. Many complained about the comments that day, and soon Landini was hearing about it in letters that he forwarded on to Bob King. "My unsolicited counsel to you (and to Bill Hodges)," Landini wrote to King just a few days after the rally, "is that the complainers should not be answered; and I see no point served in calling Bird's attention to the complaints."

But Landini couldn't take his own advice. At times, when people wrote to him that year criticizing Bird's use of the English language, Landini would circle the grammatical mistakes that the writers made in their letters, scrawl comments in the margins like the English professor he had once been—"Singular Possessive! . . . Run-on Sentences! . . . Construction"— and then fire off responses defending his famous basketball player.

"I, too, would prefer that Larry had a better command of grammar," Landini wrote at one point that spring, "but his courage, humaneness, politeness, and decency are far more important measures of the man and his character." Landini considered the complaints to be evidence of nothing less than societal decay—"Sometimes I think the whole world is mean and small-minded," Landini said—and he reminded himself to focus on the much larger batch of positive letters that he received that spring: from people writing songs about the team; from military veterans who felt inspired by the Sycamores' performance; from senior citizens who had lived in Terre Haute their whole lives and had never seen anything like it; and from Don Ohlmeyer, the executive producer at NBC Sports, who wished to congratulate Indiana State on its epic run and thank Landini, Hodges, and the two McKees for all their help in Salt Lake City.

"It was a remarkable year for the Sycamores," Ohlmeyer told Landini two days after the NCAA championship game, in late March 1979, trying to take the sting out of the loss.

What Ohlmeyer didn't mention was that it was an even more remarkable year for people like him—people looking to make money by bringing college sports to the masses. At the time, network revenue was derived almost exclusively from advertising dollars. Advertising rates were based on ratings, the data point that mattered most—"the Holy Grail," one network executive said. And the ratings that NBC earned for its game in Salt Lake City led to immediate changes in the marketplace.

Within eight weeks, the commissioner of the Sun Belt Conference down in Florida drew up a plan to expand the tournament from 40 to 48 teams, enamored by the thought that his small-market colleges could claim significant NCAA money. By August, collegiate officials approved the change, excited for more tournament basketball. Quietly, behind closed doors, the NCAA wanted to expand to even more teams. And in early 1981, Kevin O'Malley, that young executive from CBS, saw a way to build upon Bird and Magic's moment to give people what they really wanted: March Madness.

61

O'MALLEY'S VISION FOR THE tournament was as beautiful as it was simple.

He thought that NBC spent too much time promoting the Final Four and not enough time promoting the games in the early rounds of the tournament. He believed people would watch those early games if they had a reason to care. They just needed to understand the bracket, he said. They needed to be able to see the road to the Final Four, and O'Malley finally hit upon a way to show people this road. He wanted to hold a "selection show," he said, revealing the NCAA tournament bracket in real time on live TV with excitement, drama, and suspense. Under the format that O'Malley was considering, even the teams themselves wouldn't know where they were going, whom they were playing, or if they made the tournament at all until they watched the show.

In early 1981, as contract negotiations broke down between the NCAA and NBC over tournament broadcast rights, O'Malley and other CBS executives seized the moment, flying to Kansas City to pitch their ideas to NCAA executives in person. The collegiate officials liked what O'Malley was selling. They understood what CBS wanted to do, and they also knew that the network had the personnel to pull off the program that O'Malley envisioned. At the time, one of the most popular sports shows in America was *The NFL Today*, a pregame show anchored by Brent Musburger before football games in the fall on CBS. Everyone could picture a pro, sitting at a desk, directing traffic, and revealing a bracket. In early March 1981, less than two years after the game between Bird and Magic in Salt Lake, the NCAA accepted CBS's offer: $48 million to broadcast the tournament for the next three years.

It was an eye-popping sum of money—60 percent greater than what NBC had been paying for the tournament and the largest sum ever dedicated for any NCAA event—and it changed college athletic departments and the people who ran them. Schools that had once received as little as $7,000 for making the Final Four just a couple decades earlier were now poised to make 86 times that—$600,000—and this number would only grow as O'Malley's selection show debuted in 1982.

It was chaos on the set that day, O'Malley recalled later. CBS flew to Kansas City and built a makeshift studio in the ballroom of a Hyatt hotel where the NCAA committee was meeting. The committee, accustomed to working on their own schedule and calling coaches and athletic directors by phone to let them know that they had made the tournament, barely got the bracket to O'Malley in time to go on the air. Thirty minutes out, O'Malley said, the network still didn't have a single name pasted on its big board. Cardboard placards with the names of every school were scattered everywhere. And for a few minutes that day in Kansas City, O'Malley wondered if they would make their deadline. "Eventually my hair turned white," he said later. "I'm sure that moment had something to do with it."

But it all came together in the end. The show aired just before the *CBS Evening News* and *60 Minutes*. CBS ran it back again in 1983. And the selection show soon became more than just a staple of NCAA basketball coverage; it became its own cultural moment. Every March, college basketball players, cheerleaders, coaches, and students learned on live TV that they had been chosen. They were going to the tournament—or not. Either way, O'Malley's cameras were going to be there on campus to capture the reaction: the sadness or the euphoria. The tournament field quickly expanded three more times in the early 1980s. And by 1985—the first year the tournament featured 64 teams—everyone understood the stakes and the bracket. They were photocopying brackets at work, passing them around in school cafeterias, filling them out by hand, making guesses about which teams would win, wagering on the outcomes, and getting excited for the games, because, yes, they definitely cared.

CBS's $48 million deal now looked like a red-tag, bargain-basement steal. So, to renew the rights, the network doubled what it was willing to pay, putting up $96 million to keep broadcasting the tournament for another three years. Schools were now able to collect nearly a million dollars by just winning a few basketball games in March—an exciting, and also worrisome, prize. With so much money on the line, one basketball coach predicted, programs would begin cheating more. They'd do anything to win. They would start looking, he said, "for the easy way to the pot of gold."

It was an issue that would bedevil college basketball for decades to come, as scandals gutted one program after another, got coaches fired, put schools on probation, and made national headlines. But by the time basketball fans realized they had a problem, Larry Bird was long gone and burdened with a new responsibility: saving the NBA.

62

IN THE SPRING OF 1979, just weeks after the NCAA championship game in Salt Lake City, many CBS affiliates across the country didn't even broadcast the NBA playoffs. "I know it sounds brutal," one station manager said, explaining his decision at the time, "but there's simply a lack of fans."

Most Americans didn't care about the NBA, and they really didn't care about the two teams that made the finals in 1979: the Washington Bullets and Seattle SuperSonics for the second year in a row. In May of that year, with fan interest nonexistent in most markets, CBS chose to air Game Two of the NBA Finals on tape delay, shunning the Bullets and SuperSonics to give viewers a chance to watch popular prime-time shows like *The Waltons*, *Hawaii Five-O*, or a movie starring Bob Hope called *Boy, Did I Get a Wrong Number!* Fans who wanted to see the basketball game had to tune in at 11:30 that night, after their local news. And people in at least one market had to join the game in progress, 30 minutes after it started. The CBS affiliate in Milwaukee—an NBA city, the home of the Bucks—chose to air a rerun of *The Bob Newhart Show* instead of the NBA Finals.

It was an embarrassment for the league, yet another low point in a rough decade for the NBA, and Red Auerbach had tried his best to head off this disaster. That spring, he was thinking creatively yet again. As he visited Bird that March, watching his NCAA tournament games in Cincinnati and later Salt Lake City, the Celtics executive tried to convince Bird to sign an NBA contract with him as soon as Indiana State lost and finish his season playing in Boston. According to Bird, Auerbach was even willing to pay him as if he had been there the whole year.

It was a move that would have injected instant life into the sputtering league, and Bird had to admit that he was intrigued by the offer. He wanted to begin earning a paycheck; he talked about money a lot that spring. But he couldn't pull himself away from Terre Haute—not yet, anyway. Bird had obligations that he wanted to meet before leaving town.

That spring, Bird was a student teacher at West Vigo High School, the smallest high school in the county, on the outskirts of Terre Haute. It was a job he needed to complete in order to graduate, and he took it seriously. Bird taught gym class with longtime teacher and baseball coach Dick Ballinger, and he volunteered for a second position: to be an assistant coach on Ballinger's varsity baseball team. Ballinger, who was in his early 40s at the time, loved having Bird around. No one hit fungoes farther than he did. Sometimes, when hitting fly balls to the players at practice, Bird cleared the fence entirely, placing his hits on the tennis courts, where no one could catch them. But even more important to Ballinger, Bird set a good example for the baseball players. He worked hard—harder than any young man Ballinger had ever met—and made it clear to Ballinger that he was willing to do anything to help the team, regardless of his fame and his imminent fortune.

Once that spring, Craig McKee drove out to West Vigo to get Bird to sign a stack of photos for fans who kept writing letters to Indiana State, requesting autographs. When McKee arrived at the school, Bird wasn't in the gym and wasn't hitting fungoes, either. He was alone in the Indiana heat, mowing the outfield grass.

Ballinger just shrugged.

"I've got the only $3 million lawn mower in America," he liked to joke that spring.

At the end of April, while Bird was still doing his student teaching, he met a second obligation that was important to people close to him. He attended the Salute to Larry Bird dinner that Max Gibson, Lu Meis, Dick Landini, and the Larry Bird Committee had been planning for months. Technically, that night, Al McGuire was the keynote speaker, ready on the stage with his basketball anecdotes and his Brooklyn charm. But the crowd of about a thousand people came out to see Bird, Hodges, Nicks, Heaton, Miley, Gilbert, Reed, Staley, and the rest of the team one last time.

The players were all there, many in borrowed tuxedos, and several of them stepped up on the stage to speak. Bob Heaton gave thanks for Larry Bird and asked the Lord to bless him. Max Gibson presented a $22,000 check to Landini—the proceeds from the evening—in order to start a scholarship fund in Bird's name. The university retired Bird's jersey, hanging it in the rafters. Landini joked that he was going to wear the jersey for the night, just to know what it was like to be Larry Bird—a joke that played well in the room. And when the mayor of Terre Haute presented Bird with the key to the city, Bird cracked a joke of his own. "I thought he should have given me the jail key," he told the crowd, "in case I need it tonight."

He was at ease on the stage once again, as he had been at the pep rally a month earlier. At one point, he even dropped his comedy routine for a moment, thanked his mother and his grandmother, and begged the crowd to support Bill Hodges's team the following winter after Bird was gone. "Next year," he said, "regardless of what happens, I hope you are behind them."

It was an all-time-great night in the history of Terre Haute, and the next day, the festivities continued. At the invitation of Indiana State's head baseball coach, Bird suited up for the Sycamore nine and played well in a real game against Kentucky Wesleyan. He went 1-for-2 on the afternoon, with a strikeout, a single, and two RBIs. Better yet, he didn't injure himself. That would happen about a week later, in May 1979, in a men's softball game that he should have skipped. Early in the outing, Bird went to make a play in the outfield, misjudged a knuckling line drive, and snapped his right index finger while trying to make the catch.

Players on the field that day—including Bob Heaton and Geoff Shuck, the Indiana State star from 1975, now selling insurance in Terre Haute—were stunned. They believed they had just witnessed the end of Larry Bird's basketball career. The finger wasn't just broken; it appeared to be mangled. "It was going six different ways of sideways," Shuck recalled. But Heaton's prayer, asking the Lord to watch over Larry Bird, must have worked. At the hospital in Terre Haute, Bird saw the same doctor who had treated Heaton after his farm accident in December 1967. The player, known for miracles, had helped bequeath another. The surgery to repair Bird's finger was successful, and in early June 1979, a month after the softball injury and just days after the NBA Finals ended with no one caring, no one watching, Red Auerbach called a press conference in Boston to announce some news: He had signed Larry Bird to a five-year contract worth $3.25 million, the largest deal ever awarded to a rookie in any American sport.

Bird flew to Boston for Auerbach's press conference with one directive for his new agent, Bob Woolf: No reporters were to meet him at the airport. "Are there any fucking reporters here?" Bird asked as soon as he got off the plane. Woolf assured him that there were not, lying—one was standing right there—and the morning of the press conference got off to a rocky start. Bird left Woolf's house in tony Brookline, just west of Boston, to go on a run and immediately got lost on the city streets. In order to make it home, Boston's newest millionaire was going to have to stop a motorist and ask for a ride.

But on the stage a few hours later—in front of a crowd of reporters that included Mike Madden and a table overflowing with 31 microphones—Bird knew exactly what to do. He promised that he'd speak to the press "as long as nobody comes knocking at my door." He told everyone not to look at him as a savior—he said he'd studied his contract and that it didn't mention anything about saving anything. He reminded everyone that he was "just a hick from French Lick," the line he had used at the pep rally, and when reporters asked him about his record-breaking contract, he managed to make light of it.

"I forgot to tell Mr. Auerbach," Bird said, "but I would have played for nothin.'"

The room erupted in laughter. "Instant legend," Mike Madden said.

But the transition that summer and fall wasn't easy for Bird. In his new city, he chose to live right next to one of the only people he knew, Bob Woolf, in Brookline. At least one of Bird's teammates was shocked. Star athletes didn't typically choose to live next door to their agents. One reporter immediately broke the unwritten code—if not the rules that Bird had laid out for the media at his press conference in June. A writer at *Inside Sports* magazine—who had been invited into Bird's life that summer and who had sat with him in Woolf's kitchen—wrote about Larry's father, his failed marriage with Janet, and his daughter, now two years old. "Larry is a very nice person," Janet told the writer, "but sometimes he just forgets about other people. He sort of forgot about us."

Seemingly homesick, Bird called Bob Heaton around that time, asking him to come to Boston. "It was a long-distance call, I remember," Heaton said. "You know, 'Would you accept charges from a Larry Bird?'" Heaton took the call, of course, but he had to tell his friend that he couldn't fly to Boston or meet Bird anywhere else. Heaton was living off campus that fall with Tex Ritter. A new basketball season was about to begin. Heaton, a senior, was in the gym every day with the folks who remained: Hodges, Nicks, Miley, Gilbert, Reed, Nemcek, and Ritter. Bird was on his own, and whether he wanted to admit it or not, the expectations were real, especially after the Los Angeles Lakers selected Magic Johnson with the first pick in the NBA draft that year, and Magic signed his own massive, multimillion-dollar contract.

The league *was* relying on them. They *were* saviors. And everybody knew it.

"The NBA has so much at stake in Magic Johnson and Larry Bird," *The Boston Globe* declared in late 1979. "If these two great and colorful athletes do not boost the ratings, it may be lights out."

63

BACK AT CBS, KEVIN O'Malley knew what to do that fall: He put Bird and Magic on television as much as possible, and by the end of the regular season, the impact was easy for a numbers guy like O'Malley to measure. Television ratings for NBA games were up 12 percent.

But tape delay remained a problem for the NBA Finals in May 1980, even with Magic leading the Lakers to a championship as a rookie. That month, only 14 out of 200 CBS affiliates chose to air the decisive Game Six live. In Southern California, at least one station opted to broadcast a regular-season Dodgers–Pirates baseball game over the Lakers in the NBA Finals. In New York, the league's top executives—including future commissioner David Stern—couldn't watch the game live on their own televisions at home. And one year later, in May 1981, most Americans never got to see Bird win his first NBA title, as the Celtics defeated the Houston Rockets in six. It was as if that series never happened. Four of the six games aired in the netherworld of tape delay, in the dark, after the nightly news.

Stern admitted later that the situation made him question whether the NBA was truly a major sport. But what the league needed wasn't just two players; it was business acumen. It needed a new model to leverage the fame of those players. And in June 1981, just two weeks after Bird won his first title, the NBA began making changes that helped create this model. First, league executives ripped up the schedule. NBA seasons going forward wouldn't start until October 30, three weeks later than usual, and the playoffs wouldn't begin until it was almost June. Under this new format, regular season games would no longer have to compete against the World Series in October, and the Finals would no longer fall during "sweeps" week in May, when networks tried to maximize ratings for financial gain and were inclined to run a basketball game on tape delay in order to air their most popular prime-time shows. The Finals were now a stand-alone event, in June.

Next, Stern partnered with a small advertising agency to craft a $200,000 marketing campaign that the league could use to sell its big-name stars to the masses. In the first 15-second commercial that aired in the fall of 1981, the camera flipped quickly between Julius Erving, Kareem Abdul-Jabbar, Larry Bird, and Magic Johnson, as each spoke one line of praise about the other. Then Magic ended the spot, smiling as always and uttering the league's new tag line.

"Everybody's a fan of the NBA," Magic said. "It's FAN-tastic!"

League officials selected 30 players to appear in five different commercials, and as they made their list, Stern said, they were cognizant of creating an image of "diversity." White players like Swen Nater of the San Diego Clippers, Dan Issel of the Denver Nuggets, and Bird's teammate Kevin McHale all made appearances in the "FAN-tastic" campaign by the end of 1982—even though none of them were household names at the time. HOW CAN MAGIC BE A FAN OF SWEN NATER? one headline asked.

But Stern loved the campaign. He stuck with it, confident that it was helping, and he spearheaded a handful of other shrewd decisions in the early 1980s that set the league up for success. The NBA instituted a salary cap; enforced a stringent drug policy, cracking down on offenders to clean up its image; and signed a new contract with CBS that allowed it to negotiate side deals with a growing entity: cable television. Stern predicted, correctly, that cable TV revenues could be enormous in the years to come. He wanted to make sure the league was poised to claim that money. And in 1984, a series of events solidified the gains the league had made since Bird and Magic showed up together in 1979, fresh from that basketball court in Salt Lake City.

Stern became commissioner, Bird and Magic met in the NBA Finals, the series went seven games, the television ratings set a record for professional basketball, Bird predicted he would defeat Magic this time, he made good on that prediction as America watched, fans stormed the floor of the old Boston Garden, swallowing Bird as the Celtics won, and by the end of that month, June 1984, Stern found himself surrounded by a constellation of stars who were easy to market regardless of their race. Not just Bird and Magic anymore, but Isiah Thomas, Dominique Wilkins, and a new soon-to-be wunderkind selected with the third pick in the 1984 NBA draft: Michael Jordan.

By the time the Chicago Bulls selected Jordan, Bird was already back home in Indiana. For years, he spent his off-seasons there in a new home he built in West Baden, complete with a gazebo, a pool, and an asphalt basketball court nestled in a grove of trees. It wasn't uncommon in the 1980s to find Bird out there, shooting or playing pickup games against guys in town. But already it was getting harder to hang out like he once did. Crowds would mob him at airports, autograph seekers on his elbow. Sometimes, he couldn't relax in West Baden or French Lick. To get away, he started going to a new place that tourists would never find, a tavern called Butchie's, down in Dubois, a much smaller town about 15 miles south. Bird became a regular at Butchie's in the summer of 1984. And if he came in for a drink and left before closing time, he often placed money on the bar as he walked out the door with a simple directive for the bartender. "Keep the boys in beer," he'd say.

Bird would win one more NBA title and three MVPs. He'd go down as one of the greatest players to ever step on the court. He'd retire in 1992 and marry his longtime girlfriend, Dinah, in a private ceremony at Max Gibson's house, where Bird had once cut the grass. He'd later take on multiple roles with the Indiana Pacers, including head coach and president, and he'd make history that almost no one else could match by fundamentally altering almost everything he touched: Indiana State, Terre Haute, the NCAA tournament, and the NBA.

But his greatest achievement might be the thing that's been documented the least. Bird spawned an afterlife for Indiana State's one shining moment. He made 1979 last forever, at least off the court, and he changed the people who were part of that moment, giving them an afterlife, too. For better or for worse, no one who was there in 1979 would ever be able to outrun it.

64

GREG WEBB NEVER FORGOT about the free throw that he missed for New Mexico State in Las Cruces in early February 1979—the missed free throw that led to Bob Heaton's half-court miracle shot and helped preserve Indiana State's undefeated season in the desert. Over the years—as Webb became a father, a grandfather, and a longtime coach at Langston University, a historically Black college in central Oklahoma—the former New Mexico State star thought about it a lot and wondered how things might have been different if he had made the shot or contested the pass that Miley threw up the court to Heaton with three seconds to go.

In an alternative reality that Webb has imagined, he makes his free throw or blocks Miley's pass. Heaton never gets off a shot. Indiana State loses. Webb and his teammates gallop out into the night to go dancing at the Rain Forrest and the Sycamores fall apart in the final weeks of the 1979 season, as Bill Hodges always feared was possible. "If there's a chink in Indiana State's armor at that point in time," Webb said in 2025, "I think that it turns into a big dent." Maybe the Sycamores never advance to the Final Four—or maybe they do, but with a record that makes them a far less interesting story. "I don't think anybody would have really been excited about Indiana State," Webb said, "if they went into the final game 29–2."

In this way, Webb came to believe that he was an important part of college basketball lore. His missed free throw, which gutted him at the time, gave Heaton the chance to heave the ball from half-court, allowed the undefeated season to roll on, helped attract the interest of NBC executives who put Indiana State on national TV, created a moment that made an underdog team believe anything was possible, set the stage for the most-watched game in American basketball history—Bird vs. Magic in Salt Lake City in March 1979—and provided Webb with something he never would have expected after Heaton's shot fell through the net and Webb crumpled to the court: a sort of peace. "I think things happen for a reason," Webb said, "and I believe that night happened for a reason."

These days, Webb works at a middle school in Oklahoma City called Millwood Arts Academy. The school is located near the intersection of Martin Luther King Avenue and Interstate 44 on the north side of town. The students there are mostly Black and working-class. In Webb's role as dean of students, he often has to be the disciplinarian, and as a way of softening Webb's image, the principal at Millwood Arts loves to regale the kids with tales about the time that Webb—or "Coach Webb," as the kids call him—played on the biggest stage.

"What he does," Webb said, "is he makes up a story. He starts telling the kids, 'Coach Webb played against Larry Bird . . . Larry Bird dunked on Coach Webb . . .' And he has a little dance that he does, where Larry's hanging on the rim, shaking and all that, and he says, 'This is Larry Bird dunking on Coach Webb.'"

None of it's true. "Larry Bird had trouble dunking—period," Webb said. But Webb lets his principal tell his story. He lets him do it, he said, because the kids love it. They love imagining Coach Webb, now in his late 60s and not nearly as spry as he once was, going up against an icon who's known to them because of TikTok, Instagram reels, and YouTube.

It's a future that Webb never would have predicted in 1979, and Bird certainly wouldn't have predicted it, either. He believed that after he turned 40, no one would remember him anymore. But it hasn't worked out like that, and the strangest example of Bird's odd and enduring legacy might be found every fall at Millwood Arts Academy, a place Bird has never visited, 600 miles from Indiana.

When kids pass Coach Webb in the halls, they sometimes acknowledge him by simply nodding and whispering two words.

"Larry Bird."

And Webb knows what they mean.

"It's kind of their way of saying, 'OK, man. We're all cool.'"

65

BILL HODGES TRIED TO get away after the parties were over in Terre Haute in the spring of 1979. That April, he went to Daytona Beach down in Florida.

Hodges loved the beach and typically felt restored after a few days in the surf and sand. But this time was different. He couldn't stop his mind from racing. Because of Bob King's illness the previous fall, and the unusual way that Hodges had assumed the head coaching position in February after four months in limbo, he had effectively been both the head coach and the lead recruiter for the entire year. It was almost impossible to do both jobs well, especially with a young and inexperienced coaching staff around him. The Sycamores' recruiting suffered as a result. Deep down, Hodges knew it. And now he was making choices, personal decisions, that continued to keep him off the road, the place where he needed to be. "I had a family," Hodges said decades later, "and I had a wife that wanted good things." So he tried to do what he thought big-time coaches did in order to earn money. "I had a basketball camp, did a radio show, did a TV show, and didn't get on the road and recruit like I should have."

Carl Nicks, a senior that fall, living off campus with Alex Gilbert, noticed the difference right away. In the wake of the miracle season, the Sycamores didn't reel in a haul of elite high school stars; they signed three players who together would average 3.7 points per game in 1979–80. The team was now facing a math problem. All the other regulars who were still there were going to score more in the new season. And Nicks was about to have a breakout year, averaging 27 points a game. But one NBA scout called Nicks "a one-man team," and it was apparent right away that no one could replace Larry Bird. In the Sycamores' first game that November, Hodges's old employer, little Division II Armstrong State, came to Terre Haute and won, 66–63.

It was just one game, but it was a sign of things to come. The team scuffled all year, lost seven times by five points or fewer, blew games they would have won the year before, finished 16–11, and didn't get an invite to play in any sort of postseason tournament—a snub that Bird pointed out to Hodges in March 1980 when he called in one day to his radio show.

"Hey, Coach," Bird said. "How do you think the team will do in the NIT?"

"The NIT?" Hodges said.

"The Not Invited Tournament," Bird replied.

Hodges laughed off the joke. He knew Bird's brand of humor well, and by 1980, he believed he had corrected his mistakes from the spring of 1979. He was out on the recruiting trail again, working hard in the living rooms, closing deals, and signing a new prospect who had the talent to change everything—a six-foot-seven, 215-pound Indiana high school all-star named Kevin Thompson.

If anyone was ever cut from the mold of Larry Bird, it was Thompson. He averaged 21 points and 14 rebounds a game as a senior at Terre Haute South High School. He pushed himself to the point of exhaustion on the floor. He liked to pass, wanted to win, didn't look much like a ballplayer with his black eyeglasses and mustache, and he was white—the new Great White Hope in Terre Haute, the press called him.

But in the late summer and early fall of 1980, Thompson had curious rib pain that wouldn't go away. Doctors investigated and diagnosed him with cancer. As the new season began, Thompson wasn't on the floor sporting powder blue; he was in New York City, undergoing chemotherapy at a hospital better equipped to tackle his problem. Hodges had to admit that it was hard for him to think about basketball at the time. He was thinking instead about Thompson, life, death, survival—and his own problems at home. By late 1980, Bill and Connie had split up, careening toward a divorce. Bill had moved into an apartment across town.

The season this time was an unmitigated disaster. The Sycamores didn't win a game until mid-December and finished the year 9–18, their worst record in more than a decade. Thompson felt bad about it, Hodges said, and kept apologizing for "messing up his plans"—a conversation that Hodges wouldn't entertain. By the summer of 1981, he wanted to do something for Thompson, and in August that year, Hodges's 1979 team came together for the young man. Bird, Nicks, Heaton, Miley, Staley, and others stepped on the floor again at the Hulman Center to play a squad of retired Pacers in an effort to raise money for Thompson's medical treatment.

Briefly that night, it felt like old times in Terre Haute. The arena was nearly sold out. Bird scored 25 points and grabbed 29 rebounds, playing hard just two months removed from winning his first NBA title. Nicks, Gilbert, Heaton, and Miley all scored in double digits, and the '79 Sycamores beat the Pacers, 115–99. But there was no saving Kevin Thompson.

He died five months later, at age 19. His parents buried him under a tombstone in Terre Haute with a simple epitaph—"It's not the quantity of life that counts, but the quality"—and by the time they laid him in the ground in January 1982, Bill Hodges's team was struggling again. In an effort to save his job and win now, he had stocked his roster with junior college players who seemed to be in it for themselves. Many of them didn't last long. Two of them quit midseason, and Steve Reed, the last remaining regular from the 1979 team, watched it all unravel, shaking his head at how far the Sycamores had fallen. "Hodges went from making all the right moves," Reed said, "to probably making some mistakes."

Two weeks after Thompson's death, Hodges decided he'd had enough. He announced that he was resigning as head coach at Indiana State. He had lost the support of the administration. He felt a chill in the room anytime he and Landini crossed paths, and it probably wasn't his imagination.

In a note to Craig McKee in 1983, Landini accepted responsibility for failing to convert Indiana State's 1979 season into a "permanent endowment" for the university, ensuring basketball greatness every year. But it was hard for Landini not to blame Hodges, too. In that same note to McKee, Landini described Hodges as "a youthful, inexperienced, and prideful basketball coach" who had failed to make "negotiable capital" of the "astonishing tide of circumstances" that briefly lifted Indiana State all the way to the top.

Indiana State wouldn't return to the NCAA tournament for the rest of Landini's tenure—more than two decades. It would never again crack the top 20 in any basketball poll. Its time as a national power was over. And the rule changes that have revolutionized college sports in recent years—allowing athletes to get paid through name, image, and likeness money and giving them the freedom to jump from school to school—will make it harder for Indiana State, and other small schools like it, to ever reach such heights again.

In 2024, the Sycamores finally put together another great season. The men's basketball team went 32–7 that year. They advanced all the way to the championship game of a familiar tournament, the NIT, and they climbed as high as No. 23 in the national polls. But the players on that team had collectively earned just $92,500 in NIL deals. It was a pittance compared to what they could make elsewhere, especially after putting together a strong season in Terre Haute. Within weeks of the NIT championship game, seven members of the team—including the team's top five scorers—

left town, chasing bigger money. In order to retain them, Indiana State's boosters would have needed to come up with at least $2.2 million—money they didn't have. An underdog team that had thrilled local fans—and briefly reminded them of 1979—scattered like the leaves of autumn, forcing Indiana State to start over again. If it wasn't already clear that the Sycamores had missed their window long ago, it was now. And in some ways it could all be traced back to the university's missteps in the late 1970s and early 1980s. In some ways, it went all the way back to Bill Hodges, trying and failing to win after Larry Bird was gone.

After his resignation in 1982, Hodges knew where he wanted to go. To the ocean, he said, to the beach. And so, when he received a job offer that March, giving him the chance to coach at Palm Beach Junior College down in Florida, Hodges accepted it. The athletic director there was stunned. The games in Palm Beach drew about 100 people. The referees had day jobs—one managed a country club, another a spa. Hodges was going to have to take on a day job, too. Administrators expected him to teach PE classes on the side.

It was a big step down for the former national coach of the year. But Hodges was excited about the obscurity of it all. He wanted to disappear, regroup, spend time at the beach, and coach some basketball away from the media, the politics, the demands of the modern game, and what he called "the rat race." "My goals," Hodges said at the time, "are to build a good solid program and enjoy life."

Initially, Larry Bird was there to help with both, saving Hodges as Hodges had once saved him. That September in Palm Beach, Bird, who had resisted Hodges's attempts to get him to talk publicly in college, agreed to be the keynote speaker at a $75-a-plate dinner to raise money for Hodges's new basketball program. Hodges was probably the only junior college coach in America who could call on an NBA champion to do such a thing, and he was definitely the only one who was hanging out with the champion afterward.

"Hey, Hodgo," Bird said when the dinner was over, "are we playing golf tomorrow or what?"

They were, of course. Golf one day and tennis the next. For a long time, Bird and Hodges stayed close. But the obscurity that Hodges sought in 1982 lasted longer than he could have imagined at the time. After one year in Palm Beach, he bounced from job to job, never again managing to win more than 15 games in a season at a Division I school. He found himself coaching at the high school level by the 2000s, and ultimately lost touch with his friend Larry Bird. In 2009, Bird, long retired from his playing career and now serving as the president of the Indiana Pacers, didn't intervene when the team fired its director of player personnel, Mel Daniels. CeCe Daniels, Mel's wife, later said that the move drove a wedge between the two old friends. When Mel died in 2016, CeCe reported that Bird didn't even offer his condolences. "Larry never called me to say he was sorry," CeCe said. And Hodges said he couldn't hold his tongue. He had to say something to Bird about the whole Mel Daniels affair, about letting Daniels go.

"I really got on his ass," Hodges recalled. The Pacers were in disarray at the time, and in fairness to Bird, Daniels was maybe not helping. There were rumors that Daniels was dissatisfied with multiple people in the organization at the time, including the team's general manager and head coach. But Hodges believed that Bird owed Daniels—for everything Daniels had done for him in 1978 and '79, for the games they had played one-on-one after practice, for the efforts that Daniels had made to prepare Bird for the NBA, and for his friendship. "I said, 'You owe him your loyalty . . . I'm ashamed of you.' And he hasn't talked to me since." The two stubborn Indiana boys retreated to their respective corners, and there they remain almost 20 years later.

But Hodges isn't looking for anyone's sympathy. He isn't waiting around for Larry Bird's phone call, and he long ago rejected the narrative that was foisted upon him after he left Indiana State: that he lost one big game and drifted away, 33–1. Hodges never saw it like that. From the moment he walked off that court in Salt Lake City in 1979, he knew he had won, and if he ever needed reminding in the years that followed, all Hodges had to do was read the letter that he received in the mail a few days after the loss to Michigan State.

It came from UCLA's legendary head coach, John Wooden. It was written in Wooden's hand, in blue ink on a plain sheet of white paper, and it offered some advice from one coach to another.

"I am sure that you are disappointed," Wooden told Hodges, "but you conducted yourself most admirably. Disappointment may be quite painful, but it is only a temporary thing and as the great statesman, Winston Churchill, said, 'Victory is never final and defeat is never fatal.'"

Then, down below, Wooden signed off in swooping cursive.

"Best wishes for continued peace of mind . . ."

Hodges kept the letter his whole life. It hung on the wall of his office in Palm Beach. It traveled with him from job to job, and in 2025, it was still there with him. The letter was in a frame at the top of the stairs at Hodges's house in suburban Charlotte, North Carolina, leading to the room where he watched basketball at night in his favorite chair. Visitors lucky enough to watch games with Hodges in that room, or pass long evenings there, talking about the days he once spent with Larry Bird in the midst of a miracle, couldn't help but read it.

"It's over there," Hodges told one visitor in early 2025. "Right there."

"I treasure it," he said.

66

BY THE TIME HODGES moved to Palm Beach in March 1982, almost everybody from the 1979 team had left Terre Haute—graduating, moving on, or in the case of sports information director Ed McKee, taking a new job.

McKee got out early, leaving Indiana State just months after the game in Salt Lake City. He believed that the wave had crested—nothing could ever match what they had just done. He didn't want to be sitting in the sports information office in the old practice arena when everybody else figured that out, and he was eager for a new challenge after three years of wrangling Larry Bird. Al McGuire informed McKee that he could use him as a reference, if needed. The popular NBC analyst had witnessed McKee's difficult task, managing Bird up close in the trenches when the spotlight burned the brightest. And in January 1980, long before everything fell apart, McKee took a PR job with the Pacers for all of these reasons. "It's time to move," McKee told McGuire, simply.

In the years that followed, Bird and McKee never sat down and reckoned with what had happened in that little window of time in the late 1970s. But Bird did talk about it at least once, decades later at a press conference in Terre Haute, and that day, he admitted he had been wrong to have been so difficult and so quiet with the media when he was at Indiana State. "I was young," he said. "I was immature, shy, and I didn't handle it very well." Perhaps more importantly, Bird made it known to McKee that he appreciated what he had done for him. Fittingly for Bird, he managed to convey this feeling without ever saying it to McKee out loud.

After the season ended in 1979, there was some sort of party in Indianapolis, hosted by Converse shoes. Bird was the star attraction that day, McKee said, and when Bird walked into the room filled with executives and strangers, he found himself gravitating to the only two people he knew: Ed McKee and his wife, Linda. For a moment that day, McKee wasn't a PR guy trying to get Bird to talk, and Bird wasn't a star trying to make McKee's life difficult. They were just two people who knew each other, peers and maybe even friends, hanging out at a party.

A short while later, the Converse folks broke up the conversation and whisked Bird away. He had stakeholders to meet, hands to shake, and sneakers to sell. But McKee never forgot that moment at the party, or the note that Bird wrote to him before he left for Boston. Bird scrawled it on a black-and-white photo of himself, and like Hodges, McKee kept the note forever. He would be 80 years old, living with Linda outside of Denver, and still, there it was, framed and sitting on his desk, because the note on the photograph said it all.

"Ed," Bird wrote. "Thanks for all the things and work you did for me ... No one but me knows how much you did."

The players on the team were the next to go. Nicks and Gilbert both left via the 1980 NBA draft—Nicks to the Nuggets with the last pick of the first round and Gilbert to the Bucks in the middle of the sixth. Miley went off to play in Europe. Heaton parlayed his local fame as the Miracle Man into a marriage to his girlfriend, Jane Ann, a job selling insurance in Terre Haute, and a seat in the Indiana state legislature. Reed went into hospital administration. Staley and Curry became corrections officers, and other guys took the best jobs they could find in a tough economy. In 1980, Nemcek found work at an aluminum recycling plant in northern Indiana, and Heaton's senior-year roommate, Tex Ritter, went to school in Indianapolis for a while, trying to earn skills to get hired in a new and growing field: computers.

For most of them, it didn't work out. Ritter realized he didn't like computer science. Nemcek hated the factory job and desperately needed something else. And all three of the guys who tried to keep playing basketball—Nicks, Gilbert, and Miley—failed to catch on in a meaningful way. Gilbert knew what his problem was: addiction. He had never really mourned his late brother, Lindell. He had gone out hard after losing to Michigan State, and in some ways he never stopped after that. From the moment the team plane landed back in Terre Haute for the pep rally, Gilbert was partying. "I would wake up getting high and drunk," he said later. "And I'd go to sleep getting high and drunk." It felt impossible to be a student in a dorm after being a star on that stage. And this behavior continued, Gilbert said, after the Bucks drafted him in 1980. "I was 22 years old, pocket full of money, girls, the life—the NBA life at the time."

Not surprisingly, Gilbert didn't catch on with the Bucks. He didn't pan out playing overseas, either. And in the late 1980s, about a decade after his brother's death, it came full circle for him in a dark and dangerous way: Gilbert was back home in East St. Louis, he said, buying drugs at the Gompers Homes, the same public housing development where his brother had been gunned down in November 1978.

If Miley or Nicks had known what was happening with their friend, they might have intervened. But Gilbert was hiding his problem—"I never told anyone," he said—and Miley and Nicks were busy finding their own ways in the 1980s, trying to hang on to basketball. Miley played overseas for four seasons before running out of road and returning home to take a job at a sporting goods store in Indianapolis. And Nicks, always tenacious, tough, and gritty, did everything he could to hold on to his one chance in the NBA.

For a moment, in the fall of 1980, it looked like it would happen for him. The Nuggets' coach, Donnie Walsh, loved Nicks, called him "the most competitive player in the draft," awarded him a roster spot that year, and felt so good about him that he made a prediction: "He's going to make it in the NBA." But by Christmas, Walsh was fired—bad luck for Nicks. Within days of the firing, Nicks was traded to the Utah Jazz—not ideal. By the following winter, the Utah coach was fired, too. Nicks had now played for four coaches in fewer than two seasons, and in the fall of 1982, the last of those coaches cut him from the Jazz, opening a new chapter in Nicks's life: his journeyman years.

Nicks spent two seasons in the Continental Basketball Association. He played for the Billings Volcanos in Montana and the Toronto Tornados in Canada. He logged time overseas in France and Belgium, and he weathered blows that would have brought other players to their knees. He was living in sad hotels, hitchhiking when he didn't have a car, playing games in a dilapidated ice rink where the winter winds ripped through the walls, earning $350 a week—less than what Hodges was making down in Palm Beach—showering in locker rooms where the water ran cold, spending eight-hour road trips packed into minivans with his team, and stepping out at his next destination, still believing.

"I really think I'll be back in the NBA," Nicks told a reporter in 1984. "I think they want to see if I'll go through this—the van, the gyms, the locker rooms. I think they're testing me."

But it wasn't a test; it was just life. And by the 1990s, Nicks had given up on his dream. He wasn't making it back to the NBA. He was taking a job at the department of corrections, just as his teammates Staley and Curry had. He was running recreational programs for inmates. He was coaching an eighth-grade basketball team on the outskirts of Indianapolis and he was calling Larry Bird at the Pacers all the time—every week, Nicks said—asking for a job as a scout.

"I was wearing him out," Nicks admitted later. "But I had to. I was desperate. I was really desperate."

Then Nicks sat around, waiting and waiting for Bird to call him back.

67

IT COULD HAVE GONE on this way forever for the guys; it's difficult for athletes when the final buzzer sounds and the games are over. But in the late 1970s at Indiana State, they had learned that a little hard work could change one's circumstances and that these changes could happen faster than one might imagine. They still had connections with each other. All of them remained inextricably linked to Bird. And as a result of the lessons they had learned, the relationships they had formed, and their enduring legacy in Indiana, each of them found a way to a better life.

In the early 1980s, Ritter finally stopped kidding himself about working with computers and decided to do something that Larry Bird might have done. He pushed the proverbial ball up the floor and took a chance. Ritter learned to play guitar, joined a band, landed wedding gigs, moved to Nashville in the late 1980s, met his wife there as they did backing vocals together for another artist, and 35 years later they're not just married, they're a band themselves: Bomar & Ritter, out of Deputy, Indiana. Ritter isn't famous, but he's doing what he loves. And when he crossed paths with Bird at an event in Terre Haute one night about a decade ago, Ritter couldn't pass up the opportunity to say thanks.

"Right before we left," Ritter said, "I told Larry—I said, 'Man, it was an honor to be on the team with you. I'm not sure I had a whole lot to do with the success of the team, but it was an honor to play with you.'"

Bird just looked at him, Ritter said, and told him to never speak like that again.

"You had all kinds of things to do with the success of this team," Ritter recalled Bird saying. "Don't ever think that you didn't."

Ritter drove home that night in the dark, feeling moved by the interaction, and for a long time, he couldn't figure out why. But later, he hit upon the reason. They *had* been in it together. Ritter had been there, too, even if he was down at the end of the bench. And maybe, he realized, Bird was more than just an old teammate.

"Maybe," Ritter said, "I could officially consider him a friend."

Around 1982, Rich Nemcek took his own chance. He left the aluminum recycling plant to become an air traffic controller, and in the late 1980s, he got an opportunity to move up—from his post at a small airport in DuPage County, Illinois, to a big-time job at one of the busiest hubs in America: O'Hare International Airport in Chicago. By then, Nemcek didn't think very often about the 1979 team. "I had my whole career after that," he said, "my family and my kids." But he knew the team still mattered to other people, so he found a way to work the story of the 1979 championship game into his interviews at O'Hare. "Just casual references," Nemcek said. "But it helped."

Instead of discussing the prospective job—and Nemcek's résumé— they were now talking about Bird, Magic, history, greatness, and Nemcek's surprising connection to it all. He got the job. "And what was even cooler was, for a while they were replaying the game every NCAA season." Nemcek would walk into the break room at O'Hare at times, find his coworkers watching the Sycamores playing for a national title on cable TV, and would tell everybody in the break room to wait—just wait, he said—for the last three minutes of the game, when he got on the floor after Carl Nicks fouled out.

"The best guy," Nemcek liked to joke, "gets in at the end."

By the time that Nemcek was interviewing at O'Hare, Brad Miley had also leveraged 1979 to escape his own version of purgatory. He got out of that sporting goods store in Indianapolis. A businessman spotted him there in the 1980s and realized there was a better use for Miley's talents, personality, and name recognition. He offered Miley a job at a growing alcohol distribution company, selling beer, wine, and spirits. And he knew exactly where to place Miley in order to get the most out of him. He sent him to sell in Terre Haute.

Miley accepted the job and moved back to town with his young wife, Kathy. She got hired at a local bank and he got a map of the city. He began putting pushpins into this map to plot a weekly route. He started walking into Walmarts, Krogers, restaurants, and bars to meet people and sell, and he realized right away that the man who had hired him knew what he was doing. Local managers took notice when Brad Miley of the 1979 Sycamores came striding into their establishments, smiling and friendly and hoping for their business. Sales exploded. At one point, Miley said, he had close to 200 accounts, and he knew it wasn't just because of the quality of his sales pitch. It was because of who he was, what he had done, and what that achievement still meant to the community now.

"It opened a lot of doors," Miley said. "I'm not gonna lie."

The Mileys built a house on a cul-de-sac north of the city. They became a courtside presence at Sycamores games in the old Hulman Center. Students who weren't even alive when Miley played with Larry Bird began asking him for photographs. He took on a status far greater than that of a former player. He became like the mayor of Terre Haute, a connector of people. Even Kathy, his wife, benefited at times from his name. "My wife to this day comes home and says, 'I did a loan, a $300,000 loan, with somebody,' and they said, 'Are you the wife of Brad Miley that played in 1979?'" Everybody knew him. And his fame hasn't diminished over the years; it has only grown—as the team reunited every decade to mark the anniversary of 1979, as the university erected a statue for Larry Bird outside the arena in 2013, and as Larry's friend from the 1970s, Greg Gibson, built a museum in Bird's name, opening in downtown Terre Haute with great fanfare in 2024.

For the museum dedication, almost everyone came back, including Marcia Staub, one of the two cheerleaders who had appeared on the cover of *Sports Illustrated* with Bird in 1977. Staub—now Marcia Staub Murphy, a grandmother in Paris, Illinois—wanted to see the new mural that had been painted on a brick wall outside the museum: a 33-foot-tall rendering of the magazine cover that had changed Bird's life and in some ways changed hers, too.

Staub was nervous that day as she drove over from Paris with her boyfriend. She wasn't sure if she should be there or if Bird would even remember her; they hadn't seen each other in almost 50 years. But there was no reason to be anxious. When Bird spotted Staub in the crowd, he came over and gave her a hug—"a big hug," Staub said—and then the two old classmates just stood there, talking and talking about the past.

"He was so friendly," Staub said. "Like a different person. A totally different person."

68

THANKS TO THESE events—the team reunions, the statue, the museum, the 33-foot mural, and the basketball games that still happen every winter in the Hulman Center—Larry Bird has lasting value to the community. Local tourism officials estimate that he is worth at least $7 million annually to the economy of Terre Haute. Almost five decades since his last college game, Bird is still keeping the lights on, putting people in seats, drawing fans downtown, and making Terre Haute relevant, a place worth visiting to people from around the world.

But not everyone has enjoyed the ride. Over the years, Alex Gilbert grew tired of the reunions, the dedications, the hoopla, and the reporters who wanted to write stories about it all. In a surprising turnabout, Gilbert became the quiet one now. He didn't want to talk about the past, 1979, Larry Bird, or the miracle team. Sometimes, he wished the team had never existed. Maybe it would have been better for him, he said, if they had gone

19–10 that year and never achieved anything. Maybe then, he said, he could have come to terms with his brother's death, wrestled with his feelings, gotten the therapy he needed, and entered the NBA clean and sober.

"I'm always sad when I think about that," Gilbert said. "I always think, *What if?*"

Of course, there was another reason why Gilbert was reluctant to attend events in Terre Haute, especially in the 1990s. In those years, he was still hiding the truth of his drug addiction from his friends, and from Brad Miley perhaps most of all. Whenever Gilbert returned to Indiana to visit Miley, he'd hold it together. "And if I didn't hold it together," Gilbert said, "I didn't go see him." He'd stay home in East St. Louis, plumbing the darkness.

In those years, there was a lot of it. Not just one rock bottom, Gilbert said, but many. He lived at the bottom at times, lost in the undercurrents. Gilbert often wondered if he would ever break free from his addiction and reach the surface again. Then, around Christmastime 1999, a single rock-bottom moment helped shake him loose.

Alex and his future wife, Ann, had worked hard to buy Christmas presents for their nieces and nephews. "And I found some of the presents," Gilbert recalled. "I sold them for drugs. I was out all night. And my wife—she's a strong woman. I came home at four or five in the morning and she let me have it." Among other things, Ann let Alex know that they were replacing the presents, even if they had to spend money they didn't have. "Even if we had to spend the rent money."

That day, they went to a mall in the suburbs of St. Louis. And while Ann did the shopping, Alex sat down, trying to compose himself. He felt broken, he said, as if he might vomit or pass out. "I mean, I was tore out the frame. I could barely stand up." And as he was sitting there, trying to get through the trip to the mall, Gilbert heard an excited voice coming from someone in the crowd of shoppers.

"Alex Gilbert?"

The guy was a stranger, a man from East St. Louis. He had probably been about 12 years old in 1979. He had watched Gilbert play during the miracle season at Indiana State. He couldn't believe he was meeting him now at the mall, and he wanted to tell him something. "He told me I was his hero," Gilbert recalled. "He said, 'I've always looked up to you. I thought you were the best basketball player I ever saw in my life and I want my son to meet you.'" At that point, Gilbert said, the man ran off to find his son and Gilbert just sat there thinking, *What have I done to myself?*

He decided to get clean. In the years to come, it happened. He remains clean today, still married to Ann. He has returned to Terre Haute for events, including the team's 40th anniversary celebration in 2019. And while Gilbert still resists talking about 1979, due to all the complicated memories involved, he doesn't mind discussing that moment at the mall around Christmas. "If you can remember to put that in somewhere," he said in 2025, "I'd appreciate it."

The thing that had almost destroyed him—the greatness of 1979—had come back around in the end to save him.

"Like a lifeline," Gilbert said.

He latched onto it and pulled himself out of the void.

69

IN SOME WAYS, GILBERT returned just in time. In the past few years, players from the team have started to die off. Eric Curry, Nemcek's best friend, went first. Rick Shaw, the team manager, came next. Hodges was so broken up over Shaw's passing in early 2025 that he didn't want to talk. Everyone began to sense that time was growing short, and a few players, including Larry Bird, indicated that they might not return for the team's 50th reunion in 2029. They didn't want to look around and take note of the people who were missing. They didn't want to look around and realize they had all grown old. The last time they were together in Terre Haute, Nemcek said, Bird turned to him and made an announcement: "This is the last reunion I'm coming to."

But that didn't mean that Bird was giving up on his friends, on his teammates, or the people who had been there for him at the start, when his life could have gone in a different direction. Over the years, he has stayed in touch with many of them and quietly helped a few in the shadows when they needed it the most. Upon his retirement in 1992, Bird sent his former high school coach, Jim Jones, a small but heavy package in the mail. Jones opened the box to find a Celtics ring inside, with Bird's number, 33, spelled out in diamonds and framed in emerald green. Jones couldn't believe what he was holding in his hand; he would come to consider the ring one of his most prized possessions. But the note from Bird inside the box was just as important to him. Bird told his old coach that the ring was a token of his appreciation, and he signed off with a simple line.

"I hope I made you proud," Bird said.

Throughout the 1990s and into the early 2000s, Bird stayed in touch with another coach who had helped him along the way: Bob King. Not long after the 1979 season, King retired to New Mexico, the place he loved the most. And from time to time, King's phone would light up in the desert with a familiar number. Larry Bird was on the line. "Dad loved it," recalled Dianne Goldrick, King's daughter. "He was very personable and would talk with anybody about basketball." But discussing it with Bird was special for King. He'd sit there on the phone, Goldrick said, smiling as he and Bird talked about sports.

In 2004, Dianne's younger brother Brad had to call Bird with sad news: Their father had died at age 81. With the news, Bird snapped into action. He flew west for the funeral on the Pacers' private jet, asked Carl Nicks to go with him, and, at the invitation of King's family, spoke at the funeral, telling stories in front of a large crowd that packed into the gym at the University of New Mexico to pay their respects.

Nicks, by then, was working at a hospital in Indianapolis, helping troubled teens, and he was excited to fly on the plane with Bird. But he was even more excited two years later, in 2006, when Bird called him one day, just as he used to call King. Nicks was walking into the hospital when his phone rang, he said, and Bird dispensed with any small talk and got straight to the point. He had just two questions for Carl: Did he still watch college basketball? And did he know how to use a computer?

The answer to the first question for Nicks was easy. Of course he still watched college basketball; he loved it. The answer to the second question about computers was a little trickier. "I didn't even know how to log on," Nicks admitted later. "Really, I didn't." But he sensed an opportunity, so, on the phone with Bird, Nicks made the only reasonable choice. He lied. He told Bird he was all about computers, and Bird offered Nicks the job he'd been waiting on: that scout's position with the Indiana Pacers. "I went to my brother-in-law," Nicks recalled, "and did a crash course in computers." And almost 20 years later, Nicks was on a different plane in June 2025. He was flying west on the team charter to watch his Pacers play in Game Seven of the NBA Finals against the Oklahoma City Thunder. Bird had changed his life once in 1979 and he had changed it again with that phone call in 2006.

He had put Carl Nicks where he knew he belonged from the start: in the league.

"It changed everything," Nicks said. "It really did. I'm back in the NBA."

But the player who got the most from Bird didn't need a job, didn't need a diamond-encrusted ring, didn't need a note, didn't need his validation, didn't need his fame, and didn't need any of the trappings or connections that came with it. He just needed a friend.

In 2014, Bob Heaton's son, Travis, committed suicide at age 27, a devastating moment for Bob and his wife, Jane Ann. They had built a beautiful life in Terre Haute. Bob was serving in the state legislature. People recognized him at gas stations and grocery stores, and from time to time at parties, if someone started talking about 1979, or where they were when Bob hit the half-court shot in New Mexico, or what it meant to them when Bob hit the buzzer-beater to defeat Arkansas, Jane Ann would encourage Bob to roll up the sleeve of his shirt and show people the scars from his farm accident. Once again, Bob would be telling stories of miracles.

Now he and Jane Ann were reeling, swimming in pain, and one day, not long after Travis's death, Bird phoned Heaton and invited him to drive over to Indianapolis to visit with him at his office at Pacers headquarters.

Heaton made the drive, eager to see his friend, and once they were safely inside Bird's office, Bird opened up to him like he never had before. They talked about his dad, Heaton's son, questions that had no answers, and then Bird finally leveled with Heaton.

"Bob," Bird said, "to this day, I still don't understand why my dad took his life."

The conversation wasn't emotional, at least not for Bird. Heaton said Bird didn't cry. But he talked for a long time. "He wanted to talk," Heaton said. The conversation went on and on. The two old friends were going deep, and by the time Heaton stood up to leave, maybe an hour later, he was spilling over with gratitude. He drove home across the Indiana prairie to Jane Ann in Terre Haute knowing something important.

They were not alone.

70

THESE DAYS, IF FOLKS want to find Bird, it isn't easy. He moved away from West Baden more than two decades ago. He lived for a while in a gated community in Indianapolis. And when he stepped down as president of the Pacers in 2017, and stopped coming around the facility a few years later, he finally did something he'd been trying to do since the 1970s. Bird disappeared, spending half the year in Florida and the other half on a secluded ranch in rural Indiana.

To get to the ranch, visitors must be invited, and they have to know the way. There are no streets here named after Larry Bird and no statues, either. There's just a big piece of land, down a country road, with a lake for fishing and a forest for hunting mushrooms. And once Bird arrives here every spring, he doesn't like to leave. He works the land, cuts the grass, arranges visits from friends around his landscaping schedule, and doesn't even return to French Lick and West Baden like he once did, perhaps because there's not much left for him there anymore.

His mother died 30 years ago. His siblings all moved away. The old basketball court on the boulevard got plowed over in the name of progress—a McDonald's—and the court that Bird once built at his home in West Baden in that grove of trees fell into disrepair after he left for Indianapolis. The asphalt crumbled. A spiderweb of cracks fanned out to the margins. Weeds sprouted through the gaps. The nets attached to the two goals rotted in the rain and the snow. And these days, there's not much to remind visitors of what this court used to be. There's just a sign planted into the ground and a memory of a time not that long ago.

It was early September 1985, just three weeks before the Celtics were to report to camp. Bird was in the middle of a stretch in which he went to four NBA Finals in a row. The only thing stopping him from winning all of them was Magic Johnson and the Lakers. Converse was selling shoes named after both men, and the sneaker company wanted to film a commercial with Bird and Magic, right there on Bird's asphalt court in West Baden. That week in September, Bird wasn't playing pickup games against guys in town; he was playing against Magic, at least for the cameras. Crowds gathered to watch. People sat on benches, chatting with the two stars, up close and personal, and then, when it was over, Bird and Magic drove down the road to have a drink together at the tavern closest to Bird's house: the Jubil Bar.

The place where Bird's father had once whiled away the hours was, for one night, at least, the center of the basketball universe. Larry Bird and Magic Johnson were sitting together between the door and the pool table. They were knocking back beers. They were entertaining old friends and new, and they were enjoying the moment—the last days of summer in rural Indiana, just before a new basketball season began again.

ACKNOWLEDGMENTS

WRITING A BOOK IS a bit like firing up a half-court shot. Even if you've practiced it, even if you've made the shot before, it feels like a miracle every time it goes in. And so, as always, I have many people to thank for making this book possible.

For starters, I need to thank the hundreds of people who gave generously of their time, welcoming me into their homes, digging up old journals, tracking down old television and radio broadcasts, and spending hours talking about the past. There are too many people to thank by name. To see who helped me and how, I encourage you to read the notes at the end of the book. Every person mentioned in the notes was vital to making this happen. But there are a handful of people who must be mentioned here.

This book doesn't happen without the help of the two men who worked in the sports information department together in the 1970s: Ed McKee and Craig McKee. Ed spent hours with me starting in the summer of 2024, invited me into his home, allowed me to go through his personal archives, and connected me with dozens of others. Craig McKee was similarly helpful and also shared with me the journal he wrote—and the notes he kept—back in 1978–79. His memories, recorded in real time, offered a clear-eyed view of what was really happening behind the scenes, and gave me an invaluable road map for this narrative. I am grateful to both of them.

I also relied heavily on those who coached Larry Bird and the adults who knew him best when he was young: Butch Emmons, a former coach at Springs Valley; Gary Holland, Bird's coach during his senior year of high school; Jim Jones, Bird's mentor growing up; and Bill Hodges, the man who found him in French Lick, coaxed him to come to Indiana State, and was at his side during those formative years. I will always remember the tour that Emmons gave me of French Lick and West Baden; the night I spent in Holland's basement, going through his personal archive of Larry Bird recruitment letters; the afternoon I spent in Jones's kitchen in rural Indiana, talking about Larry Bird; and the many hours I passed in the company of Bill Hodges, both on the phone and inside his house in suburban Charlotte, North Carolina. Over the years, some journalists have taken pleasure in pointing out that Hodges never again recaptured the magic that he found in 1979. I think of it differently. Most of us will be lucky in this life to ever achieve a single great and notable thing. Hodges accomplished at least one, and I thank him and all the other coaches for speaking with me.

I only reached Hodges because I had first gotten to know his players, and others who were in Terre Haute in the 1970s. And so, I need to thank them most of all: Brad Miley and his wife, Kathy, for their warm welcome; Bob Heaton and his wife, Jane Ann, for their trust; Carl Nicks, for his great storytelling; Harry Morgan and his wife, Rita, for their enduring helpfulness; Steve Reed and his wife, Lisa, for their unwavering support; Alex Gilbert, for his honesty; Leroy Staley, for his kindness; Tom Crowder, Rod McNelly, Rich Nemcek, Bob Ritter, and Terry Thimlar, for their understanding and their time; John Nelson, Geoff Shuck, and Rick Williams, for their memories of the early years; Bob Behnke, for letting me inside the trainer's room; Greg Gibson, for his hospitality; the children of Bob King—Dianne, Brad, Larry, and Randy—for their enthusiasm; and Rick Shaw, for speaking to me at length even as his health declined. Shaw died in early 2025, and it saddens me to know that he never got to see this book.

Several fellow journalists—who covered the team, or Bird himself, during these early years—also helped make this book possible. Andy Amey, Len Berman, Peter Carry, Vince Doria, David Israel, Larry Keith, Skip Myslenski, Bruce Newman, Bob Ryan, Dan Shaughnessy, and Lane

Stewart each had a front-row seat to this history. They were there, and I appreciate the time they spent with me, sharing details and stories, so that I could feel like I was there, too.

In addition to these important sources, librarians and archivists played a critical role along the way, as they always do in a project like this one. I must thank Robin Coulter, who opened the archives for me at the Melton Public Library in French Lick and allowed me to spend hours there, splayed out on the floor; Arielle Craig, who assisted me time and again at the Vigo County Public Library in Terre Haute; Teddie Moreno, who knew where to find everything in New Mexico State University's library archives and special collections; Dave Shearer, who unearthed a treasure trove of original television broadcasts at WTHI-TV in Terre Haute and gave me permission to use the footage online (check it out at www.KeithOB.com); and Dennis Vetrovec, who helped me navigate the primary documents held in Indiana State University's special collections to find what I needed to tell this story. These folks saved me many times, as did John Sherman, in the athletic department at Indiana State, and research assistant Conor Howard, at Indiana University. And I would be remiss if I didn't thank two others who also assisted me: Janee Probst and Geoff Gentilini. It was with their help and guidance that I tracked down the military records for Joey Bird, filling a hole that had long existed in this story.

Lastly, I need to thank those who brought this book to life—or helped make sure that I didn't lose my moorings in the process: Yaniv Soha, my editor, who believed in me way back in 2010 and still does now; Richard Abate, my agent, who always knows what to say and do; David Brown, Jimmy Iacobelli, Erin Kibby, Abby Mohr, Kate Napolitano, and Nick Poser at Atria; Jeremy Ryan at Metamorphosis Agency; Adam Rifenberick at Press Box Publicity; the great video trailer wizard Dan Crow; the people who helped keep me sane, including David Abel, Alissa Bartkus, Jim Bartkus, Sean Biehle, Chris Blagg, Jim Callahan, Dan Chartrand, Doug Ciocca, Brett Clanton, Mandy Crow, Chris Donovan, Miruna Dospinescu, Tom Haines, Dan and Julie Hayes, Eric and Monica Heinberg,

Chris Hitler, Stacey Keane-Blagg, Gerry Lanham, Jessica Leffler, Russell Lewis, John Lilly, Beth Lousteau, Ian McNulty, Chris O'Brien, Colleen O'Brien, Keith O'Brien Sr., Terry O'Brien, James O'Byrne, Stephanie Price, Paul Rioux, Madeleine Schaberg, Jenn Serio, Steven Serio, and Dave Yu; our "PHS" crew, the Carlsons and the Moriartys; and the three people who sacrificed the most during the reporting and writing of the book: my wife, Eva, and our sons, Mac and Cal.

Thanks for always cheering for me, win or lose.

NOTES

ABBREVIATIONS USED IN NOTES

Newspapers
AJ *Albuquerque Journal*
BG *The Boston Globe*
BTM *Bedford (IN) Times-Mail*
CE *The Cincinnati Enquirer*
CJ *The Louisville Courier-Journal*
CP *The Cincinnati Post*
CT *Chicago Tribune*
DFP *Detroit Free Press*
DH *The Dubois County (IN) Daily Herald*
IN *The Indianapolis News*
IS *The Indianapolis Star*
LSJ *The Lansing State Journal*
SVH *Springs Valley Herald*
THS *The Terre Haute Star*
THT *The Terre Haute Tribune*

Books
VH L. Virginia Smith, *Larry Bird: From Valley Hick to Boston Celtic* (self-published, 1982).

Collections
PRL Records of President Richard Landini, Record Group UAR1.2.8, Indiana State University, Special Collections.

EPIGRAPH

vii **"Larry Bird, distilled":** Craig McKee, interview with author, May 9, 2025.
vii **"If Bill Hodges hadn't":** *Magic & Bird: A Courtship of Rivals*, written by Charles Olivier, directed by Ezra Edelman, aired March 10, 2010, on HBO.
vii **"I like to tell people":** Rich Nemcek, interview with author, May 4, 2025.

INTRODUCTION

1 **elbow or a punch:** Details about Indiana State's game against Rutgers in March 1978, and the altercation on the floor afterward, come from multiple sources, including: Abdel An-

derson, interview with author, March 2, 2025; James Bailey, interview with author, January 28, 2025; Bob Behnke, interview with author, September 5, 2024; Hollis Copeland, interview with author, June 29, 2025; Steve Hefele, interview with author, February 28, 2025; Bill Hodges, interview with author, March 7, 2025; Brad Miley, interview with author, September 25, 2024; Steve Reed, interview with author, August 15, 2024; Rick Shaw, interview with author, September 23, 2024; Vinni DiTrani, "Bailey to the Rescue," *Hackensack (NJ) Record*, March 15, 1978; "Belted by Bird, Student Charges," *Hackensack (NJ) Record*, March 15, 1978; T. J. Simers, "Bird's Burned-Up as Rutgers Wins," *Morristown (NJ) Daily Record*, March 15, 1978; Jim Smith, "Bailey Becomes Neutralizer for Bird," *Newsday*, March 15, 1978; "Sporting Around" and "Jim Bailey Hits in Clutch for Rutgers," *THT*, March 15, 1978; "Sycamore Year Ends at Rutgers," *THS*, March 15, 1978; Joe Calabrese, "Knights Survive in Battle of Bumbles," *Trenton (NJ) Times*, March 15, 1978; and Craig McKee, journal entry, shared with author. Finally, Bird himself acknowledged this altercation in an authorized memoir—Larry Bird and Earvin Magic Johnson with Jackie MacMullan, *When the Game Was Ours* (Mariner Books, 2009), 23. Based on Bird's account, it was an elbow. Based on other accounts, it was a punch.

3 **"Birdshit!" one fan shouted:** Accounts vary on what the fan said, but multiple sources confirm this account, including Smith, "Bailey Becomes Neutralizer"; and Copeland, interview with author, June 29, 2025.

3 **everyone saw:** Multiple sources and accounts listed above confirm these details, but two eyewitnesses had especially vivid memories that were exactly the same—Copeland, interview with author, June 29, 2025, and Shaw, interview with author, September 23, 2024.

3 **"The guy's nose":** Shaw, interview with author, September 23, 2024.

3 **"What happened?":** Simers, "Bird's Burned-Up."

4 **acquire some beer:** Brad Miley, interview with author, September 25, 2024.

4 **more than a thousand:** According to On3, a platform that tracks college players, 1,055 men's college basketball players had put their names in the transfer portal by the end of April 2025.

PART I

1.

9 **Larry Bird would spill out:** Three different people remember playing with Bird and his brothers at and around the old water plant: Kevin Carnes, interview with author, February 3, 2024; Butch Emmons, interview with author, September 13, 2024; and Dave Qualkenbush, interview with author, May 22, 2025. In addition, the author toured the old water plant with Emmons on February 3, 2024.

10 **had to let young Larry go:** This detail was confirmed by three of Bird's coaches in French Lick—Emmons, interview with author, September 13, 2024; Gary Holland, interview with author, November 25, 2024; and Jim Jones, interview with author, May 24, 2025.

2.

10 **pleasant demeanor:** Multiple sources confirm these details, including Emmons, interview with author, February 3, 2025; Gary Holland, interview with author,

February 3, 2025; Jim Jones, interview with author, May 24, 2025; Qualkenbush, interview with author, May 22, 2025; *VH*, 52; and Larry Bird with Bob Ryan, *Drive: The Story of My Life* (Doubleday, 1989), 14.

10 **Joey never finished:** The author requested the military history of Claude Joseph Bird Jr. from the National Personnel Records Center and received 77 pages of documents in April 2025. These previously unutilized and unseen records included a document signed by Joey Bird's father on April 24, 1944, giving his son permission to enlist in the US Naval Reserve before his 18th birthday; his enlistment papers signed by Joey in Indianapolis on May 1, 1944; his personal affirmation that he had never finished eighth grade or attended high school; his identification records; his transfer orders; the discipline report concerning his AWOL status from the Great Lakes naval station on August 21, 1944; the discipline report concerning his liquor consumption on a ship in Charleston, South Carolina, on March 30, 1945; his individual orders to adjust pay, showing his status as a crew messman and nothing more; his discharge papers signed July 23, 1946; his personal account of his lost belongings written and signed by him on February 19, 1947; and his status as an army infantryman during the Korean War in 1950–51. The documents offer a new window into Joey Bird never seen before. Hereafter, it shall be referred to as Claude Joseph Bird Jr., military records.

10 **filled with exciting dispatches:** The author reviewed the *Springs Valley Herald* from the spring and summer of 1944. Every day, the *Herald* carried a prominent front-page feature under the headline "News of Our Boys in Service."

11 **got into trouble:** Claude Joseph Bird Jr., military records.

11 **over in Paoli:** In *Drive*, Bird said the factory was in Paoli. In *VH*, his aunt L. Virginia Smith said it was Orleans. The author corresponded with the Orange County Historical Society to pin down that Bird's account was likely the correct one.

11 **reenlisting to go to Korea:** In addition to Joey Bird's World War II record, the author also obtained records related to his time in Korea, showing his service with the 25th Division of the US Army. According to these records, Bird joined his unit in Korea on May 11, 1950. Additional details come from *VH*, 11.

11 **a foot soldier:** Claude Joseph Bird Jr., military records; *VH*, 50; and "Former Southport Basketball Star with Marines," *IN*, September 19, 1950.

11 **shivering in a foxhole:** The author was able to pinpoint Joey Bird's service in Korea thanks to "Former Basketball Star" and an archival news story written by Joey Bird himself: "The Dough Boys in Korea," *SVH*, March 15, 1951. Additional details come from the records of the 25th Infantry Division, November 1950, Book VIII.

11 **first-person tale:** Cpl. Claude Joseph Bird Jr., "The Dough Boys."

12 **On a Saturday night:** "Bird-Kerns," *SVH*, September 27, 1951.

12 **would be a bridal shower:** Corine Conrad, "Crystal," *DH*, October 13, 1951.

12 **a concrete finisher:** John Kerns, US Census 1940 and US Census 1950.

12 **had advised against:** *VH*, 50.

12 **drinking at times to get drunk:** People in French Lick were well aware of Joey Bird's drinking at the time. But none described it more starkly than the women in his life. Georgia's sister, L. Virginia Smith, wrote that by the early 1950s, Joey "often drank enough to become intoxicated" (*VH*, 14), while Georgia Bird called Joey an "alcoholic" (Rick Woodson, "Silent Superstar Put Indiana State on the Map," Gannett News Service, February 21, 1979).

12 **lashing out at ghosts:** The author confirmed the details of Joey Bird's nightmares with three sources—Qualkenbush, interview with author, May 22, 2025; *VH*, 51; and

the HBO documentary *Magic & Bird: A Courtship of Rivals*, which included Bird's participation and was created with the help of the memoir that Jackie MacMullan cowrote, *When the Game Was Ours*.

12 **four born in four years:** The first Bird child, Mike, was born in July 1952 (Corine Conrad, "Crystal," *DH*, August 8, 1952). The fourth child, Larry, was born in December 1956.

3.

12 **Larry loved his father:** Mike Bird, interviewed in *Magic & Bird*.

12 **moved a lot:** In order to paint a picture of Bird in his early life, the author conducted interviews with more than a dozen people who knew Bird during his childhood in West Baden and French Lick. People interviewed include, but are not limited to: Carnes, interview with author, February 3, 2024; Doug Conrad, interview with author, September 23, 2024; Mike Cox, interview with author, May 22, 2025; Emmons, interviews with author, September 13, 2024, September 17, 2024, and February 3, 2025; Bill Harris, interview with author, September 26, 2024; Holland, interviews with author, August 2, 2024, November 25, 2024, and February 3, 2025; Eddie Jones, interview with author, May 22, 2025; Jim Jones, interview with author, May 24, 2025; Bill Kendall, interview with author, May 22, 2025; Ralph Purkhiser, interview with author, February 10, 2025; Qualkenbush, interview with author, May 22, 2025; Kim Rominger, interview with author, September 27, 2024; Barry Wilson, interview with author, September 13, 2024; and Gary Wyman, interview with author, May 22, 2025. Additional details about the family's moves come from *VH*, 16, and *Drive*, 12.

12 **two jobs to help pay:** Bill Jauss, "He's the Indiana State Bird!" *CT*, January 20, 1978; Rick Woodson, "Silent Superstar Put Indiana State on the Map," Gannett News Service, February 21, 1979; and multiple interviews with residents of French Lick and West Baden mentioned above.

12 **small crew of French Lick boys:** Details in this section about Bird and his friends come from interviews with two of the four boys—Mike Cox, interview with author, May 22, 2025, and Gary Wyman, interview with author, May 22, 2025.

13 **If Larry had a dream:** Bird spoke about this dream himself at a press conference in Terre Haute on May 30, 2024.

13 **wake up swinging:** *VH*, 51. In an interview with the author, Qualkenbush also confirmed Joey Bird's night terrors. Qualkenbush said he heard Joey when sleeping over at the Bird house during his childhood.

13 **the Jubil Bar:** The author confirmed the spelling of the bar name with two sources: Robin Coulter, at the Melton Public Library in French Lick, and Bill Kendall, the owner of the Jubil Bar in the 1970s.

13 **fought and even killed:** "Spencer Trial Is August 30," *BTM*, August 26, 1976, and "Treated for Knife Wound," *BTM*, February 9, 1973.

13 **"There were times":** *VH*, 16.

13 **filed for divorce:** "Facts on File," *BTM*, August 15, 1972.

14 **He got jobs:** Details about Bird's childhood jobs come from multiple sources, including: Rominger, interview with author, September 27, 2024; Wilson, interview with author, September 13, 2024; Michael Rubino, "Larry Bird's Greatest Shot Is the One He Didn't Take," *Indianapolis Monthly*, December 24, 2015; and *Drive*, 13.

14 **155 pounds:** "Springs Valley Roster," *BTM*, November 17, 1972.
14 **could take a bale:** Wilson, interview with author, September 13, 2024.
14 **saw it with their own eyes:** Carnes, interview with author, February 3, 2024; Conrad, interview with author, September 23, 2024; Cox, interview with author, May 22, 2025; Emmons, interviews with author, September 13, 2024, September 17, 2024, and February 3, 2025; Harris, interview with author, September 26, 2024; Holland, interviews with author, August 2, 2024, November 25, 2024, and February 3, 2025; Eddie Jones, interview with author, May 22, 2025; Jim Jones, interview with author, May 24, 2025; Kendall, interview with author, May 22, 2025; Purkhiser, interview with author, February 10, 2025; Qualkenbush, interview with author, May 22, 2025; Rominger, interview with author, September 27, 2024; Wilson, interview with author, September 13, 2024; and Wyman, interview with author, May 22, 2025.
15 **more than just a coach:** Bird, press conference, May 30, 2024; Emmons, interviews with author, September 13, 2024, September 17, 2024, and February 3, 2025; Holland, interviews with author, August 2, 2024, November 25, 2024, and February 3, 2025; and Jones, interview with author, May 24, 2025.
15 **the first person:** Larry Bird press conference, May 30, 2024.
15 **"those other boys":** *Drive*, 17.
15 **roused Larry himself:** Jones, interview with author, May 24, 2025.
16 **became fixtures at Flick's:** Conrad, interview with author, September 23, 2024; Cox, interview with author, May 22, 2025; and Wyman, interview with author, May 22, 2025.
16 **priced the menu:** Flick's Restaurant advertisement, *Springs Valley Herald*, October 31, 1974.
16 **"You always have":** *Drive*, 12.

4.

16 **"I'll be damned":** John Fox, "Pfc. Dave's Bliss," *Binghamton (NY) Sunday Press*, February 11, 1968.
16 **"To play for me":** Barry Levine, "A Real Dr. Jekyll Case," *New Brunswick (NJ) Home News*, February 26, 1971.
17 **"I feel that I am studying":** John Fox, "Pfc. Dave's Bliss."
17 **Bliss was learning:** Bliss would coach thirty-seven seasons of Division I basketball. He resigned from his last job at Baylor in 2003, after making payments to players and attempting to cover them up when one of those players was murdered.
17 **Knight instructed Bliss:** Many details in this section come from interviews with members of Knight's coaching staff at Indiana, including: Dave Bliss, interview with author, September 17, 2024; and Bob Weltlich, interviews with author, December 2, 2024, and December 4, 2024.
18 **Hoosier players did the unthinkable:** "Basketball Coach Quits at IU," *Evansville Press*, March 11, 1971.
18 **"I'm not bitter":** "Indiana U.'s Lou Watson Resigns," *THT*, March 11, 1971.
18 **"trouble-makers":** Max Stultz, "Indiana Flies Distress Flag," *IS*, March 12, 1971.
18 **"earthy American language":** Barry Levine, "A Real Dr. Jekyll Case."
18 **openly mock female coaches:** Mark Whicker, "Opinion," *Chapel Hill (NC) News*, August 2, 1973.

19 **On the day he was introduced:** Details of this day come from multiple sources, including: "Army's Knight New I.U. Cage Coach," *IS*, March 28, 1971; Corky Lamm, "I.U. Scores Again—Without a Shot," *IN*, March 31, 1971; and Russ Brown, "Recruiting Occupies New IU Coach Knight," *CJ*, March 31, 1971.

5.

19 **Bliss found Larry Bird:** Details in this chapter draw extensively on interviews with six coaches who were in the Springs Valley gym that winter and in Bobby Knight's coaches room in Bloomington. These sources include: Bliss, interview with author, September 17, 2024; Emmons, interviews with author, September 13, 2024, September 17, 2024, and February 3, 2025; Holland, interviews with author, August 2, 2024, November 25, 2024, and February 3, 2025; Jones, interview with author, May 24, 2025; Bill Olsen, interview with author, February 1, 2025; and Weltlich, interviews with author, December 2, 2024, and December 4, 2024. Also valuable were the recruiting letters than Holland kept from the winter of 1974 and shared with the author on February 3, 2025—hereafter referred to as Holland Personal Collection.

21 **developing the qualities:** Details in this section come from interviews the author conducted with the previously mentioned French Lick and West Baden sources who knew Bird during this window of time. Bird himself confirmed his penchant to distrust people, hold grudges, and be stubborn (*Drive*, 23).

21 **Bird borrowed the compact Chevrolet pickup truck:** Wyman, interview with author, May 22, 2025.

21 **took Bliss mushroom hunting:** Bliss, interview with author, September 17, 2024; and Tom Cushman, "Getting Indiana State's Bird to Finally Chirp," *Philadelphia Daily News*, March 15, 1979.

21 **Jones made an announcement:** Jerry Birge, "Keeping Score," *DH*, June 22, 1973.

22 **The reasons for the decision:** Jones, interview with author, May 24, 2025.

22 **felt like crying:** Cox, interview with author, May 22, 2025, and *Drive*, 30.

22 **Bliss didn't feel much better:** Bliss, interview with author, September 17, 2024.

22 **Bird grew about four inches:** This detail is well chronicled and was confirmed in multiple places, including: Emmons, interviews with author, September 13, 2024, September 17, 2024, and February 3, 2025; Holland, interviews with author, August 2, 2024, November 25, 2024, and February 3, 2025; Jim Jones, interview with author, May 24, 2025; multiple news accounts from 1978–79; and *Drive*, 31.

22 **"It wasn't even matching":** Wilson, interview with author, September 13, 2024.

22 **no one was going to make fun:** Purkhiser, interview with author, February 10, 2025.

23 **When opposing teams were inbounding:** Details about Larry's play on the floor in high school come from interviews with his previously mentioned high school teammates, coaches, and the men who recruited him—as well as interviews with four people who played against Bird while he was at Valley: Bill Butcher, interview with author, November 13, 2024; Alex Crane, interview with author, January 22, 2025; Jim Pentzer, interview with author, January 27, 2025; and Wayne Flick, interview with author, December 19, 2024.

23 **College coaches had to see:** Holland Personal Collection.

23 **a Kansas State assistant:** Marvin Adams, assistant coach, Kansas State University, letter to Jones, February 11, 1974, Holland Personal Collection.

NOTES

23 **"the highest rating"**: Olsen, letter to Holland, January 21, 1974, Holland Personal Collection.

23 **lots of people were weighing:** Emmons, Holland, and Jones spoke to the author about the pressure that Bird was feeling; Georgia Bird mentioned it in several interviews she gave in the late 1970s; and Bird himself has acknowledged it over the years (*When the Game Was Ours*, 15).

24 **on the same day:** Kenny Trivette, assistant basketball coach, University of Kentucky, letter to Holland, January 21, 1974, Holland Personal Collection.

6.

24 **Bliss and Knight drove:** Bliss, interview with author, September 17, 2024. Multiple news accounts also confirm Knight's presence in the gym that night.

24 **a world apart:** Details in this section recounting the Loogootee–Valley rivalry and their big game on January 29, 1974, come from multiple sources, including interviews with 10 people on the floor that night and multiple people in the stands: Bliss, interview with author, September 17, 2024; Butcher, interview with author, November 13, 2024; Conrad, interview with author, September 23, 2024; Crane, interview with author, January 22, 2025; Emmons, interview with author, February 3, 2025; Flick, interview with author, December 19, 2024; Holland, interview with author, November 25, 2024; Purkhiser, interview with author, February 10, 2025; Rominger, interview with author, September 27, 2024; Wilson, interview with author, September 13, 2024. The author also utilized several news accounts, including: "2 Killed at Navy Depot by Demonstration Blast," *IS*, August 19, 1972; "Two Women Killed at Crane Naval Ammunition Depot," *Mayfield (KY) Messenger*, August 19, 1972; "Peace Can Mean Job Losses at Crane," *Bloomington-Bedford (IN) Sunday Herald-Times*, December 10, 1972; "Hoosiers Played Major War Role," *Vincennes (IN) Sun-Commercial*, January 24, 1973; Russ Brown, "Springs Valley Shooting Normal," *CJ*, January 26, 1972; Russ Brown, "Alan Crane Hits Clincher for Loogootee in Tense 51–49 Upset of Springs Valley," *CJ*, January 24, 1973; Russ Brown, "Unbeaten Loogootee Faces Stiffest Test," *CJ*, January 29, 1974; Russ Brown, "Coach's Son, Bill Butcher, Puts Axe to Springs Valley," *CJ*, January 30, 1974; and Jerry Birge, "Keeping Score," *DH*, January 30, 1974.

25 **knew he was in trouble:** Holland, interview with author, February 3, 2025.

25 **Estimates would vary:** Russ Brown, "Coach's Son"; and Jerry Birge, "Keeping Score," January 30, 1974,

26 **"right in the sternum":** Flick, interview with author, December 19, 2024.

27 **an obscene gesture:** Flick, interview with author, December 19, 2024, and Holland, interview with author, February 3, 2025.

7.

27 **At least he didn't holler:** Holland, interview with author, February 3, 2025.

27 **Bird stayed positive:** Purkhiser, interview with author, February 10, 2025.

27 **celebrating each member:** *SVH*, February 21, 1974.

27 **all the stops:** "Fans L-I-N-E Up for Regional Tickets," *SVH*, March 7, 2024.

28 **"You pinch their legs":** Pentzer, interview with author, January 27, 2025, and Al Brewster, "'Cutters Cut Down Valley to Reach '16,'" *Bloomington-Bedford (IN) Sunday Herald-Times*, March 10, 1974.

28 **too slow to play in Lexington:** Billy Reed, "Bird Driven Away," *CJ*, February 21, 1979.
29 **a disappointment for Bird:** Reed, "Bird Driven Away"; "It's a Long Trip from UK to IU . . . as a Bird Flies," *CJ*, June 28, 1974; and *When the Game Was Ours*, 12.
29 **sat in a hotel:** Bliss, interview with author, September 17, 2024. Bliss's journal, shared with the author, also confirms this memory.
29 **"As long as Bird is one!":** Bliss, journal entry, March 10, 1974.
29 **The meeting happened:** Two sources confirmed the details of the meeting with Bird, Knight, and Jones—Jim Jones and his wife, Joyce, interviews with author, May 24, 2025.
29 **the very best version of Bobby Knight:** Jim and Joyce Jones, interviews with author, May 24, 2025.
29 **trying to convince:** Olsen, interview with author, February 1, 2025.

8.

30 **The morning of the trip:** Details in this section come from multiple sources, including: Holland, interviews with author, August 2, 2024, November 25, 2024, and February 3, 2025; Olsen, interview with author, February 1, 2025; *SVH*, various issues from March and April 1974; Dan Lauck, "The Changing of Denny Crum," *Newsday (Hempstead, NY)*, December 22, 1977; Kevin Sherrington, "Denny Crum," *Wichita Eagle*, March 27, 1986; and an extensive *Louisville Courier-Journal* magazine piece on Crum from the year he tried to land Bird (Billy Reed, "I'm a Competitor," *Courier-Journal and Times Magazine*, November 24, 1974).
32 **In the photo:** "Bird Doing Great as All-Star," *SVH*, April 25, 1974.

9.

32 **father was overwhelmed:** *Drive*, 15.
32 **buy rounds of drinks:** Multiple locals confirmed to the author that Joey Bird frequented the bars in French Lick and West Baden, including the owner of the Jubil Bar in the 1970s—Bill Kendall, interview with author, May 22, 2025.
32 **"in return for the drinks":** *Drive*, 15.
32 **about $20 left for himself:** *Drive*, 16.
33 **"first-class rook job":** Jerry Birge, "Keeping Score," *DH*, March 27, 1974.
33 **"I don't like the coach":** Details about Bird's frustration on the all-star team come from multiple sources, including: Bob Hammel, "Hoosiers Stars Romp by Kentucky, 110–95," *Bloomington-Bedford (IN) Sunday Herald-Times*, June 30, 1974; Jan Clark, "Overman Finds Coaching All-Stars No Picnic," *Richmond (IN) Palladium-Item*, June 30, 1974; Dane Young, "Powerful Hoosiers Out-hustle Kentucky," *Evansville Sunday Courier and Press*, June 30, 1974; Mike Chappell, "Hoosier Stars Demolish Kentucky in Two-Game Set," *Anderson (IN) Daily Bulletin*, July 1, 1974; Bob Williams, "Indiana Star's 2-Game Shooting Awesome," *IS*, July 1, 1974; Jimmie Angelopolous, "Sweep Not Without Gripes," *IN*, July 1, 1974; Mark Montieth, "All-Star Anguish Still Vivid for Bird," *IS*, February 8, 1998; and Dana Hunsinger Benbow, "Second String?" *IS*, June 2, 2024.
33 **riding in the truck bed:** Cox, interview with author, May 22, 2025; and Wyman, interview with author, May 22, 2025.

34 **"petulance born of embarrassment":** Bob Hammel, "Disappointed Bird Declines Late Role," *Bloomington-Bedford (IN) Sunday Herald-Times*, June 30, 1974.
34 **claimed to be excited:** *When the Game Was Ours*, 12.
34 **$75 in his pocket:** *Drive*, 36.
34 **McNutt had a reputation:** "Despite Policy, Dorms House Booze," *Indiana Daily Student (Bloomington, IN)*, September 13, 1974; and John Laskowski, interview with author, November 29, 2024.
34 **five future NBA players:** The author reviewed the Indiana University campus directory from the fall of 1974. According to the directory, the following basketball players lived in McNutt: Kent Benson, Larry Bird, Quinn Buckner, Mark Haymore, Scott May, Wayne Radford, and Jim Wisman. All but Haymore and Wisman would play in the NBA.
35 **Janet Condra, with long hair:** Springs Valley High School yearbook, 1974.
35 **the dormitory next door:** Indiana University campus directory, 1974.
35 **outside the dormitory walls to be bewildering:** In any interview that Bird gave later, he always said IU was too big for him to ever get comfortable.
35 **30,000 students:** Details about what they might have been doing that week come directly from the "Today on Campus" calendars and advertisements published in the *Indiana Daily Student* in August 1974.
35 **"like a whole country":** *Drive*, 39.
35 **Wisman would later earn . . . He was leaving:** The author interviewed four members of the team that fall: Bliss, interview with author, September 17, 2024; Laskowski, interview with author, November 29, 2024; team manager Larry Sherfick, interview with author, January 7, 2025; and Weltlich, interviews with author, December 2, 2024, and December 4, 2024. Additional confirmation comes from *When the Game Was Ours*, 13; Seth Davis, *When March Went Mad* (Times/Henry Holt, 2009), 54; and *Drive*, 40.
35 **back-to-back turnovers:** Dick Mittman, "Shirt-Grabbing Revisited," *IN*, February 10, 1976; and Bob Kelley, "Wisman 'Expected' Explosion," *Evansville Sunday Courier and Press*, February 15, 1976.
35 **drew the eye:** "A Hot Knight in the Old Town . . . ," *IS*, February 8, 1976.
35 **began to question their coach:** Wayne Fuson, "Knight Won Game But Lost Friends," *IN*, February 10, 1976, and "Bobby Knight: Pro, Con," *IN*, February 13, 1976.
35 **blamed Clark and the *Star*:** Robert Reed, "Coach Knight: At Least You Weren't Kicking Your Dog," *Franklin-Greenwood (IN) Daily Journal*, February 11, 1976.
35 **wanted to ban all photographers:** "'I Screwed Up,' Admits Knight," *Evansville Press*, February 11, 1974.
35 **likely ended up there together:** Bliss, interview with author, September 17, 2024.
36 **"Man, I don't have nothing":** *When the Game Was Ours*, 13.
36 **"two different worlds":** Laskowski, interview with author, November 29, 2024.
36 **"How can I keep wearing":** *Drive*, 40.
37 **treated him poorly:** In an interview with the author, Bliss conceded, "There's a certain amount of hazing that probably goes on." Additional details come from Sherfick, who recounted for the author comments that players made to—and about—Bird in the locker room; Weltlich, who recounted for the author a memory of seeing Bird, standing off to the side in the arena, not playing at all—*Drive*, 39; and *When the Game Was Ours*, 13.

37   **told no one about his intentions:** Bird made this statement in *When the Game Was Ours*. However, Bliss claims that Larry came to his office to give him the news—a story that fellow assistant coach Bob Weltlich confirmed for the author. "Unfortunately," Bliss told the author, "I remember it all too well."
37   **"He looks at me":** Sherfick, interview with author, January 7, 2025.
38   **Bird walked into his office:** Bliss, interview with author, September 17, 2024.
38   **Outside, it was starting to feel:** Details come from the *Indiana Daily Student*.
38   **"I was panicked":** Bliss, interview with author, September 17, 2024.
38   **putting down $25:** Dave "Ace" Soverly, "Dealin' in Sports," *Anderson (IN) Herald*, September 12, 1974.
38   **Bird was long gone:** Bliss, interview with author, September 17, 2024; Sherfick, interview with author, January 7, 2025; Weltlich, interviews with author, December 2, 2024, and December 4, 2024; and *Drive*, 41.
38   **hitchhiked home:** Bird wrote about this moment in *Drive*. He also spoke about it at a press conference at the Final Four on March 25, 1979. "Just hitchhiked home," he said that day. "Didn't even tell Bobby Knight."

10.

38   **"You disappoint me":** Georgia Bird confirmed her disappointment over the years in interviews she gave to multiple publications, including: Phil Hersh, "Indiana State: The Bird's Nest," *Des Moines Register*, December 20, 1977; Bill Jauss, "He's the Indiana State Bird!" *CT*, January 20, 1978; Larry Keith, "Bird Has Those Trees on Top," *Sports Illustrated*, January 23, 1978. Additional confirmation comes from Rubino, "Larry Bird's Greatest Shot Is the One He Didn't Take"; and *Drive*, 38.
38   **Larry didn't seem to understand:** *Drive*, 39.
39   **"We have accepted it":** Bob Hammel, "Bird Goes Home," *Bloomington (IN) Herald-Telephone*, September 16, 1974.
39   **taking control of his life:** Rubino, "Larry Bird's Greatest Shot"; Larry Keith, "Bird Has Those Trees on Top," *Sports Illustrated*, January 23, 1978; and *Drive*, 38.
39   **exactly as small:** Details about Northwood Institute and its history come from multiple sources, including advertisements in *IN* (February 18, 1920) and *Evansville Courier* (January 25, 1920); "West Baden Looms as Business College," *Evansville Press*, November 3, 1966; "Price Paid for Hotel Will Not Be Revealed," *IN*, November 10, 1966; Becky Hill, "Fabled Hotel to Live Again," *Bloomington-Bedford (IN) Sunday Herald-Times*, February 5, 1967; Norman Bess, "Going to College? Take Time, Lots of Cash," *IN*, April 21, 1973; "NI students take lion's share of show ribbons," *BTM*, October 1, 1973; "It Happened in Indiana," *THT*, January 12, 1974; and author tour of the facility on February 3, 2025.
40   **members of the Northwood team:** Details about Bird's time at Northwood in this section come from interviews with four different people on the team at that time, including Dave Earley, interview with author, January 17, 2025; Kent Hutchinson, interview with author, January 22, 2025; Burt Sexton, interview with author, January 21, 2025; and Glen Tow, interview with author, January 18, 2025.
40   **"Really?":** Tow, interview with author, January 18, 2025.
41   **"dead silence":** Earley, interview with author, January 17, 2025.
42   **wasting his talents:** Tow, interview with author, January 18, 2025.
42   **Bird liked working for the city:** The author confirmed this detail with multiple sources, including: Carnes, interview with author, February 3, 2025; and Hodges,

interview with author, February 12, 2025. Larry's own mother, Georgia, even confirmed it in 1979 in an interview with Mike Madden. "It don't take much to make Larry happy," she said at the time. "He liked driving that truck." Michael Madden, "The Bird Is the Word—and the Word Is Super," *BG*, January 28, 1979.

42 **a used Chevy:** In *Drive* (p. 40), Bird described it as a 1964 Chevy. Bob King later described it differently. It was "an old clunker," King said. Phil Hersh, "Terre Hautens Hot for Bird Watching," *CE*, December 18, 1977.

42 **That December:** Details about the death of Larry Bird's father come from multiple sources, including: "Facts on File," *BTM*, December 21, 1974; death certificate for Claude Joseph Bird Jr., Indiana State Board of Health, No. 75-010590, February 3, 1975; "Gun Shot Fatal to Baden Man," *SVH*, February 6, 1975; multiple author interviews with the previously listed sources who were living in French Lick and West Baden at that time; Rubino, "Larry Bird's Greatest Shot"; and *Drive*, 14–15.

PART II

11.

45 **laying him to rest:** "Gun Shot Fatal to Baden Man," *SVH*, February 6, 1975.

45 **on a hill:** The author visited the cemetery on May 24, 2025.

45 **moving in the wrong direction:** Details about Hodges's career in the winter of 1975 come from multiple sources, including: Hodges, interview with author, February 11, 2025; George Bianchi, interview with author, February 2, 2025; Connie Mosbaugh, interview with author, June 29, 2025; Rick Shuck, interview with author, February 28, 2025; and G. L. Bianchi, *7 Years an Eagle: Vol. II* (self-published, 2023), 483. Bianchi's book is a memoir of his life and recounts in detail his year with Hodges in Savannah.

45 **dead-end road:** Details about Hodges's early life and basketball career in high school come from multiple sources, including: Dave Harris, interview with author, January 27, 2025; Ralph Stacy, interview with author, January 29, 2025; Barry Templin, interview with author, September 26, 2024; Hodges, multiple interviews with author; Terry Thimlar, multiple interviews with author; Eagle Township High School yearbook, 1961; Wilson Hodges, US Census 1950; "Sheridan Tops Zionsville 92–81," *Sheridan (IN) News*, January 12, 1961; "Marshall Paces Warren Over Zionsville, 74–64," *IS*, February 1, 1961; and "Zionsville Falls Easily as Neal Pumps 31, Harp Owns 10–7 Record," *Noblesville (IN) Ledger*, February 6, 1961.

46 **fight just about anyone:** Dave Harris, interview with author, January 27, 2025; Bill Hodges, interview with author, February 11, 2025; Ralph Stacy, interview with author, January 29, 2025; and Barry Templin, interview with author, September 26, 2024.

46 **wasn't just any coach:** Details about Hugh Thimlar come from multiple sources, including: Hodges, multiple interviews with author; Terry Thimlar, multiple interviews with author; Thimlar scrapbooks, shared with author in Thimlar's home, March 5, 2025; and Jay Lawrence, "Indiana State's Hodges Lets Bird Show the Way," *Fort Myers News-Press*, January 11, 1979.

47 **selling Electrolux vacuum cleaners:** Hodges spoke to the author about the road he traveled to becoming a head coach and his brief time selling vacuum cleaners— Hodges, interview with author, February 11, 2025. Additional details can be found in Mike Myers, "The Coach from Boone County," *IN*, January 22, 1979.

47 **moved south:** The author spoke to multiple people about this time in Hodges's life, including Bill, his ex-wife, Connie, and players and colleagues who knew him during this time—Bianchi, interview with author, February 2, 2025; Hodges, multiple interviews with author; and Mosbaugh, interview with author, June 29, 2025.
48 **in a shared office:** Bianchi, interview with author, February 2, 2025; and Hodges, interview with author, March 7, 2025.
48 **didn't even have much money:** Mosbaugh, interview with author, June 29, 2025.
48 **was flying down:** Terry Thimlar, interviews with author, August 7, 2024, and March 5, 2025; and Hodges, interview with author, February 11, 2025.

12.

49 **Bob King stepped off:** Terry Thimlar, interviews with author, August 7, 2024, and March 5, 2025.
49 **rheumatic fever:** For details on Bob King's backstory, the author interviewed three of his children—Dianne Goldrick, interview with author, October 15, 2024; Brad King, interviews with author, October 18, 2024, and January 9, 2025; Larry King, interview with author, October 15, 2024. The author also received additional help from a fourth child, Randy King.
49 **"certain type of defense":** "Bob King Chosen for UNM Basketball Coach," *Santa Fe New Mexican*, March 29, 1962.
50 **"the most nowhere place in America . . . Podunk for a night?":** "*Playboy* Interview: Steve Martin," *Playboy*, January 1980.
50 **used the comments to his advantage:** Details about Martin's return trip to Terre Haute can be found in multiple sources, including: Gordon Englehardt, "'Excuuuuse me!' . . . Steve Martin Recants on Terre Haute Critique," *CJ*, December 8, 1979; Jan Carroll, "Martin Says 'Nowhere' Moved," *Chronicle Tribune (Marion, IN)*, December 8, 1979; and Mary Wade Atteberry, "The Shuffle Inn in Shambles When Martin Shuffled Out," *IS*, December 11, 1979.
50 **"Chief Oubachi":** "Oubachi Proposed as Mascot for Sycamores," *Indiana Statesman (Terre Haute, IN)*, February 13, 1969.
50 **$600 a year:** "Going to College?" *IN*, April 21, 1973.
51 **Thimlar suggested:** Terry Thimlar, interviews with author, August 7, 2024, and March 5, 2025.
51 **a walking NCAA investigation:** Details about Webster's saga come from Dick Weiss, "Byrd Lands in Miami," *Philadelphia Daily News*, October 5, 1974; Jack Willkinson, "The Byrd's Still Attractive—Even With Clipped Wings," *Miami News*, November 14, 1974; Jim Martz, "Dade-South's Evans Eyes Best-Ever Season," *Miami News*, November 26, 1974; and Henry Seiden, "Byrd Flies North to Ex-Dade South Coach," *Miami News*, July 1, 1975.
52 **with an understanding:** King never confirmed this arrangement, but Evans spoke about it with multiple people at Indiana State in the 1970s.

13.

52 **Hodges drove down:** Bianchi, *7 Years an Eagle: Vol. II*, 484; Bianchi, interview with author, February 2, 2025; Hodges, interview with author, February 12, 2025; and Thimlar, interview with author, March 5, 2025.

52 **Shuck was surprised:** Details in this section about the Shuck family's experience with Hodges come from multiple sources, including: Hodges, interview with author, March 7, 2025; Geoff Shuck, interview with author, February 1, 2025; Rick Shuck, interview with author, February 28, 2025; "5 Area Cagers Drew Collegiate Tenders," *Kokomo Tribune*, April 27, 1971; US Census records for Charles Eugene Shuck; and the 1957 Kokomo city directory.

53 **855 career wins:** When Rupp was recruiting Shuck in 1971, he had compiled 855 wins. He'd retire one year later with a total of 876.

54 **couldn't wait to introduce:** "ISU Cagers to Put On Show, Says King," *THS*, April 8, 1975, and Carl L. Bender, "King Notes Changes in ISU Basketball," *THT*, April 8, 1975.

54 **"Within three years":** Bender, "King Notes Changes."

54 **already at odds:** Hodges, interview with author, February 11, 2025. But other sources also confirmed that it was Hodges who was fixated on Bird, not Evans, including: Behnke, interview with author, September 11, 2024; and Jimmy Claus, "Sporting Around," *THT*, July 26, 1977.

14.

54 **"progressive psychosis":** Death certificate, Claude Joseph Bird Jr.

54 **time in Korea:** *VH*, 50.

55 **Social Security check:** *Drive*, 17.

55 **talked about Joey Bird's suicide:** Bird confirmed this detail in his memoir, *Drive*, 17. The author's sources in West Baden and French Lick, listed above, also confirmed this detail in interviews with the author.

55 **Hancock Construction:** Details about Bird's brief stint in the industrial league come from multiple sources, including Rick Flynn, interview with author, September 19, 2024; Gary McCooe, interview with author, September 26, 2024; Michael Rubino, "Larry Bird's Greatest Shot Is the One He Didn't Take," *Indianapolis Monthly*, December 24, 2015; and several stories from newspapers in southwestern Indiana in the winter of 1975.

55 **Larry Baird:** Norman Grissom, "Hancock Team Wins AAU Cage Crown," *Mitchell (IN) Tribune*, February 27, 1975.

55 **first tournament:** "HC's Cagers AAU Champs," *BTM*, February 24, 1975.

56 **were thrilled:** McCooe, interview with author, September 26, 2024.

56 **drew a horrible slot:** Doug Wolfson, "Regional AAU Meet Opens Today," *Des Moines Register*, March 7, 1975.

56 **best numbers:** Accounts vary as to how many rebounds Bird had. The author went with the more plausible number: 25. "State AAU Champs Lose in Iowa," *Mitchell (IN) Tribune*, March 13, 1975.

56 **hand him a towel:** McCooe, interview with author, September 26, 2024.

56 **200 coaches:** Mike Madden, "The Bird Is the Word—and the Word Is Super," *BG*, January 28, 1979.

56 **run everybody off:** This description came from Bird's mother herself—Larry Keith, "Bird Has Those Trees on Top," *Sports Illustrated*, January 23, 1978.

56 **wasn't going back to college:** Bird's feelings at the time were confirmed by Bird himself in interviews that he gave in 1977, and by his mother, who gave multiple interviews over the years confirming that Bird did not want to go back to school. Ray

Compton, "ISU Bird to Fly Away—Someday," *IN*, May 21, 1977; Bill Jauss, "He's the Indiana State Bird!" *CT*, January 20, 1978; and Larry Keith, "Bird Has Those Trees on Top," *Sports Illustrated*, January 23, 1978. As Bird said in his 1977 interviews, "If it wasn't for people like Coach King and Coach Hodges, I probably wouldn't even be in college."

15.

56 **no easy way:** This account tries to get as close as possible to what happened that day through interviews with Hodges, Holland, Carnes, and members of the Indiana State team or athletic department who were briefed about the visit in 1975, and Bird's own words from interviews he gave in the 1970s and later. The author also relied on multiple accounts that previously documented this visit, including Madden, "The Bird Is the Word"; Bill Jauss, "He's the Indiana State Bird!" *CT*, January 20, 1978; Larry Keith, "Bird Has Those Trees on Top," *Sports Illustrated*, January 23, 1978; Skip Myslenski, "Bird's Hit Tune Still Lacks Lyrics," *CT*, February 16, 1979; Rick Woodson, "Silent Superstar Put Indiana State on the Map," Gannett News Service, February 21, 1979; Michael Rubino, "Larry Bird's Greatest Shot Is the One He Didn't Take," *Indianapolis Monthly*, December 24, 2015; Dana Hunsinger Benbow, "How Hodges Got Bird to Play for ISU," *Evansville Courier and Press*, November 25, 2021; Hodges's recollections shared at a press conference with Bird in front of 200 reporters on March 25, 1979; Bird's recollections shared at a keynote speech in Palm Beach, Florida, on September 7, 1982; and Bird's interview with the *Indianapolis News* in 1977—Ray Compton, "ISU Bird to Fly Away—Someday," *IN*, May 21, 1977. Additional versions of this day can be found in *Drive*, 44; *When the Game Was Ours*, 16; *When March Went Mad*, 58; and Lee Daniel Levine, *Bird: The Making of an American Sports Legend* (McGraw-Hill, 1988), 101.

57 **best player:** Hodges, interview with author, February 11, 2025.

57 **Holland was still:** Holland, interviews with author, August 2, 2024, November 25, 2024, and February 3, 2025.

58 **weren't new to each other:** Details about Hodges and Evans, their history, and their differences come from interviews with people who knew them, including Evans's childhood friend Wayne Garee, interview with author, January 29, 2025; Hodges, interviews with author, February 11, 2025, March 7, 2025, and April 1, 2025; Mosbaugh, interview with author, June 29, 2025; and interviews with multiple people who played or worked at Indiana State in the 1970s while the two men were there.

59 **lived for lots of things:** Evans listed his hobbies and interests himself on August 30, 1966, in the US Baseball Questionnaire that he filled out for William J. Weiss Baseball Statistics and Publicity.

59 **drafted Stan Evans:** "Braves Sign Free Agents," *Atlanta Journal*, June 19, 1966.

59 **batting just .203:** "Stan Evans," Baseball Reference, https://www.baseball-reference.com/register/player.fcgi?id=evans-002sta.

59 **37–22 in two junior college seasons:** "Stan Evans Named ISU Assistant," *DH*, March 26, 1975.

59 **"If I wanted to":** Gene Williams, "In Junior College Ball, 'You Could Say We Are Renegades,'" *Miami News*, December 14, 1974.

59 **"one of the worst jobs":** Ed Lang, "Jaguar Basketball Adds Coach," *Miami News*, August 21, 1971.

59 **"It crosses my mind":** Williams, "In Junior College Ball."
60 **"Why do you want":** Henry Seiden, "Byrd Flies North to Ex-Dade South Coach," *Miami News*, July 1, 1975.
60 **couldn't decide:** Bird described his conflicted feelings in *Drive*, 16. His feelings at this time were also chronicled in *VH*, 56. His aunt wrote that the family knew Larry was unhappy, "though he didn't show his unhappiness to most people."
61 **understood the product:** Jim Morris, assistant coach for Indiana State, letter to Jim Jones, February 6, 1974, Holland Personal Collection; Jones, interview with author, May 24, 2025; and Phil Hersh, "Indiana State: The Bird's Nest," *Des Moines Register*, December 20, 1977.
61 **worked as a maintenance man:** Carnes, interview with author, February 3, 2025.
61 **long hair, mustache:** A photo of Carnes appeared in the local newspaper around this time—"Independent All-Stars Teams—Eastern Division," *SVH*, February 6, 1975.
62 **In Hodges's memory:** Hodges, interview with author, February 11, 2025.

16.

62 **"I'm working at the Sheraton":** Carnes, interview with author, February 3, 1975.
62 **Hodges kept coming:** Hodges, interviews with author, February 11–13, 2025; Carnes, interview with author, February 3, 1975; and multiple news accounts previously cited, including Rubino, "Larry Bird's Greatest Shot." Bird also independently confirmed this detail over the years on multiple occasions.
62 **felt like he was always there:** At a keynote speech on September 7, 1982, Bird said, "Every time I looked up, he was around, every night, every day. He just wouldn't let go." Sandy Keenan, "Bird Drops In," *Miami Herald*, September 8, 1982.
62 **Bird didn't mention:** Everyone the author interviewed who knew Bird during this time reported that Bird had never talked to them about his father's suicide.
62 **Hodges learned:** Hodges, interview with author, April 1, 2025.
63 **began to recruit:** Hodges said that he only recruited and signed King after he knew Bird was coming. Danny King, interview with author, May 23, 2025, and "King Signs Letter to Play for ISU," *THT*, June 6, 1975.
63 **baling hay:** Both parties confirm that they discussed the job of hay baling—Hodges, interview with author, March 7, 2025, and *When the Game Was Ours*, 16. In *Drive*, 45, Bird goes so far as to say that Hodges even stood there with him while he baled hay. To the author, Hodges remembered just discussing the work.
63 **felt confident:** Hodges believes Bird was signed well before summer—Hodges interview with author, March 7, 2025; and Bob Ibach, "Bird Got Word on Indiana State in Just Two Visits," *Baltimore Evening Sun*, March 23, 1979. However, others, including Bird, his high school coach, Jim Jones, and members of the Indiana State basketball team at the time say that Bird didn't officially commit to coming until later in the summer and that Bird didn't visit to play in the summer pickup game until sometime after June 26, 1975—the night that Bird's Hancock Construction team played the Indiana all-stars.
63 **skipping Bird's Hancock Construction game:** Sources over the years have reported that Hodges or King attended this game. Hodges informed the author that these sources are incorrect—Hodges, interview with author, April 25, 2025. However, Bird indicated in *Drive* (p. 45) that Hodges was at least there that afternoon.
63 **scored 39:** Phil Bloom, "Hancock Netters Slip Past Indiana All-Stars"; and Al Brewster, "Bird Flying for Hancock Team," *BTM*, June 27, 1975.

63 **could only shake his head:** Jones, interview with author, May 24, 2025.
63 **had to close:** It's unclear exactly when Bird visited Terre Haute with his brother Mark and his friend Kevin Carnes. Hodges believed it happened in the spring; multiple other sources, including Johnny Nelson, Geoff Shuck, and Larry Bird himself, indicate that it happened much later in the summer—Nelson and Shuck, interviews with author; *Drive*, 41.
64 **"I'll come up":** *Drive*, 45.
64 **summer pickup games:** Thimlar, interview with author, August 7, 2024.
64 **private meeting:** Geoff Shuck, interview with author, February 1, 2025; Rick Williams, interview with author, March 11, 2025.
64 **"good conversation":** Geoff Shuck, interview with author, February 1, 2025.
64 **teammates began to trickle in:** Details about Bird's day at Terre Haute come from multiple sources, including interviews with five people who were there: Carnes, interview with author, February 3, 1975; Hodges, interviews with author, February 12–13, 2025; Nelson, interview with author, September 25, 2024; Geoff Shuck, interview with author, February 1, 2025; and Rick Williams, interview with author, March 11, 2025. Bird has confirmed the general details in his memoirs: *Drive*, 45; and *When the Game Was Ours*, 16.
64 **a grand total of six shots:** Indiana State Statistics Summary for 1974–75, https://gosycamores.com/sports/2010/4/8/204924741.aspx.
65 **"that little itty-bitty guy":** Nelson, interview with author, September 25, 2024.
66 **"some itty-bitty guy":** *Drive*, 46.
66 **"We never left":** Nelson, interview with author, September 25, 2024.
66 **Shuck and Williams had to agree:** Shuck, interview with author, February 1, 2025; Williams, interview with author, March 11, 2025.
66 **"Do I still need to":** Shuck, interview with author, February 1, 2025.

PART III

17.

69 **needed to pull off:** Details about Landini's personality and state of mind in 1975 come from multiple sources, including Landini's personal records, held in Indiana State's Special Collections; his earliest speeches and comments to the press in 1975; multiple news accounts in the *Indiana Statesman*, the *Indianapolis News*, the *Indianapolis Star*, the *Indianapolis Star Magazine*, and the *Missoulian* in Montana; and an interview with a man who worked closely with him in administration in the 1970s—John Newton, interview with author, April 24, 2025.
69 **stagnant or declining:** PRL, box 3125, Statesman Towers folder, enrollment projections 1965–1975, ISU Special Collections.
69 **sat empty:** PRL, box 3125, Statesman Towers folder, ISU Special Collections.
69 **"enrollment famine":** PRL, box 3149, Landini speeches, Fall Faculty Assembly, August 27, 1975, ISU Special Collections.
69 **"do not shrink":** PRL, box 3149, Landini speeches, Fall Faculty Assembly, August 27, 1975, ISU Special Collections.
69 **shining example:** Jerry Eaton, "Dean at Litchfield Cites Need to Guide," *Arizona Republic (Phoenix, AZ)*, July 18, 1967.

70 **"relevance, reintegration"**: "Reaction to Landini Hurt Litchfield Plan," *Arizona Republic (Phoenix, AZ)*, March 23, 1969.
70 **"rebellion, reaction"**: Tom Rippey, "Senator Assails ASU Leadership," *Arizona Daily Star (Tucson, AZ)*, March 12, 1969.
70 **over their heads:** Don Bolles, "Prospects Dark for ASU Campus at Litchfield Park," *Arizona Republic (Phoenix, AZ)*, March 23, 1969.
70 **"Anything that has"**: Bolles, "Prospects Dark for ASU Campus."
70 **won over skeptics:** "Choice of New ISU President Unanimous," *IS*, February 5, 1975.
70 **If 18-year-olds:** "Presidential Appointee Landini: Falling Enrollment a Top Priority," *Indiana Statesman (Terre Haute, IN)*, February 5, 1975.
70 **"tepid fervidity"**: John Flora, "ISU's Landini: The Key Is Openness, Candor," *IN*, November 19, 1975.
70 **"At the football games"**: John Newton, interview with author, April 24, 2025.
71 **"until the last dog"**: Susan Lennis, "Richard Landini: Hoosier in Profile," *Indianapolis Star Magazine*, December 13, 1975.
71 **record enrollment:** John Fancher, "Enrollment Increase Shows IU Is Held in High Esteem," *Bloomington-Bedford (IN) Sunday Herald-Times*, September 7, 1975.
71 **admired Knight:** PRL, box 3198, Athletics, Bobby Knight, ISU Special Collections.
71 **"The fact is"**: PRL, box 3198, Athletics, Bobby Knight, undated written remarks, circa 1985.
71 **"undeserved contumely"**: PRL, box 3198, Athletics, Bobby Knight, letter from Landini to Knight, February 7, 1985, ISU Special Collections.

18.

72 **still wasn't talking:** Several people close to Bird during this time confirmed this detail, including: Cox, interview with author, May 22, 2023; Jones, interview with author, May 24, 2025; and Hodges, interviews with author, February 11, 2025, and April 25, 2025.
73 **moved Bird into:** Both Hodges and Newton confirmed Larry's living arrangements on South 22nd Street that summer—Hodges, interview with author, April 25, 2025; and Newton, interview with author, April 24, 2025.
73 **King moved into the basement:** Hodges, interview with author, February 11, 2025; Danny King, interview with author, May 23, 2025; Mosbaugh, interview with author, June 29, 2025; and Thimlar, interview with author, August 7, 2024.
73 **job as a groundskeeper:** Hodges, interview with author, February 11, 2025; Howie Johnson, interview with author, September 12, 2024; and Danny King, May 23, 2025.
74 **500 acres of farmland:** Greg Gibson, interview with author, February 8, 2025.
74 **"Man, who is this dude?"**: Greg Gibson, interview with author, February 8, 2025.
74 **married Janet:** VH, 60; "Facts on File," *BTM*, October 29, 1975.
74 **moving into married-student housing:** Indiana State student directories, 1975–1978, and interviews with Bird's teammates at the time.
74 **knew he was too young:** *Drive*, 48. In an interview later, Janet also conceded that the couple was too young to marry. Diane K. Shah, "The Bird and the B's," *Inside Sports*, October 1979.
74 **taped out "the house"**: Thimlar, interview with author, August 9, 2024.

74 **began to wonder:** Geoff Shuck, interview with author, February 1, 2025; and Williams, interviews with author, September 19, 2024, and October 2, 2024.

74 **threatened to quit:** Several versions of this story have appeared elsewhere—in *Drive*, 46; *When March Went Mad*, 83; and *When the Game Was Ours*, 17. The author's version relies on interviews with people who were there, including Tom Crowder, interview with author, December 5, 2024; Hodges, interview with author, February 12, 2025; Nelson, interview with author, September 25, 2024; Geoff Shuck, interview with author, February 1, 2025; and Williams, interview with author, September 19, 2024.

75 **one game over .500:** Carl L. Bender, "Hoosiers Lauded; ISU Dumps Aces," *THT*, March 2, 1976.

75 **Hodges would return home:** Hodges, interview with author, February 11, 2025.

75 **"One day":** Williams, interview with author, September 19, 2024.

19.

75 **The first time:** Carl Nicks, interviews with author, August 27, 2024, and September 3, 2024; and Hodges, interview with author, March 7, 2025.

76 **white men didn't show up:** Details about life in Englewood come from Carl Nicks, interviews with author, August 27, 2024, and September 3, 2024; his brother, Romero Nicks, interview with author, March 12, 2025; and several stories from the *Chicago Tribune* in the 1970s, including "Firebomb Hits Grocery," September 5, 1973; James Pearre, "Crime: One Way to Earn a Living," February 23, 1975; Monroe Anderson, "S. Side Woman Slain, 2 Wounded," June 30, 1975; Alan Merriwed, "Profile of Crime in Chicago Shows It's Skyrocketing in White Districts," September 11, 1975; David Satter, "Blacks Describe Reign of Terror in Chicago Lawn," November 4, 1975; and Stanley Ziemba, "31.5% Out of Work in Inner-City Area," January 29, 1976.

76 **almost entirely Black:** The author did not rely solely on Nicks's memory for these details; they come straight out of the Englewood High School yearbook, 1976.

76 **The Rushville senior:** Details about the recruitment of Brad Miley come from multiple sources, including: Hodges, interviews with author; Miley, interviews with author; Bob Beeler, "Lions Win Two Tough Ballgames," *Rushville (IN) Republican*, March 22, 1976; Don Snider, "Colescott Matched Robertson in Pacing 2 State Champions," *CJ*, March 28, 1976; "Senators Out, Lions Fall to Marion," *Rushville (IN) Republican*, April 14, 1976; and "Goins, Miley Named to Indiana All-Stars," *Rushville (IN) Republican*, April 17, 1976.

77 **Hodges wanted:** Hodges, interview with author, February 11, 2025.

77 **"I can do it all":** Harry Morgan, interview with author, September 18, 2024.

77 **"My offense":** Mike Chappell, "Getting Better," *Anderson (IN) Daily Bulletin*, December 8, 1976.

77 **His parents had left:** Details about Harry Morgan's family and their lives in Anderson come from multiple sources, including: Morgan, interviews with author, September 18–19, 2024; US Census records for Harry's father, Jerry, 1940 and 1950; Jerry Morgan, World War II draft card; C. Randall Shuman, "Madison Heights Remains Closed," *Anderson (IN) Herald*, November 10, 1972; C. Randall Shuman, "Racial Issue Concern Fading," *Anderson (IN) Herald*, December 6, 1972; "KKK Requests Parade Permit," *Anderson (IN) Daily Bulletin*, September 2, 1976; "KKK Street Walk" advertisement, *Anderson (IN) Daily Bulletin*, September 24, 1976; "Klan

Makes Downtown March," *Anderson (IN) Herald*, September 26, 1976; and a June 1977 series in *The Elwood (IN) Call-Leader* about Klan activities in the county, titled "Ku Klux Klan."

78 **He was playing for:** Harry and Rita Morgan, interviews with author, September 19, 2024.

78 **nothing typical about this night:** Details about this night in Evansville come from multiple sources, including: Harry Morgan, interview with author, September 18–19, 2024; Williams, interview with author, March 11, 2025; Dave Johnson, "From the ABA to Evansville," *Evansville Press*, April 13, 1976; Dave Johnson, "Former Pacer Daniels Didn't Let 'Em Down," *Evansville Press*, April 15, 1976; Larry Rusk, "Sun Oil Team Beaten in Tri-State Tournament," *Vincennes (IN) Sun-Commercial*, April 16, 1976; "Tri-State Itself May Be Biggest Loser," *Evansville Press*, April 22, 1976; and Mike Chappell, "Getting Better," *Anderson (IN) Daily Bulletin*, December 8, 1976.

78 **30 stitches:** Bruce Herron, "Suit Asking $60,000 from Mel Daniels Begins," *Albuquerque Tribune*, November 12, 1970.

78 **Bird caught a ride:** Williams, interview with author, March 11, 2025.

79 **could still see it:** The author did not rely solely on Morgan's memory here; Rick Williams confirmed the general details of this play to the author as well.

79 **"Couldn't nobody":** Morgan, interview with author, September 18, 2024.

79 **On the ride home:** Williams, interview with author, March 11, 2025.

79 **the next day:** "Indiana State Signs Carl Nicks," *IS*, April 16, 1976.

79 **Two weeks later:** "Morgan Signs," *IN*, April 28, 1976.

79 **Miley wanted:** Miley, interview with author, August 15, 2024.

20.

80 **no one knew that better:** Ed McKee, interviews with author, August 2, 6, and 7, 2024.

80 **careened off the road:** "Indiana State Football Team in Crash," *Richmond (IN) Palladium-Item and Sun-Telegram*, September 12, 1971.

80 **took him in the same draft as Mel Daniels:** Ed McKee, interview with author, August 2, 2024; and "Indiana Grabs Top ABA Draft Choice," *IS*, April 3, 1967.

81 **knew Larry Bird was good:** Ed McKee, interview with author, August 6, 2024.

81 **His name was:** Ed McKee, interview with author, August 7, 2024; and Craig McKee, interview with author, August 20, 2024.

81 **Hodges understood . . . Bird was in trouble:** Hodges, interview with author, February 13, 2025.

81 **"irretrievable breakdown":** Court order for Cause No. S-C-76-1101, the marriage of Janet S. Bird and Larry J. Bird, Vigo County Superior Court, September 24, 1976.

82 **Bird was nervous:** "Bird Feels Good About His ISU Debut," *THT*, November 20, 1976.

82 **He had 7 steals:** There is a discrepancy in the box scores about Bird's opening stat line. The author went with the one published by the *THT* on November 20, 1976.

82 **31 points with 18 rebounds:** Dennis Clark, "Sycamores Topple Chicago State," *THT*, November 28, 1976.

82 **He scored 33:** "Larry Bird Again Sparks Indiana State," *DH*, December 4, 1976.

83 **"just well known":** Craig McKee, interview with author, May 9, 2025.

83 ***ain'ts, cain'ts*, and double negatives:** Mike Madden, "The Bird Is the Word—and the Word Is Super," *BG*, January 28, 1979.

83 **The good news:** Both *The Terre Haute Tribune* and *The Evansville Press* ran features about Bird in this little window of time. Both avoided all the "out-of-bounds" topics, and both read like they could have been written by the sports information office itself, especially the one in the *Tribune*—"Bird Feels Good About His ISU Debut," THT, November 20, 1976; and Bob Kelley, "Newcomer Larry Bird: ISU Gets a Complete Player," *Evansville Press*, December 5, 1976.

83 **"If I get the shot":** Kelley, "Newcomer Larry Bird."

84 **"better every game":** Mike Chappell, "Getting Better."

84 **deserved the marquee billing:** Details about Bird's and Morgan's stats can be found in multiple places, including: Mike Chappell, "Harry: Pieces Fitting Together"; and Steve Herman, "Larry: ISU's Mr. Basketball," *Anderson Daily Bulletin*, December 1, 1977.

84 **"not taking nothing . . . See what I'm saying?":** Morgan, interview with author, September 18, 2024.

84 **stewing:** Nicks, interview with author, September 3, 2025.

21.

85 **flew charter down to Houston:** Details about the trip and the game against Houston come from interviews with people who were there, including: Behnke, interview with author, September 11, 2024; Nicks, interview with author, September 3, 2024; Hodges, interview with author, March 7, 2025; Miley, interviews with author, August 15, 2024, and March 19, 2025; Morgan, interview with author, September 19, 2025; Mosbaugh, interview with author, June 29, 2025; Nelson, interview with author, September 25, 2024; Shaw, interview with author, August 15, 2024; and Thimlar, interview with author, August 7, 2024. Additional details come from news stories, including: "Sycamores Prepare for NIT Debut" and "Sporting Around," THT, March 7, 1977; "Birdsong Not Only Problem for ISU" and "Sporting Around," THT, March 8, 1977; "ISU No Rinky-Dink Team: Lewis" and "Big Apple Eludes Indiana State," THT, March 10, 1977; and Jim Barnhart, "Illinois State Plays Houston Tonight," *Bloomington (IL) Pantagraph*, March 14, 1977.

87 **Early on that night:** Details of the game itself come from interviews with the players and coaches mentioned above, as well as WTHI radio and television broadcasts of the game.

89 **"He's the best":** Barnhart, "Illinois State Plays Houston."

89 **Birdsong agreed:** Gary Taylor, "Otis Birdsong Calls Larry Bird 'Best I've Ever Played Against,'" *DH*, March 10, 1977.

90 **Forbes wanted to:** WTHI radio and television broadcast, March 9, 1977.

91 **"We're going to send":** Hodges, interview with author, March 7, 2025; Nicks, interview with author, September 3, 2024; and Dana Hunsinger Benbow, "The Forgotten ISU Superstar," *IS*, January 18, 2019.

91 **call Morgan in his room:** Multiple members of the team confirmed Larry's prank call to Harry Morgan in Houston, including Bill Hodges, Carl Nicks, Brad Miley, and Harry Morgan himself. In addition to these interviews, the general story of the prank call was confirmed in news coverage at the time and later: "Now, a Word About Mr. Bird," *Basketball Weekly*, January 12, 1978; and Steve Marantz, "More Than Just a Passing Fancy," *BG*, December 21, 1979.

91 **"I didn't know who it was":** Morgan, interview with author, September 10, 2025.

91 **talk about it for years:** Marantz, "More Than Just a Passing Fancy."

NOTES

91 **"We was all laughin'":** Marantz, "More Than Just a Passing Fancy."
91 **offered to deliver:** Mosbaugh, interview with author, June 29, 2025.
91 **"We don't want":** THT, March 11, 1977.
92 **Bird's ex-wife:** Hodges, interview with author, February 12, 2025, and March 7, 2025.
92 **The two young men:** Greg Gibson, interview with author, February 8, 2025.

22.

92 **knew his competition well:** Jeff Judkins, interview with author, September 18, 2024.
93 **32.8 points per game:** https://www.sports-reference.com/cbb/seasons/men/1977.html.
93 **"a white guy":** This quote, and other details in this section, come from Judkins, interview with author, September 18, 2024.
93 **Bird was cool:** Judkins, interview with author, September 18, 2024; VH, 67.
94 **only watching Larry Bird:** Tom Apke, interview with author, February 27, 2025.
94 **Bird dominated:** Details in this section about the tryouts for the 1977 World University Games team come from interviews the author conducted with six people who were there: Rick Apke, interview with author, February 26, 2025; Tom Apke, interview with author, February 27, 2025; James Bailey, interview with author, January 28, 2025; Phil Hubbard, interview with author, January 25, 2025; Judkins, interview with author, September 18, 2024; and Sidney Moncrief, interview with author, February 27, 2025.
94 **"And that's when":** Hubbard, interview with author, January 25, 2025.
95 **"They were all":** Tom Apke, interview with author, February 27, 2025.
95 **"play it wide open":** "Road to Bulgaria Tough on Unprepared U.S. 5," New York Daily News, August 11, 1977.
95 **didn't want to go:** Jimmy Claus, "Sporting Around," THT, August 23, 1977; Phil Hersh, "Terre Hautens Hot for Bird Watching," CE, December 18, 1977; and VH, 67.

23.

95 **The early games:** Details in this section come from interviews with four people who played in the games: Bailey, interview with author, January 28, 2025; Hubbard, interview with author, January 25, 2025; Judkins, interview with author, September 18, 2024; and Moncrief, interview with author, February 27, 2025. Additional details come from news accounts, including "USA Cagers Open with Belgium Five," White Plains (NY) Reporter Dispatch, August 18, 1977; and "Natt, U.S. Open World Games Play," Monroe (LA) News-Star, August 18, 1977.
96 **conditions the worst:** Moncrief, interview with author, February 27, 2025.
96 **"Dear Mom":** VH, 67; Jimmy Claus, "Sporting Around," THT, August 23, 1977.
96 **landed in Bulgaria:** Details about the early games in Bulgaria, and the players' lives away from the court there, come from multiple sources, including: Bailey, interview with author, January 28, 2025; Hubbard, interview with author, January 25, 2025; Judkins, interview with author, September 18, 2024; Moncrief, interview with author, February 27, 2025; David Minthorn, "Americans Rip Belgium 136–57 in World University Games," Wausau (WI) Daily Herald, August 19, 1977; "Leonard, Glance Shoot for Record," Fresno Bee, August 20, 1977; "Calvin Natt Leads U.S. Cagers,"

Monroe (LA) Morning World, August 21, 1977; and Mike Sullivan, "Bulgaria: U.S. Team Spent a Year There Last Month," *CJ*, September 5, 1977.
- 96 **Crum's starting lineup:** "U.S. Cagers Swamp Soviets in Games."
- 96 **chaos reigned:** "U.S. Hoopers Swamp Russia, 129–95," *Oregon Statesman (Salem, OR)*, August 23, 1977.
- 96 **Crum was worried:** "U.S. Cagers Swamp Soviets in Games," *Great Falls (MT) Tribune*.
- 97 **going to miss:** Hubbard, interview with author, January 25, 2025.
- 97 **limped into the Cuba game:** Details about the Cuba game come from Bailey, interview with author, January 28, 2025; Hubbard, interview with author, January 25, 2025; Judkins, interview with author, September 18, 2024; Moncrief, interview with author, February 27, 2025; David Minthorn, "Fight Costs U.S. Cagers," *Camden (AR) News*, August 22, 1977; "Natt, U.S. Battle by Cuba, 94–78," *Monroe (LA) Morning World*, August 24, 1977; Ken O'Brien and Peter Genovese, "Rutgers Bailey Injured" and Ken O'Brien, "Hello Bulgaria, Are You There?" *New Brunswick (NJ) Home News*, August 24, 1977; Ted Lewis, "Calvin Natt Returns from Gold Medal Trip," *Monroe (LA) News-Star*, August 29, 1977; Carl Cluff, "'Free' Feeds for U.S. Gold," *Oregon Journal (Portland, OR)*, August 30, 1977; Leigh Montville, "He Was Doing Fine Until He Got to Bulgaria . . . ," *BG*, September 4, 1977; Sullivan, "Bulgaria: U.S. Team Spent a Month"; Dan Castellano, "Bailey Home, but Still Scarred," *Newark Star-Ledger*, September 5, 1977; and Bob Scott, "PU's Walter Jordan Recalls Experiences at University Games," *Vincennes (IN) Sun-Commercial*, September 21, 1977.
- 97 **"under the bench":** Moncrief, interview with author, February 27, 2025.
- 97 **"just punching guys":** Judkins, interview with author, September 18, 2024.
- 98 **"How bad is it?":** Bailey, interview with author, January 28, 2025.
- 98 **"We had to go":** Montville, "He Was Doing Fine."
- 98 **17 stitches:** The accounts vary as to exactly how many stitches Bailey received. The author went with the number reported by Bailey's hometown paper *The Boston Globe*.
- 98 **Bailey's parents:** Bailey, interview with author, January 28, 2025.
- 99 **asked King to promise:** Jimmy Claus, "Sporting Around," *THT*, September 2, 1977.
- 99 **a baby girl:** Larry's daughter was born in mid-August 1977, a detail the author confirmed through two sources: Mike Beas, "Birds of Feather Not Flocking Together," *IS*, November 8, 1994; and Indiana public records.
- 99 **a big press conference:** Jimmy Claus, "Sporting Around," *THT*, September 2, 1977.
- 99 **remained certain:** Jimmy Claus, "Sporting Around," *THT*, July 26, 1977.
- 99 **finally came around:** Nicks, interview with author, September 3, 2024.
- 99 **Student of the Year:** Peg Carlson, "Warsaw Honors 300 Students," *South Bend (IN) Tribune*, May 13, 1977.
- 99 **Mike Krzyzewski:** Reed, interview with author, August 1, 2024; Mike Krzyzewski, letters to Steve Reed, April 19, 1976, and September 7, 1976, shared by Reed with the author from his personal collection.
- 99 **off-campus party:** Two sources confirm the general details of this story—Reed, interview with author, August 1, 2024; and Miley, interview with author, August 15, 2024.
- 100 **foot of the runways:** Details about Leroy Staley, his family, and his recruitment to Indiana State come from Staley, interviews with author, August 14, 2024, September 18, 2024, and March 6, 2025; Hodges, interview with author, March 7, 2025; and Staley's personal scrapbooks, shared with the author.
- 100 **Staley cried:** Staley, interview with author, August 14, 2024.

24.

100 **freshman enrollment was up:** "Table 1, New Freshmen for All the Fall Semesters, 1971–1977," Indiana State University, Special Collections.

100 **Season-ticket sales:** Phil Hersh, "Indiana State: The Bird's Nest," *Des Moines Register*, December 20, 1977.

101 **"I'm a Bird Watcher":** "Wear It Proudly!" *Indiana Statesman (Terre Haute, IN)*, November 28, 1977.

101 **The magazine wanted to fly:** Details about the *SI* story and the trip to New York come from multiple sources, including: Ed McKee, interview with author, August 6, 2024; former Indiana State cheer coach Ruth Ann King Medworth, interview with author, March 13, 2025; Kent Hannon, email to author, September 26, 2024; Skip Myslenski, "Bird's Hit Tune Still Lacks Lyrics," *CT*, February 16, 1979; and Hersh, "Indiana State: The Bird's Nest."

101 **"*Sports*-fucking-*Illustrated*":** Lane Stewart, interview with author, March 28, 2025.

101 **wasn't so sure:** In interviews he gave that winter, Bob King told reporters that he had to "beg" and "plead" with Bird for him to work with *Sports Illustrated*. Bird also admitted his reluctance himself, in an interview with the *Chicago Daily News* ("Fans Love 'Bird' Watching in Winter," *Chicago Daily News*, December 25, 1977) and an interview with the AP's Steve Herman (Herman, "Basketball Is My Whole Life, I-State's Bird Says," *IS*, December 1, 1977). As Bird said at the time, "They knew I didn't want to do it. But I ain't the one who has the final say so." He added, "The coach told me I should, so I did."

102 **amazing week:** Based on the memories of those involved, the author was able to figure out that McKee and Bird were in New York on either October 5 or October 6, 1977. The other details come straight out of the New York newspapers that week.

102 **invited Bird and McKee:** This detail was confirmed in three places: McKee, interviews with author; Hannon, email to author; and Myslenski, "Bird's Hit Tune."

102 **size 16:** "Athletic Awards Banquet at Nasson Saturday Night," *Sanford (ME) Tribune*, May 22, 1969.

103 **a new girlfriend:** Multiple sources confirmed for the author that Dinah and Larry were together by the fall of 1977. Hannon confirmed in an email to the author that Bird wanted to return home, "because he was missing his girlfriend." Bird himself confirmed the general timing of the relationship in his memoir, *Drive*, 49. Connie Mosbaugh spoke to the author about how Dinah was different than Janet—Mosbaugh, interview with author, June 29, 2025. The author utilized public records and newspaper accounts to confirm the age difference. The Mattinglys announced Dinah's birth in the *Evansville Courier and Press* in November 1954, two years before Bird was born. And additional details come from news accounts, including "Colleen Cain Is Married to W. M. Mattingly," *Evansville Sunday Courier and Press*, August 19, 1951; "New Agent to Replace Ford Is Appointed," *THT*, June 16, 1967; and "Schulte HS Lists 133 Honor Roll Students," *THS*, November 15, 1972.

103 **secured the participation:** The author spoke with several people who were either at the *SI* photo shoot or had intimate knowledge about what happened there—King Medworth, interview with author, March 13, 2025; Ed McKee, interview with author, August 6, 2024; Marcia Staub Murphy, interview with author, February 5, 2025; and Lane Stewart, interviews with author, March 28 and April 1, 2025. Additional details come from Stewart's assignment journals; from Bill Hodges, interviews

with author; from Phil Hersh, "Indiana State: The Bird's Nest"; and from Sharon Senefeld's memories. She died in 2012, but she spoke about the photo shoot over the years in Cathy Mong, "She's Got the Jump on the No. 1 Team," *Richmond (IN) Palladium-Item*, March 11, 1979; and Ron Cook, "A Name to Remember," *Pittsburgh Press*, September 15, 1985.

103 **last Sunday of October:** Stewart kept a journal of his assignments in the 1970s. The date of the photo shoot, October 30, comes directly from this journal, shared with the author, March 28, 2025.

104 **beautiful fall morning:** According to weather reports published in newspapers in western Indiana and Chicago, it was a clear day, sunny and warm, "Indian summer."

25.

104 **The H stood for:** Details in this section come from Stewart, interviews with author, March 28 and April 1, 2025; and *Sports Illustrated* editor Peter Carry, interview with author, April 29, 2025.

105 **wasn't excited:** Details about the photo shoot come from McKee, interview with author, August 6, 2024; Staub Murphy, interview with author, February 5, 2025; Stewart, interview with author, March 28, 2025; Stewart's journals, shared with author, March 28, 2025; "Fans Love 'Bird' Watching in Winter," *Chicago Daily News*, December 25, 1977; Cathy Mong, "She's Got the Jump on the No. 1 Team," *Richmond (IN) Palladium-Item*, March 11, 1979; and Ron Cook, "A Name to Remember," *Pittsburgh Press*, September 15, 1985.

107 **"Barring some catastrophe":** Kent Hannon, letter to Ed McKee, November 9, 1977, Ed McKee personal collection.

108 **faded jeans:** Ron Maly, "Sycamores' Bird: Winning First, Personal Glory Second," *Des Moines Register*, November 23, 1977.

108 **deflect attention:** Maly, "Sycamores' Bird."

108 **basketball clinic for kids:** Steve Sinclair, "Basketball Clinic Scores Big for Bluejays," *Omaha World-Herald*, November 7, 1977.

108 **picked Indiana State:** Dean Clark, "Sycamores No. 1," *Tulsa World*, November 8, 1977.

108 **forcing King to prostrate himself:** Robin Miller, "ISU, Bird: Basketball Bullies," *IS*, November 20, 1977.

108 **"Forget Larry Bird":** "19th Hole: The Readers Take Over," *Sports Illustrated*, December 12, 1977.

108 **going to win:** Bird made this prediction in multiple places, including Ron Maly, "Missouri Valley Making Cage Comeback," *Des Moines Register*, November 8, 1977; and Ray Compton, "Sycamores Better Than Expected?" *IN*, November 29, 1977.

26.

108 **scored the first basket:** Dennis Clark, "Sycamores Too Much for Westmont," *THT*, November 27, 1977.

108 **Morgan didn't mind:** "'Obscurity Doesn't Bother Me,'" *Anderson (IN) Daily Bulletin*, January 12, 1978, and Dean Clark, "Bird, Sycamores Nesting Well," *Tulsa World*, November 7, 1977.

108 **Rita gave birth:** Harry and Rita Morgan, interviews with author, September 19, 2024.

- 108 **"can't tell him nothing"**: Larry Keith, "Bird Has Those Trees at the Top," *Sports Illustrated*, January 23, 1978.
- 108 **custom-made cape**: "Sideline Attraction," *THT*, March 4, 1978.
- 108 **had given himself a nickname**: Larry Keith, "Bird Has Those Trees."
- 110 **Bob King worked**: Ray Compton, "How Good? Purdue Tries ISU Tonight," *IN*, November 28, 1977, and "Sycamores Make Awaited Debut Tonight," *THS*, November 26, 1977.
- 110 **"We have not looked"**: Jimmy Claus, "Sporting Around," *THT*, November 23, 1977.
- 110 **"pro or college"**: "King Pleased with Win," *THT*, November 29, 1977.
- 111 **typically quiet**: The author interviewed roughly three dozen men who played against Bird in high school and college—several of whom also played against him later in the pros. No one remembered him as someone who talked trash during his time at Indiana State.
- 111 **"whip him"**: Ray Compton, "Sycamores Better Than Expected?" *IN*, November 29, 1977.
- 111 **"can do it all"**: Bruce Ramey, "Schaus: We Got Careless," *Lafayette (IN) Journal and Courier*, November 27, 1977.
- 111 **first winter storm**: "Wintry Blast Surges Across North," *THT*, November 27, 1977; "Storms Hit Midwest, East," *THS*, November 28, 1977.
- 111 **four hours before**: Jimmy Claus, "Sporting Around," *THT*, November 29, 1977.
- 112 **SOLD OUT**: *Indiana Statesman (Terre Haute, IN)*, November 29, 1977.
- 112 **six other states**: Bill Mabin, "Indiana State vs. Purdue Basketball Game Televised," *THT*, November 26, 1977.
- 112 **three and a half million people**: PRL, box 3098, Athletics-Basketball, 1976–1989, "ISU Basketball on Television" document, 1977–78.
- 112 **biggest game of our lives**: Mike Lopresti, "ISU Off the Ground about Bird and Gang," *Richmond (IN) Palladium-Item*, November 29, 1977; Joe Wolf, "Indiana State Clobbers Boilers, 91–63," *Rushville (IN) Republican*, November 29, 1977.
- 112 **opened the game**: Details from the game come from interviews with Bob Behnke, Bill Hodges, Ed McKee, Craig McKee, Brad Miley, Harry Morgan, Steve Reed, Rick Shaw, and Leroy Staley, and news accounts including: Mike Chappell, "Purdue Can't Handle Bird, Romping ISU," *Anderson (IN) Daily Bulletin*, November 29, 1977; "Sycamores Pop Purdue, 91–63," *Evansville Courier*, November 29, 1977; Max Stultz, "Syca-Much-Mores Than Riveters," *IS*, November 29, 1977; Bob Scott, "Sycamores Fall on Purdue" and "Easy Win Over Boilermakers Came as No Shocker to Bird," *Lafayette (IN) Journal and Courier*, November 29, 1977; "ISU Defense Does It to Purdue," *THS*, November 29, 1977; and Carl L. Bender, "ISU Plays Down Win Over Purdue," *THT*, November 29, 1977.

27.

- 113 **"This one," he conceded**: Bender, "ISU Plays Down Win."
- 114 **"hit real good"**: Tom Lindley, "Secret Is Out at Indiana State," *Evansville Press*, December 4, 1977; Bender, "ISU Plays Down Win."
- 114 **jumped through the ceiling**: Craig McKee recorded his thoughts in the moment in a lengthy typewritten narrative that he wrote at the time and shared with the author on September 25, 2024. The narrative was titled "Thirteen Wins, *Sports Illustrated* and Collapse." Hereafter, it will be sourced as simply "Thirteen Wins."

314 NOTES

- 114 **VOTE AS MANY:** "Wanted," *Indiana Statesman (Terre Haute, IN)*, January 26, 1978.
- 115 **ran the steps:** Multiple players confirmed this New Year's Day tradition to the author, including Brad Miley, interview with author, March 19, 2025.
- 115 **"If I get the ball":** Bender, "ISU Plays Down Win."
- 116 **locked eyes with him:** Hodges, interview with author, March 7, 2025. Additional game details come from Dennis Clark, "Larry Bird Leads ISU Past Evansville," *THT*, December 11, 1977.
- 116 **"We will work hard":** Jimmy Claus, "Sporting Around," *THT*, December 11, 1977.
- 116 **gone down on takeoff:** Details of the plane crash and its aftermath come from multiple news accounts, including: Roberta Heiman, "'Oh God, No . . . Not Him . . . Not Him'"; Herb Marynell, "Crash Site Is Called Terrible Place to Die"; and Tim Graham, "Aces Team Dies in Plane in Trouble From the Start," *Evansville Press*, December 14, 1977; "UE Basketball Team Dies in Plane Crash," *Evansville Courier*, December 14, 1977; and "Locks Are Blamed for Crash of Evansville Team's Plane," *CJ*, August 18, 1978.
- 116 **"Why wasn't it":** Reed, interview with author, September 20, 2025.
- 116 **strangely out of touch:** Craig McKee, "Thirteen Wins."
- 117 **no longer trusted:** Multiple sources who were with the team and the athletic department around this time confirmed the tension among the coaches, including: Hodges, interview with author, March 7, 2025; Thimlar, interview with author, July 14, 2025; Craig McKee, interviews with author, September 25 and 26, 2024, and October 3, 2024; and McKee's notes and journal from October 1978. McKee's narrative, written in the moment, confirms that King no longer trusted Evans by January 1978; that their disagreements were "irrevocable"; that King believed Evans was "stabbing" him in the back; that Hodges was called in to be at every game, "road and home—despite his recruiting schedule"; and that the tension was well known. As McKee wrote on October 11, 1978, the day that Evans ultimately left the basketball team: "My friend, Stan Evans, learned today that actions sometimes suffer repercussions. He made a tactical error by superseding King's authority and blasting the man to too many persons. His bitterness was not really a secret . . . He failed at tact, diplomacy, secrecy, and ass-kissing."
- 117 **well liked in the athletic office:** Behnke, interview with author, August 1, 2024; Craig McKee, interview with author, August 16, 2024; Ed McKee, interview with author, August 6, 2024; and Rick Shaw, interview with author, August 15, 2024.
- 117 **"just the tension":** Behnke, interview with author, August 1, 2024.
- 118 **seemed to want:** Bird put it this way later: "We had too many guys who wanted to shoot the ball." Bird press conference, March 25, 1979.
- 118 **"I guess it just don't":** Keith, "Bird Has Those Trees."
- 118 **local police visited:** Multiple sources recalled Richard Johnson's dealings with the police that year: Hodges, interview with author, February 11, 2025; Miley, interview with author, March 19, 2025; and Staley, interview with author, March 6, 2025.
- 118 **"I don't want to":** Steve Herman, "Basketball Is My Whole Life, I-State's Bird Says," *IN*, December 1, 1977.

28.

- 119 **Bird immediately shut down:** This detail was confirmed by multiple sources with the team, as well as Larry Keith himself—Larry Keith, interview with author, January 25, 2025.
- 119 **"She would be polite":** Keith, interview with author, January 25, 2025.

120 **"I knew where"**: Keith, interview with author, January 25, 2025.
120 **"I honestly don't think"**: Larry Keith, "Bird Has Those Trees at the Top," *Sports Illustrated*, January 23, 1978.
120 **He wasn't even sure**: Merle Jones, "Bird Flies Into Limelight, Retains Relaxed Attitude," *Southern Illinoisan (Carbondale, IL)*, January 19, 1978.
120 **frozen Carbondale**: "Amey Takes Aim on a Snowy Trip to Southern," *THS*, January 24, 1978.
120 **two feet of snow**: "We've Had Some Snow or Have You Noticed?" *THS*, January 18, 1978.
120 **called Ed's room**: Craig McKee, "Thirteen Wins."
120 BIRD HAS THOSE TREES: Keith, "Bird Has Those Trees."
120 **"the stuff"**: Craig McKee, "Thirteen Wins."
121 **as if Ed had been**: Craig McKee, "Thirteen Wins."

29.

121 **came out on fire**: Details about the game at Southern Illinois come from Merle Jones, "Salukis 'Played a Super Game'—Happy Lambert," *Southern Illinoisan (Carbondale, IL)*, January 20, 1978; "Salukis Hand I-State First Defeat," *THS*, January 20, 1978; "Illinois State next test for Sycamores" and "Sporting Around," *THT*, January 20, 1978; and *THS*, January 24, 1978.
121 **"I don't really"**: Jones, "Bird Flies Into Limelight."
121 **ugly in a hurry**: Details about the Illinois State game come from: Jim Barnhart, "Redbirds Topple Sycamores, 81–76," and Bryan Bloodworth, "ISU Spoils Larry, Harry Show," *Bloomington (IL) Pantagraph*, January 22, 1978; Mike Kiley, "One Bird No Match for Five Redbirds," *CT*, January 22, 1978; "Sycamores Suffer Second Setback," *THT*, January 22, 1978.
122 **"a very dangerous storm"**: "Blizzard Hits," *Tipton County (IN) Tribune*, January 26, 1978.
122 **10-hour odyssey**: Details about the trip to Wichita come from interviews with people on the plane, including: Behnke, September 11, 2024; Crowder, interview with author, December 5, 2024; Miley, interview with author, August 21, 2024; Reed, interview with author, September 20, 2024; and "Weary ISU Would Have Liked Snow," *IN*, January 27, 1978.
122 **"layovers everywhere"**: "Weary ISU Would Have Liked Snow."
123 **called Bill Hodges in**: Hodges recalled this detail for the author. (Hodges, interview with author, March 7, 2025.) Craig McKee's notes and journal, written in real time that season, confirmed it. (Craig McKee, "Thirteen Wins.")

30.

123 **The Aggies were everything**: Details about the Aggies come from Cyrus Cormier, interview with author, March 19, 2025; Robert Gunn, interview with author, March 20, 2025; Ken Hayes, interviews with author, March 1, 2015, and March 3, 2025; and Greg Webb, interview with author, March 18, 2025.
125 **controlled the game early**: Details about the game come from interviews with players who played in the game, including multiple members of the Indiana State team and four members of the New Mexico State squad: Cormier, interview with author,

March 19, 2025; Gunn, interview with author, March 20, 2025; Hayes, interviews with author, March 1, 2025, and March 3, 2025; and Webb, interview with author, March 18, 2025. Additional details come from the following news accounts: Bart Ripp, "Aggies Edge Indiana State in Thriller," *AJ*, February 7, 1978; Carlos Salazar, "Ags Won, but the Bird Was the Show" and "Aggies in Driver's Seat," *Albuquerque Tribune*, February 7, 1978; Harry Readel, "Ags Weave Webb Around Ind. St.," *El Paso Herald-Post*, February 7, 1978; "Late Free Throws Nip Sycamores," *THS*, February 7, 1978; and "Aggies Strengthen Hold on First," *THT*, February 7, 1978.

126 **"murdered," King said:** "Sporting Around," *THT*, February 9, 1978.

126 **"I tried to tell everyone":** "Sycamores Strive to Snap Slump on Road," *THS*, February 1, 1978.

127 **liked their chances:** Steve Sinclair, "Jays Mentally Tuned Up," *Omaha World-Herald*, March 5, 1978.

127 **"the best basketball player":** "Aggie Coach Lauds Team," *THS*, March 4, 1978.

127 **debilitating back pain:** Details about Bird's back pain before the game come from Behnke, interview with author, September 11, 2024; and news coverage, including: "Creighton Nips ISU in Title Bout," *THS*, March 6, 1978; and "Game Resembled Heavyweight Fight: Apke," *THT*, March 6, 1978.

127 **"We don't want":** "Game Resembled Heavyweight Fight: Apke," *THT*, March 6, 1978.

128 **That afternoon, Morgan carried:** Details about the Creighton game come from interviews with the Indiana State players who played in it, interviews with Behnke and Hodges, and interviews with both Apke brothers—Rick Apke, interview with author, February 26, 2025; and Tom Apke, interview with author, February 27, 2025. Additional details come from Bill Benner, "Oh, Brother What a Shot! Apke Act Stops Sycamores," *IS*, March 6, 1978; Steve Sinclair, "Jays Ready for 'Lucky' Court," *Omaha World-Herald*, March 6, 1978; "Creighton Nips ISU in Title Bout," *THS*, March 6, 1978; "Game Resembled Heavyweight Fight: Apke" and "New York Will Love Bird: Tom Apke," *THT*, March 6, 1978; and "1978 MVC Championship: Rick Apke's Buzzer Beater," posted on YouTube on October 8, 2014, by White & Blue Review.

31.

129 **"most brilliant gem":** Ralph Morrow, "NIT Loses TV, May Drop to 8 Teams," *Dayton Daily News*, December 5, 1975.

129 **expand its coverage:** "College Basketball Tourney Telecast," *Biddeford-Saco (ME) Journal*, March 10, 1973.

130 **about 32 million:** The author worked with both NBC and Nielsen to gather the historical data in order to document the growth of college basketball in the 1970s. This figure—and others noting the size of television audiences in 1972, 1973, 1975, and 1979—come directly from this data, archived NBC documents, and archived Nielsen reports. Both Dan Masonson at NBC and Lauren Pabst at Nielsen were crucial in unearthing this data. Hereafter noted as NBC and Nielsen archival data.

130 **13½ points:** Buck P. Patton, "Oddsmakers Say UCLA Will Win by 13½ Points," *Memphis Press-Scimitar*, March 26, 1973.

130 **three inevitabilities:** Associated Press, "UCLA College King Again," *Selma (AL) Times-Journal*, March 27, 1973.

130 **nine color cameras:** "Olympic Hit Olga Korbut On 'Wide World' Saturday," *Fort Lauderdale News*, March 23, 1973.
130 **37 million:** NBC and Nielsen archival data; "38 Million Saw NCAA Finals," *Nashville Tennessean*, April 10, 1973.
130 **42 million:** NBC and Nielsen archival data; Paul Henniger, "Baseball Back—So Is Gowdy," *Los Angeles Times*, April 12, 1975.
131 **hugged Bird's old roommate:** Stan Hochman, "Bobby Knight Proves He Cares," *Philadelphia Daily News*, March 30, 1976.
131 **CBS dropped:** "NIT Loses CBS Backing; Field Cut to Eight Teams," *Scranton Tribune*, December 5, 1975.
131 **Mizlou Television:** "Mizlou TV to Handle NIT," *AJ*, September 16, 1976.
131 **"Not Important Tournament":** Ron Drogo, "Abundance of Fine Teams Guarantees Quality NIT," *Hackensack (NJ) Record*, February 27, 1977.

32.

132 **that Friday night:** "Sycamores to Battle Rutgers Next," *THT*, March 11, 1978.
132 **pacing the arena:** "Sporting Around," *THT*, March 11, 1978.
132 **The game was close:** Dave Johnson, "Reserve's Basket Saves Indiana State Win," *Evansville Press*, March 11, 1978; Wayne Fuson, "On to Rutgers for Sycamores," *IN*, March 11, 1978; Max Stultz, "ISU Blasts Way Into NIT," *IS*, March 11, 1978; and "ISU, Sycamores Eye Quarterfinals," *Bloomington (IL) Pantagraph*, March 10, 1978.
132 **"would go well":** "Sporting Around," *THT*, March 11, 1978.
133 **About four million:** PRL, box 3098, Athletics—Basketball—Postseason Tournaments folder, "ISU Basketball on Television."
133 **To write their feature stories:** Vinny DiTrani, "Rutgers Hopes for Sour Note From Bird," *Hackensack (NJ) Record*, March 14, 1978; and Marty McLaughlin, "Rutgers NIT ¼-Final a Bird & Bailey Show," *New York Daily News*, March 14, 1978.
133 **rough outline of a plan:** Details about the Rutgers game come from interviews and news accounts, including: Anderson, interview with author, March 2, 2025; Bailey, interview with author, January 28, 2025; Behnke, interview with author, September 5, 2024; Copeland, interview with author, June 29, 2025; Hefele, interview with author, February 28, 2025; Hodges, interview with author, March 7, 2025; Miley, interview with author, September 25, 2024; Morgan, interviews with author, September 18–19, 2024; Shaw, interview with author, September 23, 2024; Reed, interview with author, August 15, 2024; Vinny DiTrani, "Bailey to the Rescue," *Hackensack (NJ) Record*, March 15, 1978; "Belted by Bird, Student Charges," *Hackensack (NJ) Record*, March 15, 1978; T. J. Simers, "Bird's Burned-Up as Rutgers Wins," *Morristown (NJ) Daily Record*, March 15, 1978; Jim Smith, "Bailey Becomes Neutralizer for Bird," *Newsday (Hempstead, NY)*, March 15, 1978; "Sporting Around" and "Jim Bailey Hits in Clutch for Rutgers," *THT*, March 15, 1978; "Sycamore Year Ends at Rutgers," *THS*, March 15, 1978; Joe Calabrese, "Knights Survive in Battle of Bumbles," *Trenton (NJ) Times*, March 15, 1978; and Craig McKee 1978 journal, shared with author, September 26, 2024.
136 **"We're shaking hands":** Copeland, interview with author, June 29, 2025.
136 **"you know how Larry is":** Bailey, interview with author, January 28, 2025.
136 **argued openly:** Several players in the locker room remembered the tension that day and recounted it to the author. Craig McKee also documented it in real time in "Thirteen Wins."

136 **Steve Reed blamed:** Reed, interview with author, August 15, 2024.
136 **Staley blamed:** Staley, interviews with author, August 14, 2024, September 18, 2024, and March 6, 2025.
136 **"What happened?":** T. J. Simers, "Bird's Burned-Up as Rutgers Wins," *Morristown (NJ) Daily Record*, March 15, 1978.
137 **"a white superstar":** Copeland, interview with author, June 29, 2025.
137 **"Bird or someone":** "Sycamore Year Ends at Rutgers," *THS*, March 15, 1978.
137 **"in a ruckus":** "Sporting Around," *THT*, March 15, 1978.
137 **Staley informed King:** Staley, interview with author, September 18, 2024; and Hodges, interview with author, March 7, 2025.
137 **arrested Richard Johnson:** The author confirmed this detail with multiple sources, including: Hodges, interview with author, March 5, 2025; Miley, interview with author, August 21, 2025; Staley, interview with author, March 5, 2025; "ISU's Richard Johnson Arrested for Robbery," *Vincennes (IN) Sun-Commercial*, May 9, 1978; and Johnson's Vigo County criminal case file—CR-77922, *State of Indiana vs. Richard Johnson*.
137 **met with Landini:** PRL, box 3131, Landini daily planner, 1978.

PART IV

33.

141 **Around the house on Middle Street:** The location of Magic Johnson's childhood home has been well chronicled over the years in many publications. The first reference to it appeared in *The Lansing State Journal* in 1974.
141 **no one called:** The author interviewed five people who coached or played with Johnson in college—Mike Brkovich, interview with author, March 21, 2025; Dave Harshman, interview with author, April 11, 2025; Greg Kelser, interview with author, September 27, 2024; Mike Longaker, interview with author, April 7, 2025; and Fred Paulsen, interview with author, April 2, 2025. Additional confirmation and details come from Earvin "Magic" Johnson with William Novak, *My Life* (Random House, 1992), 18.
141 **"There goes":** *My Life*, 18. Additional sources confirmed Magic Johnson's childhood nickname as "June Bug," including: Bob Talbert, "Skippers Not to Miss," *DFP*, June 3, 1984.
141 **He held multiple:** "Dwight Rich Cager Rewrites Record Book," *LSJ*, March 10, 1974.
141 **needed a nickname:** Johnson told his version of the story in *My Life* (p. 71). Stabley has told his own version over the years. Both are almost exactly the same, with one important difference—Johnson said the nickname made him uncomfortable. Greg Johnson, "Illness Can't Erase the Magic Touch," *Grand Rapids Press*, November 8, 1991; and Harry Atkins, "The Magical Birth of a Very Special Nickname," *Dayton Daily News*, November 8, 1991.
142 **hated the name:** *My Life*, 71.
142 **On a Friday night:** Fred Stabley Jr., "Everett Crushes Parkside," *LSJ*, January 25, 1975.
142 **really that young:** Dave Matthews, "Everett Express Rolls On, 80–66," *LSJ*, March 6, 1975.
142 **turned team huddles over:** "Everett Coach: 'I Am Devastated by This,'" *DFP*, November 8, 1991.

NOTES

- 142 **"once in a lifetime"**: Fred Stabley Jr., "'It's Been a Trip'—Fox," *LSJ*, April 3, 1977.
- 142 **scalped:** Dave Matthews, "Vikings Squeak Past Eastern, 63–62," *LSJ*, February 5, 1975.
- 142 **in the Pontiac Silverdome:** Lynn Henning, "Season's Finest Hour," *LSJ*, February 1, 1977.
- 142 **paying for the right:** "City's Prep Classic Battle of Top Scorers," *LSJ*, January 31, 1977; Dave Matthews, "'Eastern Win No Fluke,'" *LSJ*, February 1, 1977; and Hal Schram, "'March Madness' Starts a Day Early," *DFP*, February 28, 1977.
- 143 **132 phone calls:** Joe Falls, "Thank Goodness the Suspense Is Over," *DFP*, April 23, 1977.
- 143 **yet another crowd:** News accounts of Johnson's announcement in April 1977 can be found in multiple places, including: Mick McCabe, "Earvin Chooses MSU, but Feels Lure of Pros" and "MSU 'Tried Not to Hound Him'—Jud," *DFP*, April 23, 1977; and Bob Gross, "Challenge Sold Earvin on MSU," Fred Stabley Jr., "Jud Heathcote Just Can't Stop Smiling," and Lynn Henning, "Enjoy, Spartan Fans, but Please Don't Expect Too Much," *LSJ*, April 23, 1977.

34.

- 143 **The school roared:** Mick McCabe, "MSU 'Tried Not to Hound Him'—Jud," *DFP*, April 23, 1977; and Bob Gross, "Challenge Sold Earvin on MSU," *LSJ*, April 23, 1977.
- 144 **Heathcote didn't think:** Fred Stabley Jr., "Jud Heathcote a Real Dr. Jekyll, Mr. Hyde," *LSJ*, March 8, 1978.
- 144 **Heathcote raged:** Mike Brkovich, interview with author, March 21, 2025; Greg Kelser, interview with author, September 27, 2024; and Fred Paulsen, interview with author, April 2, 2025.
- 144 **feet propped up:** Fred Stabley Jr., "Jud Heathcote Just Can't Stop Smiling," April 23, 1977.
- 145 **"Missing by feet":** The author interviewed several players who competed in this game, including Brkovich, Kelser, and Longaker, who played for Michigan State; and Rick Robey, Jay Shidler, and Kyle Macy, who played for Kentucky. Additional details come from Joe Falls, "Johnson's Magic Just Wasn't There," *DFP*, March 19, 1978.
- 145 **"We'll be back":** Falls, "Johnson's Magic."
- 145 **reported down to Lexington:** Details in this section come from interviews with six members of this team, almost half the squad—Bailey, interview with author, January 28, 2025; Moncrief, interview with author, February 27, 2025; Kyle Macy, interview with author, April 23, 2025; Mike O'Koren, interview with author, April 2, 2025; Rick Robey, interview with author, April 7, 2025; and Jay Shidler, interview with author, April 17, 2025. Additional details come from news accounts, including: "Robey's 16 Lead All-Stars by Marathon," *CJ*, April 4, 1978; Frank Hyland, "A Taste of Moscow in Atlanta," *Atlanta Journal*, April 6, 1978; Mark Wolf, "Ford Leaves 'Em Loving It at UNC," *Charlotte Observer*, April 8, 1978; and Paul Borden, "UK's Lee Stuffs Final Points to Cap 107–82 Romp by U.S.," *CJ*, April 10, 1978.
- 145 **Magic skipped:** Lynn Henning, "Fun Night for Happy MSU Fans," *LSJ*, April 4, 1978.
- 146 **$49,000—a nice chunk:** Jack Etkin, "TV Money Has Rocketed Final Four Into Sports Stratosphere," *Kansas City Star*, April 1, 1984.
- 146 **ballooned to $240,000:** "NCAA Basketball Tourney Expanded," *IS*, August 15, 1978.

146 **the team had earned:** Steve Wilson, "NCAA Tournament Income Puts UK Basketball Over $1 Million," *Lexington Leader*, April 13, 1978.
146 **would expand from 32:** "NCAA Basketball Tourney Expanded," *IS*, August 15, 1978.
146 **three Kentucky players:** Stuart Warner, "UK Players Propel Stars Past Soviets," *Lexington Herald*, April 10, 1978.
146 **"What the hell":** Robey, interview with author, April 7, 2025.
147 **doesn't remember seeing:** Moncrief, interview with author, February 27, 2025.
147 **Jay Shidler . . . agreed:** Shidler, interview with author, April 17, 2025.
147 **one moment of greatness:** Mark Bradley, "U.S. Razzle-Dazzles Soviets," *Lexington Leader*, April 10, 1978.
147 **Red Auerbach:** *When the Game Was Ours*, 25.

35.

148 **16½-hour telethon:** "Pacers Nearing Goal on Ticket Sale Drive," *IN*, July 4, 1977, and Alex Sachare, "Telethon Contributes Heavily to Redemption," *THT*, July 10, 1977.
148 **wasn't leaving school:** Tom Reck, "Guessing Game Ends with Draft Today," *THS*, June 9, 1978; Bill Benner, "Pacers Trade Pick to Portland," *IS*, June 9, 1978; and *When the Game Was Ours*, 32.
148 **who also failed:** "Coach Gives Portland Word: Bird Staying," *IS*, June 9, 1978; and *When the Game Was Ours*, 32.
149 **He had the chance to select Larry Bird:** Details of the 1978 draft come from Bob Ryan, interviews with author, September 13, 2024, and January 29, 2025; Red Auerbach and John Feinstein, *Let Me Tell You a Story* (Little, Brown, 2004), 149–50; Francis Rosa, "Auerbach Relishes 'Victory,'" *BG*, June 10, 1978; and https://www.basketball-reference.com/draft/NBA_1978.html.
149 **ranked 442nd:** Bob Dolgan, "Former Cage Star Becomes a Rookie as Sportscaster," *Cleveland Plain Dealer*, November 26, 1978.
149 **blamed the poor ratings:** Doug Nye, "The 'Nightmare' Series," *Columbia (SC) Record*, June 2, 1978.
149 **a young vice president:** Kevin O'Malley, interviews with author, June 30, 2025, and July 4, 2025. Additional details about O'Malley's life come from his stories written about him by his hometown paper *The (Springfield, MA) Republican*: Gerry Finn, "Kevin O'Malley Made the Big Leagues at CBS," June 8, 1980; and Carlo Imelio, "Young O'Malley Fights in CBS Trenches," February 26, 1984.
149 **lots of television programs:** Mark Wolf, "NBA Playoffs Fouling Out in Ratings," *Charlotte Observer*, May 12, 1978.
149 **a show called *Superstars*:** Gary Deeb, "CBS Hopes the NBA Ratings Will Rebound," *Philadelphia Daily News*, June 2, 1978.
149 **a disconnect between viewers . . . "most urban of games":** O'Malley, interviews with author, June 30, 2025, and July 4, 2025.
150 **70 percent Black:** This figure, and other details about the racial imbalance of the league, come from investigative pieces and profiles written at the time—Jane Gross, "Racial Quotas in the NBA?" *Newsday (Hempstead, NY)*, December 27, 1978; Betsy Aaron, *CBS Evening News*, March 16, 1979; Shah, "The Bird and the B's"; and Bob Ryan, "Race: How Big a Factor?" *BG*, March 29, 1982. The author gathered additional details from interviews with Black players in the league

around this time, including Hollis Copeland—Copeland, interview with author, June 29, 2025.

150 **In the opening minutes:** John Hall, "Sneak Punch Made Kareem a Small Man," *CJ*, October 26, 1977.

150 **in intensive care:** Ted Green, "Tomjanovich Is in Intensive Care After Laker Punchout," *Los Angeles Times*, December 11, 1977.

151 **"My job," Auerbach said:** Auerbach acknowledged the importance of race in at least two places around this time—Shah, "The Bird and the B's"; and Ryan, "Race: How Big a Factor?"

151 **"unusual commodity":** Bill Jauss, "He's the Indiana State Bird!" *CT*, January 20, 1978.

151 **"White people have to have":** Stepien made this remark in 1979 to a reporter at a newsletter called *Rave*, which was distributed inside the Cavaliers' arena at the time. It was subsequently picked up by numerous publications, including Bill Nichols, "Stepien, Musselman Deserve Their 'Honeymoon,'" *Cleveland Plain Dealer*, June 15, 1980.

151 **"How many times":** Rosa, "Auerbach Relishes 'Victory'"; and Dick Mittman, "Celtics to Wait on Bird," *IN*, June 22, 1978.

151 **overjoyed when he got:** Harry Morgan, interviews with author, September 18–19, 2024.

151 **"I was hoping":** Morgan, interviews with author, September 18–19, 2024, and September 10, 2025; and Eric Losey, "Harry Morgan Thinks Positive About Making Team With NBA Spurs," *Vincennes (IN) Sun-Commercial*, June 18, 1978.

152 **The Spurs were inviting:** Morgan, interviews with author, September 18–19, 2024, and September 10, 2025; and Ben Smith, "Morgan & Taylor: Dreams Die Hard," *Anderson Daily Bulletin*, May 14, 1981.

152 **Morgan didn't make:** Morgan, interviews with author, September 18–19, 2024, and September 10, 2025; and Mike Chappell, "Just a Chance," *Anderson (IN) Daily Bulletin*, August 1, 1978.

152 **Tucson Gunners:** "Brown Slows Gunners' Cuts," *Tucson Citizen*, November 3, 1978.

152 **"I was a real scoring *machine*":** Ben Smith, "Morgan & Taylor: Dreams Die Hard."

152 **more than a thousand points:** https://www.basketball-reference.com/players/m/morgaha01.html.

152 **headed home to Anderson:** Harry and Rita Morgan, interview with author, September 19, 2024.

152 **never once heard:** Reed, interview with author, August 15, 2024.

152 **a bar called Rafters:** Gibson, interview with author, February 8, 2025.

152 **played for a softball team:** John Benton, interview with author, February 6, 2025.

152 **Huge crowds:** Details about the weekend come from Benton, interview with author, February 6, 2025; Benton's personal collection of softball scorebooks, shared with the author; and news accounts of the games that weekend, including: Earl Mishler, "Bird, Montana on Same Field?" *South Bend (IN) Tribune*, August 3, 1978; "Shoemaker Wins 1st Finals Test," *South Bend (IN) Tribune*, August 6, 1978; and Earl Mishler, "Terre Haute Team Slow-Pitch Champ," *South Bend (IN) Tribune*, August 7, 1978.

153 **In the snapshot:** John Benton personal collection, shared with author, February 6, 2025.

36.

153 **"He'll be playing for me"**: "Coach Gives Portland Word: Bird Staying," *IS*, June 9, 1978.
153 **He figured King would retire:** Hodges, interview with author, February 11, 2025.
154 **flew down to Tampa:** Staley, interviews with author, August 15, 2024, and September 28, 2024.
154 **Nicks had reported:** Hodges, interview with author, March 7, 2025; Nicks, interview with author, September 3, 2024; "GCCC Cage Drills Begin," *Panama City (FL) News-Herald*, September 18, 1977; and "GCCC Clinic, Exhibition Set," *Panama City (FL) News-Herald*, November 5, 1977.
155 **a key decision:** Hodges, interview with author, March 7, 2025.
155 **ringing Nicks up:** Hodges, interview with author, March 7, 2025; Nicks, interview with author, September 3, 2024; and Dana Hunsinger Benbow, "The Forgotten ISU Superstar," *IS*, January 18, 2019.
155 **Curry was insistent:** Rich Nemcek, interviews with author, May 5–6, 2025.
155 **Alex Gilbert:** Three sources confirmed the details about the recruiting of Alex Gilbert—Gilbert, interviews with author, February 10 and 25, 2025; Hodges, interview with author, February 12, 2025; and Staley, interview with author, March 5, 2025.

37.

157 **Heaton's ancestors:** Details in this section come from Bob Heaton, interviews with author, February 7, 2025, and May 23, 2025; Marcia Heaton Spencer, interviews with author, March 3, 2025, and May 23, 2025; Bob Heaton's personal scrapbooks, shared with the author on a visit to his house, May 23, 2025; and genealogical research the author conducted, tracing back Bob Heaton's family five generations. Important records include: birth certificate for Bob's father, Forrest Heaton, Indiana State Board of Health, No. 26731; birth certificate for Bob's mother, Betty Heaton, Indiana State Division of Public Health, No. 39491; US Census records for Bob's maternal grandparents, Carl Sparks and Kathryn Haney, 1950; US Census records for Bob's maternal great-grandparents, Frank Haney and Grace Elliott, 1910; US Census records for Bob's maternal great-great-grandfather, Aker Haney, 1900; Civil War service records for Aker Haney; and US Census records for Bob's maternal great-great-great-grandfather, Patrick Haney, 1850.
157 **In 1966:** Heaton, interview with author, February 7, 2025; and Heaton Spencer, interview with author, March 3, 2025.
157 **Two days after the Heatons opened:** Details in this section come from Heaton, interview with author, February 7, 2025; Heaton Spencer, interview with author, March 3, 2025; Mark Purdy, "Hero Heaton Anything but Pure Shooter," *CE*, March 18, 1979; Dick Rosetta, "Master 'Miracle' Maker," *SLT*, March 20, 1979, which includes a lengthy family account of what happened that day in Cory; and Heaton's multipart first-person series that he wrote for the *Terre Haute Star-Tribune* in 1980—"Bob Heaton's Story," *Terre Haute Star-Tribune*, February 24, 1980, and "Heaton Recalls His Games for Clay City, Recruiting," *Terre Haute Star-Tribune*, February 25, 1980.
159 **"I hope you can play":** Betty Heaton kept the letters, and Bob Heaton invited the author to view them at his house on May 23, 2025.

NOTES 323

159 **jagged scars:** Heaton showed his scars to the author in a meeting on February 7, 2025.
159 **starting five:** "Bob Heaton Signs With U. of Denver," *THT*, May 1, 1975.
159 **honorable mention:** "Honorable Mention List Includes Bird, Butcher," *BTM*, March 26, 1974.
159 **King wanted Heaton:** "ISU Cagers to Put On Show, Says King," *THS*, April 8, 1975; Carl L. Bender, "King Notes Changes in ISU Basketball," *THT*, April 8, 1975; and "Heaton Took Long Way to ISU," *THT*, February 25, 1979.
159 **like a lost dog:** Heaton, interview with author, February 7, 2025.
159 **Bird approached him:** Heaton, interview with author, February 7, 2025.
160 **hanging out:** The author interviewed four people who spent time at the house or knew the players well during this window of time—Bob and Jane Ann Heaton, interview with author, May 23, 2025; Shelley Keever Reyenga, interview with author, February 25, 2025; and Steve Reyenga, an Indiana State baseball player who briefly lived at the house in the fall of 1978. Reyenga, interview with author, February 24, 2025.
160 **He wanted Daniels:** "Ex-Pacer Mel Daniels to Assist King at ISU," *Rushville (IN) Daily Republican*, July 28, 1978.
160 **aired these concerns:** Both parties confirmed this conversation—Hodges, interview with author, February 11, 2025; and Nelson, interview with author, September 25, 2024.

38.

161 **The pain came on:** Details about King's heart attack and its aftermath come from multiple sources, including: Behnke, interview with author, August 1, 2024; Goldrick, interview with author, October 15, 2024; Hodges, interview with author, February 11, 2025; Brad King, interviews with author, October 18, 2024, and January 9, 2025; Larry King, interview with author, October 15, 2024; Craig McKee, interview with author, September 25, 2024; Ed McKee, interview with author, August 2, 2024; Ron Maly, "Harmon Ineligible for Iowa," *Des Moines Register*, August 3, 1978; Roger J. Ruvolo, "Former Lobo Coach King on Road to Recovery," *AJ*, August 5, 1978; Roger J. Ruvolo, "'Coach' Daniels Ready," *AJ*, August 6, 1978; Wayne Fuson, "Tennis Center Ready For '79," *IN*, August 7, 1978; Maury White (column), *Des Moines Register*, August 21, 1978; and Craig McKee journal, shared with author, September 26, 2024.
163 **"kind of concerned":** Ruvolo, "Former Lobo Coach."
163 **"I'll keep 'em":** Maury White (column).
163 **"Is he all right?":** Behnke told this story to the author, as well as to others in the athletic department at the time—Behnke, interview with author, August 1, 2024.

39.

164 **one of the highest-paid:** "Salaries of Top State Workers," *IN*, September 25, 1978.
164 **Larry Bird Committee:** PRL, box 3098, Athletics—Basketball—Larry Bird Appreciation Dinner folder, records of the Larry Bird Committee.
164 **By the Thursday:** Behnke, interview with author, August 1, 2024; Goldrick, interview with author, October 15, 2024; Hodges, interview with author, February 11, 2025; Brad King, interviews with author, October 18, 2024, and January 9, 2025;

Larry King, interview with author, October 15, 2024; Craig McKee, interview with author, September 25, 2024; Ed McKee, interview with author, August 2, 2024; and Craig McKee journal, shared with author, September 26, 2024.

165 **before it could burst:** Goldrick, interviews with author, October 15, 2024, and April 25, 2025; "ISU's King Takes Leave From Posts," THT, October 11, 1978; "Huntsman, Hodges Assume Duties at ISU," THS, October 12, 1978; and "Report Expected Today on King's Condition," THT, October 12, 1978.

165 **homecoming week:** Details about Landini's week come from multiple sources, including PRL, box 3131, Landini daily calendar, 1978; Newton, interview with author, April 24, 2025; and multiple news accounts about homecoming festivities in the *Indiana Statesman*, October 12, 1978.

165 **5:15 meeting:** PRL, box 3131, Landini daily calendar, 1978.

165 **"the man we want":** "President Landini Plays Role in Sports," THT, February 26, 1979.

166 **backing of both King *and* Bird:** Hodges, interview with author, March 7, 2025; Newton, interview with author, April 24, 2024; Dave Johnson, "Bird Is Miracle for Hodges," *Evansville Press*, March 2, 1979; and *Drive*, 49. As Bird recounted in his memoir, "Believe me, I definitely would have left if Bill Hodges wouldn't have gotten the job."

166 **Bird wanted Landini:** In 2024 and 2025, the author interviewed almost everyone off the 1978-79 Indiana State roster: coaches Bill Hodges, Danny King, and Terry Thimlar; staffers Bob Behnke, Rick Shaw, and Craig and Ed McKee; and players Tom Crowder, Alex Gilbert, Bob Heaton, Rod McNelly, Brad Miley, Rich Nemcek, Carl Nicks, Steve Reed, Bob Ritter, and Leroy Staley—17 sources in all. Hereafter, when scenes have been built, or details have been confirmed, through these interviews, it shall be referred to as: 1978–79 ISU team, interviews with author.

166 **didn't fully believe:** Hodges, interview with author, February 13, 2025.

166 **"We pray":** Indiana State press release, October 11, 1978, Craig McKee personal collection.

166 **It was 9:40:** Craig McKee was so cognizant of the importance of the moment that morning that he kept notes in real time, saved them for decades, typed up a narrative about what happened that morning in the moment, and shared it with the author—Craig McKee journal, shared with author, September 26, 2024.

166 **10:15 when Landini:** References to this meeting can be found in two places—Craig McKee journal, shared with author, September 26, 2024, and PRL, box 3131, Landini daily calendar, 1978.

40.

167 **Evans's friends . . . were stunned:** Behnke, interview with author, September 11, 2024; Craig McKee, interview with author, September 26, 2024; and McKee journal.

167 **"I didn't give up" . . . 14–12 in the upcoming:** Jim Zentmeyer, "Fate Put Hodges, Not Evans, in the Spotlight," CP, March 15, 1979.

167 **Plenty of experts:** Mal Elliott, "Bird Goes Inside This Year to Power Sycamores," *Wichita Beacon*, November 6, 1978; and "The Super Sophs," *Sports Illustrated*, November 27, 1978.

167 **dispatched Lane Stewart:** Stewart, interviews with author, March 18, 2025, and April 1, 2025; and Keith, interview with author, March 29, 2025.

NOTES

168 **the day of the shoot:** The author spoke to multiple people who witnessed or took part in the photo shoot, including: Dave Harshman, interview with author, April 11, 2025; Longaker, interview with author, April 7, 2025; Paulsen, interview with author, April 2, 2025; and Stewart, interviews with author, March 18, 2025, and April 1, 2025. Johnson himself confirmed the general details in *My Life*, 166.

168 **preseason poll:** "The Top 20," *Sports Illustrated*, November 27, 1978.

168 **McKee helped Evans:** Craig McKee, interviews with author; McKee journal, shared with author; "Evans Takes New Duties; Aide Hired," THS, October 25, 1978; "ISU Basketball Aide Takes Non-Cage Post," THT, October 25, 1978; and "Sycamore Cagers Preview Against Awesome Russian National Team," *Terre Haute Spectator*, November 18, 1978.

41.

169 **Hodges didn't understand:** Hodges, interview with author, April 25, 2025.

169 **clipped and sealed:** Details about King's surgery and his return home come from multiple sources, including: Goldrick, interviews with author, October 15, 2024, and April 25, 2025; Hodges, interview with author, April 25, 2025; Brad King, interviews with author, October 18, 2024, and January 9, 2025; and Larry King, interview with author, October 15, 2024. Additional details come from "Report Expected Today on King's Condition," THT, October 12, 1978; "King Listed Satisfactory After Surgery," AJ, October 14, 1978; "Ex-UNM Coach King Going Home," AJ, October 28, 1978; and McKee journal, shared with author, September 26, 2024.

170 **Terry Thimlar was:** Details about Thimlar, his life, and his hiring in the fall of 1978 come from multiple sources, including: Thimlar, interviews with author, August 7, 2024, August 9, 2024, August 13, 2024, and March 5, 2025; "Sidelined but Not Out," IN, July 1, 1963; Dan McDonald, "Coach's Son Shakes Polio, Becomes Star," *Fort Myers News-Press*, November 25, 1973; and "ISU Adds Thimlar to Basketball Staff," IS, October 25, 1978.

170 **special connection:** "Ex-UNM Coach King Going Home," AJ, October 28, 1978.

170 **The site was:** Details about media day 1978 come from multiple sources, including: Hodges, interview with author, February 13, 2024; Ron Maly, "Pass the Word: Bird Is Returning to D.M.," *Des Moines Register*, November 3, 1978; Ron Maly, "Bird Here for Missouri Valley Tipoff Meeting," *Des Moines Register*, November 5, 1978; Ron Maly, "Drake's Cagers Picked 7th in Missouri Valley," *Des Moines Register*, November 6, 1978; Steve Sinclair, "Bird Tabs Apke No. 1 Coach; Valley Polls Put Jay at No. 5," *Omaha World-Herald*, November 6, 1978; "King Says Hurricane's Improved, but Saluki Cagers Valley Favorites," *Tulsa World*, November 6, 1978; Elliott, "Bird Goes Inside"; and Ron Maly, "Highly Prized Bradley Freshman Nearly Accepted Hawkeyes' Bid," *Des Moines Register*, November 7, 1978.

171 **molding this team:** Details about the team's practices in October and November 1978 come directly out of Hodges's typed and handwritten practice plans and notes, recorded in the moment in the fall of 1978 and shared with the author on March 7, 2025. Additional details come from interviews the author conducted with the people who participated in those practices—1978–79 ISU team, interviews with author.

173 **wasn't recovering:** Goldrick, interview with author, October 15, 2024; Hodges, interview with author, April 25, 2025; and Brad King, interviews with author, October 18, 2024, and January 9, 2025.

42.

173 **"If we win"**: "New Coaches at SIU and ISU Will Soon Learn About Pressure," *Evansville Press*, November 9, 1978.

173 **The Soviets arrived:** Details about the Soviet tour of the US in November 1978 come from multiple sources, including author interviews with 15 players and coaches who faced the Soviets that month; Carlos Salazar, "Russians Sidestep Politics for Music," *Albuquerque Tribune*, November 3, 1978; Greg Hansen, "From Russia With Laughter?" *Albany (OR) Democrat-Herald*, November 6, 1978; "Beavers Edge Russians on Steve Johnson's Layup," *Corvallis (OR) Gazette-Times*, November 6, 1978; Bart Ripp, "Russian Bombers Silence Lobos' Popguns," *AJ*, November 7, 1978; Matt Lindsey, "Russians Just Too Big," *Albuquerque Tribune*, November 7, 1978; "Russians Learn Lessons Well; Notre Dame Cagers Fall, 90–75," *IS*, November 11, 1978; "The Big Red Wins, 68–55, Only It Was the Other Guys," *IS*, November 12, 1978; Dick Ham, "Russians Elude Boilermakers 65–61," *Lafayette (IN) Journal and Courier*, November 14, 1978; Fred Stabley, "'Simple Plan' Nets Super Basketball Victory" and Keith Gave, "After-Game Party Lesson in Detente," *LSJ*, November 15, 1978; Dick Kaegel, "Russian Cavalry Overtakes Illini," *St. Louis Post-Dispatch*, November 17, 1978; and Grant Overstake, "Soviets React to Hearty Crowd by Outrunning Kansas 87–84," *Wichita Beacon*, November 21, 1978.

174 **"We're showing"**: Kaegel, "Russian Cavalry."

175 **"This Johnson"**: Gave, "After-Game Party."

175 **retired to the home:** Gave, "After-Game Party."

175 **"We aren't changing"**: "Indiana State Faces Soviet Cagers Today," *THT*, November 19, 1978.

176 **Hodges didn't seem nervous:** 1978–79 ISU team, interviews with author.

176 **almost unshakable:** Nicks, interview with author, September 9, 2024.

176 **the Sycamores struggled:** Details about the Indiana State game against the Soviets come from multiple sources, including: "Sporting Around," "Russians Coach Talks Candidly About ISU," and "Nicks, Gilbert Shine as Russians Defeated," *THT*, November 20, 1978; Overstake, "Soviets React to Hearty Crowd"; and 1978–79 ISU team, interviews with author.

176 **wouldn't have survived:** 1978–79 ISU team, interviews with author.

177 **"our 11th game"**: Dave Overpeck, "ISU Saves Hoosier Face in Victory Over Soviets," *IS*, November 20, 1978.

177 **"Your team is very good"**: *THT*, November 21, 1978.

177 **"We want to go on"**: *THT*, November 21, 1978.

177 **The game in West Lafayette:** Details about the Purdue game in late November 1978 come from multiple sources, including: 1978–79 ISU team, interviews with author; WTTV television coverage of the Purdue–Indiana State game, November 27, 1979, viewed in its entirety by author; "Sporting Around," *THT*, November 26, 1978; "Sycamores, Boilers Renew Hot Rivalry," *THT*, November 27, 1978; Mike Chappell, "Even in Pivot, Bird Does Thing as ISU Trims Purdue," *Anderson (IN) Daily Bulletin*, November 28, 1978; Jeff Washburn, "Bird's 22 Leads ISU Over Purdue, 63–53," *Lafayette (IN) Journal and Courier*, November 28, 1978; and "Sporting Around" and "ISU Keeps Poise to Beat Purdue," *THT*, November 28, 1978.

43.

178 **broadcasters were surprised:** WTTV television coverage of the Purdue–Indiana State game.
178 **the team bus:** "ISU Keeps Poise to Beat Purdue," *THT*, November 28, 1978.
179 **ISU DOESN'T DO MUCH:** Mike Lopresti, "ISU Doesn't Do Much, but It's Enough at Purdue," *Richmond (IN) Palladium-Item*, November 28, 1978.
179 **fully believing:** "ISU Keeps Poise to Beat Purdue," *THT*, November 28, 1978, and Anne Harter, "Aces Out to Stop Bird, ISU," *Evansville Press*, December 2, 1978.
179 **"kind of a rookie":** "Sycamores Dominate Play Here; Purdue Comes Next," *THT*, November 26, 1978.
179 **bad news:** Details about the death of Alex Gilbert's brother, Lindell, come from multiple sources, including: Hodges, interview with author, March 7, 2025; Gilbert, interviews with author, February 10, 2025, and February 25, 2025; Miley, interviews with author, August 21, 2024, and March 19, 2025; Thimlar, interview with author, August 9, 2024; the criminal case file for the man charged in Lindell's death, Spencer Lee Lowery Jr., St. Clair County, Illinois, case No. 79-CF-122; Pete Swanson, "Indiana State's Alex Gilbert Travels Road of Tragedy and Glory This Season," *Evansville Sunday Courier and Press*, January 28, 1979; and "Charged in Killing in East St. Louis," *St. Louis Post-Dispatch*, February 15, 1979.
180 **In front of a sold-out:** "Sycamores Battle Evansville Tonight," *THS*, December 2, 1978; Pete Swanson, "Bird Flies Past Aces," *Evansville Press*, December 3, 1978; "Illinois State at Hulman Center Tonight," *THS*, December 4, 1978; and "ISU Winner in Close One," *THT*, December 3, 1978.
180 **With 10 minutes:** "Sycamores, 'Birds Clash Anew Tonight," *THT*, December 4, 1978; Mike Kiley, "Bird Flies Over Ill. State Again," *CT*, December 5, 1978; Bryan Bloodworth, "Indiana State, Fouls Beat Redbirds, 78–76," *Bloomington-Normal (IL) Daily Pantagraph*, December 5, 1978; Robin Miller, "Sir Larry of Indiana State Slays Illinois Brutes, 78–76," *IS*, December 5, 1978; "Sycamores Claw Way to 78–76 Victory," *THS*, December 5, 1978; and WTHI coverage of the Illinois State–Indiana State game, December 4, 1978, viewed in its entirety by author.
181 **"Indiana State can't hit":** WTHI television coverage of the Illinois State–Indiana State game.
181 **no one was questioning:** 1978–79 ISU team, interviews with author.
181 **Hodges invited King:** Mike Myers, "ISU Defense Shines as Bird Soars," *IN*, December 18, 1978; and Hodges, interview with author, March 7, 2025.
182 **won by 38:** "Bird Scores 48—Blasts Butler," *Elwood (IN) Call-Leader*, December 18, 1978; and Bill Benner, "Bird, ISU Trample Butler," *IS*, December 17, 1978.
182 **"We couldn't have stopped":** "Bird Scores 48," *Elwood (IN) Call-Leader*.
182 **They cheered:** WTHI coverage of Creighton–Indiana State game, January 27, 1979, viewed in its entirety by author; and 1978–79 ISU team, interviews with author.
182 **Before each game:** Pete Swanson, "Indiana State Loose as (Golden) Goose," *Evansville Sunday Courier and Press*, February 18, 1979; and 1978–79 ISU team, interviews with author.
182 **31,683 fans:** Fred Stabley Jr., "Dome-Dull Spartans Need Rally to Win," and Lynn Henning, "Wild Fans Lap It Up Under Silverdome," *LSJ*, December 20, 1978.
182 **feeling good about themselves:** 1978–79 ISU team, interviews with author.

183 **spent an afternoon:** Details about the day on the Heaton farm and the tractor incident were confirmed by three different players, including Crowder, interview with author, December 9, 2024; Heaton, interview with author, February 7, 2025; and Ritter, interview with author, December 5, 2024.

44.

183 **Auerbach . . . hadn't meddled:** Francis Rosa, "Auerbach Relishes 'Victory,'" *BG*, June 10, 1978.

183 **Auerbach flew to Indiana:** Details of Auerbach's visit to Terre Haute recounted in this section were confirmed through multiple sources, including: Behnke, interview with author, September 11, 2024; Shaw, interview with author, August 15, 2024; Len Berman, interview with author, May 5, 2025; Kim Rogers, "Auerbach High on His Flyin' Bird," *IN*, January 4, 1979; Robin Miller, "Sycamores Win Valley Opener," *IS*, January 4, 1979; "Sycamores Beat Stubborn Tulsa," *THT*, January 4, 1979; "10–0 Sycamores 1–0 in Valley," *THS*, January 4, 1979; Will McDonough, "Sox Make Offer That Twins Find Hard to Refuse," *BG*, January 5, 1979; and "Sporting Around," *THT*, January 5, 1979.

184 **compared Tulsa:** "Sporting Around," *THT*, January 4, 1979.

184 **"Everything we do":** "Questions Answered, Others Remain," *THT*, November 21, 1978.

184 **two million subscribers:** John G. Watson, "Pay Cable TV: More Than a Link and a Promise," *Los Angeles Times*, January 28, 1979.

184 **"This is the state bird":** HBO coverage of the New Mexico State–Indiana State game, January 15, 1978, viewed in its entirety by author.

186 **wasn't superstitious:** "ISU Wins 14th 73–69 Over Aggies," *Indiana Statesman (Terre Haute, IN)*, January 16, 1979.

186 **the Aggies didn't feel:** The Aggies' impressions of Indiana State and Terre Haute come from interviews with four members of that team—Cormier, interview with author, March 19, 2025; Gunn, interview with author, March 20, 2025; Hayes, interviews with author, March 1, 2025, and March 3, 2025; and Webb, interview with author, March 18, 2025.

186 **Temperatures hovered around zero:** "Weather," *THS*, January 15, 1979.

186 **As Ken Hayes took:** Hayes, interview with author, March 1, 2025.

186 **The game that night:** 1978–79 ISU team, interviews with author; Cormier, interview with author, March 19, 2025; Gunn, interview with author, March 20, 2025; Hayes, interviews with author, March 1, 2025, and March 3, 2025; and Webb, interview with author, March 18, 2025; "ISU, New Mexico State Collide Tonight," *THS*, January 15, 1978; "Sycamores, Aggies Square Off Tonight," *THT*, January 15, 1979; "I-State Downs Aggies in 73–69 Debate," *THS*, January 16, 1979; Skip Myslenski, "Bird's Hit Tune Still Lacks Lyrics," *CT*, February 16, 1979; and WTTV coverage of New Mexico State–Indiana State game.

187 **"If I miss":** Ray Compton, "I-State in 'Valley' Driver's Seat . . . If," *IN*, January 16, 1979.

187 **an official complaint:** Hayes, interview with author, March 3, 2025.

187 **snowbank:** Myslenski, "Bird's Hit Tune."

187 **Red Auerbach made a move:** Larry Whiteside, "Finally, Celtics Make Deal: Knight for Robey," *BG*, January 17, 1979; and Dick Mittman, "Pacers Deal Robey for Knight," *IS*, January 17, 1979.

188 **Bird might sign:** Mike Madden, "The Bird Is the Word—and the Word Is Super," *BG*, January 28, 1979.

45.

188 **had again stopped talking:** Bird's silence with the media was one of the main story lines of the 1978–79 season. It was noted in every profile written about him that season, and witnessed by everyone in the locker room, especially by those in the sports information office, Ed and Craig McKee—1978–79 ISU team, interviews with author; Craig McKee, multiple interviews with author; Ed McKee, multiple interviews with author; and McKee journal, shared with author, September 26, 2024.
188 **in a whirlpool:** "On Cue, Bird Shows His Best," *CT*, February 26, 1979.
189 **"They all want to":** Bruce Newman, "Flying to the Top," *Sports Illustrated*, February 5, 1979.
189 **"Used to be":** "Larry Bird Talks About Cage Season," *THT*, November 7, 1978.
189 **"People that try":** Bird, HBO television interview with Len Berman, January 3, 1979.
189 **"How's he going to":** Myslenski, "Bird's Hit Tune."
189 **"It'll hit him":** Tom Cushman, "Bird-Watchers See Lot, Hear Little," *Philadelphia Daily News*, February 14, 1979.
189 **"Mainly because":** Cushman, "Bird-Watchers See Lot."
190 **"excluding Larry Bird":** Craig McKee, multiple interviews with author; Ed McKee, multiple interviews with author; and Warren Collier, "Fifth Quarter," *Muncie (IN) Evening Press*, December 14, 1978.
190 **appeared to be losing weight:** Cushman, "Bird-Watchers See Lot."
190 **feeling unwelcome:** Ed McKee, interview with author, February 23, 2025.
190 **"He's afraid":** Myslenski, "Bird's Hit Tune."
190 **"The doctors just . . .":** PRL, box 3131, Landini daily calendar, January 1979; Dave Koerner, "Indiana State's King Won't Return as Coach," *CJ*, January 20, 1979; and "It's Official! Bill Hodges New Indiana State Head Coach Cage," *THT*, February 3, 1979.
190 **"Whether he's right":** Dave Koerner, "Bird Remains Silent, So His Play Does the Talking," *CJ*, January 28, 1979.
191 **"first team":** Gene Policinski, "'Conservative'—Watchword in Statehouse," *Lafayette (IN) Journal and Courier*, January 26, 1978.
191 **"I can knock":** Koerner, "Bird Remains Silent."
191 **Mike Madden:** Details about Madden and his work come from interviews with his editor and three of his colleagues—Vince Doria, interview with author, January 29, 2025; Dan Shaughnessy, interview with author, January 26, 2025; and Ryan, interviews with author, September 13, 2024, and January 29, 2025. Additional details come from Madden's obituary—Bryan Marquard, "Michael Madden, 73; Was Longtime *Globe* Sports Columnist," *BG*, April 16, 2017.
191 **In the 1980s:** Details about Madden's reporting on the Elks Club come from multiple sources, including: Doria, interview with author, January 29, 2025; Shaughnessy, interview with author, January 26, 2025; Madden's story ("Tacit Complicity?" *BG*, March 15, 1985); and a follow-up story, "Harper's Firing: Sox Dishonor," *BG*, December 28, 1985.
192 **From the moment:** Madden, "The Bird Is the Word"; Mike Madden, "A Week in the Heartland of Basketball," *BG*, February 4, 1979; and Dave Smith, "Cage Star Rattled by 'the Press,'" *Richmond (IN) Palladium-Item*, March 4, 1979.

192 **a sneak peek:** "Bird Featured in *Sports Illustrated* Again," *THT*, January 30, 1979.
192 **used his local connections:** Newman, "Flying to the Top"; and Bruce Newman, interview with author, February 24, 2025.
192 **Hodges was livid:** Details about Hodges's reaction come from multiple sources, including "Hodges Glad to Be Back Home Again," *THS*, February 6, 1979; "*Sports Illustrated* Displeases Hodges," *THT*, February 6, 1979; Hodges, interview with author, April 25, 2025; Newman, interview with author, February 24, 2025; and 1978–79 ISU team, interviews with author.
192 **Heathcote so angry:** Details about Heathcote's reaction after the Northwestern loss come from multiple sources, including: Brkovich, interview with author, March 21, 2025; Harshman, interview with author, April 11, 2025; Kelser, interview with author, September 27, 2024; Longaker, interview with author, April 7, 2025; and Paulsen, interview with author, April 2, 2025.
192 **bused three hours:** Bob Ryan column, *Basketball Weekly*, February 8, 1979.

46.

193 **Hayes couldn't stand:** Hayes, interviews with author, March 1, 2025, and March 3, 2025.
193 **fast start:** Webb, interview with author, March 18, 2025.
193 **stay out of:** Gunn, interview with author, March 20, 2025.
193 **had made a gumbo:** Cormier, interview with author, March 19, 2025.
193 **the Rain Forrest:** The spelling of the nightclub's name was confirmed by the author, with the help of Mindy Del Campo, a librarian with the Las Cruces Public Library. She found old advertisements in the library archives, confirming the spelling.
193 **a record crowd:** Details about the game recounted in this section and the next two sections come from multiple sources, including: Cormier, interview with author, March 19, 2025; Gunn, interview with author, March 20, 2025; Hayes, interviews with author, March 1, 2025, and March 3, 2025; Webb, interview with author, March 18, 2025; 1978–79 ISU team, interviews with author; KOB and WTHI broadcasts of the game, February 1, 1979, viewed in their entirety by author; Jeff Coy, "Aggies Face Sycamores," and Frank Maestas, "Sycamores Lose Practice Court Battle at NMSU," *AJ*, February 1, 1979; Richard Stevens, "Spotlight Focuses on Las Cruces," *Albuquerque Tribune*, February 1, 1979; Tim Morris, "Aggies, Sycamores in Key MVC Match," *Santa Fe New Mexican*, February 1, 1979; "New Mexico State Will Host ISU" and "New Mexico State Set for Big Confrontation," *THT*, February 1, 1979; Jeff Coy, "Sycamores Edge Aggies," and Frank Maestas, "Indiana State 'Very Lucky,'" *AJ*, February 2, 1979; Richard Stevens, "It Was Just Nothing but Luck: ISU's Heaton," and "Larry Bird Not No. 1 to Aggie Fans," *Albuquerque Tribune*, February 2, 1979; Tim Morris, "Miracle Shot Helps Sycamores Set Down Aggies 91–89 in OT," *Santa Fe New Mexican*, February 2, 1979; "Half-Court Shot Spurs ISU Victory," *Round Up*, February 2, 1979; and "ISU Rallies After Seemingly Dead," *THT*, February 2, 1979.
194 **100 feet away:** KOB and WTHI broadcast of game.
195 **drawn blood:** KOB and WTHI broadcast of game; "Larry Bird Not No. 1," *Albuquerque Tribune*, February 2, 1979; and *Swastika*, Volume 73 (the 1979 yearbook of New Mexico State University), 207.
195 **"quick left hook":** The author interviewed student photographer José R. Lopez, who shot the game that night for the Associated Press. Lopez, who would later go on

NOTES

to a long career with *The New York Times*, shot a series of photographs that captured the incident. Lopez, interview with author, September 11, 2025. Additional confirmation comes from "Larry Bird Not No. 1," *Albuquerque Tribune*, February 2, 1979.

195 **"Everybody's standing"**: KOB and WTHI broadcast of game.
196 **"It don't make"**: KOB and WTHI broadcast of game.
196 **"It's kind of hard"**: "Half-Court Shot Spurs ISU Victory," *Round Up*, February 2, 1979.
196 **break the spell**: Hal McCoy, "Who Is This Coaching Man Who Is Bird's Alter Ego?" *Dayton Daily News*, February 18, 1979.
196 **"You just have to"**: Hodges, interview with author, February 13, 2025.
197 **wasn't even really listening**: Heaton, interview with author, February 7, 2025.
197 **"18-1"**: KOB and WTHI broadcast of game.
197 **"Don't give up"**: Heaton, interview with author, February 7, 2025; and Danny King, interview with author, May 23, 2025.
197 **Greg Webb had felt**: Webb, interview with author, March 18, 2025.
198 **the worst shot**: Indiana State 40-year reunion event, January 19, 2019.
198 **picked up the phone**: Craig McKee, interview with author, September 25, 2024.
198 **Hayes . . . couldn't believe it**: Maestas, "Indiana State 'Very Lucky.'"
198 **"IT'S GOING IN!"**: "Sporting Around," *THT*, February 4, 1979.
199 **"still in my craw"**: Hayes, interviews with author, March 1, 2025, and March 3, 2025.
199 **went out on the town**: 1978–79 ISU team, interviews with author.
199 **cowboy hats**: 1978–79 ISU team, interviews with author.
199 **"wasn't so hard"**: 1978–79 ISU team, interviews with author—especially Heaton, interview with author, July 15, 2025.

47.

200 **impromptu pep rally**: "ISU Wins 20th, 66–56 at Tulsa," *Indiana Statesman (Terre Haute, IN)*, February 6, 1979.
200 **slipped away**: Danny King, interview with author, May 23, 2025; and Hal McCoy, "Look, Up in the Sky . . . It's a Bird; No, It's the Bird," *Dayton Daily News*, February 13, 1979.
200 **Bob Heaton Day**: "SGA to Dedicate Monday to 'Miracle Man' Bob Heaton," *Indiana Statesman (Terre Haute, IN)*, February 6, 1979.
200 **not many people**: Bob Heaton and Jane Ann Heaton, interviews with author, May 23, 2025.
200 **rang again and again**: Pete Swanson, "Bird Plays Second Fiddle to Heaton, His Roommate—ISU's 'Miracle Man,'" *Evansville Sunday Courier and Press*, February 11, 1979; "Sycamores Hope Need for 'Miracle' Baseless," *THT*, March 17, 1979.
200 **pick out cowboy hats**: 1978–79 ISU team, interviews with author.
200 **"I'm still King's"**: "Hodges Views Himself as Assistant," *THT*, January 12, 1979.
201 **Landini decided to end . . . he announced**: "Hodges Gets Coaching Contract," *THS*, February 3, 1979.
201 **everyone who mattered**: The author spoke to at least four people who attended these parties that winter—Hodges, interview with author, March 7, 2025; Mosbaugh, interview with author, June 29, 2025; John Newton, interview with author, April 24, 2024; and Bob Warn, interviews with author, January 30, 2025, and January 31, 2025.

201 **"we pray"**: "Sporting Around," *THT*, January 24, 1979.
201 **"Take away"**: David Benner, "Sycamores Clinch Tie for Title," *IS*, February 11, 1979.
201 **"Bird Cage Defense"**: "Bradley's 'Bird'-Cage Upsets ISU's Hodges," *IS*, February 12, 1979; and "Braves Blank Bird, but Sycamores Win," *THT*, February 11, 1979.
202 **Auerbach was sending**: Leigh Montville, "Celtics Had Better Get This Bird in Hand," *BG*, February 26, 1979.
202 **that night in Terre Haute:** The author spoke with all three Celtics who made this visit—Dave Cowens, interview with author, August 16, 2025; Judkins, interview with author, September 18, 2024; and Robey, interview with author, April 7, 2025—as well as members of the Indiana State team who went out with them that night. Nemcek, interview with author, May 5, 2025.
202 **students slept**: Gary Niemier, "Sycamore Fever Hits," *South Bend Tribune*, February 25, 1979.
202 **started selling tables**: PRL, box 3098, Athletics—Basketball—Larry Bird Appreciation Dinner folder, Larry Bird Committee minutes from the meetings on February 6, February 21, and March 7, 1979.
202 **"You've got to play"**: Mike Madden, "A Week in the Heartland of Basketball," *BG*, February 4, 1979.
202 **defeated Kansas by 24:** Curt Sylvester, "Spartans Look Like Champs in Smashing Kansas, 85–61," *DFP*, February 5, 1979; and Lynn Henning, "More Raves for 'Magic,'" *LSJ*, February 13, 1979.
203 **"The question I tire of"**: Pete Donovan, "'Magic': Disappearing Act Up His Sleeve?" *Los Angeles Times*, February 27, 1979.
203 **congressional investigation:** "SGA Elections Funded; Calls for AP, UPI Investigations," *Indiana Statesman (Terre Haute, IN)*, February 23, 1979.
203 **Network executives announced:** "Sycamores on TV," *Evansville Sunday Courier and Press*, February 11, 1979.

48.

203 **having a moment:** Details about Packer, McGuire, and NBC's ratings boom come from multiple sources, including Billy Reed, "McGuire Decided to Quit After Three 'Cracks,'" *CJ*, December 31, 1977; Larry Dorman, "McGuire a Winner as Broadcaster, Too," *Palm Beach Post-Times*, March 25, 1978; Matt Lindsey, "Witty Al McGuire a Silver Dollar in a Sea of Nickels," *Albuquerque Tribune*, February 15, 1979; and Larry Keith, "Two Mouths Are Better Than Anyone," *Sports Illustrated*, March 5, 1979.
203 **Bill Paczkowski:** New York State Birth Index, No. 1232, lists his birth name as "Anthony Paczkowski," February 25, 1940.
204 **"some high school"**: Ray Compton, "Sycamores Don't Need Packer," *IN*, March 13, 1979.
204 **"Al McGuire for President"**: Russ Corbitt, "Wichita State Amid No. 1 Excitement in Terre Haute," *Wichita Eagle and Beacon*, February 25, 1979.
204 **for an NBC interview:** Phil Bloom, "Larry Bird Talks . . . to NBC and Al McGuire," *BTM*, February 5, 1979.
205 **"He called me"**: Gary Shutt, "Sideline Action Muscles Out Game Play," *Tulsa World*, February 4, 1979; and Bill Jauss, "Toughest Opponent for Indiana State? Pressure," *CT*, March 3, 1979.

205 **"The rulebook states":** Mike Kiley, "Bradley Holds Bird to 4, but Indiana State Rolls," *CT*, February 11, 1979.
206 **"No. 1," Ortegel said:** Ron Maly, "Sycamores Survive Amid Fracas: Coaches 'Jaw' Over Organ Music," *Des Moines Register*, February 21, 1979, and "Drake's Organist Only Attempting to Support Bulldogs," *Des Moines Register*, February 22, 1979.
206 **wasn't feeling any pressure:** Jauss, "The Toughest Opponent."
206 **"a pretty good player":** This quote, and others in this section, come directly out of David Israel's column, "Tell Us, Larry Bird, Can You Bear the Silence?" *CT*, February 22, 1979.
206 **upset everyone:** 1978–79 ISU team, interviews with author.
207 **bad weather moved in:** "City Paralyzed by Dense Fog," *IS*, February 24, 1979; Dan Carpenter and Susan M. Anderson, "Move Over, Blizzard of '78," and "Indiana Reels Under Blows of Fierce Winter Weather," *IS*, February 25, 1979; and NBC telecast of the Wichita State–Indiana State game, February 25, 1979, viewed in its entirety by author.
207 **began to leak:** Craig McKee, interview with author, May 9, 2025; Ed McKee, interview with author, May 14, 2025; and NBC telecast of Wichita State–Indiana State game.
207 **Larry Bird Week in French Lick:** Details about the week's festivities come from photos and stories published in the *Springs Valley Herald* over three issues—February 15, February 22, and May 3, 1979.
207 **"A defeat," Hodges said:** McCoy, "Who Is This Coaching Man."

49.

208 **Gene Smithson, had managed:** "Smithson Back Home," *THT*, February 25, 1979.
208 **"Welcome to Larry's world":** NBC telecast of Wichita State–Indiana State game.
208 **the lyrics:** These lyrics appeared in print on T-shirts and on television that winter—NBC telecast of Wichita State–Indiana State game; and Dave Dorr, "Indiana State Ode to Billy Packer Wrapped In Tissue," *St. Louis Post-Dispatch*, February 25, 1979.
209 **Alex Gilbert won:** Details of the game against Wichita State come from multiple sources, including: 1978–79 ISU team, interviews with author; NBC telecast of Wichita State–Indiana State game; "On Cue, Bird Shows His Best," *CT*, February 26, 1979; Wayne Fuson, "ISU Proves Worthy of No. 1 Spot," *IN*, February 26, 1979; Dave Overpeck, "Bird Carves Legend in Sycamores," *IS*, February 26, 1979; Gordon S. White Jr., "Indiana State, Bird (49) Roll," *New York Times*, February 26, 1979; "Bird, ISU Stage No. 1 Show for Nation," *THS*, February 26, 1979; "Bird Saves Best for Last, Pouring in Record 49 in Victory," "ISU Can Concentrate on League Playoffs," and "ISU Has Good Shot at Final Four: White," *THT*, February 26, 1979; and Russ Corbitt, "Bird, ISU Rip Shockers, 109–84," *Wichita Eagle*, February 26, 1979.
211 **"Bob King is responsible":** Fuson, "ISU Proves Worthy."
212 **"I'll see ya!":** NBC telecast of New Mexico State–Indiana State game.
212 **In the locker room:** 1978–79 ISU team, interviews with author; WTHI news footage from March 3, 1979, viewed by the author; Gibson, interview with author, February 8, 2025; and Bill Jauss, "Bird's Clinic Keeps Indiana State Unblemished," *CT*, March 4, 1979.

50.

212 **his left thumb:** Behnke, interview with author, September 16, 2024; Shaw, interview with author, August 16, 2024; Jauss, "Bird's Clinic"; Pete Swanson, "Sycamores Survive Bird's Injury," *Evansville Sunday Courier and Press*, March 4, 1979; "About THE Thumb" and "Sycamores 29–0; On to the NCAA," *THT*, March 4, 1979; and NBC telecast of postgame celebration, March 3, 1979, viewed by author.

213 **"kinda like letting":** John Bansch, "All's Ecstasy, Not Aggie-ny for ISU," *IS*, March 4, 1979.

214 **"Bob Hodges, Tom Hodges":** Details about the Naismith ceremony, Hodges's comments that day, and Bird's comments come directly from the two Atlanta newspapers at the time—Jesse Outlar, "The Bird Is No. 1—Ask Him," *Atlanta Constitution*, March 5, 1979; and David Davidson, "Bird Brings National Notice to Unheralded Indiana State," *Atlanta Journal*, March 5, 1979. In addition, the author spoke with one of the two print reporters who managed to interview Bird that day—David Davidson, interview with author, June 2, 2025.

215 **more pressing concerns:** Details about the Virginia Tech game come from multiple sources, including NBC's telecast of the Virginia Tech–Indiana State game, March 11, 1979, viewed in its entirety by author; 1978–79 ISU team, interviews with author; "ISU Cooks Gobblers; Sooners Next on Menu," and Ray Compton, "Bird Shows 'Em He's a 'Tough Individual,'" *IN*, March 12, 1979; and "Virginia Tech Coach Admits I-State Is for Real" and "I-State Passes First NCAA Test," *THS*, March 12, 1979.

215 **reported to Hodges:** Thimlar, interview with author, August 7, 1979.

215 **Behnke had crafted:** Details about the thumb and the team's concerns about the thumb come from multiple sources, including: Behnke, interview with author, September 16, 2024; Hodges, interview with author, March 7, 2025; Shaw, interview with author, August 16, 2024; Bill Madden, "Bird & Co.," *New York Daily News*, March 9, 1979; Mike DeArmond, "Eyes Focus on Left Thumb of Larry Bird," *Kansas City Star*, March 11, 1979; Dan Lauch, "Indiana State Hopes It's Thumbs Up," *Newsday (Hempstead, NY)*, March 11, 1979; and Roy Damer, "Indiana State Still Flying," *CT*, March 12, 1979.

216 **shook him off:** Compton, "Bird Shows 'Em"; Lauch, "Indiana State Hopes"; and Reed, interview with author, August 20, 2025.

216 **Packer pointed out:** NBC telecast of Virginia Tech–Indiana State game.

216 **Gilbert had been living:** Gilbert, interview with author, February 25, 2025.

51.

217 **"I don't talk":** The locker room scene was best described in two articles—Joe McGuff, "Ta-da-da-da-dah-dahhhh!—The Bird Speaks—Sort Of," *Kansas City Star*, March 12, 1979, and Dan Lauck, "It Was the Bird's Foes Who Felt the Pain," *Newsday (Hempstead, NY)*, March 12, 1979.

218 **The AP awards:** Details of the ceremony in Chicago come from multiple sources, including: Joe Mooshil, "'Great White Hope'? Bird Ponders Pros," *Anderson Daily Bulletin*, March 12, 1979; Wayne Fuson, "Bird, Hodges Get Year's Top Honors," *IN*, March 12, 1979; "Award Makes Bird Talkative," *IN*, March 13, 1979; "Hodges, Bird Score Clean Sweep," *IS*, March 13, 1979; "Hodges, Bird Receive Top AP Awards," *THS*, March 13, 1979; Roy Damer, "Bird Finally Talks to Press—About Bulls and

Gilmore," *CT*, March 13, 1979; and most importantly, the enterprising reporting of AP sportswriter Wick Temple, who was at the airport that morning when Bird, Hodges, and Landini landed and gained behind-the-scenes access to Bird. Temple's story hit the wire in March 1979 and appeared in newspapers across the country.

218 **"no Oxford don"**: PRL, box 3098, Athletics—Basketball, 1976–1989 folder, Ray Moscowitz, "Big Bird Will Never Be Oxford Don," *Columbus (IN) Republic*, May 3, 1979.

52.

220 **Landini was thrilled**: PRL, box 3098, Athletics—Basketball, 1976–1989 folder.

220 **that week in Cincinnati**: Details of the Oklahoma–Indiana State game come from multiple sources, including: 1978–79 ISU team, interviews with author; Bliss, interview with author, September 27, 2024; Gibson, interview with author, February 8, 2025; Newton, interview with author, April 24, 2025; NBC telecast of game, March 15, 1979, viewed in its entirety by author; Mark Purdy, "What's Sauce for the Bird Is Sauce, Etc," and Tim Sullivan, "Basketball New to Oklahomans, But All Know How to Cage Bird," *CE*, March 15, 1979; "Sooners Talk for Bird" and Michael Graham, "Tournament Time," *CP*, March 15, 1979; Tom Cushman, "Getting Indiana State's Bird to Finally Chirp," *Philadelphia Daily News*, March 15, 1979; Dean Clark, "OU, Porkers Get 'Semi' Serious," *Tulsa World*, March 15, 1979; Bill Ford, "'All-World' Bird and ISU Rout Sooners, 93–72," *CE*, March 16, 1979; Mike Sullivan, "Bird's Talent Rubs Off on the Sycamores, 93–72, Victim Learns," *CJ*, March 16, 1979; Dave Johnson, "The Two Sides of Bird," *Evansville Press*, March 16, 1979; Wayne Fuson, "I-State Seeks 32d Straight vs. Arkansas," *IN*, March 16, 1979; Lynda Fillmore, "No. 1 Indiana State Routs OU," *Daily Oklahoman (Oklahoma City, OK)*, March 16, 1979; and Dean Clark, "Bird Wings It, Flings It Past OU," *Tulsa World*, March 16, 1979.

220 **5½-point favorite**: "Football-Proud Sooners Take on ISU," *Evansville Press*, March 14, 1979.

221 **Both CBS and NBC News prepared**: President Landini and other high-ranking ISU administrators chronicled, in detail, the excitement on campus in the days leading up to the games in Cincinnati in many memos, notes, and letters that are held in Landini's collection at Indiana State: PRL, box 3098, Athletics—Basketball—Postseason Tournaments folder.

221 **looked into the cameras . . . "Great Hope—period"**: Betsy Aaron, *CBS Evening News*, March 16, 1979.

221 **thousands of fans flocked**: Graham, "Tournament Time."

221 **Almost 200 reporters**: "No Pronounced Favorite in Cincinnati," *THT*, March 15, 1979.

221 **Red Auerbach and front office executives**: "Tournament Time," *CP*, March 15, 1979; and Michael Graham, "Bird Watcher," *CP*, March 16, 1979.

221 **largest crowds to ever**: NBC telecast of the Oklahoma–Indiana State game.

221 **Landini was planning to stay**: PRL, box 3098, Athletics—Basketball—Postseason Tournaments folder. Critical documents include Don Roberts, memo to Landini, March 14, 1979; and secretary, note to Landini, March 12, 1979.

221 **"Buy your seeds!"**: Graham, "Bird Watcher."

222 **"win, lose, or draw"**: Jim Zentmeyer, "ISU's Hodges Can't Relax," *CP*, March 16, 1979.

336 NOTES

222 **tried to pretend:** "Coach to Press: 'Tough Bippy,'" *Daily Oklahoman (Oklahoma City, OK)*, March 18, 1979; and Bob Queenan, "Bird Silent, but Coach Takes Shot at Reporter," *CP*, March 19, 1979.
223 **Down in Arkansas:** "Day for Moncrief Confirms State's Most Loved Athlete," *Arkansas Gazette (Little Rock, AR)*, April 17, 1979.
223 **wanted to cover:** Sidney Moncrief, interview with author, February 27, 2025.
223 **debated the plan:** Billy Reed, "'Trashy' Ending Sweet for Ind. State," *CJ*, March 18, 1979.
223 **Hodges didn't want to:** Hodges, interview with author, March 7, 1979.
223 **a sore throat:** Nicks, interview with author, September 16, 2024; and NBC telecast of Arkansas–Indiana State game.
223 **Coliseum . . . were quiet:** 1978–79 ISU team, interviews with author.

53.

223 **NBC executives:** The details and figures come straight from the NBC research files, shared with the author by NBC spokesperson Dan Masonson.
223 **A rising star:** NBC telecast of Arkansas–Indiana State game, March 17, 1979.
224 **Arkansas nearly ran away:** Details about the game come from multiple sources, including author interviews with eight players who played in the game—Gilbert, Hastings, Heaton, Miley, Moncrief, Nicks, Reed, and Staley; author interviews with two Indiana State coaches, Hodges and Thimlar; author interviews with Indiana State staffers Ed and Craig McKee; the NBC telecast of the game; "Sutton: Too Bad It Couldn't Have Been Tie," *Arkansas Gazette*, March 18, 1979; Bill Ford, "Coaches Agree: It's Too Bad Someone Lost," and Tim Sullivan, "ISU's Heaton Hits Winner With 2 Seconds on Clock," *CE*, March 18, 1979; Roy Damer, "Sub's Ragged Shot Saves Indiana State," *CT*, March 18, 1979; "'Other' Miracle Worker Saves Day for Ind. State," *CJ*, March 18, 1979; Dan Lauck, "Indiana St. Wins on Last Shot," *Newsday (Hempstead, NY)*, March 18, 1979; "No. 1 ISU Going to Salt Lake City," *THT*, March 18, 1979; Bob Queenan, "Final Step Was Fatal for Arkansas' Reed," *CP*, March 19, 1979; Leal Beatti, "Bird's Roommate Earns a Big (Left) Hand," *Dayton Journal Herald*, March 19, 1979; and "Heaton Fires Shot Heard Round World," *THS*, March 19, 1979.
227 **like a phantom pain:** Scott Hastings, interview with author, February 27, 2025.
227 **"It's a miracle, I guess":** Sullivan, "ISU's Heaton Hits Winner."

54.

227 **Hodges had stashed:** Nemcek, interview with author, May 6, 2025; and Ritter, interview with author, June 10, 2025.
228 **wanted beer:** Multiple players shared this memory with the author, including: Nemcek, interview with author, May 6, 2025; Nicks, interview with author, July 10, 2025; and Ritter, interview with author, June 10, 2025.
228 **"It's destiny":** NBC telecast of Arkansas–Indiana State game, March 17, 1979.
228 **massive crowd waiting:** 1978–79 ISU team, interviews with author.
228 **"like a fever":** Bill Brighton, interview with NBC, March 17, 1979.
228 **Callers overwhelmed:** "'Sycamore Fever' Has Become Widespread Affliction," *Indiana Statesman (Terre Haute, IN)*, March 6, 1978.

NOTES

228 **up 15 percent:** PRL, box 3098, Athletics—Basketball, 1976–1989 folder; and "ISU: Basketball Team Creates New Pride," *Columbus (IN) Republic*, May 2, 1979.

228 **cheering from the press box:** In addition to Al McGuire's comments during NBC broadcasts, network executives and broadcasters sent three notes to the university in March 1979, singing the team's praises: PRL, box 3098, Athletics—Basketball—Postseason Tournaments folder.

228 **"I'm sorry," he scrawled:** "NBC Commentator Billy Packer Changes Mind Slightly," *Indiana Statesman (Terre Haute, IN)*, March 20, 1979.

228 **"even 'veteran' broadcasters":** PRL, box 3098, Athletics—Basketball—Postseason Tournaments folder, Simpson memo to Ed McKee, March 22, 1979.

228 **finalized a deal:** PRL, box 3098, Athletics—Basketball—Larry Bird Appreciation Dinner folder, Larry Bird Committee, minutes from the meeting on March 21, 1979.

228 **"I don't do anything":** "The Pre-Ordained Wavemaker," *Los Angeles Times*, February 1, 1979.

229 **Heathcote had noticed:** Brkovich, interview with author, March 21, 2025; Harshman, interview with author, April 11, 2025; Kelser, interview with author, September 27, 2024; Longaker, interview with author, April 7, 2025; and Paulsen, interview with author, April 2, 2025.

229 **"Not ready," Digger said:** Curt Sylvester, "MSU's Magic Steamroller Flattens Irish, 80–68," *DFP*, March 19, 1979.

229 **"We're unbeatable":** "Closed Doors," *IN*, March 21, 1979.

229 **eight-point favorite:** "The Latest Line," *New York Daily News*, March 20, 1979.

229 **grew to 10:** "The Latest Line," *New York Daily News*, March 22, 1979.

230 **even Al McGuire:** Gene Quinn, "Al McGuire Picks Michigan State," *Philadelphia Daily News*, March 23, 1979.

230 **"I'd love to play Larry":** Curt Sylvester, "Magic vs. Bird?" *DFP*, March 20, 1979.

230 **closed his practices:** "Closed Doors," *IN*, March 21, 1979; Jack Wilkinson, "Michigan St. Coach Turns Off Magic," *New York Daily News*, March 23, 1979; and Jud Heathcote with Jack Ebling, *Jud: A Magical Journey* (Sagamore Publishing, 1995), 12.

230 **"We should go over the top":** Rudy Martzke, "Bird Breaks Ice With Help," *Rochester (NY) Democrat and Chronicle*, March 21, 1979.

230 **understood why his counterparts at NBC:** O'Malley, interview with author, July 4, 2025.

230 **sent Landini a telegram:** PRL, box 3098, Athletics—Basketball—Postseason Tournaments folder, Chet Simmons, president NBC Sports, mailgram to Richard Landini, March 20, 1979.

231 **awash with requests:** These requests, demands, and questions are all chronicled in detail in Landini's papers: PRL, box 3098, Athletics—Basketball—Postseason Tournaments folder.

231 **about $25,000:** "Tickets to NCAA Finals Have Been Purchased; Problem Now Is Getting to Salt Lake City," *THT*, March 20, 1978.

231 **"Don't expect me":** Queenan, "Bird Silent."

232 **every reporter who had ever crossed:** The author spoke with three of these reporters—David Israel, interview with author, March 10, 2025; Keith, interviews with author, January 25 and March 29, 2025; and Newman, interview with author, February 24, 2025. The dateline on Madden's stories that week confirm his presence there, too.

232 **"I'm missing":** Jack Wilkinson, "Bird Speaks . . . Knicks, Nets, Bulls, Celts & $," *New York Daily News*, March 21, 1979.

338   NOTES

232 **Hodges hated the idea:** Bill Madden, "Bird & Co."
232 **The team gathered:** "ISU, All the Way," THS, March 22, 1979.
232 **"This is Bird Country":** Indiana State University, Salt Lake City photo collection.
233 **take turns rallying:** The author spoke to nearly 20 people who were on this plane.
233 **believed in fate:** Mark Purdy, "Hero Heaton Anything but Pure Shooter," CE, March 18, 1979.

55.

233 **since 1942:** Jack Ledden, "Seen and Heard in the Sport Realm," *South Bend (IN) Tribune*, April 15, 1942.
233 **written a book:** Ray Meyer, *Basketball as Coached by Ray Meyer* (Prentice-Hall, 1967).
233 **Chicago behind him:** Skip Myslenski, "A City Welcomes Its Heroes: 'We Are De Paul,'" CT, March 19, 1979.
233 **Ray Meyer *was* Chicago:** WMAQ-TV, Chicago, March 23, 1979.
233 **"the most heralded":** Ray Meyer with Ray Sons, *Coach* (Contemporary Books, 1987).
233 **anywhere between:** John Husar, "Star or Not, Aguirre Pays Meyer's Price," CT, December 10, 1978.
233 **playing on a hoop:** Mark Aguirre, interview with author, January 29, 2025.
233 **averaged 33 points:** Jerry Shnay and Larry Casey, "Aguirre Decides to Attend DePaul," CT, April 12, 1978.
233 **one coach offered:** Skip Myslenski, "Mark Aguirre," *CT Magazine*, November 16, 1980.
234 **churchgoing women:** Aguirre, interview with author, January 29, 2025.
234 **"turned me off":** Myslenski, "Mark Aguirre."
234 **inside Lollino's house:** *Coach*, 166.
234 **"He never, ever lied":** Aguirre, interview with author, January 29, 2025.
234 **Meyer was upset:** Husar, "Star or Not."
234 **missed the team bus:** "W. Michigan Dumps DePaul," CT, February 1, 1979; and *Coach*, 168.
235 **"A kid like this":** Husar, "Star or Not."
235 **"How do you feel, Ray?":** NBC telecast of UCLA–DePaul game, March 17, 1979, viewed by author.
235 **let Bird get his points:** "Ray Meyer's Tourney Diary: 'Team's So High It Worries Me,'" CT, March 24, 1979; "Heathcote Disputes Sycamores' Claim," THT, March 23, 1979; and *Coach*, 174.
235 **defensive-minded guard:** Mal Florence, "Michigan St. Puts 'Magic' to Work," *Los Angeles Times*, March 24, 1979.
235 **half-sister:** Emily Langer, "Cissy Houston, Grammy Winner and Whitney Houston's Mother, Dies at 91," *Washington Post*, October 7, 2024.
235 **Israel was ghostwriting:** Israel, interview with author, March 10, 2025.
235 **no depth:** Hodges, interview with author, March 7, 2025; Thimlar, interview with author, August 13, 2024.
235 **It wasn't clear:** Bill Jauss, "Watkins News Bolsters All but the Oddsmakers," CT, March 24, 1979.
236 **Sycamore players were relaxed:** 1978–79 ISU team, interviews with author.

236 **"I'm not going pro":** Two sources confirmed this interaction with Auerbach—Nemcek, interview with author, May 6, 2025; and Ritter, interview with author, June 10, 2025.
236 **lob their basketballs:** 1978–79 ISU team, interviews with author.
236 **"I sure hope":** Shaw, interview with author, August 16, 2024.
236 **NCAA rule and mandate:** Mark Purdy, "Another Step in Awakening of Larry Bird," CE, March 26, 1979.
236 **half the team went:** "Bird Wings It With Press in Salt Lake," THT, March 24, 1979.

56.

236 **Penn never had a chance:** NBC telecast of the Penn–Michigan State game, March 24, 1979, viewed in its entirety by author.
236 **"We want Bird!":** Dan Lauck, "Michigan State Overwhelms Penn," *Newsday (Hempstead, NY)*, March 25, 1979.
237 **in the second half:** Details about the DePaul–Indiana State game come from multiple sources, including: 1978–79 ISU team, interviews with author; Aguirre, interview with author, January 29, 2025; NBC telecast of DePaul–Indiana State game; Bill Jauss, "Bird Ends DePaul's Flight," David Israel, "Back to Reality, Shedding No Tears," and Bob Logan, "Bird Plan Bad Judgment: Mitchem," CT, March 25, 1979; Curt Sylvester, "Bring On Bird! Spartans Fly, 101–67," and George Puscas, "No Word Describes Spartans, Except GREAT," DFP, March 25, 1979; "The Bird vs. Magic," *New York Daily News*, March 25, 1979; Joe Gergen, "Positive Game Ends Negatively," *Newsday (Hempstead, NY)*, March 25, 1979; Lex Hemphill, "Bird: Anything You Can Do, I Can Do Better," and Tom Wharton, "Ray Meyer Displays Poise in Defeat," *Salt Lake Tribune*, March 25, 1979; and "Heaton Puts in Another Game-Winner," THT, March 25, 1979.
238 **was wide open:** *Coach*, 175.
238 **"Oh, goodness":** Aguirre, interview with author, January 29, 2025.
238 **"leaned on him":** Aguirre, interview with author, January 29, 2025.

57.

239 **wasn't fond:** Details on the Spartans' lodging situation come from interviews with members of the coaching staff and the team—Brkovich, interview with author, March 21, 2025; Harshman, interview with author, April 11, 2025; Kelser, interview with author, September 27, 2024; Longaker, interview with author, April 7, 2025; and Paulsen, interview with author, April 2, 2025.
239 **rang without end:** Lynn Henning, "Heathcote Hears Bells as MSU Prepares for Penn," LSJ, March 23, 1979, and *Jud*, 12.
239 **wrong fight song:** Harshman, interview with author, April 11, 2025; and Paulsen, interview with author, April 2, 2025.
239 **Hall of Fume:** Marion Dunn, "NCAA Coaches List Priorities: DePaul Needs Housing," *Provo (UT) Herald*, March 22, 1979.
239 **had to admit:** Curt Sylvester, "'Magic' vs. 'Bird'; Spartans Get the Match They Want," *Philadelphia Inquirer*, March 25, 1979.
239 **"man-and-a-half" defense:** Brkovich, interview with author, March 21, 2025; Harshman, interview with author, April 11, 2025; Kelser, interview with author,

September 27, 2024; Longaker, interview with author, April 7, 2025; and Paulsen, interview with author, April 2, 2025.
240 **have Magic pretend:** This topic came up at the noon press conference on Sunday, March 25, 1979, and is well chronicled in the coverage that day.
240 **"something negative":** *Jud*, 13.
240 **out of bed:** Hodges publicly talked about this detail that Sunday to reporters.
240 **didn't care:** Bird's closest friends confirmed his lack of interest in personal accolades and the trophies that came with them—Heaton, interview with author, February 7, 2025; and Gibson, interview with author, February 8, 2025.
241 **Craig McKee found himself:** Craig McKee, interview with author, September 26, 2024.
241 **Bird walked inside:** Details about Bird at the press conference come from multiple sources, including: Craig McKee, interview with author, September 26, 2024; multiple news reports published on March 26, 1979, including Mark Purdy, "Another Step in Awakening of Larry Bird," *CE*; John Schulian, "6-9 'Sphinx' Talks," *Chicago Sun-Times*; Bill Jauss, "It's Magic vs. the Bird," *CT*; Leal Beattie, "Bird's Chirping Now—and Drawing Some Laughs," *Dayton Journal Herald*; "Magic Calls Bird Phenomenal Star," *IN*; Lynn Henning, "Indiana State's Bird Innocent Young Kid," *LSJ*; Dave Anderson, "Herb Shriner With a Jumper," *New York Times*; Tom Cushman, "Larry Bird Can Talk, Too," *Philadelphia Daily News*; Chuck Newman, "City Kid Meets Country Boy," *Philadelphia Inquirer*; Bill Brill, "Larry Bird Goes Head-to-Head With Press," *Roanoke Times & World-News*; Bob Padecky, "Bird ... Even His Opponents Flock to Praise Him," *Sacramento Bee*; "Bird Hopes to Make Best of Last Shot," *THT*; and Dan Denlinger, "Attention Is One Thing Bird Can't Handle Well," *Washington Post*; and *When the Game Was Ours*, 52.
241 **"I'm loving this":** Denlinger, "Attention Is One Thing Bird Can't Handle Well."
242 **"I'll probably dream":** "Magic Calls Bird Phenomenal Star," *IN*, March 26, 1979.
242 **and he didn't want to:** *When the Game Was Ours*, 52.
242 **"like when I'm asked":** Anderson, "Herb Shriner."
242 **"low-rent slob":** Schulian, "6-9 'Sphinx.'"
242 **"hayseed":** Anderson, "Herb Shriner."
243 **Nicks desperately wanted:** Nicks, interview with author, September 16, 2024.
243 **Jud Heathcote struggled:** Brkovich, interview with author, March 21, 2025; Harshman, interview with author, April 11, 2025; Kelser, interview with author, September 27, 2024; Longaker, interview with author, April 7, 2025; and Paulsen, interview with author, April 2, 2025.
243 **How would they would ever cover:** Paulsen, interview with author, April 2, 2025.
243 **"If we play":** Harshman, interview with author, April 11, 2025.
243 **right outside their windows:** This detail was confirmed by multiple people, including: Hodges, interview with author, March 7, 2025; Nicks, interview with author, September 16, 2024; and Thimlar, interview with author, July 14, 2025.
243 **down to the front desk:** Hodges, interview with author, March 7, 2025.
243 **"I ain't feeling it":** In his memoir with Magic Johnson, written with Jackie MacMullan, *When the Game Was Ours*, Bird recalled saying, "I feel sick, like I always do" (p. 55). But three sources who were there in the locker room recall him saying that he wasn't feeling it, as the author recounts here—Heaton, interviews with author, February 3, 2025, and July 15, 2025; Miley, interview with author, August 28, 2024; and Shaw, interview with author, August 16, 2024. A fourth source, Bob Behnke, agreed

that Bird was notably different that night before the game started—Behnke, interview with author, September 16, 2024. Previous reporting has also confirmed this general version of events. See *When March Went Mad*, 206.

58.

244 **streets were quiet:** To write these lines, the author interviewed more than a dozen people who were in these cities the night of the game. Additional details come from Bill Pittman, "Sycamores Still No. 1 With Fans," *IN*, March 27, 1979; *Springs Valley Herald*, March 29, 1979; *THS*, March 27–28, 1979; and *THT*, March 27–28, 1979.

244 **In Cleveland:** Judkins, interview with author, September 18, 2024.

244 **In Florida:** O'Malley, interview with author, June 30, 2025.

244 **In New Mexico:** Webb, interview with author, March 18, 2025; and Gunn, interview with author, March 20, 2025.

244 **an hour ahead:** Bud Lang, "City Starting Work on Next Budget," *LSJ*, March 26, 1979.

244 **Fifty million people:** NBC and Nielsen archival data.

244 **started badly:** Details about the game come from the author's interviews with more than 20 players, coaches, and staffers on the floor that night, as well as NBC's broadcast of the game, March 26, 1979.

59.

246 **all of 30 seconds:** NBC broadcast of the Indiana State–Michigan State game, March 26, 1979.

246 **"Get your head up":** Mike Lupica, "A Grounded Bird Exits Sobbing," *New York Daily News*, March 27, 1979.

247 **Bird wasn't talking:** 1978–79 ISU team, interviews with author. Additional details come from news accounts, including Joe Gergen, "No Final Word From the Bird," *Newsday (Hempstead, NY)*, March 27, 1979.

247 **Heaton had dinner . . . Reed went out:** Heaton and Reed, interviews with author.

247 **Miley and Nicks:** Miley, interview with author, March 19, 2025; and Nicks, interview with author, July 10, 2025.

247 **Gilbert went out:** Gilbert, interview with author, February 25, 2025.

247 **double-fisting:** Multiple sources saw Bird at the party, but this detail comes from photographs in Terry Thimlar's personal collection, shared with the author, March 5, 2025.

247 **"The word is out":** "Did Bird Fold? Some Believe So," *Sacramento Bee*, March 28, 1979.

247 **Bird refused to use:** *Drive*, 64.

247 **Heaton was worried:** Heaton, interviews with author, February 3, 2025, and May 23, 2025.

247 **locals had flocked:** Pittman, "Sycamores Still No. 1."

248 **a flyby:** PRL, box 3098, Athletics—Basketball—Postseason Tournaments folder, "One Victory Away From Destiny," narrative written by Indiana State fan Jack Otten after the championship game. Additional details come from Kim Rogers, "No Tears at Terre Haute," *IN*, March 28, 1979.

248 **stepped off:** 1978–79 ISU team, interviews with author.
248 **"I can't believe it":** "'They're Splendid,'" *THS*, March 28, 1979.

PART V

60.

251 **Bird didn't just speak:** 1978–79 ISU team, interviews with author; Rogers, "No Tears"; Dave Benner, "ISU Fans Say Bye-Bye to Bird," *IS*, March 28, 1979; Steve Pionski, "No Sad Songs at ISU," *Richmond (IN) Palladium-Item*, March 28, 1979; "'They're Splendid,'" *THS*, March 28, 1979; and "Sycamores Return to Cheering Hordes," *THT*, March 28, 1979.
252 **"My unsolicited counsel":** PRL, box 3098, Athletics—Basketball—Postseason Tournaments folder, Landini, memo to King, April 2, 1979.
252 **circle the grammatical mistakes:** PRL, box 3098, Athletics—Basketball—Larry Bird, 1979–80 folder, Mrs. Max Poorman, letter to Landini, August 17, 1979.
252 **"I, too, would prefer":** Landini, memo to King, April 2, 1979.
252 **"It was a remarkable":** PRL, box 3098, Athletics—Basketball—Postseason Tournaments folder, Don Ohlmeyer Jr., executive producer, NBC Sports, letter to Landini, March 28, 1979.
253 **Within eight weeks:** Bill Buchalter, "Bubas: 'NCAA Tournament Can Effectively Expand,'" *Orlando Sentinel Star*, June 16, 1979.
253 **behind closed doors:** Kevin O'Malley, interview with author, June 30, 2025.

61.

253 **O'Malley's vision:** O'Malley, interview with author, June 30, 2025. O'Malley also wrote about the experiences in his own words—"How CBS Snared the NCAA Tourney Rights From NBC 40 Years Ago—in a Competitive World of 3 Networks," *Sports Business Journal*, April 4, 2021.
254 **$48 million:** Stan Isaacs, "CBS Coup: Gaining NCAA Rights," *Newsday (Hempstead, NY)*, March 10, 1981.
254 **as little as $7,000:** Jack Etkin, "TV Money Has Rocketed Final Four Into Sports Stratosphere," *Kansas City Star*, April 1, 1984.
254 **barely got the bracket:** O'Malley, interview with author, June 30, 2025; and Kevin Mulligan, "TV Weekend," *Philadelphia Daily News*, March 9, 1984.
255 **$96 million:** Peter Alfano, "CBS Puts Over a Basketball Coup," *New York Times*, November 22, 1983.
255 **"the pot of gold":** Etkin, "TV Money Has Rocketed."

62.

255 **"sounds brutal":** Fred Rothenberg, Associated Press, "Backdoor TV Treatment for NBA's Premier Show," *IN*, May 24, 1979.
256 **shows like *The Waltons*:** The author identified these shows through TV listings published in newspapers showing what CBS was broadcasting instead of the NBA Finals.
256 **chose to air a rerun:** Rothenberg, "Backdoor TV Treatment."
256 **tried to convince Bird:** *Drive*, 70.

256 **talked about money:** Bird referenced money twice in public appearances, before and after the NCAA championship game—at his press conference in Salt Lake City on March 25, 1979, and at the pep rally in Terre Haute on March 27, 1979.

256 **student teacher:** Details about Bird's time as a student teacher come from multiple sources—Dick Ballinger, interview with author, June 30, 2025; Craig McKee, interview with author, August 16, 2025; and "Larry Bird, Salute to a Legend," *IS*, November 1, 1992.

257 **came out to see:** Details about the appreciation dinner in April 1979 come from interviews with more than a dozen people who were there and multiple press accounts, including: Jimmy Claus, "Sporting Around," and Carl L. Bender, "City Honors Larry Bird," *THT*, April 27, 1979; Andy Amey, "Bird Scholarship Fund Established," *THS*, April 28, 1979; and Jimmy Claus, "ISU Accepts Championship Trophy," *THT*, April 28, 1979.

258 **went 1-for-2:** Details about Bird's day with the baseball team come from press accounts and the author's interviews with the head baseball coach, Bob Warn—Warn, interviews with author, January 30, 2025, and January 31, 2025; and "Sycamores Take Twinbill," *THT*, April 29, 1979.

258 **his right index finger:** The author interviewed three people who witnessed Bird's injury during the softball game—Benton, interview with author, February 6, 2025; Heaton, interview with author, February 7, 2025; and Geoff Shuck, interview with author, February 28, 2025.

258 **"six different ways of sideways":** Shuck, interview with author, February 28, 2025.

259 **"any fucking reporters":** Diane K. Shah, "The Bird and the B's," *Inside Sports*.

259 **on the stage:** Michael Madden, "Larry Bird: Boston's Newest Celebrity," Will McDonough, "No Savior, Says Bird," and Bob Ryan, "Bird Plays Team Game," *BG*, June 9, 1979.

259 **wasn't easy for Bird:** In 1994, shortly after Bob Woolf's death, Bird spoke about the challenges of transitioning to life in the NBA—and how Woolf helped him through this time. "When I first came to Boston from the small town of French Lick, Indiana, I felt a little overwhelmed with the size of the city and the demands that were immediately placed on me," Bird said. "Having to talk to the press every day, learning a whole new system of basketball, being away from my hometown friends, meeting so many new people each day—I was just trying to keep up with it all." (Larry Bird, "Remembrances of Bob Woolf, America's First Sports Agent," *Villanova Sports & Entertainment Law Forum*, 1994).

259 **shocked:** Shah, "The Bird and the B's."

259 **broke the unwritten code:** Local reporters at the time were well aware that the *Inside Sports* writer had run afoul of the code. Steve Marantz of the *Boston Globe* acknowledged it in a large feature that he did on Bird in December 1979

260 **"a very nice person":** Shah, "The Bird and the B's."

260 **Seemingly homesick:** Heaton, interview with author, February 7, 2025.

260 **"If these two great":** Jack Craig, "TV Ran Gamut From Great Closeups to Trash Sports," *BG*, December 28, 1979.

63.

260 **Back at CBS:** O'Malley, interview with author, July 4, 2025.

260 **up 12 percent:** Ron Alridge, "Back in the Game," *CT*, May 2, 1980.

260 **only 14 out of 200:** Fred Rothenberg, Associated Press, "NBA Ratings Are Going Down the Tube," *Harrisburg Evening News*, May 7, 1981.

260 **Dodgers–Pirates:** Ron Yukelson, "Inside TV-Radio Sports," *Palm Springs Desert Sun*, May 16, 1980.
261 **on their own televisions:** Johnette Howard, "Rx for NBA: A Bird, Magic, Some Savvy," *Dayton Daily News*, May 30, 1986.
261 **Four of the six games:** Jack Craig, "For CBS, the Playoffs Don't Rate," *BG*, May 3, 1981; Steve Duin, "CBS Delay of Game Fouls NBA," *Portland Oregonian*, May 5, 1981; Rothenberg, "NBA Ratings"; Jonathan Rand, "Basketball Has Trouble Closing Act," *Kansas City Times*, May 14, 1981; and Mark Leary, "The Thrill of (Live) Victory, the Agony of Tape Delay," *Fort Myers News-Press*, May 23, 1981.
261 **made him question:** Howard, "Rx for NBA."
261 **in June 1981:** Gary Deeb, "NBA Bosses Swallow Pride, Make Wise Decision," *Lexington Herald*, June 7, 1981.
261 **"Everybody's a fan":** Will Grimsley, Associated Press, "NBA Tries to Promote Itself," *Holyoke (MA) Transcript-Telegram*, December 3, 1981.
261 **30 players:** Brian Wicker, "NBA Commercials: How Can Magic Be a Fan of Swen Nater?" *Fargo (ND) Forum*, December 12, 1982.
262 **a new contract:** Steve Duin, "Pact Leaves Room for Cable," *Portland Oregonian*, December 29, 1981.
262 **cable TV revenues:** Larry Stewart, "Penn State's Upset Win Made It a Happier Year for NBC," *Los Angeles Times*, December 31, 1981.
262 **set a record:** "NBA: Game 7 Sets TV Ratings Mark," *BG*, June 15, 1984.

64.

263 **Greg Webb never forgot:** Details in this section about Webb today come primarily from two sources—Gunn, interview with author, March 20, 2025; and Webb, interview with author, March 18, 2025.
265 **after he turned 40:** Bird press conference, May 30, 2024.

65.

265 **tried to get away:** Dave Nightingale, "Bill Hodges Tries to Start Over," *CT*, March 7, 1980.
265 **"I had a family":** Hodges, interview with author, March 7, 2025.
266 **noticed the difference:** Nicks, interview with author, September 24, 2024.
266 **"one-man team":** Sam Goldaper, "NBA Draft: Nicks' Turn Finally?" *Spokane Spokesman-Review*, June 9, 1980.
266 **"Hey, Coach":** "Sycamores, Hodges Tumble from Limelight," *Valparaiso (IN) Vidette-Messenger*, March 20, 1980.
266 **Kevin Thompson:** Details about Thompson come from multiple sources, including Hodges, interview with author, March 7, 2025; Bob Williams, "Thompson Follows Mate," *IS*, June 7, 1980; Ray Compton, "ISU's Hodges: 'I Lost Support,'" *IN*, January 27, 1982; Pete Swanson, "Resignation Was Certain a Month Ago," *Evansville Sunday Courier and Press*, January 31, 1982; and Sandy Keenan, "That Championship Season," *Tropic (Miami Herald* magazine), April 3, 1983.
267 **split up:** Hodges, interview with author, March 7, 2025; and Mosbaugh, interview with author, June 29, 2025.
267 **"messing up his plans":** Keenan, "That Championship Season."

267 **like old times:** The author interviewed several people who played in this game, including Nicks, Gilbert, Heaton, Miley, Staley, and Ritter. Also "Bird Stars for 9,100 at Benefit," *Bloomington-Bedford (IN) Sunday Herald-Times*, August 9, 1981.
267 **five months later:** "Kevin Thompson Dies; Was All-Star," *IS*, January 8, 1982.
267 **"It's not the quantity":** The tombstone can be found at New Harmony Cemetery in Terre Haute.
268 **"Hodges went from":** Reed, interview with author, August 20, 2024.
268 **He announced that he was resigning:** Compton, "ISU's Hodges."
268 **felt a chill:** Hodges, interview with author, March 7, 2025; and Keenan, "That Championship Season."
268 **"permanent endowment":** Landini, letter to McKee, February 9, 1983, Craig McKee personal collection.
268 **"a youthful, inexperienced":** Landini, letter to McKee, February 9, 1983, Craig McKee personal collection.
268 **never again crack:** Data compiled for the author by Frank Labombarda, head of research at the Elias Sports Bureau.
268 **just $92,500:** John Newton, the man who worked with Landini in the 1970s, is still alive today and oversees Crossroad of Champions, the university's name, image, and likeness partnership, which finances NIL deals. Newton shared this figure, and others listed here, in an interview with the author on April 24, 2025.
268 **seven members of the team:** Matthew Glenesk, "Indiana State Basketball Is in Complete Rebuild Mode. Meet the 8 New Sycamores Players," *IS*, May 15, 2024.
269 **excited about the obscurity:** Details about how Hodges felt about his job in 1982 come from multiple sources, including: Hodges, interview with author, March 7, 2025; Steve Hummer, "For Hodges, No. 1 Wasn't Worth It," and Chuck Otterson, "PBJC Names Hodges," *Palm Beach Post*, March 9, 1982; Jim Martz, "Hodges Trades Bird, Big Time for Peace at Junior College," *Miami Herald*, January 13, 1983; Pete DiPrimio, "Former ISU Coach 'Enjoying Life' at Florida Junior College," *Evansville Press*, February 8, 1983; and Keenan, "That Championship Season."
269 **"My goals":** Jeff Rude, "From NCAA Final to Palm Beach," *Florida Today*, December 14, 1982.
270 **"Hey, Hodgo":** Sandy Keenan, "Bird Drops In," *Miami Herald*, September 8, 1982.
270 **"Larry never called me":** CeCe Daniels, interview with author, August 23, 2025.
270 **"got on his ass":** Hodges, interview with author, March 7, 2025.
270 **There were rumors that Daniels was dissatisfied:** Bob Kravitz, "Pacers Fire Daniels," *IS*, October 24, 2009. CeCe Daniels also confirmed the tension in her interview with the author.
271 **"I am sure that you are disappointed":** The author viewed this letter for himself on a visit to Hodges's house on March 7, 2025.
271 **"over there":** Hodges, interview with author, March 7, 2025.

66.

271 **got out early:** Ed McKee, interview with author, August 7, 2024.
272 **"time to move":** McKee, letter to McGuire, May 9, 1979, Ed McKee personal collection.
272 **"I was young":** Bird press conference, May 30, 2024.
272 **some sort of party:** McKee, interview with author, August 7, 2024.

273 **"Thanks for all the things":** The author viewed this note himself on a visit to McKee's home on February 23, 2025.
273 **next to go:** 1978–79 ISU team, interviews with author.
273 **Ritter realized:** Ritter, interview with author, December 5, 2024.
273 **Nemcek hated:** Nemcek, interview with author, May 6, 2025.
273 **Gilbert knew:** Details about Gilbert's addiction come from Gilbert himself in interviews with the author on February 10 and February 25, 2025.
274 **"the most competitive":** John Mossman, "Nuggets Happy With Forward, Guard Picks," *Grand Junction (CO) Daily Sentinel*, June 11, 1980.
274 **journeyman years:** Details about Nicks's life after the NBA come from Nicks, interview with author, September 24, 2024; and reporter Sam Smith's detailed profile of Nicks for the *Chicago Tribune* in 1984—"Final Shot," *CT*, February 26, 1984.
275 **"wearing him out":** Nicks, interview with author, July 10, 2025.

67.

275 **they had learned:** 1978–79 ISU team, interviews with author.
276 **"Right before we left":** Ritter, interview with author, December 5, 2024.
276 **"I had my whole":** Nemcek, interview with author, May 6, 2025.
277 **Brad Miley had also leveraged:** Miley, interview with author, September 25, 2024.
278 **For the museum dedication:** 1978–79 ISU team, interviews with author.
278 **Staub was nervous:** Staub Murphy, interview with author, February 5, 2025.

68.

278 **$7 million annually:** Karen Dyer, executive director of the Terre Haute Convention and Visitors Bureau, ran this calculation, based on visits to the Larry Bird Museum alone, and shared the data with the author on June 3, 2025.
278 **Gilbert grew tired:** Details in this section come from Gilbert, interview with author, February 25, 2025, with confirmation from his wife, Ann. The author also spoke with Gilbert's close friends, Carl Nicks and Brad Miley, about what they knew at the time.

69.

280 **Eric Curry . . . went first:** David Hughes, "Player on ISU's Iconic 1978–79 Team, Eric Curry, Dies at 66," *Terre Haute Star-Tribune*, January 5, 2024.
280 **Rick Shaw . . . came next:** https://www.hamptongentry.com/obituaries/rick-shaw.
280 **so broken up:** Hodges, comment to author, February 16, 2025.
280 **"This is the last":** Nemcek, interview with author, May 6, 2025.
281 **Upon his retirement:** On May 24, 2025, the author visited the home of Jim Jones and saw the ring and note for himself.
281 **King's phone would light up:** The author received extensive help from four of King's children—Dianne Goldrick, Brad King, Larry King, and Randy King. Details in this section come from their memories.
281 **flew west:** Brad King, interview with author, January 9, 2025; and Nicks, interview with author, July 10, 2025.

281 **Bird called him one day:** Nicks, interview with author, September 24, 2024.
282 **committed suicide:** Bob and Jane Ann Heaton, interview with author, May 23, 2025, and Bob Heaton, interview with author, July 15, 2025.

70.

283 **gated community in Indianapolis:** Dana Hunsinger Benbow, "'He Kept It Meticulously': Someone Just Bought Larry Bird's $2.3 Million Indianapolis Mansion," *IS*, September 17, 2019.
283 **visitors must be invited:** In order to describe Bird's ranch and the rhythms of his life there, the author spoke to multiple people who have visited him at the ranch.
284 **just three weeks:** In 1985, Celtics training camp opened on September 27.
284 **That week in September:** Details about the Converse commercial and the night at the Jubil Bar come from multiple sources, including news coverage in the *Springs Valley Herald*, September 11, 1985; "Drive Nets Couple Visit With Bird," *Evansville Press*, September 12, 1985; and interviews with three people who confirmed the scene in the Jubil Bar: Annette Wolfington, the owner of the bar at the time; Mike Cox, Bird's childhood friend, who had knowledge of the gathering; and Barry Wilson, Bird's high school teammate, who drank beers with Bird and Magic that night at the bar. At the time, Bird was well known for bringing his NBA friends to the Jubil, as Dan Shaughnessy recorded. Shaughnessy, *Wish It Lasted Forever* (Scribner, 2021), 195.

BIBLIOGRAPHY

Auerbach, Red. *Let Me Tell You a Story*. With John Feinstein. Little, Brown, 2004.

Bianchi, G. L. *7 Years An Eagle, Vol. II*. Self-published, 2023.

Bird, Larry. *Drive*. With Bob Ryan. Doubleday, 1989.

Bird, Larry, and Earvin "Magic" Johnson. *When the Game Was Ours*. With Jackie MacMullan. HarperCollins, 2009.

Davis, Seth. *When March Went Mad*. Times/Henry Holt, 2009.

Heathcote, Jud. *Jud: A Magical Journey*. With Jack Ebling. Sagamore Publishing, 1995.

Johnson, Earvin "Magic." *My Life*. With William Novak. Random House, 1992.

Levine, Lee Daniel. *Bird: The Making of an American Sports Legend*. McGraw-Hill, 1988.

Meyer, Ray. *Basketball as Coached by Ray Meyer*. Prentice-Hall, 1967.

Meyer, Ray. *Coach*. With Ray Sons. Contemporary Books, Inc., 1987.

Shaughnessy, Dan. *Wish It Lasted Forever*. Scribner, 2021.

Smith, L. Virginia. *Larry Bird, from Valley Hick to Boston Celtic*. Self-published, 1982.

PHOTOGRAPH CREDITS

INTERIOR

Part I: Indiana Basketball Hall of Fame
Part II: Courtesy of the Martin Family Photo Collection, Vigo County Public Library Archives
Part III: Indiana State University Athletic Department
Part IV: Associated Press
Part V: Getty Images

INSERT

Page 1 (top) Photo by Rich Clarkson/NCAA Photos via Getty Images
Page 1 (bottom left) Courtesy of the Indiana State University Athletic Department
Page 1 (bottom right) Courtesy of the Indiana State University Athletic Department
Page 2 (top) Associated Press
Page 2 (bottom) Courtesy of Ed McKee
Page 3 Photo by Lane Stewart/*Sports Illustrated* via Getty Images
Page 4 (top) Associated Press
Page 4 (bottom) Associated Press
Page 5 (top) Photo by José R. Lopez
Page 5 (center) Associated Press
Page 5 (bottom) Provided by Indiana State University Libraries
Page 6 (top) Associated Press
Page 6 (center) Shelley Keever Reyenga

PHOTOGRAPH CREDITS

Page 6 (bottom) Photo by Michael E. Keating
Page 7 (top) Provided by Indiana State University Libraries
Page 7 (center) Associated Press
Page 7 (bottom) © Malcolm Emmons—Imagn Images
Page 8 (top) Provided by Indiana State University Libraries
Page 8 (center) Provided by Indiana State University Libraries
Page 8 (bottom) Associated Press

INDEX

Page numbers in italics refer to photos.

A

AAU tri-state tournament, 1976, 78–79, 160
Abdul-Jabbar, Kareem, 150, 261
Aguirre, Mark, 233–35, 237–38
Anderson, Abdel, 134
Anderson, Indiana, 2, 77–78, 152
   Ku Klux Klan in, 77, 78
   Madison Heights High School basketball, Harry Morgan and, 77
Apke, Rick, 94, 95, 128
Apke, Tom, 94, 95, 128, 171
Arizona State University, 69–70
Arkansas Razorbacks, 212, 222–27
   See also Moncrief, Sidney
Armstrong State, 45, 48, 266
Army Black Knights, 16, 17–18, 99
Associated Press Awards, 218–20
Auerbach, Red, 147, 183
   addressing lack of fan interest in the NBA, 150–51, 256, 321n151
   Bird signs Celtics contract, 258–59
   brings Bird's friends Judkins and Robey to Boston, 187
   estimation of Bird, 185, 221
   firsts in NBA basketball by, 150
   interest in drafting Bird, 147, 149, 151, 183–85, 201–2, 211, 221
   at NCAA tournament, 1979: Indiana State–DePaul game, 236, 256

B

Bailey, "Jammin'" James, 93–96, 98–99, 133–34, 136, 146, 310n98
Ballinger, Dick, 256–57
Bayh, Birch, 212
Bedford High School, Indiana, Stonecutters vs. Springs Valley basketball game, 28
Behnke, Bob "Doc," 117, 122, 127, 163–64, 188, 213, 215–16
Benson, Kent, 36, 37, 150
Berman, Len, 184
Bird, Georgia Kerns (mother), 11–13, 15–16, 41, 42, 207, 208, 291n12, 292n12, 298–99n42
   on Bird's dodging publicity, 189
   on Bird quitting the Hoosiers, 38
   recruiters and, 56, 58
   Sports Illustrated article and, 119–20
Bird, Joey (father), 10–14, 24, 32–33, 291n10, 291n11, 291n12
   relationship with Bird, 12, 13, 32–33
   suicide, 42, 45, 54–55, 62, 72
Bird, Larry
   agent, Bob Woolf, 259, 343n259
   belief in his own ability, 21, 75
   benefit for Kevin Thompson, 267
   birth date, 292n12
   Boston Celtics career, 259–63, 343n259
   Boston Celtics record-breaking contract, 258–59

354 INDEX

Bird, Larry (*cont.*)
  character and personality, 9, 21, 27, 33, 60, 72–73, 82–83, 93, 106, 217–19, 242, 251, 256–57, 266
  chewing tobacco by, 181
  child with ex-wife, 92, 99, 310n99
  courage of, 97–98
  epic trash-talk, 111
  fame and fans, 262
  fighting by, 27, 97–98, 136, 194–95
  girlfriend, later wife, Dinah Mattingly, 103, 160, 200, 263, 311n103
  height and strength, 14, 22, 60, 124
  Indiana Pacers and, 263, 270, 283
  "just a hick from French Lick," 251, 259
  NBC's Packer and McGuire, opposing opinions about, 204
  old friendships, 269–70, 275–76, 278, 280–83
  playing style, 20, 23, 66, 94
  poor grammar, vulgarities, and slang of, 83, 214, 219, 220, 251, 252
  as prankster, 91, 308n91
  privacy issues, vii, 2, 21, 60, 100–102, 119–21, 133, 188–92, 259–60, 262–63, 308n83, 343n259
  ranch in rural Indiana, 283–84
  retirement, 263, 283–84
  saving the NBA and, 255, 256
  sports played besides basketball, 96, 152–53, 256–57, 258
  teenage marriage and divorce, 35, 74, 81–82
Bird, Larry: 1956–74, early years, high school basketball, and the Hoosiers, 7
  choosing a college: recruiters and, 23–24, 28–32, 295n23
  dreams about basketball, 13, 75
  father and, 12, 13, 32–33, 42
  father's suicide and, 42, 45, 54–55, 60, 62, 72, 283, 303n62
  first car, 42, 299n42
  French Lick basketball court, 14, 15
  French Lick "crew," 12–13, 14, 34
  French Lick home, 9, 12–14, 39, 41, 58

  Hancock Construction basketball team and, 55–56, 60, 63, 303n63
  hay baling, odd jobs, 14, 63, 303n63
  Hoosiers signing ceremony, 32
  Hoosiers three weeks: what happened, 34–38, 204–5, 297n37, 298n37, 298n38
  Indiana High School All-Stars, behavior and complaints, 33–34
  Indiana State visit, pickup game, and enrollment at, 63–66, 304n63
  job trash collecting, 42, 60, 204, 298–99n42
  lack of expectations for, 13
  Louisville coach Crum and a game of H-O-R-S-E, 31–32, 212
  Northwood Institute basketball and, 39–41, 42, 60
  problems at home, 10–15, 28, 32–33, 291–92n12
  recruiter Bliss (Indiana Hoosiers), 19–22, 24–27, 29, 30, 221
  recruiter Hodges (Indiana State), vii, 54, 56–66, 73–74, 303n62, 303n63
  reluctance to return to college, 56, 58, 60–62, 63, 301–2n56
  siblings, 9, 12, 292n12
  solace in basketball, 36–37, 41, 74
  sportswriters' underestimation of, 33
  Springs Valley High basketball, 14–15, 21–28, 32–34, 57–58
  two things he liked, 34
  West Baden Springs, first basketball court, 9, 14, 36–37, 60, 97, 284, 290n9
Bird, Larry: 1975–78, Indiana State years under Bob King, 1–3, 67, 72–138, *139*
  1975–76 season, 74–75
  1976–77 season, 82–85, 90
  1977–78 season, 1–4, 100, 110–38
  college All-Stars at Lexington, Kentucky, crossing paths with Magic Johnson, 138, 145–47
  dreams of going pro, 75, 93
  first college game, 82

first-team All-American, 1, 127
housemates with Heaton, 159–60
King's heart attack and, 163
media and his reluctance or refusal to talk with, 83, 99, 101–4, 114, 118–21, 122, 133–37, 232
Missouri Valley Conference tournament: Creighton game, 126–29
national recognition, 101
NBA draft and Celtics pick, 147–49, 151, 152
NIT, 1977, Houston Cougars game, 85–89, 91
NIT, 1978, Rutgers game and fan fight, 1–4, 132–38, 239–40, 289–90n1
practice and belief in himself, 75
practicing tired, motive for, 154
Purdue Boilermakers game, 110–13
Sports Illustrated article by Keith and angry reaction, 118–21, 186
Sports Illustrated cover, 1, 2, 101–8, 311n101
stardom and fame, 108–9
summer job and playing softball, 152–53, 171
Terre Haute businessman Max Gibson and, 74, 92, 152, 263
World University Games, 92–99
See also specific games
Bird, Larry: 1978–79, Indiana State years under Hodges
AP Player of the Year and awards ceremony, 218–20
attitude toward awards, trophies, and plaques, 240–41
Auerbach and, 183–85, 187–88, 201–2, 221, 256
baseball game and career-threatening injury, 258
Boston Celtics recruitment and his future, 220, 256, 258–60
Boston Globe story by Mike Madden, 191–92
Bradley Braves game and "Bird Cage Defense," 201, 205

broken thumb, 213, 214, 215–16, 220, 223, 232, 237
Butler game, 182
CBS-Cronkite story, 221
celebrity and, 202, 203
Chicago Tribune explosive column by David Israel, 206–7
critics of, 247
Eastman Award, 240–41
exhibition game against the Soviets, 173–77
"Great White Hope" label and, 207, 220, 221
HBO and national exposure, 184
Illinois State Redbirds game, 180–81
Missouri Valley Conference tournament, teams played and trophy, 212
Naismith Trophy, 213–14
as national scoring leader, 183
NBC interview with McGuire, 204–5
NCAA tournament, 1979, 5, 215–17, 220, 222–27, 235–38
NCAA tournament, 1979, championship game, Indiana State–Michigan State Spartans, vii, 4, 5, 239, 243–46, 264, 340–41n243
NCAA tournament, 1979, championship loss, reaction and speech, 246–48, 251–52
NCAA tournament, 1979, press conference, 241, 242
New Mexico State game and rematch, 185–87, 193–99, 212
New Mexico State rematch, Bird–fans fight, 194–95, 330–31n195
postseason obligations, 256–57
practice and strategy, 171–73
Purdue game, 177–79
response to media and reporters, 170–71, 188–92, 204–7, 213–15, 217–20, 236, 241–43, 246, 329n188
Salute to Larry Bird dinner and speech, 258
Sports Illustrated exposé by Newman and reaction, 192

Bird, Larry: 1978–79 (cont.)
   team cohesion and, 182, 183
   team confidence, 200
   trash talk and, 172
   Tulsa game, 183–85
   visit to Heaton's farm and close call, 183
   West Vigo High School, student teaching, 256–57
   Wichita State game and postgame press, 207–11
Bird, Linda (sister), 12
Bird, Mark (brother), 9, 12, 13, 15, 63, 65, 290n9
Bird, Mike (brother), 9, 12, 15, 152, 290n9, 292n12
Birdsong, Otis, 86, 87, 88, 89
Birge, Jerry, 33
Bliss, Dave, 16–18, 220–22
   Bird's quitting the Hoosiers and, 38, 297n37, 298n37
   recruitment of Bird, 16, 19–22, 24–27, 29, 32, 36, 57, 221
Bloomington, Indiana, 19, 20, 34, 35
Bloomington Daily Herald-Telephone, 39
Boston Celtics, 20, 64, 244, 283
   Bird's contract, 258–59
   Bird's first press conference, 259
   Bird's transition to, 259–60, 343n259
   Judkins signed by, 151, 187
   NBA Championship, 1981, 261
   NBA Finals, Bird–Magic matchup, 1984, 262
   recruiting Bird, 16, 19–22, 24–27, 29, 32, 36, 57, 147, 149, 151, 183–85, 187–88, 201–2, 221
   trade to acquire Rick Robey, 187
   See also Auerbach, Red
Boston Globe
   Madden's story on Bird, 191–92
   NBA expectations for Bird and Magic, 260
   NCAA tournament, 1979, 232
Bradley Braves, 201, 205
Brkovich, Mike, 175, 229
Buckner, Quinn, 36

Butcher, Bill, 25, 26, 63
Butler Bulldogs, 182

C
Carnes, Beezer, 26–27
Carnes, Kevin, 61, 62, 63, 65, 290n9
Carroll, Joe Barry, 178
CBS
   biggest shows, 1970s, 149
   Cronkite's story on Bird, 221
   NBA aired by, 149–50, 204, 260–61
   NBA ratings, 255–56, 260
   NCAA "selection show," 253, 254
   NCAA tournament contract, 254–55
   NFL on, 149
   The NFL Today, 254
   O'Malley and, 149, 204, 244, 253–55
Chicago Bulls, 262
Chicago Tribune
   column on Bird, 206–7, 219, 235
   NCAA tournament, 1979, and, 232
   "Ray Meyer's Tourney Diary," 235
Cincinnati Post: article on Hodges, 222, 231
Clark, Jerry, 35
Clemons, Monk, 55, 63
Cleveland Cavaliers, 151
Clinton, Bill, 223
college basketball
   booster clubs, 4, 5
   contemporary players, signing of, 4
   flawed system, 4
   Landini's ideas and, 71
   money generated by, 5
   NBC starts airing games, 202–3
   NCAA dunking rule change, 82, 156
   NCAA prize money and scandal, 255
   payment for athletes, 268–69
   popularity, 1970s, 130, 316n130
   professionalization of college sports and, 5
   recruitment, 5
   shot clock and three-point shot, 84
   transfer portal, March, 4, 290n4
   unsavory recruitment tactics, 233–34
   See also specific teams

Condra, Janet, 35, 74, 81–82, 92, 99
  daughter with Bird, 99, 259–60
Converse and Bird–Magic ad, 272, 284
Copeland, Hollis, 134, 135, 136, 137
Cormier, Cyrus, 124, 186, 193, 196
Cory, Indiana, 157, 183, 187, 227
Corzine, Dave, 93
Cowens, Dave, 202
Cox, Mike, 12–13, 22, 72
Creighton Blue Jays, 94, 95, 126–29, 171
Crowder, Tom, 122, 172, 182
Crum, Denny, 23, 29–31, 94, 212, 221
  Bird and a game of H-O-R-S-E, 31–32, 212
  World University Games, 1977, 92, 94, 95, 97–98
Curry, Eric, 155, 172, 182, 196, 273, 275, 280

D
Daniels, CeCe, 270
Daniels, Mel, 78–79, 169, 251, 270
  Indiana State assistant coach, 160, 172, 184, 215
  New Mexico State–Indiana State game, 1979, 194–95, 198
Denver Nuggets, 134, 261, 273, 274
DePaul Blue Demons, 223, 229, 235–38
Detroit Tigers, 105
Drake Bulldogs, 201, 205–6
Dubois, Indiana: Butchie's tavern, 262–63
Dubois County Daily Herald, 33
Duff, Mike, 115–16, 122
Duke University Blue Devils, 168, 179

E
Earley, Dave, 40, 41, 60
Edeshko, Ivan, 174
Emmons, Butch, 9–10, 14, 37, 290n9
Englewood High, Chicago, 75–76
Erving, Julius, 141, 261
Evans, Stan, 51–52, 54, 58–59, 110
  Bird's privacy issues and, 122
  conflict with Bob King, 117, 123, 137, 153, 160, 314n117
  head coach position expected by, 52, 117, 165, 167
  Hodges and, 58–59, 61, 62, 136
  King's heart attack and, 162, 163
  NIT, 1977, and, 86, 87, 88
  NIT, 1978, and, 132, 136
  player Webster and, 52, 59–60
  recruitment of Bird, 54, 56–62
  recruitment of Miley, 76–77
  resignation, 166–67
Evansville Purple Aces, 115, 116, 122, 179, 180

F
Fidrych, Mark "The Bird," 105
Fisher, Roger, 10
Flick, Wayne, 25, 26, 27
Florida State Seminoles, 130
Fontanet, Indiana, 74, 83, 92, 152
Forbes, Bob, 89–90, 162
Ford, Phil, 148
Fox, George, 142
French Lick, Indiana, 9, 11–14, 22–24, 36–37, 56, 284
  basketball court in, 14, 15
  Bird dismissed from eighth-grade basketball, 10, 12, 290n10
  Bird returns from Hoosiers, 39
  Bird–Kern home on Washington Street, 13–14, 39, 41, 58
  Emmons as teacher and basketball coach, 10, 290n10
  Flick's Restaurant, 15–16
  Hoosier recruiter and, 16, 19–22
  Larry Bird Boulevard, 207, 211, 249
  Larry Bird Week, 207
  NCAA championship game, 1979, and, 244
  suicide of Joey Bird and, 55
  See also Springs Valley Blackhawks

G
Gallon, Ricky, 92
Garland, Gary, 235, 237–38
Gibson, Greg, 74, 92, 152, 231, 277

Gibson, Max, 164, 167
  Bird and, 74, 92, 152, 263
  as Indiana State booster, 73–74
  Indiana State's Missouri Valley Conference win and, 212
  Larry Bird Committee, 164, 167, 202, 228
  New Mexico State–Indiana State rematch, 1979, and, 193, 199
  Salute to Larry Bird dinner and, 257
  summer jobs for players, 156
  Wichita State–Indiana State game and NBC televising, 208
Gilbert, Alex, 155–56, 160, 172, 236, 257, 266, 267, 278–79
  addiction and, 273–74, 278–80
  death of brother, 179–80
  enrolls in Indiana State, 156
  Indiana State games, 1978–79, 172, 176–77, 178, 185, 193–94, 209
  Indiana State games, 1979–80, 260
  NCAA championship loss, Bird's emotional response and, 246
  NCAA tournament games, 216–17, 225, 231, 247
  signs with Milwaukee Bucks, 273
Gilbert, Lindell, 156, 179–80, 216
Golden State Warriors, 148
Gomelsky, Alexander, 174–77
Gottfried, Joe, 201
Griffith, Darrell, 92, 96, 98
Gulf Coast Community College, Florida, 91, 99, 154–55
Gumbel, Bryant, 224, 246
Gunn, Robert, 124, 125, 171, 186, 193, 194, 196, 213, 244

H
Hall, Joe B., 28–29, 31, 145, 146
Hammel, Bob, 34
Hancock, Jerry, 55–56
Hancock Construction basketball team, 55–56, 60, 63, 303n63
Hannon, Kent, 102–3, 107–8
Hastings, Scott, 222, 225, 226–27
Havlicek, John, 20

Hayes, Elvin, 16, 86, 141
Hayes, Ken, 124, 126, 127, 186, 187
  Indiana State–New Mexico rematch, 1979, and, 193, 194, 198, 199
HBO, 184, 291–92n12
Heathcote, Jud, 144, 175, 229, 236, 239
  NCAA championship game, 1979, 239–40, 243, 245
  NCAA tournament, 1979, 230
Heaton, Bob, 157–60, 187, 202, 236, 257, 267
  Bird shares house, 159–60, 200
  Bird's friendship and, 260, 282–83
  childhood farm accident, 157–59, 187, 227, 258, 282
  girlfriend, later wife, Jane Ann, 160, 200, 215, 231, 247, 273, 282
  Indiana State 1978–79 season games, 172, 173, 177, 178, 186–87, 193–94, 196–99, 263
  Indiana State, 1979–80 season, 260
  joins Indiana State, 1977, 159
  life after basketball, 273
  "miracle shot" against New Mexico, 198–201, 205, 244, 263, 282
  NCAA championship game and aftermath, 245, 247–48
  NCAA tournament, 215, 226–27, 231, 235, 237, 282
  prayer for Bird and, 257, 258
  son's suicide, 282
  team visit to his farm and Bird's close call, 183
Hefele, Steve, 134, 135, 136
Heinsohn, Tommy, 184
Hodges, Bill, vii, 60, 81, 90, 110
  background, 45–54, 58, 172
  Bird's senior year promise and, 153
  career and life after Bird, 265–71
  character, 46, 47, 58, 231–32
  coaching jobs, 123, 153–54, 160–61
  connection to the players, 166, 170
  daughter, Zoie, 45, 48, 53
  Evansville's Mike Duff and, 115–16
  Indiana State hiring of, 52–53, 54
  King's heart attack and, 161–62, 163

letter from John Wooden, 271
marital problems and divorce, 267
NIT, 1978, and, 132, 134, 136
recruiting and mentoring Bird, vii, 54, 56–66, 73–74, 81, 92, 303n62, 303n63
recruiting Danny King, 62–63, 73, 303n63
recruiting philosophy, 48
recruiting players to fit with Bird, 75–79, 91, 99
relationship with Evans, 58–59, 61, 62, 136
Tennessee Tech and, 45, 47–48, 52–53, 57
Thimlar and, 46–47, 48, 51, 57, 59, 100, 170
Hodges, Bill: 1978–82, Indiana State head coach
1978–79 season games, 177–211
1978–79 season problems, 153–54
1979–80 season, 260, 266–67
1981–82 season, 267–68
AP Coach of the Year, 218–19
Bird and Naismith Trophy, 213–14
Bird's refusal to attend Eastman Awards ceremony and, 240–41
Bird's refusal to meet with reporters and, 191
Chicago Tribune column attacking Hodges and Bird, 206–7
Cincinnati Post criticism, 222
coaching changes from King's approach, 171–72
Drake Bulldogs game and fight with their coach, 205–6
exhibition game against the Soviets, 175–77
made acting, then head coach, 165–66, 201, 324n166
Missouri Valley Conference tournament, 184, 212–13
NCAA tournament, 215–17, 222–27, 235–38
NCAA tournament, Michigan State championship match, 239, 243–46
NCAA tournament, welcome home, 248, 251
New Mexico State rematch, final seconds play, 196–99
press demands and, 231–32
Purdue game, 177–79
resignation, 268
Salute to Larry Bird dinner and, 257
Sports Illustrated article by Newman on Bird's secrets and, 192
Thimlar's son, Terry, as assistant coach, 170, 215, 243
tragedy of Kevin Thompson, 266–67
transformation of his life, 201
Tulsa game, 183–85
Wichita State game, 207–11
Hodges, Connie, 45, 47, 48, 53, 58, 86, 91, 153, 193, 201, 232, 248, 267
Hodges, Wilson, 46
Holland, Gary, 22, 23–27, 57–58
college recruiters for Bird and, 23–24, 30, 57–58, 62
Hoosiers signing of Bird and, 32
Houston Cougars, 16, 85, 86–89
See also Lewis, Guy
Houston Rockets, 150, 261
Howell, Bailey, 204
Hubbard, Phil, 92, 94, 96, 97
Hutchinson, Kent, 40

I

Illinois State Redbirds, 85, 121–22, 132, 180–82
Indiana Pacers, 78, 148, 267, 272, 282
Bird as president, 263, 270, 283
Indiana State
affordability for students, 50
alumni donations and basketball, 228
arena, Hulman Center, 50, 111–12, 182, 186, 202, 207, 208, 232
Ballyhoo Tavern, 50, 114, 244
basketball after Bird, 265–69
benefit for Kevin Thompson in 1981, reunion of 1979 players, 267
Bird as a financial asset, 100, 119, 120, 164, 167, 191, 202

Indiana State (*cont.*)
  Bird as Indiana's biggest celebrity, 191, 202
  Bird enrolls, 1975, 66
  Bird's jersey retired, 257
  Bird's lasting impact, 263
  enrollment and, 69, 100, 228
  fans' behavior, 186, 187, 202, 228
  as former Teachers College, 50
  Landini hired as president, revitalization plans, 69–72
  location at Terre Haute, 49–50
  married-student housing, 74, 84
  NCAA championship game and team welcome home, 244, 247–48
  NCAA Final Four costs and transportation problems, 231
  NIT, 1978, as financial boon, 132
  scholarship fund in Bird's name, 257
  school color, 100, 193, 194, 197, 215, 232, 241, 248, 267
  school mascots, 50, 86, 103
  statue of Larry Bird, 277
  working-class student body, 50
  See also Landini, Richard; Terre Haute, Indiana
Indiana State Sycamores: 1975–78, Bird and the Bob King years, 1–3, 66, 72–183, 139
  1975–76 season, 74–75, 79–80
  1976–77 season, 82–85, 90
  1977–78 season, 1–4, 100, 109–38
  assistant coach Daniels, 160, 172, 184, 215
  athletic trainer Behnke, 117, 122, 127, 163–64, 188, 213, 215–16
  Bird enrolls, 64–66, 304n63
  Bird recruitment, 54, 56–66, 73–74, 303n62, 303n63
  Bird stays for senior year, 152, 153
  Bird's first game, 82, 307n82
  Bird's first regular-season game, 82
  Bird's stats and scoring rank, 82, 83
  dangerous plane flight, 122
  dissention on the team, 84–85
  "Harry and Larry Show," 2, 67, 83–84, 91, 109, 125
  King's coaching fundamentals, 74–75
  King's "four-corners stall" strategy, 125, 128, 135, 171
  King's heart attack and aneurysm, coaching career ends, 161–65, 190
  King's rebuilding the basketball program, 48, 49, 51–52, 54, 73–75
  losing streak, 1978, following *Sports Illustrated* article on Bird, 121–26
  manager Shaw, 3, 85–86, 87, 117
  media attention, 80, 82–84, 108, 110, 111, 115, 118, 132, 178, 179
  New Mexico State game, 123–26
  Missouri Valley Conference member, 95, 100
  Missouri Valley Conference tournament: Creighton game, 126–29
  national recognition, 114
  NIT, 1977, Houston game, 85–89
  NIT, 1978, Illinois State game, 131–32
  NIT, 1978, Rutgers game and Bird–fan fight, 1–4, 132–38, 239–40, 289–90n1, 290n3
  Purdue game, 110–13
  ranking in polls, 85, 110, 115, 120
  recruitment of players, 51, 52–53, 56–66, 75–79, 99–100
  Sports Illustrated cover on Bird, 1, 2, 101–8, 311n101
  summer pickup games, 64
  televised games, 112
  Westmont game, 1977 season opener, 109–10
  See also specific players
Indiana State Sycamores: 1978–79, Bird and the Bill Hodges years, 173–247
  assistant coaches, 179, 172, 179
  Bird's high scoring, 182, 183
  Bird's problems with the media, 170–71, 188–90, 192–93, 207, 213, 214–15, 217–20, 232
  Curry starts a new tradition, 182
  death of Gibert's brother, 179–80

exhibition game against the Soviets, 173, 176–77
Hodges becomes coach, 165–66, 201, 324n166
Hodges changes strategy, 171–73, 181
Lawrence College, season opener, 177
longest road trip, 192–200
media underestimation of Hodges and the team, 179
Missouri Valley Conference media day, 171–72
Missouri Valley Conference tournament, 212
NCAA tournament, vii, 4, 5, 215–46
NCAA tournament, games, 215–17, 220, 222–27, 235–38
NCAA tournament, Michigan State championship match, 238–47, 340–41n243
NCAA tournament, press demands, 231–32
New Mexico State game and rematch, 185–87, 193–99
New Mexico State rematch and Bird-fans fight, 194–95, 330–31n195
players, 1978–79 season, 137, 155–57, 172
practice regimen, 172
pressure on players and coach, 205–6
Purdue game, 177–78
rise in the polls to No. 1, 167, 182, 183, 187, 188, 192, 202, 207, 211
specific plays designed for Bird, 172
team cohesion and, 182, 183, 200
team manager Shaw, 185, 188
Tulsa game, 183–85
undefeated status, 187, 199, 201, 202, 207, 212, 227, 238
Wichita State game, 203, 207–11
Wichita State postgame honoring of Bob King, 211
See also specific players
Indiana University at Bloomington, 49
Hoosier's winning and record enrollment, 71
size of student body, 35

Indiana University Hoosiers, 1, 18, 174
1973–74 season, 34
1974–75 season, 71
arena, Assembly Hall, 37
assistant coach Weltlich, 297n37, 298n37
Big Ten Conference, 18
Bird arrives in Bloomington, 34
Bird recruitment, 19–22, 24–27, 29, 30, 32, 221
Bird's roommate and, 35–36
Bird's signing ceremony, 32
Bird's three weeks as a Hoosier: what happened, 35, 36–38, 204–5, 297n37, 298n37
coach Watson, 18, 19
future NBA players and, 34
Knight as head coach, 16, 18–19, 35, 38, 49
NCAA championships, 18, 131
team members in McNutt Quad, 34–35
Indianapolis News
on Bird's ability, 88
covering 1977 NIT, 86, 88
Indianapolis Star
coverage of Knight-Wisman incident, 1976, 35
photographer Jerry Clark, 35
Inside Sports magazine, 259–60
Israel, David, 206–7, 215, 219, 232, 235, 242
Issel, Dan, 261

J

Jacksonville Jaguars, 213
Johnson, Earvin "Magic," 141–47
Big Ten championship, 145
college All-Stars in Lexington, crossing paths with Bird, 145–47
college recruiters and, 142–43
height, 144, 243
high school basketball, 141, 142
Lakers career, 260, 261
media and reporters, 141–42, 145, 171, 202–3, 217–20, 230, 241–42, 246, 247

Johnson, Earvin "Magic" (*cont.*)
  Michigan State Spartans and, 143, 144–45, 188, 203–4, 212
  NBA scouts and, 147
  NCAA tournament, 1979, 212, 229, 230, 239, 243–46, 264
  nickname created, 141, 318n141
  personality, 142, 143–44, 145, 147
  playing with Bird, 138, 230, 239
  Soviet team and, 175
  Sports Illustrated cover, 167–68
  stats for, 202
  turning pro and, 203
  weakness in game, 144, 145
Johnson, Richard, 100, 118, 123, 125, 132, 135, 137
Jones, Albert "Slab," 124, 125–26, 186, 187, 194
Jones, Jim, 14–15, 231
  Bird and, 15, 66, 72, 281
  Bird's college recruitment and, 20–21, 23, 29, 32, 61, 63
  as Springs Valley basketball coach, 15, 21–22, 24, 37, 115
Jones, Tom, 20, 22
Jordan, Michael, 262
Jordan, Walter, 110–11, 112, 114
Judkins, Jeff, 92–95, 97, 99, 151, 244
  Celtics acquire, 151, 188
  relationship with Bird, 202
Jukes, Ed, 148, 164

K

Kansas City Royals, 102–3
Kansas State Jayhawks, 18, 23–24, 156
  NCAA tournament, 1979, at Allen Fieldhouse, 213, 215, 216
Keith, Larry, 118–21, 133, 186, 232
Kelser, Greg, 144, 202–3, 229, 239, 240, 243, 245
Kentucky Wesleyan baseball, 258
Kentucky Wildcats, 24, 28–29, 31, 53, 145, 146, 212
Kerns, Granny, 13, 14, 15, 39, 60, 207
King, Bernard, 150

King, Bob
  appearance, 49, 89
  background, 49–52
  belief in Bird's potential, 81
  Bird and *Sports Illustrated*, 101–4
  Bird as star player, 99
  Bird stays for senior year, 153
  Bird's friendship and, 281
  Bird's recruitment, vii, 54, 56–66, 73–74, 303n62, 303n63
  Bird's reluctance to talk to reporters and, 101–2, 108, 133, 136, 311n101
  coaching background, 49, 79
  coaching career ends, 173, 190
  coaching players/teaching defense to Bird, 74, 83
  conflict with Evans, 117, 123, 137, 153, 160, 314n117
  Daniels hired as assistant coach, 160
  death of, 281
  defensive strategies and "four-corners stall," 49, 83, 121, 125, 128, 135, 171
  Evans's deal for accepting the assistant coach job, 52
  head coach, Sycamores, 1976–77 and 1977–78 seasons, 1–2, 49, 51–52, 74–75, 79–80, 84–85, 110–38
  health issues, 1, 49, 89, 117, 173
  heart attack/aneurysm, 161–66, 169
  Hodges hired, 52–53, 123
  Hodges replaces as head coach, 165–66, 181–82, 201, 324n166
  Indiana State basketball program, rebuilding by, 48, 49, 51–52, 54, 73–75
  interview with WTHI's Forbes, feelings about the 1977 season, 89–90
  losing streak, 1978, 122–23, 126
  Missouri Valley Conference tournament, 1978, 127–29
  Missouri Valley Conference tournament, 1979, trophy awarded to King, 212
  New Mexico State game, 1978, 124–26
  NIT, 1977, 86–89

INDEX 363

NIT, 1978, 131–37
post-NCAA tournament, 1979, welcome home, 248
Purdue game, 1977, and, 110–14
Wichita State game, 1979, and postgame honoring of, 208, 211
wife, Sharel, and family, 161, 163–64
See also specific games and players
King, Danny, 62–63, 73, 169, 197, 198, 303n63
King, Jim, 205
Knight, Bobby, 1, 2, 16–20, 38, 49, 71
  as Army coach, 16, 17–18
  Bird's recruitment, 24–27, 29, 32, 36
  Bird's signing ceremony, 32
  Bird's three weeks as a Hoosier and, 38, 39, 57, 204–5
  Bliss and, 16–18, 19, 24–27, 29
  coaching style, 16–17, 19, 30, 34
  Hoosiers hire, 18–19
  NCAA championship, 1975, 131
  salary, 30
  Wisman incident, 1976, 35
KOB-TV (Albuquerque), 195, 196
  airing of Indiana State–New Mexico State game/Bird fight, 193, 195
Krzyzewski, Mike, 99, 116

L

Land, Steve, 20, 22
Landini, Richard, 80, 86, 100, 117
  Bird as an asset, 119, 120, 164, 191
  on Bird's AP Award speech, 219, 220
  on Bird's grammar, 252
  on Bird's sincerity and depth, 219, 252
  Hodges becomes head coach, 165–66, 190, 201
  Hodges's losing seasons and resignation, 265–69
  Indiana State enrollment, 69, 100, 228
  Indiana State hiring of and his revitalization plans, 69–72
  Indiana State wins 1979 Missouri Valley Conference, celebration, 212
  King and team problems, 137
  King's heart attack and, 162, 164
  Larry Bird Committee, 164, 167, 202
  media attention to Sycamores, 188
  NBC Sports gala invitation, 230–31
  NCAA tournament, 1979, 215, 221–22
  NCAA tournament, 1979, Final Four costs and transportation, 231
  NCAA tournament, 1979, welcome home, 248
  New Mexico State rematch, 1979, final seconds play, and, 198
  NIT, 1978, and, 132, 133
  Salute to Larry Bird dinner, 257–58
  Sycamore fans and, 187
  Wichita State game, and NBC televising, 208
Langston University, 263
Lansing, Michigan, 141, 142, 244, 246
  See also Michigan State Spartans
Lansing State Journal: reporter interviews Magic Johnson, 141–42
Laskowski, John, 36
Lawrence College Vikings, 177
Leonard, Bobby "Slick," 18, 148
Lewis, Guy, 86, 88, 89
Lollino, Frank, 234
Loogootee, Indiana, and Loogootee Lions basketball, 24, 25, 26
  Springs Valley game, 1974, 24–28
Lopez, José R., 330–31n195
Los Angeles Lakers
  NBA championship, 1980, 260
  NBA Finals, 1984, Bird–Magic matchup, 262
  signing Magic Johnson, 260
  Washington–Tomjanovich fight, 150
Louisville Cardinals, 23–24, 29–31, 221, 222

M

MacMullan, Jackie, vii
Madden, Mike, 191–92, 232, 259
Maravich, Pete, 86
Maris, Roger, Jr., 99

364 INDEX

Marquette Golden Eagles, 131, 203, 222
Martin, Steve, 49–50
Mattingly, Dinah, 103, 160, 200, 263, 311n103
May, Scott, 36
McCooe, Gary, 56
McGuire, Al, 131, 203–5, 211, 222, 226, 231, 246, 272
  Bird interview, 204–5, 214, 272
  NCAA tournament, 1979, and, 224, 225, 226, 246
  Salute to Larry Bird speaker, 257
  Wichita State–Indiana State, NBC televising and, 208–11
McHale, Kevin, 261
McKee, Craig (Indiana State sports information intern), vii, 81, 83, 84, 99, 100, 162
  Auerbach and, 184
  Bird and *Sports Illustrated*, 120
  Bird's fame and, 257
  Bird's refusal to talk to reporters and, 215
  Evans's resignation and, 168
  Hodges as head coach, 166, 324n166
  King–Evans conflict and, 117
  Landini's note of 1983, 268
  NCAA tournament, 1979, press conference and Bird, 241
  New Mexico State–Indiana State game, 1979, 198
  NIT, 1978, and, 132
  Purdue–Indiana State game, 1977, 112, 114, 313n114
McKee, Ed (sports information director), 80–81, 83, 84, 99, 100
  Auerbach and, 184
  Bird and reporters, 122, 188–90, 218, 247, 272–73
  Bird and *Sports Illustrated*, 102–4, 106, 107, 119
  Bird stays for senior year, 152, 153
  career and life after Bird, 271–73
  Hodges as acting head coach, 166
  info package for Alex Gilbert, 156
  King–Evans conflict and, 117

King's heart attack and, 162
  NIT, 1978, and, 132
  Purdue–Indiana State game, 1977, 112, 114
  Simpson's thank-you note, 228
  Yankees–Royals game and, 102–3
McNelly, Rod, 172
Meis, Lucien "Lu," 73, 164, 193, 200, 231, 257
Memphis State Tigers, 130
Meyer, Joey, 234
Meyer, Ray, 229, 233–35, 237, 239
Michigan State Spartans, 144, 179
  advantages as a team, 240, 242
  Big Ten championship, 1978, 145
  coach Heathcote, 144, 175, 229, 236
  Jenison Field House, 142, 144, 167
  Magic Johnson and, 143, 144–45, 182, 202–3
  NCAA championship game, 1979, vii, 4, 5, 229, 238, 243–46, 264, 340–41n243
  NCAA tournament, 1979, 212, 223–24, 229, 236, 240
  ranking in polls, 188, 192, 202, 211
  televised games, 202, 264
Miley, Brad, 76–77, 99–100, 160, 212, 236, 251, 257, 267
  career and life after basketball, 273, 277
  Gilbert's friendship, 156, 180, 279
  Indiana State enrollment, 79
  Indiana State games, 83–84, 87, 88, 112, 113, 132, 135, 172, 176, 186–87, 193–98, 205, 260
  NCAA tournament, 1979, 216, 217, 237, 238, 243, 247
Mills, John, 12–13
Millwood Arts Academy, 264–65
Milwaukee Bucks, 273
Missouri Valley Conference, 95
  Indiana State, conference champions, 1978 and 1979, 126–29, 212
  media day, 1977, 100–101, 108
  media day 1978, 170–71
  New Mexico State and, 1978, 123
  predictions for 1978–79, 167

INDEX 365

Mizlou Television, 131, 133
Moncrief, Sidney, 93–99, 146, 147, 212, 219, 221, 223, 224
    NCAA tournament, 1979, Indiana State game, 222–26, 243
Montana, Joe, 153
Morgan, Harry, 2, 3, 77–79, 90, 100
    AAU tri-state tournament, 78–79
    "Harry and Larry Show," 2, 84, 91, 109
    Indiana State games, 82–84, 109–10, 112, 113, 114, 118, 125–26, 137
    media and reporters, 101, 108
    Missouri Valley Conference championship, 1978, 128
    NBA hopes, 109–10, 151–52
    NIT, 1977, 87–88
    NIT, 1978, 132, 135
    Pizza Hut All-American, 114
    pranked by Bird, 91
    wife and family, 78, 84, 109, 152
Musburger, Brent, 254
Myshkin, Anatoly, 177

N

Nater, Swen, 261–62
National Invitation Tournament (NIT), 86, 129, 131, 133
    1977: Indiana State–Houston, 86–89
    1978: Indiana State–Rutgers, 1–4, 129, 131–37, 289–90n1
    2024: Indiana State advances, 268
    tagged "Not Important Tournament," 2, 131
Natt, Calvin, 94
NBA, 318n141
    Auerbach's basketball firsts, 150
    Bird and Magic, expectations for, 260
    Bird and the media, 189, 207
    Bird's contract, 258–59
    Black players and, 150–51, 320n150
    cable TV deals, 262
    CBS Sports broadcasting deal, 149
    changes in policy, 1980s, 261–62
    commissioner O'Brien, 150
    decline, 1970s, 149–50, 255–56, 258
    draft picks, 148, 178, 262
    "FAN-tastic" campaign, 261–62
    Finals, 1978, 149
    Finals, 1984, Bird–Magic matchup, 262
    Johnson's contract, 260
    signing white players, 1970s, 150–51, 320–21n150
    Stern's marketing campaign, 261–62
NBC
    airs NCAA Division I games, 5, 129–30
    cost of ads for NCAA games, 204
    executive producer Ohlmeyer, 252
    Gumbel, Simpson, and Packer at 1979 Final Four, 224, 225, 226
    Indiana State as "Cinderella in middle America," 230
    Indiana State–Wichita game and, 203, 205, 207–11
    loses NCAA contract, 253–54
    Magic–Bird matchup and, 230, 238
    Michigan State games and, 202
    NCAA championship game, 1979, Bird vs. Magic, 244, 264
    NCAA tournament, 1979, gala, Salt Lake City, 230–31
    NCAA tournament, 1979, Indiana State–Arkansas game, 223–27
    NCAA tournament, 1979, viewership, 223–24, 229, 244, 253
    Packer and McGuire on, 203–5, 228
    play-by-play man Simpson, 208, 210
NCAA Division I men's basketball tournament, 4, 155–56, 205
    at-large bids, 130
    CBS–O'Malley's vision for, 253–55
    CBS "selection show," 254–55
    expansions, 130, 146, 212, 253
    Final Four, 1976, 93
    Final Four, 1978, 145, 222
    Final Four, 1979, 227–38
    Hoosiers championships, 18, 131
    Indiana State games in, 1979, 215–17, 220, 222–27, 235–38
    Indiana State loses spot, 1978, 129

NCAA Division I men's basketball tournament (cont.)
Indiana State–Michigan State championship match, 1979, vii, 4, 5, 229, 238–47, 264
Krzyzewski and, 99
mandatory interviews, Bird and Magic, 214, 236, 239, 241–42
Marquette championship, 131
NBC televising and schedule change, 5, 129–31, 202–3, 216, 220, 316n130
press demands for players, 231–32
prize money, 146, 254
UCLA championships, 130
Nelson, Johnny, 64–66, 160–61, 201
Nemcek, Rich, vii, 202, 227–28, 236, 244, 260
Indiana State enrollment, 155
Indiana State games, 1979, 155, 172, 182, 194, 198–99
life after basketball, 273, 276
Netolicky, Bob, 78, 79
New Mexico State Aggies, 123–24, 125, 167, 171, 193, 212
coach Hayes, 124, 186–87, 193, 199
Indiana State game, 1978, 124–26
Indiana State game, 1979, 185–87
Indiana State rematch, 1979, and Bird–fans fight, 193–99, 263, 330–31n195
New York Knicks, 148
New York Yankees, 102–3
Newman, Bruce, 192, 232
Newton, John, 71, 72–73, 115, 304n69, 305n73, 345n268
NFL Today, The (CBS), 254
Nicks, Carl, 75–76, 84–85, 88, 118, 170, 233, 236, 257, 260, 266, 267
Bird's dodging publicity, 189
Bird's friendship, 282
career and life, 273–75, 281–82
enrolls in Indiana State, 1976, 79
Indiana State, 1978–79, season play, 172, 176–78, 186–87, 193–95, 201, 209, 210

NCAA tournament, 1979, 217–18, 223, 225–26, 231, 237–38, 243, 245, 247
sent back to community college, 1977, 90–91, 99, 154–55
Northwood Institute, West Baden, Indiana, 39–41, 42, 60
Notre Dame Fighting Irish, 49, 168, 174, 179, 182, 202, 212, 224, 229
ranking, 188, 192, 202, 211
See also Phelps, Digger

O
O'Brien, Larry, 150
Ohlmeyer, Don, 252
Oklahoma City Thunder, 282
Oklahoma Sooners, 220, 222
Olsen, Bill, 23, 24, 29, 30
Olympics 1980, 174
O'Malley, Kevin, 149, 204, 230, 244, 253–55, 260
Ortegel, Bob, 201, 205–6
Overman, Kirby, 33, 34

P
Packer, Billy, 203–5, 208–10, 216, 217, 224, 225, 228, 230, 236, 246
Indiana State students' jingle, 208–9
Palm Beach Junior College, 269
Parish, Robert, 64
Penn Quakers, 223, 229, 236, 245
Pentzer, Jim, 28, 33, 81
Phegley, Roger, 93
Phelps, Digger, 49, 168, 202, 212, 215, 218, 229
Pizza Hut All-American showcase, 1978, 114
Portland State, 93
Portland Trail Blazers, 148
Purdue Boilermakers, 49, 83, 174
Indiana State game, 1977, 109–14, 132
Indiana State game, 1978, 177–79
See also Schaus, Fred

Q
Qualkenbush, Dave, 290n9

INDEX

R

Reed, Steve, 99–100, 116, 123, 136, 170, 236, 257, 268
   Indiana State, 1978–79 season games, 172, 176–78, 185, 193–96, 198, 201, 209–11
   Indiana State, 1979–80 season, 260
   life after basketball, 273
   NCAA tournament, 1979, 216, 217, 225–27, 238, 245, 247

Reed, U. S., 222, 225

Richardson, Michael Ray, 148

Ritter, Bob "Tex," 172, 183, 227–28, 236, 260
   life after basketball, 273, 275–76

Robert Morris College, 82

Robertson, Oscar, 86

Robey, Rick, 28, 146, 148, 187, 202

Rose, Pete, 104–5

Rosston, Indiana, 45–46, 47–48, 58, 60

Rupp, Adolph, 53

Rushville, Indiana, 76, 77, 84

Rutgers University Scarlet Knights, 93, 133–34
   coach, Tom Young, 133
   NIT, 1978, Indiana State game and Bird–fan fight, 1–4, 5, 132–38, 194, 195, 239–40, 289–90n1
   See also Bailey, Jammin' James

Ryer, Ronnie, 210

S

Sacramento Kings, 148

San Antonio Spurs, 151–52

San Diego Clippers, 261

Schall, Steve, 222, 226, 227

Schaus, Fred, 49, 110–11, 114

Schultz, Mike, 88

Seattle Supersonics, 149, 256

Senefeld, Sharon, 103–4, 105–8

Shaw, Rick, 3, 85–86, 87, 117, 185, 188, 246
   death of, 280
   New Mexico State rematch, 1979, 196

Sherfick, Larry, 37, 297n37

Shidler, Jay, 147

Short, Purvis, 148

Shuck, Geoff, 52–53, 64, 66, 74, 75

Simpson, Jim, 208, 210, 224

Smith, Jimmy, 88–89, 112, 114, 136, 137

Smithson, Gene, 208, 211

Southern Illinois Salukis, 120, 121, 167, 171, 201, 212

Soviet men's national basketball team, 145, 147, 174, 175, 176–77

Sports Illustrated
   article on Bird's "secrets" by Bruce Newman, 1979, 192
   basketball issue, 1977, Bird, McKee, and, 101–3
   Bird cover, 1977, 1, 2, 103–4, 105–8, 278, 311n101
   "Bird Has Those Trees at the Top" (Keith), 1978, 118–21, 186
   cover shot of Mark "The Bird" Fidrych, 105
   cover shot of Pete Rose, 104–5
   importance to athletics, 101
   Indiana State cheerleaders, Bird cover and, 103–8
   Magic Johnson cover, 1978, 167–68
   NCAA Tournament, 1979, coverage, 232
   photographer H. Lane Stewart, 104–7
   preseason poll, 1978, 168
   readership, 101

Springs Valley Blackhawks, French Lick, Indiana, 14–15, 19–22, 37
   Bird makes all-star team, 33–34
   Bird's final game, 28, 81
   Bird's game with Loogootee Lions and Hoosier recruitment, 24–27
   Bird's scoring records, 22–23
   coaches, 14–15, 21–24, 32, 57–58

St. Ambrose College, 82

St. John's Red Storm, 223, 229

Stabley, Fred, Jr., 141

Staley, Leroy, 100, 110, 114, 118, 123, 125, 212, 236, 257, 267
   court squabble with Bird, 172
   Indiana State 1978–79 season games, 172, 173, 177, 184–87, 196, 211

Staley, Leroy, (*cont.*)
  life after basketball, 273, 275
  NCAA tournament, 1979, 216–17, 224, 238
  NIT, 1978, 135, 136
  quits Indiana State, 137
  returns to Indiana State, 154
Staub, Marcia, 103–4, 105–8, 278
Stepien, Ted, 151, 321n151
Stern, David, 261–62
Stewart, H. Lane, 104
  Sports Illustrated cover for Bird, 105–7
  Sports Illustrated cover for Magic Johnson, 167–68
  Sports Illustrated covers for Pete Rose and Mark Fidrych, 104–5
Sutton, Eddie, 223, 224, 225

T
Tennessee Tech, 52
  Evans coaching at, 59
  Hodges coaches and recruits for, 45, 47–48, 52–53, 57
  Hodges's recruitment of Shuck, 53
Terre Haute, Indiana, 43
  Bird awarded the key to the city, 258
  Bird living in, 72–73
  Bird playing 500 Platolene softball in, 152–53, 171
  Bird's impact on tourism earnings, 278, 346n278
  Bird's speech following NCAA championship loss, 251
  Bird's *Sports Illustrated* cover, 109
  Indiana State's NIT, financial boon for, 132
  Indiana State team boosters and local business support, 73–74, 92, 152, 156, 164, 167, 193, 199, 200, 208, 212, 231, 257
  as joke punch line, 49–50
  Larry Bird Committee, 164, 167, 202, 228, 257
  Larry Bird Museum, 277–78, 346n278
  media attention and Indiana State basketball, 188
  Miley's fame and life in, 277
  NCAA championship game, 1979, and welcome home, 232, 244, 247–48
  Rafters, 202
  Salute to Larry Bird dinner and next day festivities, 257–58
  summer jobs for Bird and Danny King, 73
  team of 1979 reunions, 277, 278, 280
  US senator Birch Bayh and, 212
  weather, 186, 207
Terre Haute Star
  on 1978 NIT and Bird-fan fight, 137
  Bird refuses to speak to, 188
Terre Haute Tribune
  on 1978 NIT and Bird-fan fight, 137
  Bird refuses to speak to, 188, 189
  news of Bob King's heart attack, 162
Thimlar, Hugh, 46–48, 51, 57, 59, 100, 170
Thimlar, Terry, 170, 215, 243, 246
  support for Alex Gilbert, 180
Thomas, Isiah, 262
Thompson, Kevin, 266–67, 268
Thompson, Mychal, 148
Tkachenko, Vladimir, 174, 175, 176
Tomjanovich, Rudy, 150
Tow, Glen, 40, 42, 60
Tulsa Golden Hurricane, 183–85, 199
  coach Jim King, 205
  Hodges's anger and argument during Indiana State game, 205
Turner, Scott, 172

U
UCLA Bruins, 30, 168, 179, 182, 202
  NCAA championships, 130, 131
  NCAA tournament, 1979, 183–85, 212, 223, 229, 235
  ranking in polls, 1978–79, 211
University of Denver, 82
University of Missouri, 156
University of Montana, 70

INDEX

University of New Mexico, 49, 78
University of Tennessee, 51

V
Versace, Dick, 201, 205
Vincent, Jay, 144, 202–3
Virginia Tech Gobblers
    NCAA tournament, 1979, 213, 215–17

W
Walls, Wayne, 110–11, 112, 113, 114
Walsh, Donnie, 274
Walton, Bill, 130
Warsaw, Indiana, 99
Washington, Kermit, 150
Washington Bullets, 149, 256
Watkins, Curtis, 235–36, 237
Watson, Lou, 18, 19
Webb, Greg, 124, 126, 186, 244, 263–65
    New Mexico State–Indiana State game, 1979, 193–99, 263–64
Webster, DeCarsta, 72, 83, 84, 88, 128, 135, 137
    Evans two-for deal in accepting Indiana State job offer and, 51–52, 59–60, 66
Weltlich, Bob, 297n37, 298n37
West Baden Springs, Indiana, 284
    Bird and the basketball court in, 9, 14, 36–37, 60, 97, 284, 290n9
    Bird's return, 1980s, home built in, 262, 283
    Converse commercial with Bird and Magic, 1985, 284
    hometown of Bird's father, Joey, 10, 11–12
    Jubil Bar, 13, 14, 15, 27, 37, 39, 55, 60, 284, 292n13, 292n32, 347n284
    NCAA championship game, 1979, and, 244
    Northwood Institute in, 39–42, 60
    suicide of Joey Bird and, 55
West Texas Buffaloes, 123, 212
West Vigo High School, Terre Haute, 256–57
Westmont Warriors, 109–10
Wichita State Shockers, 121, 122
    Bird and Indiana State's last regular-season home game, 1979, 203, 207–11
    Indiana State spectators for Indiana State game, 208
    See also Smithson, Gene
Wilkins, Dominique, 262
Williams, Freeman, 93, 96, 102
Williams, Rick, 64, 66, 74, 75, 78, 79
Wilson, Barry, 14
Wisman, Jim, 35–36, 131
Wooden, John, 30, 130, 131, 244
Woolf, Bob, 259, 343n259
Woolridge, Orlando, 229
World University Games, 1977, 92–99
    Bailey's injury, 98
    Bird tryout in Louisville, 92–95
    European teams and rules, 95–96
    Jordan as Bird's teammate, 111
    US–Cuba game and melee, Bird's ability to fight, 97–98
    US team, 95–96, 98, 102
WTHI (Terre Haute)
    Indiana State coach Bob King interviewed by Forbes, 89–90
    NIT, 1977, televised by, 86, 87
    Purdue–Indiana State game, 1977, televised by, 112
WTTV (Indianapolis)
    Purdue–Indiana State game, 1977, televised by, 112
    Purdue–Indiana State game, 1978, televised by, 177, 178
Wyman, Gary "Herbie," 12–13, 14, 34
    anecdote about Bird borrowing his pickup, 21

Y
Young, Tom, 133–35

Z
Zahn, Alan, 222, 224, 227